# Building Market Institutions in South Eastern Europe

# Building Market Institutions in South Eastern Europe
## Comparative Prospects for Investment and Private Sector Development

Harry G. Broadman, James Anderson, Constantijn A. Claessens, Randi Ryterman, Stefka Slavova, Maria Vagliasindi, and Gallina A. Vincelette

THE WORLD BANK
Washington, D.C.

# Contents

Figures

# Foreword

A decade and a half has now passed since the collapse of communism in Central and Eastern Europe. In that period, countries of the region have had to overcome the legacy of an inefficient socialist economy and to adopt market principles. The challenges have been enormous, especially in South Eastern Europe. Bosnia and Herzegovina, Croatia, the former Yugoslav Republic of Macedonia, and Serbia and Montenegro have had to deal with internal conflict, and all of the countries—including Albania, Bulgaria, Moldova, and Romania—have faced, to varying degrees, high rates of poverty, political uncertainty, and an infrastructure weakened by years of neglect.

The struggle has been unique in each country. And considerable progress has been made. Bulgaria and Romania look forward to accession to the European Union in 2007, and the European Commission has recommended that the European Council open membership negotiations with Croatia. The other South Eastern European countries recognize the need for further economic reform and are poised to meet the challenge. This book—a collaborative effort between the World Bank and the European Bank for Reconstruction and Development—not only assesses how each South Eastern European country is faring, but also provides guidance regarding where they need to turn next in their efforts to build a market economy. The book points out that to restore and consolidate peace and stability in the region, the countries must raise their levels of domestic and foreign investment. A weak investment climate undermines the prospects for economic growth and poverty reduction and jeopardizes the stability of the region. But to create a climate that will attract investors, the countries must first establish robust and enduring basic market institutions.

The book takes an innovative empirical approach to examining the issue and integrates and analyzes data from three sources. The authors developed data from a set of 40 original, enterprise-level business case studies, which were carried out in the field in each of the eight countries of South Eastern Europe in 2002. Data and perceptions from two rounds of the European Bank for Reconstruction and Development–World Bank *Business Environment and Enterprise Performance Survey*, which was conducted in 1999 and 2002, are also used. The findings from the business case studies and the surveys are buttressed by official statistics. Working from this comprehensive set of data, the authors identify regionwide and country-specific trends, impediments, and successes. They then suggest policy reforms to solve the problems diagnosed.

Solutions must differ from country to country. Yet each country can learn from its own experiences and from the experiences of others. Indeed, creating lasting stability and prosperity in the region will demand that the countries work together in building market institutions even as they compete to attract investment. Thus, in time, by proceeding with market reforms, the countries of South Eastern Europe can expect to complete their integration into the global economy.

Pradeep Mitra
Chief Economist
Europe and Central Asia Region
The World Bank

Willem Buiter
Chief Economist and Special
Counsellor to the President
European Bank for Reconstruction
and Development

# Acknowledgments

This book was prepared by a team led by Harry Broadman. The authors of the chapters are as follows: Overview—Harry Broadman and Gallina Vincelette; chapter 1—Gallina Vincelette and Harry Broadman (with extensive contributions from Maria Vagliasindi); chapter 2—Gallina Vincelette, Maria Vagliasindi, and Harry Broadman; chapter 3—Harry Broadman (with the statistical assistance of Gallina Vincelette); chapter 4—Maria Vagliasindi; chapter 5—James Anderson and Constantijn Claessens; and chapter 6—Stefka Slavova and Randi Ryterman. Harry Broadman integrated and edited the chapters. Sandra Craig assisted the team.

The study is a collaborative effort between the World Bank and the European Bank for Reconstruction and Development (EBRD). From the outset, the team benefited from discussions with, exchanges of ideas with, and comments on the manuscript from colleagues from both institutions. We appreciate the assistance of these individuals at the World Bank: Jean-Luc Bernasconi, David Bernstein, Marcelo Bisogno, Oscar de Bruyn Kops, Henk Busz, Bruce Courtney, Mansour Farsad, Bernard Funck, Kathryn Funk, Cheryl Gray, Simon Gray, Daniela Gressani, Mohinder Gulati, Ardo Hansson, John Hegarty, Joel Hellman, Ronald Hood, Joseph Ingram, Erika Jorgensen, Daniel Kaufmann, David Kennedy, Pascale Kervyn, Ioannis Kessides, Iftikhar Khalil, Ali Mansoor, Massimo Mastruzzi, Katarina Mathernova, Pradeep Mitra, Alia Moubayed, Helga Muller, Kari Nyman, Gael Raballand, Anand Seth, Khaled Sherif, Martin Slough, Rory O'Sullivan, Kyle Peters, Rosalinda Quintanilla, Andrew Vorkink, Marina Wes, and Lubomira Zimanova Beardsley. We would like to express our gratitude to these individuals at the EBRD: Willem Buiter, Hsianmin Chen, Elisabetta Falcetti, Steven Fries, Michel Nussbaumer, Peter Sanfey, Anita Taci, Kamen Zahariev, and Alexei Zverev.

In addition to data from the EBRD–World Bank *Business Environment and Enterprise Performance Surveys* (BEEPS) of 1999 and 2002, which covered approximately 1,600 firms in South Eastern Europe, primary data for this study were gathered from 40 original firm-level business case studies developed during several missions in the spring, summer, and fall of 2002 in the eight South Eastern European countries (SEE8). The business case studies were conducted in the field as follows:

- *Albania* in September 2002 by Anita Taci (EBRD) and Gallina Vincelette (World Bank)
- *Bosnia and Herzegovina* in July 2002 by Harry Broadman (World Bank) and Gallina Vincelette (World Bank)
- *Bulgaria* in September 2002 by Harry Broadman (World Bank) and Gallina Vincelette (World Bank)
- *Croatia* in June 2002 by Harry Broadman (World Bank) and Gallina Vincelette (World Bank)
- *Former Yugoslav Republic of Macedonia* in May 2002 by Harry Broadman (World Bank) and Gallina Vincelette (World Bank)
- *Moldova* in May 2002 by Maria Vagliasindi (EBRD)
- *Romania* in September 2002 by Harry Broadman (World Bank), Elisabetta Falcetti (EBRD), and Gallina Vincelette (World Bank)
- *Serbia and Montenegro* in July 2002 by Harry Broadman (World Bank) and Gallina Vincelette (World Bank).

The missions would not have been possible without the excellent organization and help the team received from our colleagues in the local offices of the World Bank and EBRD. Special thanks go to Juela Haxhiymeri (Albania); Samra Bajramovic and Stevan Raonic (Bosnia and Herzegovina); Sanja Madzarevic-Sujster (Croatia); Stella Ilieva and Galia Kondova (Bulgaria); Evgenij Najdov (FYR Macedonia); Maya Sandu, Octavian Costas, and Marisa Manastirli (Moldova); Catalin Pauna, Raluca Banioti, Corina Anton, and Simona Bucurei (Romania); and Miroslav Frick (Serbia and Montenegro).

Members of a workshop held in Budapest in June 2003—who came from the private sector, academia, and the government in each of the SEE8, as well as from the international donor community—commented on the preliminary findings of this study. Their insights were extremely helpful in sharpening the analysis and "reality testing" the study's conclusions.

The peer reviewers were Simeon Djankov, Orsalia Kalantzopoulos, Daniel Kaufmann, and Anand Seth. The team thanks them for their comments and suggestions.

We would also like to thank the World Bank publications team for their help and professionalism in preparing this book for publication.

# Building Market Institutions in South Eastern Europe— An Overview

Albania, Bosnia and Herzegovina, Bulgaria, Croatia, the former Yugoslav Republic of Macedonia, Moldova, Romania, and Serbia and Montenegro have emerged from the communist era to face the social and political challenges of making an economic transition, building market institutions, and enacting wide-ranging policy reforms to promote private sector development and investment. The eight countries of South Eastern Europe (SEE8) trail their Western European neighbors in income and in other measures of development, but the differences among the SEE8 are as striking as their similarities.

Already a functioning market economy in the eyes of the European Union (EU), Bulgaria has made progress in overcoming the legacy of inefficient socialist economic practices and has avoided tumultuous political revolutions. Romania's record of economic reform is somewhat weaker but not far behind. Both countries aspire to join the European Union in 2007. From the relative prosperity of Josip Broz Tito's time, Yugoslavia's economy was severely undermined in the 1990s by civil wars that split the country and disintegrated its industries and infrastructure. Bosnia and Herzegovina, Croatia, FYR Macedonia, and Serbia and Montenegro all bear the scars of war. Albania and Moldova, like most of the former Yugoslav republics, are challenged today by poor infrastructure, high rates of poverty, political fragility, and economic isolation—problems that also affect the rest of the SEE8 to varying degrees.

*Building Market Institutions in South Eastern Europe* examines how the countries of the region are developing, how well the good intentions and policy reforms of their governments have been translated into results, and where the process can be effectively improved. The book assesses the progress under way and offers recommendations on how best to retool production and commerce while improving the capacity of institutions to regulate markets and deliver public services.

This study is based in reality, integrating and analyzing data and perceptions from a set of 40 original enterprise-level business case studies, which were carried out in each of the eight countries in 2002, and from the two rounds of the European Bank for Reconstruction and Development (EBRD)–World Bank *Business Environment and Enterprise Performance Survey* conducted in 1999 (BEEPS1) and 2002 (BEEPS2), which covered approximately 1,600 firms in South Eastern Europe (SEE). The surveys complement traditional, official data from SEE8 governments, providing a deeper, qualitative assessment of the characteristics, trends, and relationships among economic and government institutions and the enterprise sector. They also provide results that challenge the conventional wisdom and assumptions.

This book starts from the premise that further development and reform of basic market institutions in SEE are the key to increasing domestic and foreign investment and, thus, to accelerating economic growth and reducing poverty. Although the economic recovery of the region has started, it will stall unless greater progress is made in the institutional environment for investment. Improving the investment environment also is essential to the integration of the SEE8 into the European structures. These two mutually reinforcing objectives—accelerating growth and reducing poverty, on the one hand, and integrating with Europe, on the other—are critical to achieving long-lasting peace and prosperity for all people of the region.

The objective of the study is to assess, empirically and in detail, the nature and extent of the institutional constraints to improving the environment for investment in the SEE8 and to develop policy recommendations to ease those constraints. The book focuses on four policy areas:

1. Competition and economic barriers to business entry and exit
2. Access to regulated utilities and services
3. Corporate ownership, financial transparency, and access to finance
4. Commercial dispute resolution

Institutional aspects of the South Eastern European economy and background on the scope and methodology of the study are presented in chapter 1. Institutional reform to date and remaining challenges are the topics of chapter 2. Chapter 3 deals with interenterprise competition and the conditions that hamper or promote it. Chapter 4 covers access to regulated infrastructure utilities and resources and their effect on enterprise development and better public service. Corporate ownership, financial transparency, and access to finance are the subjects of chapter 5, which also explores how those issues are linked to successful market development, investment, and business growth. Chapter 6 examines changes in courts and legal systems aimed at creating a healthy environment for effective business dispute resolution.

## Seizing a Historic Opportunity for Growth

South Eastern Europe's dramatic transition from command economies to market structures is occurring alongside a similarly ambitious effort to restore peace and social stability in a region traumatized by ethnic strife. Success in both arenas depends on market institutions that encourage investment and growth by facilitating commerce, enhancing job creation and poverty reduction, and integrating the region's domestic markets with the world economy.

The 1990s were characterized by dramatic collapses of output in SEE. Economic stability, when achieved, was backed by subsidies to the state-owned industrial sector or by extensive borrowing from abroad. By 2001, the region had reached only 74 percent of its pretransition (1989) level of economic activity. In comparison, the five most developed Central European transition economies (the Czech Republic, Hungary, Poland, the Slovak Republic, and Slovenia) had increased their combined output to 115 percent of 1989 levels.

South Eastern Europe has now recovered from the recession of the 1990s. The region as a whole grew by 4.2 percent in 2002—faster than the 2.5 percent growth rate of the world economy—and by 3.5 percent in 2003. The region's economic rebound has been fueled primarily by private activity, which by 2001 was generating more than half of total output across the SEE8. In most countries in the region, privatization of small and medium-size enterprises has been completed. At the same time, the role of foreign aid and loans has declined even in the western Balkan states, where it constituted 7 percent of the five countries' gross domestic product (GDP) in 2002.

However, a quicker and more robust rebound of output and economic growth has been impeded by the slow pace of restructuring in industry, agriculture, and services—which is in turn caused in part by the absence of effective market-based institutions to protect property rights, fair competition, and financial discipline. In addition, low levels of domestic and foreign investment have hindered economic development in SEE. Abundant evidence—from anecdotal sources to more systematic diagnostic studies and surveys—suggested that the risks and costs of doing business in SEE were excessively high and, along with other problems common to state-run economies, were discouraging private investment. Recognizing this, the countries of SEE and their development partners began efforts to improve the investment framework in the region.

Those efforts are urgent. The European Union has greatly expanded trade access to the single European market not only for the accession countries (Bulgaria and Romania), but also for the western Balkan states (Albania, Bosnia and Herzegovina, Croatia, the federal Yugoslav Republic of Macedonia, and Serbia and Montenegro) and Moldova. Simultaneously, intraregional trade liberalization has found new momentum with the signing of the SEE8 Memorandum of Understanding on Trade Liberalization and Facilitation. The opportunities created by those developments will be realized only if investment increases substantially and counteracts the region's high unemployment, insufficient job creation, and stubborn poverty.

Chapter 1 conveys the message that a favorable institutional framework for domestic and foreign investments is essential to sustainable growth and poverty alleviation in the region. The chapter also presents the scope, methodology, and approach for understanding the role of the institutional environment that affects enterprise development and growth in SEE.

## Institutional Reform in South Eastern Europe— Achievements and Challenges

The business environment in the SEE8 improved between 1999 and 2002, according to the BEEPS data and EBRD transition indicators, although progress across the region varied. Government reform policies have targeted some of the underlying institutional problems in each of the countries, but major institutional challenges remain. To better explain those challenges, chapter 2 presents a disaggregated analysis of the impediments to further institutional reform.

Reform efforts in the SEE8 come up short in two important ways. First, the development of key market institutions has been partial and slow. Second, institutional reforms already undertaken have not been effectively implemented and enforced. Traditional ways of doing things must catch up to the reforms, from recognizing the validity of contracts to paying for utilities, and from achieving financial transparency to establishing a credible judicial system.

Chapter 2 highlights the deficiencies in the development of the four market institutions that are explored in the subsequent chapters: the institutions governing competition, regulated infrastructure utilities, corporate ownership and finance, and commercial dispute resolution.

### Still Weak Interenterprise Competition

Most countries have adopted policies for removing administrative barriers, for example, by streamlining business licensing and registration procedures. In many of these countries, however, failure to operationalize the improved registration or licensing requirements in a predictable manner and inconsistent interpretation of laws and regulations lead to discrimination between different types of investors—and thus to deficiencies and corruption. More important, few of the countries have strengthened the fundamental market institutions that protect firms from anticompetitive structures and conduct. Although some of the countries have sound competition laws, there is almost universal neglect of the use of these instruments to reduce economic barriers to entry. On the exit side, the restructuring or liquidation of large loss-making enterprises has not been facilitated sufficiently, in part because key legislation has not been implemented.

## Severe Infrastructure Bottlenecks

The SEE8 are dealing with severe infrastructure bottlenecks caused by years of poor maintenance and, in some cases, conflict. The severity of the problem varies by country and by sector. But the development of predictable and transparent regulatory frameworks to ensure users' access to competitively priced, high-quality services and to engender investment in the utility sectors is lagging in all countries. Indeed, the inefficient pricing and cross-subsidies embedded in many sectors stifle the incentives that otherwise would attract investors and improve quality and access of utility services.

## Insufficient Financial Transparency, Accountability, and Protection of Ownership Rights

The governments of the SEE8 have shifted away from divesting state assets to insiders, instead relying increasingly on more transparent methods of privatization. However, although some countries have adopted International Accounting Standards (IAS) and independent financial audits for enterprises, most are still in the process of doing so. Use of such instruments needs to be complemented by training managers to properly interpret and use the financial information for improving enterprise performance. At the same time, in most countries enforcement of commercial legislation is still ineffective in protecting minority shareholders and in imposing the needed discipline of financial disclosure and transactional transparency. As a result, there are weak checks and balances on managerial performance.

## Compromised Institutions for Resolution of Business Disputes

Legal frameworks in all of the SEE8 protect property rights and the integrity of contracts. But the functioning of the associated institutions is limited by lengthy procedures, lack of qualified and independent judges, and weak enforcement mechanisms. Alternative out-of-court administrative channels for dispute resolution—such as arbitration—are underdeveloped in all eight countries. In addition, inefficient land and property rights registration systems present another source of disputes and barriers to investment in most of the region.

The following sections present summaries of the main findings of each of the four core topics of the book: competition, regulated infrastructure utilities, corporate governance and finance, and commercial dispute resolution.

## Interenterprise Competition—The Key to Growth

Chapter 3 investigates the incentives and constraints on competition in the SEE8 and recommends policies for reform, focusing on the fundamental determinants of competition and on the power of competition to multiply the benefits of reforms. Deeper diagnosis of how basic market institutions affect interenterprise competition in SEE is essential for the design of enduring policy reforms.

### Noncompetitive Market Structures and Business Conduct

After a decade of privatization and the establishment of new private firms, changes in enterprise ownership in SEE have yet to produce competitively structured markets and competitive business operations. Weak incentives in market institutions and policy frameworks in all of the SEE8 have produced little restructuring of large state-owned enterprises. Many firms with dominant sectoral positions continue to operate unchecked by a competitive market structure.

### Vertical Integration across Sectors, Ownership Forms, and Countries

The degree of vertical integration of South Eastern European firms, upstream and downstream, varies significantly across sectors, ownership forms, and countries. In terms of downstream integration, the BEEPS data for the region show that an average of 11 percent of firms' output transactions actually occur internally or are made to related parties. This level of vertical integration is generally much lower than the level case studies indicate for upstream integration. About two-thirds of the surveyed SEE8 firms indicate that they have at least four suppliers for their "main material inputs." According to the BEEPS data and the enterprise-level case studies, proportionately more de novo firms than privatized or state-owned firms buy their inputs in markets populated with more suppliers, hence suggesting that new businesses are most able to benefit from upstream competition. Overall, the evidence suggests that, although privatized and private firms shop around for distributors and customers more than state-owned enterprises do, the converse is true for input purchases.

## Barriers to Business Entry and Exit

In assessing the extent of entry and exit barriers to private sector development in the SEE8, this study distinguishes between two different types of barriers: those that are (a) economic in nature, principally determined by technology, and those that are (b) institutionally determined, policy driven, or administratively induced. The need for policy intervention to deal with economic barriers generally arises when such barriers are chronically high and in markets in which there is already significant horizontal or vertical dominance.

Evidence from the business case studies and the BEEPS data suggests that generic economic policy uncertainty—understood to be unanticipated or unilateral changes in the rules of the game—and macroeconomic instability are the most serious obstacles to new business formation in SEE, implying that governments can proactively carry out policy reforms to reduce barriers to entry in the region. Other important perceived entry barriers are high tax rates, high cost of credit, corruption, and anticompetitive practices of other businesses. Interestingly, the data give less support to what has become the conventional wisdom—that administrative barriers are the major impediments to business development in transition economies. For example, the surveyed SEE8 businesses do not perceive access to land, titling or leasing of land, business licensing and permits, and tax administration as major impediments.

Exit barriers need to be low to make economic space for new entrants and to rechannel productive assets bottled up in inefficient firms to new ventures in which employment can be expanded and new products developed. Creating such an environment calls for hard budget constraints to engender improved enterprise competitiveness from viable firms and to expose firms that are no longer commercially viable. The case studies suggest that in many of SEE8 economies budget constraints are soft and barriers to exit are in some cases appreciable.

The BEEPS data show that, for the region, 11 percent of the firms closed at least one plant since 1998—a rather low share by international standards, especially when taking into account that many SEE8 firms are not commercially viable. On a net basis, about 9 percent of the firms indicated opening at least one plant. The infrastructure sector had the largest percentage of firms reporting plant closures and very few net new plant openings. State-owned enterprises reported both the greatest proportion of gross plant closures and the greatest proportion of closures on a net basis. New firms had the smallest proportion of plant closures, and on a net basis they indicated the largest share of plant openings.

The average surveyed SEE8 firm indicated that it received subsidies from national government entities amounting to 9.5 percent of sales revenues and received subsidies from regional and local governments amounting to 17.7 percent of sales revenues. State-owned enterprises receive the greatest amount of subsidies as a proportion of sales revenues, followed by privatized firms and then by new private firms (except for FYR Macedonia and Moldova, where privatized firms receive the largest share of subsidies as a percentage of sales revenues). The largest recipients of subsidies are firms in the services and infrastructure sectors; firms in the trade, mining, and hotel and restaurant sectors are the smallest recipients of subsidies. With regard to tax forbearance, the regional average of tax arrears is 12 percent of sales revenues, not an insignificant amount.

## Competition, Firm Growth, and Performance

Changes in sales revenues, exports, employment, investment in fixed assets, and profit margins serve as measures of business performance of surveyed SEE8 firms over the period 1995–98 and 1998–2001. In recent years, there has been considerably less cross-country uniformity in all firm-level performance dimensions except profit margins. Employment growth jumped in Albania and Moldova, whereas firms in Albania, Croatia, and Romania exhibited sizable spurts in sales revenues. Albania and Croatia also experienced above-average growth in investment in fixed assets. Compared with 1995–98, export growth diminished significantly in 1998–2001.

On a sectoral basis, in 1995–98 growth in investment in fixed assets was particularly high in the services, transportation, and manufacturing sectors. In these same sectors firms generally indicated high growth rates of employment in the later period. Whereas firms in the service sector—and to a lesser extent power generation—registered significantly higher profit margins than those in other sectors in 1998, there was more uniformity in profit margins across sectors in 2001. The examination of performance across ownership types yields a striking variance: new private firms outperformed privatized and state-owned enterprises in all five dimensions measured in 1995–98. In 1998–2001, new private firms again generally outperformed the two other ownership types. The gap in employment growth rates between (a) new private firms and (b) privatized and state-owned firms considerably widened, whereas performance differences between privatized firms and state-owned enterprises narrowed considerably along all dimensions.

Times are tough for many South Eastern European businesses. Examining data on the dispersion of firm profitability in 2001 shows that the greatest proportion of loss-makers is concentrated in Bosnia and Herzegovina (11 percent), Bulgaria (8 percent), and Croatia (4 percent). Moreover, a substantial share of surveyed firms in all countries (except for Albania and Romania) indicated zero profits. Most of the surveyed firms indicated a profit-to-sales ratio in the 1 to 10 percent range. Across countries, the distribution of firms with profitability rates above 10 percent varies significantly. Across most sectors, there is more uniformity in the distribution of firm profitability—except for the mining and hotel and restaurant sectors. Across ownership types, loss-makers and those earning zero profits are most heavily represented in the state-owned enterprise category. Privatized firms have the next-largest proportion of firms in those two categories.

Multivariate regressions on approximately 1,600 surveyed South Eastern European firms suggest that higher firm profitability is associated with increased market share, greater vertical integration, lower level of subsidies, absence of state ownership (now or in the past), and more intensive research and development spending (a measure of a barrier to entry). These findings are consistent with analyses of the determinants of business performance in other regions of the world, which show that profit differentials are likely driven by the structural competitiveness of markets. The econometric results also point to country-specific factors that explain the variance in firm profitability across SEE.

## Need for Proactive and Effective Competition Policies

A proactive policy approach is needed that includes (a) economywide institutional and structural reforms, and (b) reforms in competition policy. Such a two-pronged approach will facilitate the entry of new businesses and will foster the horizontal and vertical restructuring of anticompetitive incumbent firms. Among the specific policy recommendations, the chapter outlines the following:

- Make structurally dominant markets contestable for new entrants. Priority attention and resources should be directed at preventing further horizontal and vertical consolidation through mergers and acquisitions in markets in which concentration and structural dominance are already excessive. Explicit, well-defined, and transparent merger guidelines should be developed that establish general policy parameters for distinguishing between procompetitive and anticompetitive mergers.
- Foster proactive competitive restructuring or exit of value-subtracting incumbents by facilitating reorganization and bankruptcy—including, when necessary, liquidation of insolvent firms.

- Review the missions of SEE8 government current competition policy agencies with a view to strengthening their rules-based incentive structures and to improving their implementation and enforcement capacities.
- Promote market-oriented policies for developing small and medium-size enterprises (SMEs), such as nongovernmental support programs (sponsored by commercial banks or international donors) that include (a) providing equity participation in venture capital and investment funds, (b) funding of local banks that provide commercial-based credit to SMEs, and (c) cofinancing with local banks of SME projects.
- Establish independent monitoring systems, based on widely publicized and anonymous feedback channels for enterprises to report violations, as a check on reform implementation to oversee success.
- Enhance "behind-the-border" competition to facilitate international trade and foreign direct investment (FDI) in SEE, and continue to bring policy regimes governing FDI in line with international best practice: (a) national treatment for foreign investors; (b) binding international arbitration for investor-state disputes; (c) substantial reduction in restrictions and limitations on FDI; (d) freedom for profit remittances; (e) expropriation for only a bona fide public purpose and with prompt, adequate compensation; and (f) absence of trade-related investment measures.
- Establish mechanisms that give individual countries incentives to compete for reform progress in the region. To jumpstart competition in reform among South Eastern European countries, governments could propose appropriate measures to assess reform progress, together with a simple survey methodology.
- Enhance public education efforts to foster a culture of competition in SEE by undertaking initiatives aimed at ensuring that consumers at large, as well as all enterprises, especially start-ups, are aware of the importance of the competitive process in practice and of the objectives and content of competition law.

## Access to Regulated Infrastructure Utilities

Bottlenecks in telecommunications, transportation, electrical power, and water are particularly severe in SEE because of inadequate maintenance, which is aggravated, in many cases, by conflict. Some needed and obvious changes include the following:

- De-monopolizing and privatizing existing infrastructure networks, as well as introducing competitive forces where natural monopoly conditions no longer exist, will help create the appropriate incentives for innovation by service providers and business users.

- Establishing appropriate regulatory rules will remove a significant obstacle to the development and expansion of business, as well as to regional trade and integration.
- Developing predictable and transparent regulatory frameworks will ensure users' access to competitively priced, high-quality services and will engender investment in the infrastructure sectors.

With the notable exception of FYR Macedonia, where progress appears to be limited, the SEE8 report a major improvement in infrastructure services. Chapter 4 disaggregates the perceptions of enterprises across each of the infrastructure sectors and presents cross-country and cross-sectoral variations. For the region as a whole, the power sector is perceived as the most severe infrastructure barrier to market entry and to expansion of real sector enterprises, followed by transportation and telecommunications. This finding is driven largely by the fact that businesses in Albania (together with those in Bulgaria and Romania) perceive access to electricity as a severe obstacle for entry and expansion. For Bosnia and Herzegovina, Croatia, FYR Macedonia, and Moldova, transportation is considered as the most relevant infrastructure-related barrier to entry. In most of those countries, the road network has been broken by war and has been degraded by severe underinvestment. For Serbia and Montenegro, the telecommunication sector represents the greatest barrier to entry and expansion (likely related to the highly politicized privatization of the Serbian telecommunication operator in the Slobodan Milosevic era).

Access to infrastructure is also an impediment to exit. There is strong evidence that privatized and state-owned enterprises are by far the greatest beneficiaries of soft budget constraints through nonpayment of utility services, confirming the presence of an uneven playing field tilted against the private sector.

Thirteen percent of privatized and 20 percent of state-owned enterprises are not paying infrastructure providers on time, compared with only 5 percent of new private enterprises. The disparities across different ownership categories emerge strongly from the case studies and from official data as well. Among the utilities, arrearages are the most recurrent problem in the energy sector. Energy cash collection (in terms of percentage of total collections) averages only 67.5 percent, and commercial losses (defined as nonbilled consumption) are at 20 percent. Cash collection is particularly low for industrial consumers, blunting incentives for industrial restructuring.

Nonpayment results in a variety of problems: propping up state-owned enterprises at the expense of private companies, discouraging private investment in utilities, and preventing essential improvements in technology and service.

## Poor Quality of Infrastructure Services

The quality of infrastructure service is poor. Across SEE, power outages of more than 11 days per year stand out as the major quality problem, followed by water cutoffs (9 days) and suspension of telecommunication services (5 days). Telecommunication services are characterized by higher waiting times, but they are on average more reliable. The opposite holds for electricity.

By understanding the relevance of broader regulatory reforms, including greater private sector involvement and more independent rulemaking, policymakers can effectively address these challenges in access and quality of infrastructure services. The very low payment discipline in the region is a powerful reason for accelerating private sector involvement—especially through foreign investment. A private firm owned or managed by a foreign strategic investor will have strong incentives to enforce payment discipline. It also will have the technical knowledge and finance required for essential remetering programs, computerization of billing, and other measures that can help improve payment and collection. Experience to date suggests that, in cases in which the private sector has entered power distribution, collections have gone up. Yet to successfully enhance efficiency, privatization requires complementary institutional changes, including restructuring to create scope for competition and to enhance the commercial viability of the privatized utility. It also requires changing public attitudes about low-cost energy as an entitlement.

The regulatory regime adopted for privatized network utilities is likely to encompass several dimensions, one being the establishment of an independent regulator—vital for settling market disputes and dealing with policy and other regulatory issues. Two key decisions for any newly established agency are the development of pricing rules and the choice of appropriate rate regulation. In South Eastern European countries with an independent regulator in the electricity sector, waiting times for service are a fraction of those in countries with no independent regulator. A similar pattern characterizes the telecommunication sector: countries with an independent regulator have very low waiting times (fewer than 2 days), compared with the waiting times in other countries (more than 7 days). But even if an independent regulator exists, the difficult challenge facing the national government is to endow that regulator with technically competent people and give them the authority and budget needed to implement its mandate effectively.

## Improving Infrastructure Services

Better infrastructure services could offer tremendous opportunities to reduce costs and to increase revenues in the real sector; conversely, innovation downstream has been severely constrained by inadequate infrastructure upstream caused by poor regulation. Policy recommendations to break the vicious cycle include the following:

• Sequence infrastructure reforms appropriately, establishing sound regulatory frameworks *before* privatizing utilities.
• Promote further private sector involvement by commercializing, restructuring, and ultimately privatizing key utility sectors. Wherever possible, involve strategic investors to maximize privatization revenues, to secure finance for necessary investments, and to strengthen incentives for improved efficiency.
• Establish an independent, transparent, and publicly accountable regulatory oversight process and institutions. Strengthen the independence and financial viability of the newly created regulatory agencies. Balance independence against accountability and requirements for monitoring and assessing regulatory effects.
• Coordinate the work of regulatory institutions. With the creation of independent sector regulatory agencies, competition authorities would no longer be responsible for tariff-setting processes and supervision, leaving technical and pricing regulation to specialized agencies. Competition authorities could thus play a more forceful role in determining the appropriate scope of regulatory authority and the appropriate market structure, as well as in controlling anticompetitive conduct by dominant enterprises.
• Create a more competitive environment for delivery of infrastructure services by establishing fair, transparent, and nondiscriminatory terms of access to regulated utilities.
• Develop alternative institutional frameworks for improving performance of infrastructure services, including regional and cross-sectoral approaches to regulation.

## Corporate Ownership, Financial Transparency, and Access to Finance

The private ownership of productive assets that characterizes capitalism relies on an institutional foundation not found in recent postcommunist systems. In particular, capitalist systems provide legal protections that allow the pooling of capital with controlled risk for investors, which encourages a potentially important new source of financing for productive entities. Building these systems, however, requires reforms much more profound than stroke-of-the-pen passage of laws. Investor confidence—indeed, fundamental fairness—requires corporate transparency and accountability. In the West, systems that have existed for centuries have yet to be perfected, a fact made clear by the wave of governance and

BUILDING MARKET INSTITUTIONS IN SOUTH EASTERN EUROPE

accounting scandals of the past several years. The relative infancy of the systems in transition countries poses an even greater challenge. In this vein, chapter 5 focuses on the themes of corporate ownership, financial transparency, and access to finance in SEE.

## Forms of Ownership

The BEEPS2 sample exhibits variation in forms of ownership:

- Croatia and Romania have very few firms describing themselves as sole proprietorships, but large numbers that call themselves corporations.
- Bosnia and Herzegovina and Bulgaria stand out for the large numbers of firms that said their shares were listed on the stock exchanges. Larger firms are, predictably, more likely to report a corporate form of organization and listing on stock exchanges.
- Overall for the region, most of the surveyed firms are completely owned either by the state or by domestic or foreign owners exclusively. Mixed ownership, such as joint ventures, is less common. Among larger firms, however, mixed ownership is much more prevalent.

The continuation of state involvement in partially privatized firms does not come without costs. Managers may continue to feel pressured to deliver on the programs of politicians, rather than to deliver profits to shareholders.

## Degrees of Financial Transparency

The degree of transparency and accountability evident in the way the firms present their financial statements is also examined. Among medium-size and large firms (firms with at least 50 full-time employees) that took part in BEEPS2, the use of IAS is highest in Croatia and Moldova, both of which also reported the most widespread use of IAS in BEEPS1. For both countries, the survey suggests that IAS have become the norm and are used by some 90 percent of firms. At the lower end of the scale are FYR Macedonia, Romania, and Serbia and Montenegro; less than half of the medium-size and large firms in those countries report using IAS. The low levels of compliance are in part explained by simple adherence to rules placed on firms by authorities. Within the SEE8 there has been little change in the prevalence of IAS between the 1999 BEEPS and the 2002 BEEPS, except in Bulgaria, which showed a marked increase.

The BEEPS data suggest that larger firms and foreign-owned firms are more likely than smaller firms and domestically owned firms to use IAS and external audits. However, variation in the observed use of IAS and external audits in the SEE8 is most significant across countries. Apparently, firms adopt IAS because external factors, such as requirements embodied in laws, force them to do so rather than because it is inherently a better business practice. Ownership concentration is important for explaining the use of external audits in FYR Macedonia and Moldova, and in both countries it is firms with smaller degrees of concentration that are more likely to use external audits, even after controlling for form of ownership. This finding is consistent with the use of external audits as a tool for diffuse ownership to check the performance of management.

## Terms and Modes of Sale, Purchase, and Finance

Firms in countries with less-developed formal financial systems are less likely to transact business in any manner other than spot exchange. Within the region, both prepaid and credit sales are strongly negatively correlated with the EBRD indicator on banking reform and interest rate liberalization. In addition, the BEEPS data show that alternative means of transacting business, such as barter, bills of exchange, and debt swaps, are common in most of the SEE8. Firms in the former Yugoslav republics that participated in the BEEPS were especially likely to report the use of barter; the business case studies present a similar story. After firms switch from bartering to monetary payments, both sellers and buyers achieve better pricing and value.

For both working capital and investment purposes, firms throughout the region continue to use primarily their own retained earnings. In Croatia and FYR Macedonia, firms were significantly more likely to bring in new equity as a means of financing operations, and in FYR Macedonia firms were also the most likely to make use of informal credit sources. Croatian firms were the most likely to use formal credit arrangements, consistent with the more developed level of banking in that country. Albania and Serbia and Montenegro demonstrated the highest levels of financing through retained earnings. The BEEPS data suggest also that the use of new equity for financing investment has increased in Bosnia and Herzegovina and in FYR Macedonia, whereas use of informal credit has expanded in Bulgaria and Romania.

## Financial Transparency, Investment, and Growth

At a national level, countries with deeper penetration of IAS and external audits tended to grow faster in 2002. Nevertheless, building true financial transparency will continue to be a formidable challenge, and the case studies have already suggested that problems with formal finance are pushing firms to look elsewhere for the funds needed to invest and grow.

In simple regressions, firm reports of adopting IAS and external auditing are correlated with firm-level investment. However, much of this relationship derives from the fact that countries with deeper penetration of IAS and external audits also had higher levels of investment, on average, among firms in the survey. After controlling for country effects, both IAS and external audits cease to be important for explaining investment. This finding is consistent with the idea that financial transparency has an important external effect: when firms are generally more transparent, the atmosphere of trust that is so essential for arm's-length investing is strengthened, and all firms benefit. Ease of access to finance is important for explaining investment intensity across surveyed firms, even after controlling for cross-country and other differences. Surveyed firms with more competition and larger firms tended to report lower levels of investment, but the relationships were generally not significant at conventional levels.

Firms that said they adopted IAS had much higher average sales growth than firms that did not, a finding that remains even after controlling for country effect. However, when access to finance, size, competition, and other factors are accounted for, the link between IAS and firm sales growth weakens considerably. It is notable that access to finance, itself determined in part by financial transparency, remains significant at a very high level.

## Higher Standards and Fuller Disclosure

Analysis of the survey data and case studies suggest the following policy directions:

- Deepen the separation between politicians and firms. Policy measures to achieve this separation range from promoting further privatization in countries where significant portions of the productive economy remain partially or fully state owned, to establishing clear governance mechanisms that moderate conflicts of interests. Albania, Bosnia and Herzegovina, and Serbia and Montenegro all need to continue the privatization work that was delayed by conflict. Several countries, including Bosnia and Herzegovina and Romania, have adopted legislation that would strictly control conflicts of interest by requiring directors to choose between their public office and their board seats.
- Monitor public disclosure of financial statements. Vigilant monitoring is needed to ensure that firms required to disclose their financial statements in fact do so. For the many publicly traded firms that do not yet obtain external audits, public disclosure of financial statements should be the first step in reforms, with or without reforms in accounting systems.

- Push for widespread adoption of IAS and the use of independent external audits. Financial transparency builds trust in financial statements on the part of banks, investors, regulators, and others, but without a push most firms will not undertake the necessary reforms.
- Train people to interpret financial statements prepared according to international standards. Many professionals in the public and private sectors must be able to read financial statements accurately if financial markets are to function efficiently. Maintaining training and education programs that produce qualified accountants will be essential to building investors' confidence in the integrity of financial statements.
- Set down clear rules on conflict of interest in the accounting profession. In building institutions of financial transparency from the ground up, the SEE8 can learn from the experience of others, including the United States, which was recently rocked by accounting scandals. Conflicts arise when auditors want to please their customers; when investment-banking firms are also investment advisers; when executive officers are also board members; and when regulatory authorities, such as stock exchanges, are governed by the firms they regulate. Some of these situations are specific to each country, but the general point is that envisioning the ramifications of potential conflicts of interest when laws and regulations are being drafted can help prevent the erosion of investor confidence that has recently damaged industrial markets.

## Commercial Dispute Resolution, Contract Enforcement, and the Courts

A fundamental aspect of commerce is trust: trust that products and services have the expected quality and integrity; that services and products will be delivered and paid for; and that contracts, partnerships, credit arrangements, and other agreements will be adhered to. Although the history of commerce is built on trust, commerce is also subject to risks of all sorts. For that reason, business and commerce rely on enforceable rules and contracts, agreed-upon ways of resolving disputes, and instruments of justice. Part of the legacy of the state-run economies of SEE is the debasement of trust, the lack of enforceable rules, and a court system without credibility. These problems are all in the process of correction.

Chapter 6 analyzes the quality of the investment climate throughout SEE from the perspective of commercial dispute resolution. This subject includes a spectrum of institutions, as well as formal and informal mechanisms, that promote the reliability of business activities and serve to enforce contracts, such as the courts, business associations, social networks, private protection firms (legal and criminal), government intervention, and public channels.

Although contract enforcement can be mediated through a variety of means—relationships based on trust, self-enforcement through repeat transactions, third-party enforcement based on reputation, private enforcement, administrative (governmental) intervention, and court enforcement (litigation)—courts are the main institution enforcing contracts and resolving business disputes. Without efficient courts and the expectation that courts will uphold contractual rights and obligations, firms will be less willing to deal with new clients and suppliers, and fewer transactions will take place.

## Transitional Techniques for Enforcing Good Commercial Practices

To avoid and resolve disputes in this period of transition from a system no one trusted to new institutions that must win credibility, firms in SEE follow several strategies. These strategies include refusing to extend credit to existing or new customers; requiring prepayment before releasing the objects of the contractual exchange; and relying on business associations, the government, political parties, or private protection services. The BEEPS2 data reveal the varied effectiveness of these techniques.

- To avoid disputes, the region's firms use bilateral mechanisms, such as prepayment and nonextension of credit, that significantly reduce the probability of running into payment disputes.
- Business association membership and donations to political parties are not found to reduce the incidence of disputes; indeed they are correlated with greater recourse to courts. In fact, 84 percent of surveyed firms indicate that the business association to which they belonged provided no value at all—or at best negligible value—in helping them resolve disputes with the same third parties.
- Firms avoid disputes by forgoing trade with unknown suppliers, even when such trade would be on more beneficial terms than existing suppliers could offer, and by forging long-lasting relationships with suppliers and customers, even at a higher cost of doing business. This cost reflects lost opportunities to trade with alternative firms on better terms or to facilitate the entry of new firms into the market.

## The High Cost of Formal Dispute Resolution

Court enforcement of commercial debt contracts in the SEE8 is slow and costly, especially in comparison with court enforcement in other transition economies. On the ease of resolving contractual disputes in court, the SEE8 show considerable differences. To resolve the same case before a first-instance court in the country's largest city, Serbia and Montenegro imposes the most procedural steps (40), followed by

Albania and Moldova (35), and Croatia (20). Moving that case through the court takes longest in Serbia and Montenegro (more than 1,000 days).

There are significant differences in the cost of court proceedings. Albania has the highest costs of legal procedure before the first-instance courts—1.5 times the claim amount. Clearly, if fees exceed the claim amount, firms will not take cases to court. Court procedures are also expensive in Bosnia and Herzegovina, FYR Macedonia, and Serbia and Montenegro, with total attorneys' and court fees ranging from 40 to 80 percent of the claim value. The least costly of the SEE8 jurisdictions are Bulgaria and Croatia, where total costs come to approximately 13 percent of the claim value.

Overall, chapter 6 emphasizes that firms tend to use the court system when it is less formal, less expensive, and faster in resolving disputes, and that those firms that regularly use the courts to enforce contracts are the ones that perform better. But what types of firms do go to court to resolve their business disputes? Three findings emerge:

- Small firms use courts the least.
- State-owned firms file more cases and have a higher proportion of payment disputes resolved in court than do private firms.
- New firms file significantly fewer cases with the courts and report a significantly lower proportion of payment disputes resolved by court proceedings than do older firms.

In addition, several key observations arise from assessing firms' perceptions about the performance of the court system. First, respondents seldom rate the judicial system of their jurisdiction as performing well. Second, court delays are seen as a major symptom of court inefficiency. And third, despite their generally low assessments of the courts, firms tend to register somewhat higher scores when asked about their confidence in the legal system.

Although old firms have a more favorable perception of the speed of court justice than do new firms, the differences are not statistically significant. However, large and state-owned firms tend to believe that the courts are faster than do small and private firms. Naturally, firms that are larger generally have the resources to absorb longer legal procedures than smaller firms.

Judicial corruption remains a significant problem. New firms, small firms, and private firms pay bribes to court officials and judges more frequently than do old firms, large firms, and state-owned firms. Frequent bribe payments raise the costs of "judicial capture" to the firm. Small and medium-size firms suffer higher costs of judicial capture; firm age also affects costs of capture positively and significantly. Interestingly, judicial formalism is found to significantly raise the frequency with which firms pay bribes to the courts, when other factors are controlled for. This finding lends support to the argument that higher procedural formalism and complexity create opportunities for corruption.

## The Burden of Judicial Complexity

There is significant cross-country variance in judicial complexity. Only FYR Macedonia makes the use of lawyers for legal representation mandatory in debt collection before a first-instance court, although in practice many plaintiffs in the other countries do hire lawyers at this stage. Also, all SEE8 jurisdictions impose written requirements for filing, service of process, judgment, and enforcement; three countries require that the defendant's opposition be in written form; and two insist that all evidence be in written form and that final arguments be submitted in writing. These requirements present an additional hurdle for businesses, because they have to seek legal advice before filing a complaint.

The regulation of evidence delays contract enforcement. While six of the SEE8 have statutory regulations on out-of-court statements and the recording of evidence, none has regulations on the admissibility of irrelevant evidence or requires that oral interrogation be conducted exclusively by the judge. In each of the eight jurisdictions, enforcement is suspended if an appeal is filed, and the suspension lasts until the appeal is resolved. Furthermore, all jurisdictions allow comprehensive review on appeal and most, apart from Croatia and Moldova, allow appeal during trial. Thus, a debtor who wants to delay execution can file appeals, even if no reasonable chance of a successful appeal outcome is expected.

## Advancing Judicial Reform

Contract enforcement mechanisms, both formal and informal, are essential for the smooth functioning of commercial contracts. Therefore, any policy aimed at strengthening the enforceability of commercial contracts and the resolution of commercial disputes needs to address judicial reform together with mechanisms for informal enforcement. Policymakers could pursue several types of reform that have been found to improve the enforcement of commercial contracts in various jurisdictions worldwide. These measures include concrete policy recommendations, which are outlined below:

- Establish information-sharing institutions. Create enforcement mechanisms such as credit bureaus, the media, nongovernmental organizations, and intermediaries such as accountants and auditors. Such institutions perform important functions in ensuring that contracts are enforced and that obligations between business partners are met.

- Improve judicial statistics to identify bottlenecks in court performance and signal to policymakers the direction of future reforms. Collecting judicial statistics is a necessary step in improving court administration and case management systems, which are in need of modernization and reform in all of the SEE8.
- Remove nondispute cases from the courts and transfer noncontentious matters such as company or property registration to relevant administrative agencies to improve court efficiency and free resources.
- Make judicial processes less burdensome and simpler for the parties in order to improve the speed and transparency of litigation. This measure could involve (a) moving away from written to oral procedures to prevent interruptions and delays, (b) limiting the need for legal justification in straightforward commercial cases, (c) changing procedural laws to allow more discretion on the part of the judge in admitting evidence and using it to ease the judicial process, (d) improving the enforceability of the first-instance judgment and limiting the scope for appeals without due cause, and (e) improving the system of court notifications of parties and witnesses to reduce the burden of procedural notifications.
- Establish specialized courts such as small claims courts and specialized commercial courts to reduce procedural complexity, to speed disposition, and to reduce legal costs.
- Strengthen existing or introduce alternative dispute resolution mechanisms such as mediation and commercial arbitration, especially in overburdened courts with significant case backlogs.
- Increase court resources to enhance training of judges and judicial support staff; improve the poor state of judicial buildings and office equipment; and improve the case assignment, case filing, and case tracking systems.

# Conclusion

South Eastern Europe has made considerable progress in establishing an environment for the formation and operation of private enterprises. However, substantial challenges remain to be tackled everywhere in the region. This study emphasizes the importance of developing key market institutions to further the growth of a vibrant enterprise sector in the region. Boosting domestic and foreign investment in the SEE8—thereby accelerating growth, reducing poverty, and tightening the region's integration with its European neighbors—depends on raising competition, reducing economic barriers to entry and exit, improving firms' access to regulated utilities and services, restructuring corporate ownership, increasing financial transparency, widening access to finance, and strengthening and streamlining commercial dispute resolution.

# Abbreviations

| | |
|---|---|
| ADR | Alternative dispute resolution |
| ANRC | Romanian Communication Regulatory Authority (Autoritatea Nationala de Reglementare in Comunicatii) |
| ATP | Autonomous Trade Preference |
| BEEPS | *Business Environment and Enterprise Performance Survey* |
| BSE | Bucharest Stock Exchange |
| BTC | Bulgarian Telecommunications Company |
| CEE5 | The Czech Republic, Hungary, Poland, the Slovak Republic, and Slovenia |
| CEFTA | Central European Free Trade Agreement |
| CEO | Chief executive officer |
| CIDA | Canadian International Development Agency |
| CIS | Commonwealth of Independent States |
| CMS | Corruption Monitoring System |
| CRC | Communications Regulation Commission (Bulgaria) |
| DSL | Digital subscriber line |
| EBRD | European Bank for Reconstruction and Development |
| ESM | Elektrostopanstvo na Makedonija |
| EU | European Union |
| FDI | Foreign direct investment |
| FESAL II | Second Financial and Enterprise Sector Adjustment Program |
| FIAS | Foreign Investment Advisory Service |
| FIC | Foreign investors' council |
| FTA | Free trade agreement |
| GDP | Gross domestic product |
| GNI | Gross national income |
| GSM | Global System for Mobile Communications |
| HEP | Hrvatska Elektroprivreda |
| IAS | International Accounting Standards |
| IFI | International financial institution |
| INA | Industrija Nafte |
| ISP | Internet service provider |

| IT | Information technology |
|---|---|
| KESH | Korporata Elektro-energjetike Shqiptare |
| KfW | Kreditanstalt für Wiederaufbau |
| LLU | Local loop unbundling |
| LRMC | Long-run marginal cost |
| MEBO | Management-employee buyout |
| OECD | Organisation for Economic Co-operation and Development |
| R&D | Research and development |
| ROSC | Report on the Observance of Standards and Codes |
| SAA | Stabilization and association agreement |
| SEE | South Eastern Europe |
| SEE8 | Albania, Bosnia and Herzegovina, Bulgaria, Croatia, the former Yugoslav Republic of Macedonia, Moldova, Romania, and Serbia and Montenegro |
| SEEPAD | South Eastern European Partnership on Accountancy Development |
| SMEs | Small and medium-size enterprises |
| SOEs | State-owned enterprises |
| USAID | U.S. Agency for International Development |
| VAT | Value added tax |
| WTO | World Trade Organization |

# 1
# Institutional Aspects of the South Eastern European Economy: Introduction, Trends, and Scope of the Study

## Background

Accelerating growth and reducing poverty through the establishment of a stable, transparent, and uniform investment framework are key to restoring and consolidating peace and stability in South Eastern Europe (SEE). Low levels of domestic and foreign investment have constrained economic development in the region. Evidence from enterprise surveys and diagnostic studies, as well as from many anecdotal sources, shows that the cost of doing business in SEE is too high and discourages private investment.

South Eastern European countries and their development partners have recognized explicitly the importance of improving the investment framework in the region. All of the beneficiary members of the Stability Pact—which is a political declaration of commitment and a framework agreement on international cooperation among more than 40 partner countries and organizations—have committed to developing a shared strategy for stability and growth in SEE.[1] As part of the Stability Pact, the countries of SEE intend to implement the Investment Compact, which includes important legislative and administrative commitments for advancing the region's economic and business environment.[2] Improving the investment framework in SEE not only is important; it also is urgent for two reasons. First, the European Union (EU) has greatly expanded trade access to the single European market, both for the accession countries (Bulgaria and Romania) and for the five western Balkan states (Albania, Bosnia and Herzegovina, Croatia, the former Yugoslav Republic of Macedonia, and Serbia and Montenegro) and Moldova. Simultaneously, liberalization of intraregional trade has gained new momentum with the signing of the Memorandum of Understanding on Trade Liberalization and Facilitation by Albania, Bosnia and Herzegovina, Bulgaria, Croatia, FYR Macedonia, Moldova, Serbia and Montenegro, and Romania. Only if investment increases substantially will it be possible to seize the opportunities created by these developments.

The second reason for urgency is the close association of high unemployment rates and insufficient job creation with high rates of persistent poverty throughout the region, which endangers social stability and could thus undermine the prospects for growth.

In the study that is the focus of this book, we analyze eight countries (the SEE8): Albania, Bosnia and Herzegovina, Bulgaria, Croatia, FYR Macedonia, Moldova, Romania, and Serbia and Montenegro.[3] We cover the institutional impediments to investment and private sector development in the SEE8 and suggest policy reforms to ease these constraints. The premise of the study is that an institutional framework that is favorable for domestic and foreign investments is essential to achieve sustainable growth and alleviate poverty in the region.

In this chapter, we describe the recent economic trends in the SEE8 and their prospects for international and intraregional integration. We present our understanding of the role of the institutions and economic environment that affect enterprise development and growth in the SEE8 and describe the objectives, scope, and organization of the study.

## Trends in the SEE8 Economies

### Dynamics of Output by Sector

The recent progress in privatization and structural reforms in South Eastern Europe indicates that the region has recovered from the deep and lengthy recession of the 1990s. Most of the economies of the region have experienced relatively sustained growth, although in some cases that growth is still somewhat fragile, especially since the end of the Kosovo conflict in 1999 (see table 1.1).

Most of the 1990s were characterized by dramatic collapses of output. The occasional periods of economic stability were backed by subsidies to the state-owned industrial sector, which increased fiscal and current account deficits, or by extensive borrowing from abroad. In 2001, the SEE8 had reached only 74 percent of its pretransition (1989) level of economic activity.[4] In comparison, in 2001 the five most developed Eastern European transition economies (the Czech Republic, Hungary, Poland, the Slovak Republic, and Slovenia) had recovered and grown to a combined output of 115 percent of 1989 levels. Despite the slow and erratic

## Table 1.1  Output in the SEE8, 1998–2002

| | Real GDP growth by sector (%) | | | | | Value added by sector (% of GDP) | | | | |
|---|---|---|---|---|---|---|---|---|---|---|
| | 1998 | 1999 | 2000 | 2001 | 2002 | 1998 | 1999 | 2000 | 2001 | 2002 |
| *Albania* | | | | | | | | | | |
| Annual GDP growth | 7.9 | 7.3 | 7.8 | 6.5 | 4.7 | | | | | |
| Agriculture | 5.0 | 3.7 | 4.0 | 1.4 | 3.0 | 54.5 | 37.2 | 35.9 | 34.2 | 32.4 |
| Industry | 12.1 | 10.8 | 11.4 | 10.7 | 5.5 | 24.5 | 22.3 | 22.7 | 23.4 | 22.7 |
| Manufacturing | 4.1 | 6.4 | 5.0 | 6.5 | 6.0 | 11.9 | 13.5 | 13.2 | 13.2 | 12.8 |
| Services | 11.2 | 13.0 | 13.3 | 13.6 | 7.4 | 21.1 | 40.5 | 41.4 | 42.4 | 44.9 |
| *Bosnia and Herzegovina* | | | | | | | | | | |
| Annual GDP growth | 15.6 | 9.6 | 5.6 | 4.5 | 3.9 | | | | | |
| Agriculture | −0.1 | −3.4 | −8.3 | — | — | 14.8 | 13.3 | 11.7 | 14.3 | — |
| Industry | 16.7 | 9.0 | 5.7 | — | — | 26.0 | 24.4 | 24.9 | 29.6 | — |
| Manufacturing | −7.5 | −0.5 | 7.2 | — | — | 16.2 | 14.9 | 15.1 | — | — |
| Services | 10.2 | 14.1 | 9.4 | — | — | 59.2 | 62.3 | 63.4 | 56.1 | — |
| *Bulgaria* | | | | | | | | | | |
| Annual GDP growth | 4.0 | 2.3 | 5.4 | 4.0 | 4.3 | | | | | |
| Agriculture | 1.2 | 5.5 | −10.3 | 0.5 | 1.1 | 19.1 | 16.6 | 14.2 | 13.9 | 13.3 |
| Industry | 7.9 | −6.3 | 10.6 | 4.2 | 3.1 | 31.0 | 28.6 | 29.7 | 29.0 | 28.9 |
| Manufacturing | 6.5 | −5.9 | 19.5 | — | — | 19.4 | 17.2 | 18.1 | 17.8 | 17.9 |
| Services | 0.6 | 5.3 | 6.7 | 4.2 | 4.9 | 49.9 | 54.8 | 56.1 | 57.1 | 57.8 |
| *Croatia* | | | | | | | | | | |
| Annual GDP growth | 2.5 | −0.9 | 2.9 | 3.8 | 5.2 | | | | | |
| Agriculture | 5.6 | −2.0 | 1.3 | 0.7 | — | 9.8 | 9.8 | 9.9 | 9.7 | — |
| Industry | 4.7 | 0.1 | 1.5 | 4.3 | — | 33.1 | 33.4 | 34.1 | 34.2 | — |
| Manufacturing | 5.3 | 4.1 | 4.1 | 6.0 | — | 22.2 | 22.6 | 24.1 | 24.3 | — |
| Services | 2.1 | −0.3 | 5.0 | 4.8 | — | 57.0 | 56.8 | 56.0 | 56.1 | — |

*(Table continues on the following page.)*

3

## Table 1.1  (continued)

| | Real GDP growth by sector (%) | | | | | Value added by sector (% of GDP) | | | | |
|---|---|---|---|---|---|---|---|---|---|---|
| | 1998 | 1999 | 2000 | 2001 | 2002 | 1998 | 1999 | 2000 | 2001 | 2002 |
| *Macedonia, FYR* | | | | | | | | | | |
| Annual GDP growth | 3.4 | 4.3 | 4.5 | −4.5 | 0.3 | | | | | |
| Agriculture | 3.3 | 0.9 | 1.0 | −10.8 | 2.1 | 13.2 | 12.9 | 12.0 | 11.7 | 12.1 |
| Industry | 2.6 | 3.3 | 8.0 | −6.4 | −5.6 | 33.8 | 32.6 | 33.7 | 32.1 | 29.7 |
| Manufacturing | 0.5 | 2.4 | 9.4 | −3.9 | −5.4 | 20.9 | 20.5 | 20.7 | 20.3 | 18.6 |
| Services | 3.6 | 6.3 | 2.3 | −1.6 | 3.6 | 53.0 | 54.5 | 54.3 | 56.1 | 58.2 |
| *Moldova* | | | | | | | | | | |
| Annual GDP growth | −6.5 | −3.4 | 2.1 | 6.1 | 7.2 | | | | | |
| Agriculture | −6.2 | −3.9 | 2.3 | 4.3 | 2.0 | 30.5 | 27.9 | 29.0 | 26.0 | 25.1 |
| Industry | −15.2 | −3.5 | 6.6 | 17.5 | 6.0 | 23.5 | 22.7 | 21.7 | 24.1 | 24.2 |
| Manufacturing | −16.4 | −6.1 | 15.9 | 17.8 | 6.0 | 16.5 | 14.7 | 16.3 | 18.2 | 18.2 |
| Services | 0.6 | 5.9 | −3.8 | −0.5 | 4.4 | 46.1 | 49.4 | 49.2 | 49.8 | 50.7 |
| *Romania* | | | | | | | | | | |
| Annual GDP growth | −4.8 | −1.2 | 0.6 | 5.3 | 4.3 | | | | | |
| Agriculture | −10.4 | 3.3 | −18.2 | 21.2 | 3.0 | 16.2 | 15.2 | 12.5 | 15.0 | 14.8 |
| Industry | −8.7 | −1.7 | 6.2 | 7.4 | 7.0 | 35.4 | 33.9 | 34.1 | 34.6 | 35.6 |
| Manufacturing | −5.3 | −7.1 | 6.2 | — | 8.0 | — | — | — | — | 25.7 |
| Services | −0.5 | −3.4 | 6.8 | — | — | 48.4 | 51.0 | 53.4 | 50.4 | 49.6 |
| *Serbia and Montenegro* | | | | | | | | | | |
| Annual GDP growth | 1.9 | −15.7 | 5.0 | 5.5 | 4.0 | | | | | |
| Agriculture | — | 1.2 | −20.0 | — | — | — | 10.1 | 17.6 | — | — |
| Industry | 3.6 | −22.5 | 10.9 | — | — | — | 43.1 | 37.6 | — | — |
| Manufacturing | — | — | — | — | — | — | — | — | — | — |
| Services | — | — | — | — | — | — | 46.8 | 44.8 | — | — |

*Sources:* World Bank (2003c) and national statistical authorities.
*Note:* — = not available; GDP = gross domestic product.

4

recovery in output since the fall of the socialist regime, by the end of the 1990s, growth rates in the SEE8 had been restored. In 2002, the region grew 4.2 percent, on average—faster than the 2.5 percent growth rate of the world economy. For 2003, the average regional growth for the SEE8 also was positive, at 3.5 percent (EBRD 2003).

The economic rebound of the SEE8 has been fueled primarily by private means as resources have moved from the state to the private sector. In 2002, the private sector generated at least one-half of the output across the region, except in Bosnia and Herzegovina and Serbia and Montenegro (see figure 1.1). The privatization of large-scale enterprises advanced slowly for most of the 1990s, which suggests that the emerging private sector and the small and medium-size enterprises (SMEs) were the vehicles of recent growth in the SEE8. Although SME privatization has been completed in most of the countries in the region, in Bosnia and Herzegovina, Moldova, and Serbia and Montenegro, ownership divestiture programs are still under way (EBRD 2002). At the same time, the role of foreign aid and loans has declined even in the western Balkans, where it constituted a

**Figure 1.1   Progress in the Transition of the SEE8: Small-Scale Privatization, Large-Scale Privatization, and Private Sector Share in Output**

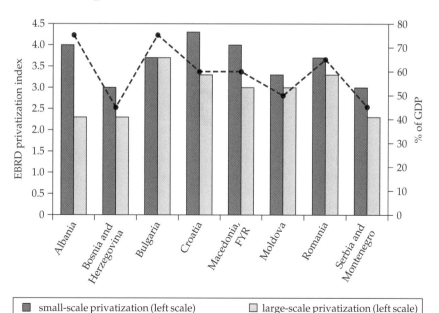

small share (7 percent) of the five countries' gross domestic product (GDP) in 2002 (European Commission 2003b, p. 10).

INDUSTRY

Despite progress with initial reforms such as small-scale privatization, price liberalization, and foreign exchange and trade liberalization, industrial output in the SEE8 has recovered on average only 45 percent of its 1989 level, except in Bosnia and Herzegovina, which registered only 12 percent recovery of its 1989 output level (UNECE 2002). Before the fall of the socialist regime, the industrial sector generated most of the output in these countries. However, traditional industrial sectors, such as base metals, textiles, footwear, and food processing, declined in many of the SEE8, partly because of the market transformation and the lack of competitiveness of many export sectors, and partly because of the war and regional conflicts of the Yugoslav succession. The failure to attract domestic and foreign investment has left large-scale manufacturing, especially the heavy industries such as metallurgy, heavy-machine building, and mining, with outdated equipment and technology. This lack of up-to-date technology has hampered the competitiveness of the region's industrial products.

Although the recovery of the industrial sector in the SEE8 has been anemic, in the past decade small-scale manufacturing has remained a major component of output. The recent industrial recovery throughout the region was led primarily by the export-oriented light industries for consumer goods such as food and beverages, textiles and clothing, leather goods and footwear, light machinery and equipment, chemical products, wood products, and electrical appliances.

The construction industry also grew in parts of the region. In the 1990s, it became one of the most dynamic sectors of the economies of Albania and Bosnia and Herzegovina. However, because it was funded primarily by remittances and foreign aid for rebuilding the countries that suffered from regional conflicts, the sector became heavily dependent on foreign projects. Construction financed by the domestic private sector in Bosnia and Herzegovina, for example, has been negligible since the war there ended in 1995 (EIU 2002). In the rest of the region, the construction industry was hit by the transitional recession but mostly recovered and grew in the late 1990s.

The acute need in the SEE8 for improvements in physical infrastructure, housing, and tourism suggests the potential for further development of the industrial sector, but growth in the region will require a favorable investment climate.

AGRICULTURE

Agricultural output also shrank during the first decade of market transformation in the SEE8. On average, the agricultural sector made up less than 18 percent of GDP in 2001. Albania and Moldova were the only countries among the eight where agriculture represented a larger share of output in 2002: in Albania close to 33 percent of GDP, and in Moldova 25 percent of GDP (see table 1.1). The high level of agricultural output in both countries is due not only to their large rural populations, but also to the slower progress in the development of the services sector and industry restructuring. With the notable exception of Albania, agricultural labor productivity also declined substantially in the region since 1990.[5]

Although agricultural prices were liberalized early in most of the SEE8, the agricultural sector throughout the region suffered from a reform policy stalemate and from neglect. The decomposition of agro-industrial cooperatives and the restitution of land were often disrupted by political controversy regarding divestiture strategies and the pace of the process. Only in Bulgaria and part of Romania was restitution—the return of farmland to precommunist owners—used as a privatization strategy. In Albania, Moldova, and the remainder of Romania, a distribution strategy allocated farmland to either collective farm workers or the whole population.[6] In the countries that emerged from the former Yugoslavia, privatization of land was not required because farmland was privately owned before 1990 (EBRD 2002, pp. 76–78).

A vibrant land market in the SEE8 has yet to evolve because disputes, lengthy procedures, and corruption have delayed the distribution of land titles. In addition, records held by the land registers and the cadastre are frequently inconsistent, and difficulties in identifying the real owners have jeopardized the upholding of property rights. For example, 70 percent of the issued land titles in Romania have ended up in litigation (FIAS 2001a). As a result, using land as collateral in business transactions in the SEE8 is rare. Serbia and Montenegro's central bank has assigned land value as zero in its accounting books (FIAS 2001b).

The slow development of land reforms has impeded market exchanges and has hampered the growth of the agricultural sector. Across the region, the new owners of agricultural land have not yet achieved pre-1989 production capacity. For example, Romania, once a major agricultural producer, has experienced a steady decline in the livestock sector—the production of meat and crops—since 1989 (EIU 2001b). Although agriculture still accounts for over a quarter of GDP in Moldova, yields for vegetables have decreased by 64 percent (44 percent for sugar beets alone) since 1990 (data for 2000, EIU 2001a). The level of livestock production has also come down drastically in the past 10 years in Moldova.[7] Similar trends exist in Bosnia and Herzegovina, FYR Macedonia, and Serbia and Montenegro.

The liberalization of the agricultural markets in the SEE8 and the removal of protectionist prices exposed domestic agricultural products to the competitive pressure of imports. Many of the SEE8 are currently net food importers, including Albania, Bosnia and Herzegovina, Croatia, FYR Macedonia, Romania, and Serbia and Montenegro, which further suggests the uncompetitive state of the domestic agricultural market.

SERVICES

With the decline of production in agriculture and industry, the services sectors became the leading generators of output in the transition economies of Eastern Europe. Transition trends from Eastern Europe indicate that, in general, services had grown to about half of GDP in these countries by the end of the 1990s. The composition of SEE8 output had similar dynamics; however, the high share of services in the SEE8 does not necessarily reflect a postindustrial structure to their economies. The high share of services in the GDP of these countries instead reflects qualitative deficiencies in the economy: government services and utilities represent a large share of those services. For most of the 1990s, regulated utilities were a vehicle for cross-subsidies and soft lending to nonrestructured firms, and only recently have governments begun breaking up monopolies and privatizing those services.[8]

As a result of recent restructuring efforts in some services sectors, services such as communications and tourism have increased their economic significance in the region. For example, the liberalization of telecommunications in the region has resulted in investments in improved telecommunication networks. As a result, the number of fixed lines has increased, old analog networks have been replaced with digital networks, privatization of state-owned monopolies has begun, and the market for mobile services has expanded. The tourism industry has gained economic significance for the region as well. For example, in Croatia 5.7 percent of total employment is concentrated in tourism, and the sector generates close to 5.1 percent of GDP (2002, constant market prices).

The trade sector also has expanded. For the period 1990–2002, the share of GDP in wholesale and retail trade and repair of motor vehicles grew from 7.8 percent to 10.4 percent in Bulgaria, from 14.8 percent to 16.4 percent in Croatia, and from 5.2 percent (in 1993) to 8.1 percent in Romania in 2001.[9] In fact, retail trade has emerged as one of the most attractive sectors for new private companies. For example, in Albania, 52 percent of the businesses operate in retail trade. Local and European retail chains such as Metro, Mercator, and Billa have spread throughout the region too.

The financial sector plays an integral part in the evolution of the services sectors and of the overall economy by providing a payment mechanism for the intermediation of resources. There is abundant evidence that the development of the financial sector provides a critical boost to economic growth (see, for example, Levine 1996). However, although the SEE8 have taken the initial steps to reform their financial sectors, only a few have financial sectors capable of providing significant lending to private enterprises.

Although most commercial banks in the region have been privatized, competitive intermediation of financial resources has yet to effectively reach entrepreneurs.[10] The financial sector is burdened by bad loans and lending based on common relationships. Such lending crowds out other productive investments. Also, the big spread between interest rates for deposits and lending in the SEE8 suggests that most banks operate inefficiently. Moreover, the lack of modern, risk-based screening and monitoring mechanisms leads banks to make uninformed decisions. As a result, banks are not investing in the private sector. For example, in the SEE8 in 2002, only in Croatia was the level of domestic credit to the private sector slightly over 45 percent of GDP; the level was only 4 percent in Albania, and in Serbia and Montenegro it was 5.6 percent (EBRD 2002).[11] The lack of affordable financial resources appears to have become one of the major obstacles to business development in the region, especially in the absence of alternatives to bank financing.[12]

Overall, the economic trends for output in the SEE8 show a sluggish recovery. The delayed restructuring in industry, agriculture, and services, which was caused in part by the lack of effective market-based institutions that would protect property rights, fair competition, and financial discipline, impeded a quick rebound of output and slowed economic growth in the SEE8. Although growth rates have finally begun to rebound regionwide, improving the business and investment environment through strengthened market institutions is essential for sustaining the recent growth and for reducing poverty in the region.

## Human Development Aspects of the SEE8 Transition

Unemployment in the SEE8 in the 1990s has been high and continues to increase as a result of slow job creation, structural disruptions, and the lack of well-functioning market institutions in the region. For example, in 2002 registered unemployment in Bosnia and Herzegovina and FYR Macedonia was 41 percent and 32 percent of the total labor force, respectively. In the other Balkan countries, the unemployment rate varied between 7 and 8 percent in Moldova and Romania and 29 percent in Serbia and Montenegro (see figure 1.2).[13]

However, country-level labor and household surveys suggest that the actual level of unemployment in the region is much lower than the data in figure 1.2 indicate, given the size of the informal economy in the region. Estimates of the "gray economy" are difficult to gauge and vary significantly from country to country, but experts estimate that it represents about a third of GDP in most of the SEE8 and close to half of GDP in

## Figure 1.2    Registered Unemployment in the SEE8, 1994–2001

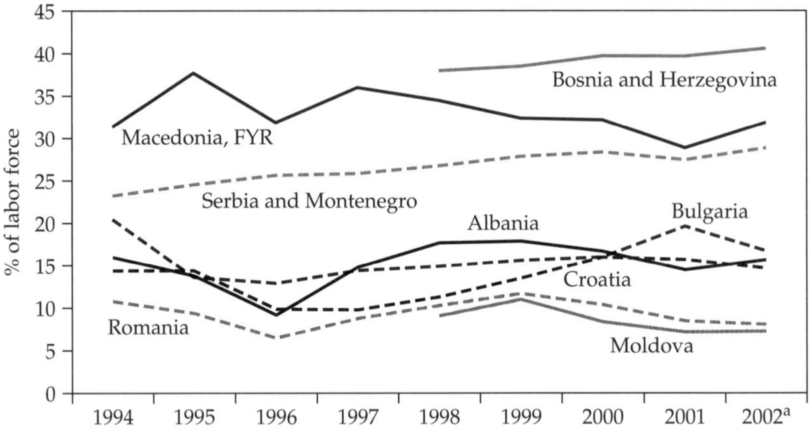

*Source:* EBRD (2003).

FYR Macedonia and Moldova.[14] According to a 2001 labor force survey, only 40 percent of the registered jobless in Bosnia and Herzegovina were in fact unemployed, and the informal sector provided jobs for 36 percent of the employed (World Bank 2002a, p. xi). More than half of the registered unemployed in Serbia and Montenegro had jobs in the informal sector (World Bank 2002a, p. 13). In the late 1990s, the informal sector of Bulgaria was assessed at about 25 percent of output (Nenovsky and Hristov 2000). In FYR Macedonia, the 2001 labor force survey showed that over 57 percent of those who were unemployed in 2000 in fact held jobs in the informal sector (European Commission 2003a, p. 15). In Romania, the informal sector represented 30 to 40 percent of GDP in 2000, according to a report of the European Commission (EIU 2001b). The rise of unemployment in the region is not an isolated problem; it should be considered in relation to output recovery, privatization, and new business creation. Labor hoarding (or overstaffing) and low labor productivity are typical during transition periods in many economies. At the outset of reform across Eastern Europe, the labor market was structurally distorted, with nearly full employment but low wages. Employment figures in all of the SEE8 declined because of a variety of factors, such as the initial collapse of output, the consequent (albeit limited) restructuring of public enterprises, the reduction of direct and indirect subsidies from the state, and the partial hardening of the budget constraints. As a result, job cuts have become typical for public enterprises in the region. Simultaneously, as the privatization of public enterprises gained momentum in the SEE8, the productivity of such firms increased, which also ultimately contributed to the layoffs.

SOUTH EASTERN EUROPEAN ECONOMY

Labor market rigidities also emerged from the heavily regulated and protected formal sector. These regulations presented large and inflexible barriers to employment and impeded labor mobility. In addition, the slow pace of new business development in the SEE8 could not quickly offset the loss of jobs. Thus, job dynamics, measured by net growth in employment, have been slow, with job destruction outweighing the gains from job creation. For example, in Bosnia and Herzegovina the job flow rate in companies with more than 100 employees showed that, on average, 4.2 jobs per 100 existing jobs were created in 1997–99, while 5.3 jobs were lost (World Bank 2002a, p. 30). Even in the countries where the business environment has improved in the past few years, unemployment has been rising because labor deficiencies are being reduced through privatization, increased productivity, and slow job creation. For example, in Bulgaria, new businesses created 36 percent of all new jobs in 2000, and the job creation rate in the micro enterprises was 27 percent, as opposed to 2.1 percent in the large firms (World Bank 2002b). Similarly, during 1995–97 in Romania, the job destruction rate in firms of more than 100 workers was more than twice as high as the rate of job creation, leading to an overall decline in employment (World Bank 2002b, p. 30).

Ironically, although unemployment is generally rising, the labor markets remain overregulated and often hostile to new business formation; however, the dynamics of the SEE8 markets vary significantly. Employment protection in the western Balkan states is very strictly regulated, with lengthy and costly dismissal procedures, restrictions on temporary employment, and inflexible wage structures determined by insiders (Rutkowski 1998, 2003). Bulgaria and, to a lesser extent, Romania have slightly more flexible labor codes in comparison with the countries formed after the split of Yugoslavia, although the laws could amplify the rigidity of the market and the increases in labor costs. In Croatia, the labor law introduced in 2003 has contributed substantially to improving the flexibility of the labor market. The outlier in the group is Moldova, which has not yet developed a market-oriented labor policy to expose and tackle its unemployment problem. Overall, employees are overly protected throughout the region, not only because of the written labor rules, but also because of the judicial interpretation of labor legislation.

Achieving greater labor mobility and encouraging job creation will require that decisive steps be taken to improve labor legislation throughout the region. Deregulation, decentralization of collective bargaining to firm-level dialogue, improved flexibility of dismissal procedures, simplified wage adjustment and overtime pay, and introduction of fixed-term contracts are some of the reforms being debated to improve the transparency and functioning of the labor institutions in the region. Such initiatives, as well as formalization of the gray economy, are key to fighting the unemployment problem in the SEE8.

## International and Intraregional Integration

TRADE

After the fall of the socialist regimes in Eastern Europe, trade flow and structure were disrupted. Price and structural distortions, outdated technologies, labor-intensive production, and trade restrictions made it difficult to identify and boost the most competitive sectors of the region so it could benefit from trade. As a result, merchandise trade slowed, growing only moderately after overcoming the initial postcommunist decline in output (see figure 1.3).[15] Conflicts and war in the Balkans have also affected the supply side of trade and have reduced the opportunities for diversifying exports. For example, exports from Croatia and FYR Macedonia remain subdued because of the conflict. After the end of the war in Bosnia and Herzegovina and Serbia and Montenegro, trade increased, but it has not yet reached prewar levels. The value of exports from Bulgaria, Moldova, and Romania fluctuated sharply in the 1990s because of the slow recovery of output and the initial loss of markets. Albanian exports nearly tripled in the past 10 years, but from a negligible base.

The systemic changes spurred two major shifts in the 1990s: (a) the loss of common markets in the other former socialist countries and (b) the liberalization of trade with the industrial world. Together these shifts changed the direction of SEE8 trade. Except for Moldova, the European Union has become the SEE8's biggest trading partner. The volume of exports from the SEE8 to the European Union doubled from US$7.5 billion to US$15.3 billion during 1994–2001 (IMF 2002). Imports from the European Union more than doubled during the same period. The change in trade flows for the eight countries' merchandise trade is shown in figure 1.3.

Exports of the SEE8 are concentrated in only a few products. Two main product groups are reaching European and world markets: (a) textiles and clothing and (b) heavy manufacturing. Of the latter, transportation equipment and metal processing accounted for over 50 percent of exports in Bosnia and Herzegovina, Croatia, FYR Macedonia, and Serbia and Montenegro at the end of the 1990s. Basic metals have also been important exports for Bulgaria and Romania, in addition to low-value-added, labor-intensive products in textiles, clothing, footwear, and furniture. The textile sector has become a leading export sector for Albania as well as Moldova, where it has gained a steady share (18 percent in total exports in 2000). Overall, textiles and clothing from the SEE8 composed 1.6 percent of total EU imports in 2000. Agricultural exports, on the other hand, have played a minor role in the SEE8 trade, except in Moldova, where food, beverages, and tobacco products accounted for 42 percent of total exports in 2000, and in Serbia and Montenegro, where they accounted for 22 percent of exports in 2002.

## Figure 1.3    Direction of Trade in the SEE8

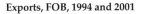

Exports, FOB, 1994 and 2001

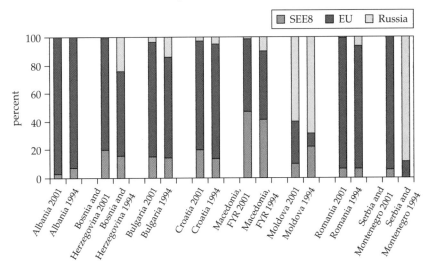

Imports, CIF, 1994 and 2001

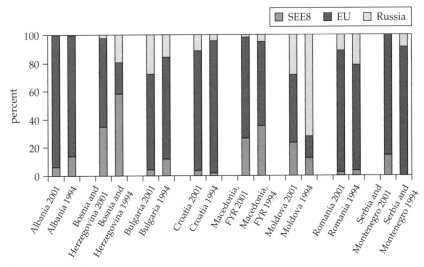

*Source:* IMF (2002).
*Note:* FOB = free on board; CIF = cost, insurance, and freight.

The sectoral composition of exports in the SEE8 did not shift markedly in the 1990s. In Serbia and Montenegro, the share of manufactured goods declined and the share of raw materials and other goods with limited processing increased. The reverse happened in Albania, Bulgaria, and

Romania because of textile processing. The underlying reasons for this lack of change were the delayed economic reform in the industrial sector and the slow creation of new businesses in the SEE8. These two factors negatively affected supply and caused losses of markets (Michalopoulos 2001). In addition, the governments' provision of political and financial support to noncompetitive industries in the region slowed economic recovery and hampered international integration.

Intraregional trade among the SEE8 remained at negligible levels during the 1990s, not exceeding 10 percent (EBRD 2003). The pace and scope of SEE8 trade relationships have varied. Although each of the Bosnia and Herzegovina entities (the Federation of Bosnia and Herzegovina and Republika Srpska) has a strong trading relationship with another former Yugoslav state (the Federation of Bosnia and Herzegovina with Croatia, and Republika Srpska with Serbia and Montenegro), they maintain little trade with each other. Similarly, FYR Macedonia and Serbia and Montenegro have had a strong trading relationship, but as of early 2001, little trade existed between Croatia and Serbia and Montenegro, between Albania and most of the rest of the SEE8, and between Moldova and the rest of the SEE8. To a large extent, this situation reflected the legacy of political tensions and the high risks associated with trade transactions during the war and with international sanctions.

These trends in trade reflect the dynamics of intraregional and international trade policies. After the war and the lifting of sanctions in Serbia and Montenegro, a regional initiative to liberalize trade among the South Eastern European countries emerged under the Stability Pact. The pact has become an important step in boosting regional exchanges and overcoming the politically driven disruption of trade between some of the countries (for example, between Croatia and Serbia and Montenegro, and between Bosnia and Herzegovina and Serbia and Montenegro).

In June 2001, under the Stability Pact's Working Group on Trade Liberalization and Facilitation, Albania, Bosnia and Herzegovina, Bulgaria, Croatia, FYR Macedonia, Romania, and Serbia and Montenegro signed a Memorandum of Understanding on Trade Liberalization and Facilitation. (Moldova has since associated itself with the memorandum, signing it in 2002.) The aim of the memorandum of understanding was to promote free trade among the South Eastern European countries. Recognizing the political difficulties surrounding the creation of a single free trade agreement (FTA) in the region, the memorandum settled for a less ambitious goal of establishing a network of bilateral FTAs, which led to the creation of a "virtual" free trade area that covers all the South Eastern European countries.[16] The main principles outlined in the memorandum are (a) to establish over a 6-year transitional period a network of bilateral FTAs based on a product coverage rule of at least 90 percent; (b) to work to deepen integration through liberalization of services; and (c) to take steps to harmonize legislation and regulations—including those on competition, investment, and standards—and to bring them closer to those of the European Union.

For the past 3 years, the memorandum has been the centerpiece of trade integration efforts in the region, and the working group has focused on monitoring the implementation of the commitments made by the countries and on exploring ways to deepen their integration efforts. As of March 2004, 24 bilateral FTAs had been signed or ratified among the SEE8. The short-term objectives are to ensure that these FTAs comply with the terms of the memorandum and to ensure that they are fully and efficiently implemented, including provisions that eliminate nontariff barriers, that identify the scope of use and management of tariff quotas and specific duties on agriculture, that impose consistency in the application of trade remedies, and that effectively implement preferential rules of origin. In the medium term, the signatories are working toward harmonizing the scope of their FTAs, the rules and procedures governing competition policy, and sanitary and phytosanitary measures, as well as toward further liberalizing services.[17]

Observers consider the memorandum to be a useful step forward in intraregional integration; however, a number of unresolved issues remain, including the level of liberalization of the overall trade regimes (World Bank 2003b). The long-term vision of integrating SEE into the European and international markets requires the consolidation of the FTAs into a larger grouping or even into a single FTA with common rules and exceptions. In addition, a system of cumulative rules of origin is needed that will foster intra-industry trade and investments across the European Union and the Balkans. An alternative arrangement to the numerous bilateral FTAs would be the Central European Free Trade Agreement (CEFTA), which some of the SEE8 have already joined.[18]

The evolving relationships of SEE8 with the European Union have greatly enhanced their integration into the global economy. In September 2000, the European Union introduced special measures for duty- and quota-free access for exports within the framework of the Autonomous Trade Preference (ATP) scheme for the western Balkan states (Albania, Bosnia and Herzegovina, Croatia, FYR Macedonia, and Serbia and Montenegro).[19] The measures are considered by experts to be "generous in providing market access opportunities to these five countries" (Michalopoulos 2001). The European Union also launched the stabilization and association process to parallel the ATP scheme. This process represents the European Union's commitment to enter into a bilateral stabilization and association agreement (SAA) with each of the five countries, combined with a promise of some type of association with the European Union. The SAAs establish the legal framework for future economic and political relationships between the European Union and the five countries and envisage the establishment of free trade areas among the five countries and with the European Union within 10–12 years. The SAAs also cover economic and institutional reform, cooperation of political and judicial entities, and harmonization of legislation with EU law in the areas of investment, competition, the environment, and standards. In addition, the SAAs call for intensifying regional cooperation among the five western Balkan countries to encourage the deepening of regional trade and investments flows.

The trade relationships between the European Union and Bulgaria and Romania have been of a different nature. Both countries are associate members of the European Union and candidates for full membership. Numerous agreements and documents between these two countries and the European Union have resulted in a fairly liberal trade regime across a wide range of sectors and have made exchanges easier.[20] Trade in both directions has been steadily increasing. As a result, in 2001 over 55 percent of Bulgaria's total exports reached EU destinations, and half of its imports originated in the European Union (see figure 1.3). Bulgaria's major trade partners have been Germany, Greece, and Italy. Romania's trade flows are also dominated by the more attractive European markets. Close to 68 percent of Romania's total exports reached the single European market (mainly France, Germany, and Italy), and the country received over 57 percent of its imports from the European Union (see figure 1.3).

Moldova has not yet reached its full trade integration potential with the European Union. As a former Soviet republic, Moldova has not greatly changed its trade patterns in the past decade, and the Russian Federation has remained its main trading partner. The Commonwealth of Independent States has accounted for close to two-thirds of Moldova's total export revenues since the country became independent (EIU 2001a). The composition of Moldovan exports has been very similar to that of other South Eastern European countries, consisting mainly of food products, beverages and tobacco, machinery and transportation equipment, and textiles. However, these products are reaching EU markets at a much slower pace in contrast with the much deeper penetration by the other South Eastern European countries. Now that Moldova has become a full-fledged member of the Stability Pact, the country will inevitably foster trade and investment links with the rest of the region and with the European Union. Liberalization of trade and regional integration are expected to bring opportunities for diversification of exports and new markets for Moldovan products. At the same time, exports will face the fierce competition and demand for quality on the world market, which would be difficult to meet if structural reforms in Moldova are slowed.

Membership in the World Trade Organization (WTO) is also a means to further the international integration of the SEE8. There is a compelling argument that nonmember countries (Bosnia and Herzegovina and Serbia and Montenegro) should use WTO accession to further reduce their existing trade controls (see, for example, World Bank 2003b, pp. 80–85). Opportunities exist for the liberalization of tariffs as well as services. The WTO accession process gives governments a means to push forward "behind-the-border" measures that would otherwise be difficult to implement, especially from a political perspective.

Two main points can be made from the discussion above. First, although cross-border trade is gaining momentum in the SEE8 as bilateral FTAs proliferate, the major challenge continues to be effective implementation of those agreements. Existing nontariff barriers and cumbersome procedures must be abolished to facilitate the process of international and intraregional integration. In addition, establishing of a single free trade area will lead to more intensive trade and investment flows in the region. Second, achieving a sustainable path of economic recovery and establishing a supportive business environment in the region are necessary to spur a supply response from the private sector. These two approaches would allow the SEE8 to better exploit their competitive advantages and would foster trade and exchanges among one another and with the rest of the world.

FOREIGN DIRECT INVESTMENT

As in other emerging markets, the experience of Eastern Europe has shown that foreign direct investment (FDI) has been the primary vehicle for advancing a country's economic structure, for creating new jobs, and for fostering economic growth (Broadman, Bergsman, and Drebentsov 2000; World Bank 2003a). However, a major gap exists between the South Eastern European region and the more advanced transition countries of Eastern Europe with regard to cumulative FDI flows. This gap suggests that the Balkans have not benefited much from the flow of foreign capital and know-how during the past decade. For example, although the flow of FDI to Poland has been US$38.5 billion since 1990, in Romania— the SEE8 country that has attracted the most FDI—the cumulative inflow for the same period has been less than one-quarter of Poland's (see table 1.2 and figure 1.4). The comparison of FDI flows of the SEE8 and the more advanced Eastern European countries on a per capita basis is also striking. For example, from 1990 to 2002, the cumulative per capita inflow of FDI was much higher in the Czech Republic (US$3,554) and Hungary (US$2,253) in comparison with that in even the largest recipients of FDI in the SEE8—that is, Bulgaria (US$560), Croatia (US$1,419), or Romania (US$415) (EBRD 2003, p. 65).

### Table 1.2    Foreign Direct Investment in the SEE8, 1989–2002

| Country | Cumulative FDI inflows (US$ millions) 1989–2002 | Cumulative FDI inflows per capita (US$) 1989–2002 | FDI inflows per capita (US$) 2001 | FDI inflows per capita (US$) 2002 | FDI inflows (% of GDP) 2001 | FDI inflows (% of GDP) 2002 |
|---|---|---|---|---|---|---|
| Albania | 936 | 303 | 66 | 44 | 4.8 | 2.8 |
| Bosnia and Herzegovina | 753 | 198 | 34 | 61 | 2.7 | 4.4 |
| Bulgaria | 4,390 | 560 | 79 | 55 | 4.7 | 2.8 |
| Croatia | 6,296 | 1,419 | 316 | 86 | 7.2 | 1.7 |
| Macedonia, FYR | 935 | 476 | 221 | 50 | 12.9 | 2.7 |
| Moldova | 849 | 199 | 37 | 25 | 10 | 6.6 |
| Romania | 9,008 | 415 | 52 | 50 | 2.9 | 2.4 |
| Serbia and Montenegro | 1,717 | 206 | 20 | 67 | 1.4 | 3.6 |

*Source:* EBRD (2003, p. 65).

### Figure 1.4    Inflows of Foreign Direct Investment in the SEE8, 1991–2003

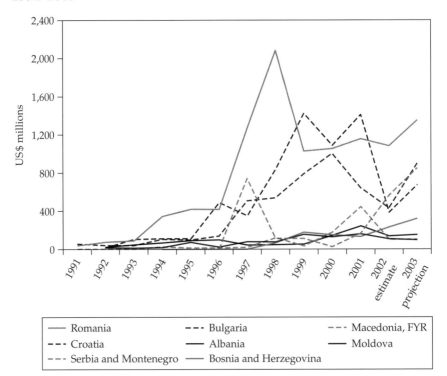

*Source:* EBRD (2003, p. 65).

The nature of the flow of FDI to the SEE8 also varies in comparison with that of the more advanced Eastern European countries. In the Balkans, both the volume and the composition of FDI inflows have been linked mostly to large-scale privatization transactions in telecommunications, banking, and heavy industry. In contrast, greenfield FDI has been mainly in low-technology, labor-intensive, but export-oriented industries such as leather, textiles, and clothing. Greenfield investments in SEE have been very limited and directed primarily at servicing the domestic market (Demekas 2002). However, most recent data on Bulgaria and Romania suggest a shift in this trend as industries take advantage of lower production costs. Overall, the low level of greenfield investment in the SEE8 suggests that once the sell-off of state-owned enterprises is completed, the amount of FDI in the SEE8 may be small, unless an institutional environment that supports private investment takes hold.

The main source of FDI in the region has been the Organisation for Economic Co-operation and Development (OECD) countries, which account for over 90 percent of FDI inflows in Bulgaria, Croatia, and Romania. Non-OECD countries, especially Russia, are active investors in the energy sector. However, intraregional investment in common commercial and supply networks has a negligible presence in the SEE8. The lack of such investment is a critical bottleneck in the creation of greater "economic space" in SEE, and it both reflects and contributes to the limited interenterprise competition and limited entry of new enterprises in the SEE8.

Foreign direct investment in the Balkans is limited both structurally and institutionally. As figure 1.5 conveys, there is a positive association between institutional development and the cumulative inflow of FDI per capita in the SEE8.[21] Countries such as Albania, Bosnia and Herzegovina, Moldova, and Serbia and Montenegro, where restructuring was delayed, have not been able to attract foreign capital. Similarly, those countries with weaker business frameworks have been less attractive to foreign investors because of uncertain property rights and contracts, poor corporate governance incentives, underdeveloped infrastructure and utilities, and corruption.

Recent improvements in legislation and strengthening of market institutions have started to produce positive results by increasing the flow of FDI to the SEE8. Bulgaria, Croatia, and Romania have benefited from more foreign investment than the rest of the SEE8, as a result of their recent progress in restructuring and privatizing the state-owned enterprises and because of improvements to their institutional environment. These early results should encourage policymakers from the region to vigorously pursue their reform agendas for strengthening the institutional aspects of the business climate.

## Figure 1.5    Institutional Development of the Business Sector and Foreign Direct Investment in the SEE8

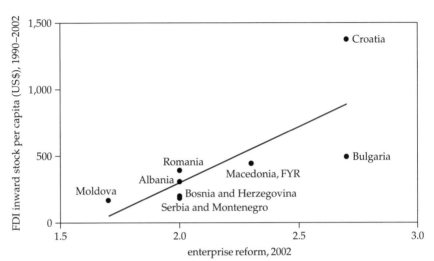

*Sources:* EBRD (2002, 2003) and UNCTAD (2003).
*Note:* The enterprise reform index is EBRD's governance and enterprise restructuring index. It ranges from 1 (indicating lax credit and subsidies that weaken financial discipline at the enterprise level and few reforms to promote corporate governance) to 4+ (indicating standards and performance typical of industrial economies and effective corporate control exercised through domestic financial institutions and markets, thereby fostering market-driven restructuring). (See EBRD 2002, p. 21.)

Stimulating intraregional trade and investment is a key challenge for the SEE8. To date, initiatives within the Stability Pact present some of the most important policy instruments for advancing the institutional climate for business and investment in the region and for strengthening intraregional cooperation. These steps toward intraregional cooperation are important. They address the need for further reform of the policy and institutional frameworks within the SEE8.

As we have shown, progress in trade and FDI in the region has been disappointing, slowing the process of international integration. Although trade has recovered for all of the SEE8, the composition of trade by product group has not shifted significantly in the past decade. Also, the levels of domestic and foreign investment in the SEE8 lag substantially behind those found in the more advanced formally socialist economies of Eastern Europe. Both of these observations reflect that, because of weaknesses in the institutional climate in the SEE8, insufficient economic restructuring has occurred, and new investment has not yet expanded the countries' capacity to trade and grow (Michalopoulos 2001).

# Scope and Methodology of the Study

This study starts from the premise that further development and reform of basic market institutions in the SEE8 hold the key to increasing domestic and foreign investment in these countries and, thus, to reducing poverty and accelerating their economic growth. The main message of this chapter is that, although the economic recovery of South Eastern Europe has started, its growth will not be sustained without progress in reforming the institutional framework for investment. In addition, improving that framework is essential to the integration of the SEE8 countries with the structures of the European Union. These two mutually reinforcing objectives—reducing poverty and accelerating growth on the one hand and integrating with Europe on the other—are critical to achieving long-lasting peace and prosperity for all people of the region.

The objective of the study is to empirically assess the nature and extent of the institutional constraints to improving the investment environment in the SEE8 and to develop policy recommendations to ease those constraints. The study focuses on four policy areas:

1. Competition and economic barriers to entry and exit
2. Access to regulated utilities and services
3. Corporate ownership, financial transparency, and access to finance
4. Commercial dispute resolution

The study systematically investigates these four topics across the SEE8 to allow for cross-country comparisons and to develop a regional perspective on the corresponding policy challenges. The study's integrated approach addresses the interactions of the institutions that affect the structure of incentives for enterprise development. Without a theoretical framework, the study would risk focusing on a limited class of issues— for example removing administrative barriers or improving dispute resolution—rather than tackling the systemic problems. Removing administrative barriers to entry is necessary, but it is unlikely to be sufficient to foster investment, as it fails to address the fundamental problems of anticompetitive market structures and conduct. Similarly, improving dispute resolution is important, but such reforms alone would be insufficient to encourage investment without complementary measures such as greater financial transparency, accountability, and disclosure. The study's approach provides a rationale for pursuing structural reforms and avoiding partial fixes. It encourages the establishment of priorities for building or strengthening key institutions that will reduce firms' transaction costs and facilitate business development and expansion.

# Data Sources

OFFICIAL STATISTICS
To analyze the institutional constraints to improving the investment environment in the SEE8, the study relies on official data from the eight countries to assess the characteristics of and trends in infrastructure, investment, employment, and trade. However, an analysis of economic progress that is based solely on official statistics could not adequately assess the challenge of improving the investment climate in the region. To minimize the risk of being superfluous and short-sighted, the study uses two additional instruments: a set of enterprise-level case studies and the two European Bank for Reconstruction and Development (EBRD)–World Bank *Business Environment and Enterprise Performance Surveys* (BEEPS). Both instruments cover all eight countries.

CASE STUDIES
In the summer of 2002, we conducted 40 in-depth case studies (representing five enterprises in each of the eight countries). The case studies were intended to qualitatively assess the nature and extent of institutional barriers and their interrelationships in the business environment of the SEE8. The focus of the case studies reflects the four policy areas identified above, and the design provides for the development and testing of alternative hypotheses. To achieve intra- and intercountry comparisons, we selected the business cases based on a set of specific criteria, such as firm size, sectoral representation, firm location, direction of trade, enterprise ownership structure, and age of firm. Firms were chosen from sectors that had relative economic importance in SEE, but we also allowed for the diversity of firms within each country and selected firms that represented certain common characteristics across the countries. The case studies were conducted in the software, textile, food retail, construction, and metalworking industries. Table 1.3 summarizes the sectors and characteristics of the interviewed firms.

BUSINESS ENVIRONMENT AND ENTERPRISE PERFORMANCE SURVEY
The study also uses the results of a survey developed by the EBRD and the World Bank and the EBRD. The survey instrument covers nearly 6,000 firms in 26 postcommunist transition countries. The BEEPS complements the methodology described above as well as captures the magnitude of the institutional barriers faced by enterprises, thus providing a quantitative assessment of the relative importance of those barriers.[22]

The BEEPS was conducted in two rounds: BEEPS1 in 1999, and BEEPS2 in the summer of 2002. BEEPS became a primary vehicle for this study. More than 1,600 SEE8 enterprises took part in BEEPS2. The firms operated in industrial sectors such as mining, construction, or

## Table 1.3  Enterprise-Level Case Studies
*(number of interviewed firms)*

| Sector | Type of enterprise | | | Origin of main owner | | | Size | | | Main market | | |
|---|---|---|---|---|---|---|---|---|---|---|---|---|
| | De novo | State-owned | Privatized state-owned | Domestic | Foreign | Mixed | Small[a] | Medium[b] | Large[c] | Foreign | Domestic | Both |
| Software | 7 | | 1 | 8 | | | 4 | 4 | | 1 | 5 | 2 |
| Textile | 3 | 1 | 3 | 7 | | | 3 | 2 | 2 | 3 | 1 | 3 |
| Food retail | 5 | | 3 | 7 | | 1 | 1 | | 7 | | 8 | |
| Construction | 5 | | 3 | 6 | | 2 | | 3 | 5 | | 6 | 2 |
| Metalworking | 1 | 4 | 4 | 4 | 3 | 2 | 1 | | 8 | 3 | 3 | 3 |
| Total | 21 | 5 | 14 | 32 | 3 | 5 | 9 | 9 | 22 | 7 | 23 | 10 |

*Source:* Authors' enterprise-level case studies.

*Note:* During the summer of 2002, 40 companies were interviewed in Albania, Bosnia and Herzegovina, Bulgaria, Croatia, FYR Macedonia, Moldova, Romania, and Serbia and Montenegro. The identity of the firms is confidential.

a. Fewer than 50 employees.

b. Between 50 and 249 employees.

c. More than 249 employees.

manufacturing or were active in services such as transportation, trade, real estate and business, or tourism. In designing the sample, the creators of the BEEPS relied on predetermined respondents' quotas. Hence, smaller firms were overrepresented in all of the surveyed countries, including the SEE8.

The age and ownership of the surveyed companies, for which the BEEPS creators also established sample quotas, also differ. Among the respondent firms are representatives of state-owned, privatized, and start-up (de novo) firms. State-owned firms are strongly represented in the manufacturing, transportation, storage, and communication sectors, whereas the surveyed de novo and privatized firms are mainly in whole-sale and retail trade and in manufacturing. The profile of the surveyed enterprises in the SEE8 is presented in tables 1.4 and 1.5.

## Structure of the Study

The study is organized in five more chapters. Chapter 2 focuses on the overall assessment of progress made by the SEE8 governments in improving the business and investment climate. It also assesses the unfinished reform agenda in the eight countries using the four core policy areas. To evaluate the progress to date and to highlight the remaining reform challenges for the region, we juxtapose recent reform initiatives in the SEE8 against the perceptions of the business community in the region.

Chapter 3 focuses on the institutional impediments to interfirm competition within the SEE8. The chapter analyzes the nature and determinants of barriers to entry and exit. In so doing, it assesses the effects of horizontal and vertical elements of market structure on competition as well as assessing the role that government policies and institutions play in facilitating market exchanges and fair play. It also analyzes the extent to which certain aspects of competition affect firm performance and explores why particular sectors, ownership forms, or countries are more competitive than others.

Chapter 4 investigates businesses' access to regulated utility and infrastructure services, including prices paid for, access to, and quality of services provided by regulated utility suppliers. It explores the links between procompetition regulations and improved performance. It delves into the economywide effects of private sector delivery of utility services and of the privatization of such services. In addition, the chapter establishes links between infrastructure development and investments on the one hand, and opportunities for regional integration on the other.

Chapter 5 sheds light on the issues of property rights, corporate governance, and financial transparency in the SEE8. It reviews the channels

# Table 1.4 Characteristics of SEE8 Firms Participating in BEEPS2

| BEEPS2 sample structure | Albania | Bosnia and Herzegovina | Bulgaria | Croatia | Macedonia, FYR | Moldova | Romania | Serbia and Montenegro | Total |
|---|---|---|---|---|---|---|---|---|---|
| *Industrial sector (number of firms)* | 83 | 83 | 71 | 65 | 62 | 55 | 106 | 91 | 616 |
| Mining and quarrying | 2 | 3 | 3 | 3 | 2 | . | . | 4 | 17 |
| Construction | 19 | 12 | 19 | 24 | 13 | 5 | 24 | 18 | 134 |
| Manufacturing | 62 | 68 | 49 | 38 | 47 | 50 | 82 | 69 | 465 |
| *Services sector (number of firms)* | 87 | 99 | 179 | 122 | 108 | 119 | 149 | 159 | 1,022 |
| Transportation, storage, and communications | 14 | 12 | 25 | 15 | 14 | 11 | 20 | 22 | 133 |
| Wholesale, retail, and repairs | 42 | 57 | 93 | 59 | 63 | 74 | 68 | 74 | 530 |
| Real estate and business | 9 | 7 | 22 | 28 | 11 | 3 | 26 | 27 | 133 |
| Hotels and restaurants | 13 | 15 | 21 | 10 | 14 | 9 | 17 | 18 | 117 |
| Other community, social, and personal services | 9 | 8 | 18 | 10 | 6 | 22 | 18 | 18 | 109 |
| *Size (number of firms)* | | | | | | | | | |
| Small (2–49)[a] | 121 | 111 | 174 | 125 | 120 | 118 | 154 | 155 | 1,078 |
| Medium (50–249) | 31 | 42 | 38 | 34 | 28 | 35 | 63 | 51 | 322 |
| Large (250–9,999) | 18 | 29 | 38 | 28 | 22 | 21 | 38 | 44 | 238 |
| *State ownership (number of firms)* | 18 | 23 | 37 | 28 | 6 | 27 | 38 | 42 | 219 |
| *Private ownership (number of firms)* | 143 | 159 | 207 | 139 | 163 | 145 | 211 | 197 | 1364 |
| De novo enterprise | 130 | 114 | 162 | 111 | 134 | 109 | 172 | 170 | 1102 |
| Privatized state-owned enterprise | 13 | 45 | 45 | 28 | 29 | 36 | 39 | 27 | 262 |
| *Age (year established)* | | | | | | | | | |
| Oldest | 1930 | 1885 | 1892 | 1884 | 1944 | 1944 | 1800 | 1898 | 1897 |
| Youngest | 1999 | 1999 | 1999 | 1999 | 1999 | 1999 | 1999 | 1999 | 1999 |
| Average | 1992 | 1984 | 1983 | 1982 | 1987 | 1990 | 1988 | 1983 | 1986 |
| Median | 1995 | 1995 | 1992 | 1992 | 1990 | 1995 | 1993 | 1991 | 1993 |
| *Year privatization completed (median)* | 1995 | 2001 | 1998 | 1993 | 1998 | 1996 | 1997 | 1999 | 1997 |

*Source:* EBRD and World Bank (2002).

*Note:* Because of missing values, the total number of total firms for each category is not equal.

a. Sole proprietorships were not included in BEEPS2.

## Table 1.5  Characteristics of SEE8 Firms Participating in BEEPS1

| BEEPS1 sample structure[a] | Albania | Bosnia and Herzegovina | Bulgaria | Croatia | Macedonia, FYR | Moldova | Romania | Total |
|---|---|---|---|---|---|---|---|---|
| *Industrial sector (number of firms)* | 68 | 84 | 95 | 68 | 83 | 84 | 67 | 549 |
| Farming, fishing, and forestry | 2 | 1 | 19 | 0 | 2 | 42 | 2 | 68 |
| Mining and quarrying | 2 | 1 | 2 | 0 | 3 | 0 | 2 | 10 |
| Construction | 9 | 23 | 8 | 3 | 13 | 8 | 4 | 68 |
| Manufacturing | 53 | 58 | 66 | 64 | 65 | 34 | 58 | 398 |
| Power generation | 2 | 1 | 0 | 1 | 0 | 0 | 1 | 5 |
| *Services sector (number of firms)* | 84 | 108 | 35 | 59 | 52 | 54 | 58 | 450 |
| Transportation, storage, and communications | 7 | 5 | 9 | 9 | 1 | 9 | 0 | 40 |
| Wholesale, retail, and repairs | 51 | 74 | 21 | 14 | 42 | 34 | 40 | 276 |
| Real estate and business services | 17 | 26 | 3 | 3 | 9 | 7 | 0 | 65 |
| Financial services | 4 | 3 | 2 | 6 | 0 | 3 | 0 | 18 |
| Personal services | 5 | 0 | 0 | 27 | 0 | 1 | 18 | 51 |
| *Size (number of firms)[b]* | | | | | | | | |
| Small | 89 | 135 | 67 | 31 | 88 | 50 | 77 | 537 |
| Medium | 40 | 35 | 21 | 39 | 24 | 42 | 26 | 227 |
| Large | 13 | 22 | 41 | 57 | 24 | 47 | 22 | 228 |
| *State ownership (number of firms)* | 30 | 56 | 25 | 27 | 25 | 25 | 25 | 213 |
| *Private ownership (number of firms)* | 109 | 135 | 103 | 100 | 111 | 104 | 100 | 762 |
| De novo enterprise | 81 | 133 | 77 | 34 | 97 | 47 | 85 | 554 |
| Privatized state-owned enterprise | 28 | 2 | 26 | 66 | 14 | 57 | 15 | 208 |
| *Age (year established)* | | | | | | | | |
| Oldest | 1920 | 1885 | 1909 | 1827 | 1882 | 1825 | 1899 | |
| Youngest | 1999 | 1999 | 1999 | 1999 | 1999 | 1999 | 1999 | |
| Average | 1990 | 1988 | 1975 | 1987 | 1969 | 1987 | 1988 | |
| Median | 1994 | 1994 | 1991 | 1993 | 1987 | 1994 | 1992 | |

*Source:* EBRD and World Bank (1999).

*Note:* Because of missing values, the total number of total firms for each category is not equal.

a. The BEEPS1 sample includes some firms in sectors not covered in BEEPS2. These are farming, fishing, and forestry; power generation; and financial services. BEEPS1 does not include firms from the hotel and restaurant sector; other community, social, and personal services; or real estate services. The table presents the characteristics of all SEE8 firms that participated in BEEPS1.

b. Sole proprietorships were included in BEEPS1.

through which the current ownership structure in the region has evolved. Stock exchanges, laws, and regulations, as well as the state of the financial and the state-owned sectors, are viewed as key forces, which shape the corporate governance and ownership structures in the region. The chapter assesses the links between corporate performance and various ownership and governance structures.

Chapter 6 looks at the experience and strategies of the business community in the SEE8 in resolving commercial disputes. The chapter investigates the factors that influence the use of courts in business disputes and establishes that judicial formalism reduces the demand for bringing a dispute to court.

In chapters 3 through 6, we also include recommendations for policy reform. We designed the recommendations to help government policymakers remove obstacles to private investment in the region as well as to provide input to policy dialogue and policy-based lending to the international donor community. The recommendations also inform the strategy for the next phase in implementing the Stability Pact's Investment Compact.

# Endnotes

1. The Stability Pact for South Eastern Europe was adopted on June 10, 1999, in Cologne, Germany, at the European Union's initiative. There are three political instruments (working tables) in the pact: (a) Working Table I on Democratization and Human Rights; (b) Working Table II on Economic Reconstruction, Cooperation, and Development; and (c) Working Table III on Security Issues. Working Table III has two subtables: one on Security and Defense, and one on Justice and Home Affairs. Members are (a) countries from the South Eastern European region (Albania, Bosnia and Herzegovina, Bulgaria, Croatia, FYR Macedonia, Moldova, Romania, and Serbia and Montenegro); (b) countries outside the region (the European Union member states, Canada, Japan, Norway, the Russian Federation, Switzerland, Turkey, and the United States); (c) international organizations (the United Nations, Organization for Security and Co-operation in Europe, European Council, United Nations High Commissioner for Refugees, Northern Atlantic Treaty Organisation, and Organisation for Economic Cooperation and Development); (d) international financial institutions (the World Bank, International Monetary Fund, European Bank for Reconstruction and Development, European Investment Bank, and Council of Europe Development Bank); and (e) regional initiatives (the Black Sea Economic Co-operation, Central European Initiative, South East European Co-operative Initiative, and South East Europe Co-operation Process). All members are on an equal footing in shaping initiatives and policies on the future of the region and in setting priorities concerning the content of all three areas studied by the working tables. Further information on the Stability Pact for SEE can be accessed at http://www.stabilitypact.org.

2. The Investment Compact is an initiative of Working Table II on Economic Reconstruction, Cooperation, and Development. It was launched in February 2000 in Skopje. It takes a three-phase approach: (a) diagnosis of current investment conditions in the countries of the region (already finished); (b) development of country-specific policy recommendations and design of regional policy initiatives; and (c) monitoring of progress in policy implementation, in improvement of the investment conditions, and in investment performance in South East Europe. For more information see http://www.investmentcompact.org.

3. Given the special institutional treatment and weaker knowledge base pertaining to Kosovo, we did not include it in this study.

4. Data are from the UNECE. These data were averaged for the South Eastern European region (with the exception of Bosnia and Herzegovina) using simple averaging (UNECE 2002).

5. Agricultural output in Romania has been positive too, but not labor productivity. See EBRD (2002, p. 76) for a detailed discussion about agriculture in transition.

6. Farmland in Albania and Romania was distributed to farm workers or rural households on an equal per capita basis (EBRD 2002, p. 77).

7. Levels shrank by 61 percent for pigs, by 55 percent for cattle, and by 30 percent for sheep and goats (EIU 2001a, p. 59).

8. For example, in Romania in the 1990s, nonpayment for energy became a chronic practice for the state-owned enterprises. Payments were made through mutual settlement of dues, by barter, and by promissory note. Moreover, energy companies continue to direct funds to selected state enterprises as bank lending to loss makers has declined. Similarly, most of the 44 large enterprises in Serbia have debts and arrears to the utility suppliers. These borrowers do not have the financial capacity to serve their obligations and have amassed approximately 18 percent of total liabilities in debt to suppliers, including the utilities sector. As a result, the natural monopolies have become one of the most burdensome features of the transition to markets, not only fiscally impeding the governments in these countries, but also slowing their enterprise restructuring.

9. Figures are share in GDP (constant market prices). Data for Croatia and Romania are from the national statistical institutes in each country.

10. For a succinct discussion, see Berglof and Bolton (2003) and Meyer and Nash (2002).

11. Data for Serbia and Montenegro for 2001. See EBRD (2003, p. 190).

12. For an interesting discussion, see Bukvič and others (2001).

13. The registered unemployment data presented in figure 2 reflect the International Bureau of Labor unemployment statistics for Moldova (see EBRD 2003, p. 175). The labor force survey of 1999 shows that unemployment in Moldova was 14 percent of the labor force in the first quarter of 1999 (Rutkowski 2000).

14. For estimates of the informal sector in SEE, see Schneider (2002).

15. This section draws extensively on the findings of a major World Bank trade study covering the western Balkans (see World Bank 2003b). The official

merchandise trade statistics are an important source for drawing the trends in the region. However, the reliability of the data is questionable because of the size of the gray economy in some of the countries as well as the common practice of smuggling goods in an environment with a weak customs system. Goods have been imported and traded in the South Eastern European countries, bypassing the requirements for declaration and duties at the point of entry. Observers report that, in Kosovo and FYR Macedonia, for example, such trading practices are associated with tariff evasion and weak customs administration. Customs delays and widespread demands for bribes to speed up the administrative procedures in the movement of goods have become a major obstacle to trade in the region.

16. The trade initiative of the Stability Pact complements the ongoing EU processes—the accession process for Bulgaria and Romania, the stabilization and association process for the five western Balkan states, and the partnership and cooperation process for Moldova. The stabilization and association process explicitly links liberalization of trade with the European Union to regional cooperation and liberalization among the five western Balkan countries, as stated in an EU Council regulation (No. 2007/2000) of September 2000.

17. See results of the Rome ministerial meeting at http://www.stabilitypact.org/trade/default.asp.

18. Bulgaria joined CEFTA in 1998, Croatia joined in March 2003, and Romania joined in 1997. The effects of joining CEFTA should not be overexaggerated, however, as five of the eight CEFTA members are planning to join the European Union in May 2004, leaving only the South Eastern European countries (Bulgaria, Croatia, and Romania) in the agreement.

19. Bilateral agreements for duty- and quota-free access govern trade in textile products between the European Union and each of the western Balkan countries except for Serbia and Montenegro. In November 2003, the European Union and Serbia and Montenegro also reached an agreement for duty- and quota-free access for textiles.

20. Important exceptions exist for Eastern European products, including agricultural products, iron and steel, and textiles, on which the EU has imposed restrictions. Such sensitive areas represent a considerable portion of trade flow for the SEE8 and restrict the potential volume of trade with the European Union.

21. The association between institutional development and cumulative inflow of FDI per capita is even stronger if Croatia is excluded from the sample.

22. See EBRD (2002, chapter 2) for a discussion of the business environment in the transition countries and the BEEPS.

# References

Berglof, Erik, and Patrick Bolton. 2003. "The 'Great Divide': Financial Architecture in Transition." CEPR Discussion Paper 3476. Centre for Economic Policy, London.

Broadman, Harry, Joel Bergsman, and Vladimir Drebentsov. 2000. "Improving Russia's Foreign Direct Investment Policy Regime." Policy Research Working Paper 2329. World Bank, Washington, D.C.

Bukvič, Vladimir, Will Bartlett, Andrej Rus, Djevad Sehic, and Vesna Stojanova. 2001. "Barriers to SME development in Slovenia, Bosnia and Macedonia." Final report PHARE/ACE P97-8089-R.

Demekas, Dimitri G. 2002. "Building Peace in South East Europe: Macroeconomic Policies and Structural Reforms since the Kosovo Conflict." A joint World Bank–International Monetary Fund paper presented at the Second Regional Conference for South East Europe, Bucharest, October 25–26, 2001.

EBRD (European Bank for Reconstruction and Development). 2002. *Transition Report 2002: Agriculture and Rural Transition.* London.

———. 2003. *Transition Report 2003: Integration and Regional Cooperation.* London.

EBRD and World Bank. 1999. *Business Environment and Enterprise Performance Survey* (BEEPS1). London and Washington, D.C. Data available online at http://info.worldbank.org/governance/beeps.

———. 2002 *Business Environment and Enterprise Performance Survey* (BEEPS2). London and Washington, D.C. Data available online at http://info.worldbank.org/governance/beeps2002.

EIU (Economic Intelligence Unit). 2001a. *Country Profile 2001: Moldova.* London.

———. 2001b. *Country Profile 2001: Romania.* London.

———. 2002. *Country Profile 2002: Bosnia and Herzegovina.* London.

European Commission. 2003a. "Former Yugoslav Republic of Macedonia: Stabilisation and Association Report 2003." Commission Staff Working Paper. Brussels. Available online at http://europa.eu.int/comm/external_relations/see/sap/rep2/com03_342_en.pdf.

———. 2003b. "Report from the Commission: The Stabilization and Association Process for SEE. Second Annual Report." Brussels.

FIAS (Foreign Investment Advisory Services). 2001a. *Administrative Barriers: Romania.* Washington, D.C.

————. 2001b. *The Climate for FDI: Serbia.* Washington, D.C.

IMF (International Monetary Fund) Bureau of Statistics. 2002. *Direction of Trade Statistics Yearbook.* Washington, D.C.

Levine, Ross. 1996. "Financial Development and Economic Growth: Views and Agenda." Policy Research Working Paper 1678. World Bank, Washington D.C.

Meyer, Edward C., and Nash, William L. 2002. *Balkans 2010: Report of an Independent Task Force Sponsored by the Council on Foreign Relations Center for Preventive Action.* New York: Council on Foreign Relations.

Michalopoulos, Constantine. 2001. "The Western Balkans in World Trade." World Bank, Washington D.C. Processed.

Nenovsky, Nikolay, and Kalin Hristov. 2000. *Currency Circulation after Currency Board Introduction in Bulgaria.* BNB Discussion Paper 13. Sofia: Bulgarian National Bank.

Rutkowski, Jan. 1998. "Employment Adjustment and the Wage Structure in FYR Macedonia." World Bank, Washington D.C. Processed.

————. 2000. "Active Labor Market Policies in Moldova: Current State and Planned Changes." World Bank, Washington D.C. Processed.

————. 2003. "Does Strict Employment Protection Discourage Job Creation? Evidence from Croatia." Policy Research Working Paper 3104. World Bank, Washington D.C.

Schneider, Friedrich. 2002. "The Value Added of Underground Activities: Size and Measurement of the Shadow Economies of 110 Countries All over the World." Johannes Kepler University, Linz, Germany. Processed.

UNCTAD (United Nations Conference on Trade and Development). 2003. *World Investment Report 2003. FDI Policies for Development: National and International Perspectives.* United Nations: New York and Geneva.

UNECE (United Nations Economic Commission for Europe). 2002. *Economic Survey of Europe No.1.* New York and Geneva: United Nations. Available online at http://www.unece.org/ead/pub/surv_021.htm.

World Bank. 2002a. *Labor Market in Postwar Bosnia and Herzegovina. How to Encourage Businesses to Create Jobs and Increase Work Mobility.* Washington, D.C.

————. 2002b. *Bulgaria: A Changing Poverty Profile.* Washington, D.C.

————. 2003a. *Global Economic Prospects and the Developing Countries: Investing to Unlock Global Opportunities.* Washington, D.C.

————. 2003b. *Trade Policies and Institutions in the Countries of SEE in the EU Stabilization and Association Process.* Washington, D.C.

————. 2003c. *World Development Indicators 2003.* Washington, D.C.

# 2
# Institutional Reform Progress to Date and Remaining Challenges in South Eastern Europe

As shown in chapter 1's review of the economic trends in South Eastern Europe (SEE), output recovery and integration of the region into the world markets have been insufficient for sustainable growth. A successful transition process hinges on a well-functioning institutional environment for investment that safeguards property rights and contracts, supports day-to-day business transactions, creates jobs, accelerates poverty reduction, and helps integrate the region into the world economy.

To assess the progress of institutional reform and to highlight the remaining challenges, we present in this chapter an overview assessment of each of the four core issues that will be analyzed in detail in the book: competition, regulated infrastructure utilities, corporate ownership, and resolution of commercial disputes.

The chapter is organized as follows. First, we review in the aggregate the state of market institutions that influence the business environment in the eight countries that are the focus of this study (the SEE8). Next, we present a more disaggregated analysis of the institutional impediments and the reform progress to date of the eight governments in each of the four policy areas. The last section sets the stage for the in-depth comparative analyses in chapters 3 to 6.

## Aggregate Assessment of the Business Environment in SEE

The snapshot analysis of the business environment in SEE based on the two European Bank for Reconstruction and Development (EBRD)–World Bank *Business Environment and Enterprise Performance Surveys* (BEEPS1 and BEEPS2) suggests that the 2002 investment climate in the region has improved in comparison with the climate in 1999. Figure 2.1 presents how the surveyed SEE8 enterprises perceived in 1999 and 2002 the relative

34                    BUILDING MARKET INSTITUTIONS IN SOUTH EASTERN EUROPE

# Figure 2.1    Aggregate Assessment of Institutional Barriers in the Business Environment in the SEE8, 1999 and 2002

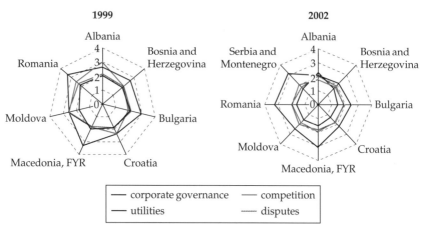

*Sources:* EBRD and World Bank (1999, 2002).
*Note:* The term *corporate governance* includes financial transparency (for firms with more than 50 workers) and access to financing. *Regulated infrastructure utilities* includes infrastructure services (telecommunications, electricity, transportation, and access to land). *Competition* includes entry barriers (macroeconomic stabilization, legal barriers, and structural barriers) and exit barriers (arrears). *Business disputes* includes attributes of the court system in resolving business disputes. A simple average of the components is calculated for each of the four dimensions. On the scale from 1 to 4, 4 represents the most severe obstacle.

importance of policy-related problems in each of the four thematic areas described above. The responses of the enterprises are averaged by country and are normalized on a scale from 1 to 4, with 4 representing the most severe obstacle. The chosen graphical representation is particularly effective because it allows us to capture (a) intertemporal variations in the perceptions of the surveyed firms, (b) changes across and within countries with respect to each policy issue, and (c) the severity of the problems in the four areas of the study.

As figure 2.1 shows, access to regulated infrastructure utilities has significantly improved in the eight countries.[1] Nonetheless, remnants from the old system, such as inefficient pricing, cross-subsidies, and lack of competition on the utilities market, have caused bottlenecks for the development of the private sector and have discouraged investment in SEE. Moreover, for countries such as Albania, access to regulated utilities still represents one of the major obstacles hindering expansion and growth of enterprises.

One striking observation from figure 2.1 is that, almost universally, corporate governance problems and access to financing remain rated among the most prevalent obstacles throughout the region. In the area of corporate governance, implementation of international accounting standards and financial audits has been the weakest in FYR Macedonia, Romania, and Serbia and Montenegro. This finding reflects a low level of transparency in privatization and a high level of state interference in FYR Macedonia and Serbia and Montenegro. For Romania, the finding is related to the low number of enterprises to adopt independent financial audits before 2003. A change in legislation at the beginning of 2003 required all companies listed on the Romanian stock exchange to adopt local accounting standards that are based on international accounting standards (IAS). Enterprises in Bulgaria and Moldova experience more obstacles in obtaining access to financing than the other countries in the region do. Financial regulation has been stringent with respect to bank lending in Bulgaria, especially after the crash of the banking sector in early 1997, and banks generally use more conservative methods in making loans now than they did during the period of lax lending before the crisis.

The business disputes data in figure 2.1 indicate that the judicial systems in the SEE8 have only slightly improved from 1999 to 2002. The region's weak institutional and governance capacity, including its inability to enforce its laws and regulations, is widely recognized. As the competition indicator in figure 2.1 shows, barriers to entry are also perceived as a major obstacle to business development in the SEE8. The problem is most pronounced in Albania and Moldova. There is limited cross-country variation in the area of exit barriers in the eight countries in 2002. The presence of subsidies and arrears has gradually declined since 1999, most likely because of an improved institutional environment, which includes the enforcement of bankruptcy and liquidation.

Figure 2.2, which is based on the EBRD transition indicators, shows the progress the countries have made in carrying out institutional reforms in each of these four policy areas during 1999 and 2002. Compared with the performance indicators shown in figure 2.1, the transition indicators in figure 2.2 show a somewhat stronger cross-country and intertemporal variance. The leaders in terms of institutional reforms are Bulgaria, Croatia, and Romania. FYR Macedonia and Moldova are still lagging behind but have made more progress than Albania, Bosnia and Herzegovina, and Serbia and Montenegro. Relatively speaking, FYR Macedonia has substantially strengthened its institutions to reduce barriers to entry and exit. In contrast, Albania, Bosnia and Herzegovina, and Serbia and Montenegro have made no progress on competition policy reform since 1999.

In the area of business dispute resolution, Bulgaria, Moldova, and Romania have adopted more comprehensive commercial legislation; these countries have the highest scores in the region (see figure 2.2). Albania and Bosnia and Herzegovina have also improved their commercial law frameworks to promote investment and growth; however, the observed progress

## Figure 2.2    Institutional Progress in the SEE8, 1999 and 2002

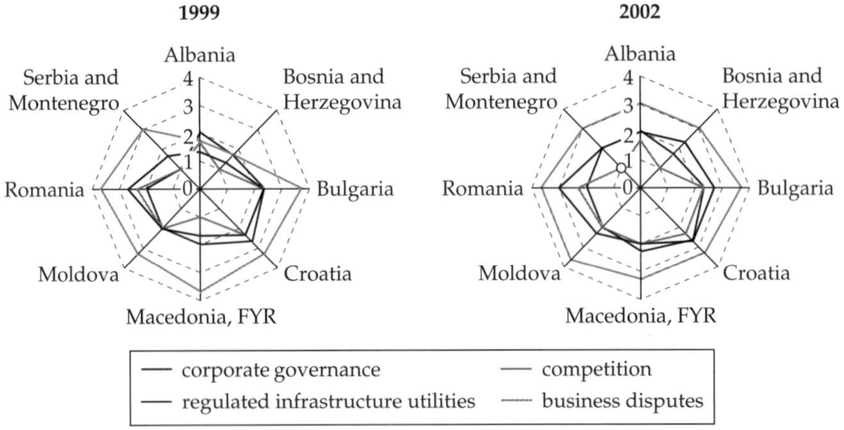

1999

Albania

Serbia and     4     Bosnia and
Montenegro    3     Herzegovina

Romania          Bulgaria

Moldova          Croatia

Macedonia, FYR

2002

Albania

Serbia and     4     Bosnia and
Montenegro    3     Herzegovina

Romania          Bulgaria

Moldova          Croatia

Macedonia, FYR

—— corporate governance      —— competition
—— regulated infrastructure utilities    —— business disputes

*Source:* EBRD (2002).
*Note:* To maintain consistency with the perception indicators used in the BEEPS1 and BEEPS2, we have constructed corporate governance, regulated infrastructure utilities, and competition indicators for 1999 and 2002 from composite indexes of the European Bank for Reconstruction and Development transition indicators. The business disputes indicator is based on the EBRD Legal Transition Team's assessment of surveys directed at lawyers and legal experts from each of the countries (see Ramasastry 2002). The scale for each indicator ranges from 1 (indicating a poor institutional framework in the respective area) to 4.33 (indicating that the institutional framework in the respective area is comparable to those found in industrial countries).

must be measured against poor initial conditions in 1999. As figure 2.2 shows, Romania has the highest rating on the infrastructure indicator for 2002, although Albania and Bosnia and Herzegovina have made the strongest steps forward in improving their infrastructure regulatory frameworks. In the area of corporate governance, the indicators in figure 2.2 suggest that much more effort is needed in all countries if they are to achieve substantial improvements in hardening budget constraints and promoting more rigorous and transparent financial accounting and auditing practices.

A comparative analysis of the two sets of indicators—the one derived from the perceptions of the business community through BEEPS1 and BEEPS2 (see figure 2.1) and the one reflecting the institutional assessment (see figure 2.2)—reveals two interesting features. First, policy seems to have been appropriately targeted on the underlying institutional problems. In the case of entry and exit, reforms appear to be more advanced in Bulgaria and Croatia, the countries where the obstacles are rated the highest (as evident in figure 2.1). Similarly, Albania and Bosnia and Herzegovina have targeted institutional reforms in the infrastructure sectors in response to low access to utilities. Second, these countries appear to have carried out reforms to alleviate the barriers in ways that have limited effectiveness. This issue will be explored and presented in more detail in the following section.

## Institutional Impediments to Investment and Growth

All eight countries face institutional impediments to investment and growth, but the severity is different in each country. In this section, we will discuss these impediments as they relate to the four core issues: competition, regulated infrastructure utilities, corporate ownership, and resolution of commercial disputes.

### *Interenterprise Competition*

To encourage interenterprise competition, the SEE8 need to concentrate reform efforts in four areas: (a) eliminating impediments to business entry and growth, (b) hardening budget constraints and removing exit barriers, (c) strengthening the bankruptcy regime, and (d) reforming the tax code.

ELIMINATING IMPEDIMENTS TO BUSINESS ENTRY AND GROWTH
New small businesses, especially in trade and services, have emerged rapidly in the 1990s across the region. Entrepreneurs have engaged in small-scale, labor-intensive sectors of the economy such as textile, footwear, timber, and furniture making, often through subcontracting and process-ing for foreign firms. Many of these new firms were created through the breakup of larger enterprises and through the sale of smaller units as small- and medium-scale privatization picked up momentum in the second half of the 1990s.[2]

As noted in chapter 1, because of the layoffs caused by the transitional recession, self-employed workers (for example, sole proprietors) and employees in small and medium-size enterprises (SMEs) have, in the past decade, become the main new job drivers in the SEE8. For example, self-employed workers in Romania accounted for 25.4 percent of total employ-ment in 2001.[3] The share of the self-employed in the other countries is smaller, but still significant.

As figure 2.3 shows, throughout the region, job creation among the surveyed firms is significantly higher for de novo and privatized enter-prises than for state-owned enterprises, which registered a negative rate of employment growth from 1999 to 2002. Only in Albania did surveyed state-owned enterprises create more job opportunities than the de novo

## Figure 2.3   Changes in Average Employment by Enterprise Ownership, 1999–2002

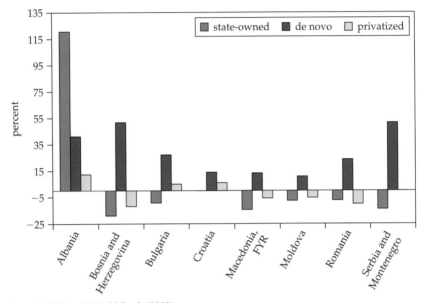

*Source:* EBRD and World Bank (2002).

and privatized establishments in the period between 1999 and 2002. The job creation rate for surveyed de novo enterprises ranges from 11 percent (in Moldova) to 52 percent (in Bosnia and Herzegovina and Serbia and Montenegro) over the same period of time (see figure 2.3). Surveyed state firms (excluding those in Albania) have contracted at a rate of −10 percent on average since 1999.

Despite the growth of the SME sector and self-employment, the trends in the economic output suggest that the creation of new enterprises and new jobs has fallen short of expectations in the region. This finding can be explained partially by the persistence of severe entry regulations. To start and operate a business, entrepreneurs need to obtain a myriad of the necessary permits and licensing and need to fulfill all the legal requirements and procedures. Currently, the process is costly, time consuming, and poorly administered in most of the SEE8, as illustrated by table 2.1. For example, it takes 74 business days, the equivalent of US$664 in fees, and 12 separate but interdependent procedures to legally start a business in Bosnia and Herzegovina. Similarly, in Albania, the same process takes 62 days, US$719 in fees, and 11 procedures. In contrast, opening business in Bulgaria involves 30 days, US$120 in fees, and 10 procedures.

## Table 2.1 Business Entry

| Country | Number of procedures | Duration (business days) | Local cost (US$) |
|---|---|---|---|
| Albania | 11 | 62 | 718.98 |
| Bosnia and Herzegovina | 12 | 74 | 663.73 |
| Bulgaria | 10 | 30 | 120.38 |
| Croatia | 13 | 51 | 798.01 |
| Moldova | 11 | 41 | 123.15 |
| Romania | 9 | 48 | 543.39 |
| Serbia and Montenegro | 16 | 71 | 200.11 |

Source: World Bank (2003a).
Note: FYR Macedonia was not included in the survey.

Regardless of the peculiarities of the eight countries, all governments in the region have engaged in programs designed to foster new business creation and development and to reduce barriers to entry in the South Eastern European market. Improvement is needed even in the countries that have most successfully streamlined the process. For example, although administrative procedures for registering a firm have been reduced in Bulgaria, numerous permits are still required. Government efforts to reduce the current number of permits by half and to simplify the procedures have been established, but across-the-board results are yet to be seen.

Other countries are also dealing with the issue of excessive licensing requirements and permits. In Bosnia and Herzegovina, the authorities are finalizing an action plan to streamline business registration and licensing procedures by introducing a single business registration system across both entities (the Federation of Bosnia and Herzegovina and Republika Srpska) and by eliminating approval duplication at the five levels of government (state, entity, canton, city, and municipality). In addition, both entities are working on ways to simplify business entry by implementing a state law on foreign direct investment and by harmonizing their company laws.[4] In early 2003, 500 businesspeople in Bosnia and Herzegovina, with the assistance of representatives of the international financial institutions, formed the Bulldozer Committee. The committee's mandate was to identify the main obstacles to the business environment in the country and discuss ways to remove them. In May 2003, the parliament enacted approximately 50 of the Bulldozer Committee's proposals in the areas of harmonizing standards among entities, establishing rates of taxation, and simplifying procedures for foreign direct investment (FDI).

Another institutional solution for overcoming the administrative burden of opening up a business venture is to establish one-stop shops for business registration. Such shops have been created in FYR Macedonia and Romania to ease the constraints of business entry. A "consent by silence" rule has also been enforced in FYR Macedonia, under which consent for certain regulatory approvals and licenses is automatic after an 8-day period. Similarly, the principle of "silent approval" also has been introduced recently in both Bulgaria and Romania and allows businesses to assume official consent for new permits or certificates (but not licenses) should the relevant authorities not respond within 30 days of the applications (see EBRD 2003, pp. 129, 181). Yet during case study interviews of enterprises in the SEE8, businesses share concerns that the one-stop-shop model is rigid and inflexible.

Merely simplifying the administrative requirements for business creation is not sufficient to stimulate entrepreneurship. Few of the countries have strengthened the fundamental market institutions that protect firms from anticompetitive structures and conduct. Although some of the countries have sound competition laws, they almost universally neglect using these instruments to reduce economic barriers to entry. Some efforts have been undertaken to strengthen institutional support for SME development and greenfield investments. In January 2001, Romania established a dedicated Ministry for Small and Medium-Size Enterprises and Cooperatives with the goal of developing an SME policy and strategy for the country. After the government's reshuffle in June 2003, the ministry was abolished and replaced by a state agency that reports directly to the prime minister. Notwithstanding these institutional changes, an action plan to remove regulatory barriers for SMEs and to create a State SME Credit Guarantee Fund are under way.

Similarly, in Albania, a special program to establish SMEs and to promote foreign investment and exports was launched after the 1997 crisis. The government has already approved a strategic document for SME development (Albanian Council of Ministers 2001). This document contains measures such as the approval of a special law on SMEs, the improvement of microcrediting schemes, and the establishment of an SME promotion agency. An Albanian Investment Promotion Agency that would provide one-stop facilities for foreign investors and credit information bureaus was launched in April 2002.[5]

To foster entry and new business development, the government of Croatia adopted a program to support SMEs. Under the program, SMEs receive financing on favorable terms and technical advice that can boost technology and market development. Also, Croatia is revising its Law on Competition to strengthen its Agency for Market Competition and to bring the country into conformity with European Union (EU) practice. The agency is also upgrading the technical skills of its staff members and improving enforcement procedures.

In Serbia, drafts of an enterprise law, a foreign investment law, and an antitrust law are advancing, although simplifications in incorporation and registration procedures are yet to fully materialize. In 2000, Montenegro approved a new foreign investment law that guarantees, among other provisions, the right to repatriate profits.

Besides the initiatives on the national level to improve the environment for start-ups and SMEs, efforts at the regional level to foster small business growth are also visible. The Stability Pact has created new initiatives to address problems of starting up and developing a business. In July 2003, the ministers of economy of the SEE8 attended the second ministerial conference of the Stability Pact. At the conference, which was held in Vienna, the ministers issued a joint statement that commits the countries to further removal of the obstacles to investment in SEE. Specifically, taking into consideration the legal situation in each country, the ministers agreed to implement key measures over the coming years in the following areas: reducing licensing and approval procedures; simplifying acquisition of real estate for productive purposes; reducing unnecessary reporting requirements for investors; establishing more transparent laws, regulations, and procedures; streamlining residence permit procedures for key personnel for investment; and removing specific obstacles to investment in the service sectors (Stability Pact 2003c).

In June 2003, the countries of the western Balkans (Albania, Bosnia and Herzegovina, Croatia, FYR Macedonia, and Serbia and Montenegro) endorsed the European Charter for Small Enterprises at the EU Western Balkans Summit in Thessaloniki (see box 2.1). By committing to the charter's principles, the five countries join 29 other European countries (including Bulgaria and Romania) in an effort to reinforce business development and good practice in a wider Europe. The charter provides a framework for international and intraregional cooperation on enterprise development, with the aims of overcoming the local challenges of a receding and reforming state sector and of exploiting the opportunities arising from the introduction of market reforms in SEE.

Although Bulgaria and Romania have been proactive for years in forming investors' organizations (such as the Bulgarian International Business Association and the Romanian Foreign Investors Council) for assisting in policy reform and attracting investments, efforts to establish similar organizations in the rest of the region have begun only recently. In July 2003, during the second ministerial conference of the Stability Pact, all of the SEE8, with the support of the Organisation for Economic Co-operation and Development (OECD), agreed to establish a regional network of foreign investors' councils (FICs) and to fill the gap in communicating key policy issues affecting the business environment in the

## Box 2.1  The European Charter for Small Enterprises

The EU leaders at the Feira European Council approved the European Charter for Small Enterprises on June 19–20, 2000. The charter calls on member states and the commission to take action to support and encourage small enterprises in 10 key areas:

1. Education and training for entrepreneurship
2. Cheaper and faster start-ups
3. Better legislation and regulation
4. Greater availability of skills
5. Improved online access
6. Improved benefit from the European single market
7. Taxation and financial support
8. Strengthened technological capacity of small enterprises
9. Access to successful e-business models and to top-class small business support
10. Stronger, more effective representation of small enterprises' interests at EU and national levels

The EU candidate countries endorsed the European Charter for Small Enterprises at the landmark conference in Maribor, Slovenia, on April 23–24, 2002. The candidate countries will be included in the charter reporting system from 2003 onward on an equal footing with the member states. In June 2003, the countries of the western Balkans (Albania, Bosnia and Herzegovina, Croatia, FYR Macedonia, and Serbia and Montenegro) also endorsed the European Charter for Small Enterprises at the EU Western Balkans Summit in Thessaloniki. For the western Balkan countries, the commission will issue a separate report, which will likely include targets and benchmarks.

*Source:* European Commission (2003b).

region. As outlined by the Stability Pact (2003b), the general objectives of local FICs are

- to improve the investment and business development climate;
- to assist members in expressing business and operational difficulties and in proposing suitable reform measures to relevant authorities;
- to formulate concrete proposals to improve the business environment and to provide constructive feedback to government on policies;
- to cooperate with government authorities in undertaking action to implement policies.

FICs have been established in Albania, Bosnia and Herzegovina, FYR Macedonia, Romania, and Serbia and Montenegro, and discussions are currently under way to establish an FIC in Moldova. The regional network will complement the efforts of individual countries to attract new businesses and investment.

HARDENING BUDGET CONSTRAINTS AND REMOVING EXIT BARRIERS
Despite the institutional improvements to foster new business creation, many incumbent enterprises in SEE continue to operate under nonmarket conditions and to enjoy soft budget constraints. Soft budgets breed business inefficiencies, undercut restructuring efforts, and distort competition. Distortions arise, among other reasons, when some enterprises within the same industry are entitled to special privileges in terms of both price setting and access to infrastructure, which likely diverge from socially desirable outcomes. Hardening of budget constraints for all firms in the region is vital if the SEE8 are (a) to induce nonviable firms to exit the market or restructure, (b) to reallocate resources toward more productive uses, and (c) to create economic space for new entrants.

Soft budgets in the region have been perpetuated in numerous ways, the most direct one being by means of budgetary subsidies. Direct forms of subsidies have gradually declined since the mid-1990s, yet indirect forms of support (such as the tolerance of tax arrears, suppliers' arrears, nonpayment of utility bills) remain sizable and, in some cases, are increasing.

From information provided in BEEPS1 and BEEPS2, figure 2.4 reports the average proportion of SEE8 enterprises with subsidies and arrears on

**Figure 2.4   Firms with Subsidies and Arrears in the SEE8 under BEEPS1 and BEEPS2**
*(percentage of total firms)*

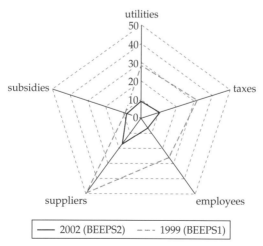

*Sources:* EBRD and World Bank (1999, 2002).

an intertemporal basis—1999 compared with 2002. Although the average level of arrears among the surveyed firms has contracted substantially since 1999, suppliers' arrears have remained the most recurrent ones on average, followed by arrears in payments for taxes, receivables, utilities, and worker compensation. Disaggregated cross-country data reveal that every fourth surveyed firm in Croatia and every fifth in Albania and Bosnia and Herzegovina reported payments to material input suppliers that were overdue by more than 90 days. Arrears to the utilities companies among the surveyed firms were most pronounced in Albania and Bosnia and Herzegovina, whereas the interviewed firms in Bosnia and Herzegovina, Bulgaria, and Romania were characterized by substantial incidence of tax arrears. For example, in Romania, overdue taxes account for 20 percent of total annual sales for many surveyed enterprises.

Figure 2.4 shows that, in 1999, surveyed firms indicated that direct subsidies were less prevalent than arrears, as suggested above. However, the share of firms receiving government subsidies in 2002 was not appreciably lower than in 1999. Indeed, there was less progress in reducing subsidies than in reducing all other categories of arrears.

Institutional reforms in SEE to harden budget constraints and to encourage the exit of nonviable firms have focused on several fronts. In two areas, government actions are critical: (a) making bankruptcy regimes more effective and (b) enforcing tax collection and reforming tax structures to minimize tax privileges and reduce investment distortions.

STRENGTHENING THE BANKRUPTCY REGIME
A good bankruptcy regime provides either the institutional tools for restructuring an enterprise's debts and capital structure to restore its economic viability or the sale of the enterprise's assets to new owners capable of using them in a productive way. The existing bankruptcy systems in the region generally do not fully meet these objectives. Creditors lack control over the process and have little expectation of seeing repayment of even a portion of their debts within the foreseeable future. The courts and bankruptcy managers are inexperienced and have been subject to significant pressure to act in the interests of insiders rather than creditors. As with all other court procedures, bankruptcy is extremely slow—further dissipating the value of assets available to pay creditors.

As table 2.2 summarizes, the average time for carrying out bankruptcy cases in the region is close to 3.5 years, and the cost reaches as much as 38 percent of the asset value (see World Bank 2003a for assumptions and definitions). According to the data, only in Albania and Serbia and Montenegro does the insolvency regime deliver efficient outcomes (meaning that the insolvency results in foreclosure, in liquidation, or in a successful rehabilitation of the business under new management). Nevertheless, although the actual time for carrying out bankruptcy in Albania

## Table 2.2    Bankruptcy Indicators

| Country | Actual time[a] (in years) | Actual cost[b] (% of assets) | Preservation of absolute priority[c] | Efficiency of outcome[d] |
|---|---|---|---|---|
| Albania | 2.0 | 38 | 0.67 | 1 |
| Bosnia and Herzegovina | 1.9 | 8 | 0.67 | 0 |
| Bulgaria | 3.8 | 18 | 1.00 | 0 |
| Croatia | 3.1 | 18 | 1.00 | 0 |
| Romania | 3.2 | 8 | 0.33 | 0 |
| Moldova | 2.8 | 8 | 0.67 | 0 |
| Serbia and Montenegro | 7.3 | 38 | 0.33 | 1 |

*Source:* World Bank (2003a).

a. Actual time is expressed in years and includes all delays caused by legal derailment tactics that parties to the insolvency may use. It captures the average duration that insolvency lawyers estimate as necessary to complete a procedure.

b. Actual cost is defined as the cost of the entire bankruptcy process—including court costs; insolvency practitioner's costs; and the cost of independent assessors, lawyers, accountants, and so forth. It excludes the cost of bribes. Range of costs is expressed as the percentage of asset value and includes ranges of 0–2 percent, 3–5 percent, 6–10 percent, 11–25 percent, 26–50 percent, and more than 50 percent.

c. Preservation of absolute priority is scaled so that higher values imply stricter observance of priority. A value of 1.00 means that secured creditors are paid before court costs, labor claims, and tax claims. A value of 0.67 means that secured creditors are paid second, and a value of 0.33 means they are paid third. A value of 0.00 means that secured creditors are paid after all court costs, labor claims, and tax claims are satisfied.

d. Efficiency of outcome documents the success of the insolvency regime in reaching economically efficient results. A designation of 1 means that the insolvency process results either in (a) foreclosure or liquidation with a going-concern sale or (b) successful rehabilitation by maintaining the business but hiring new management. A designation of 0 means that neither of the options in the first designation was met.

is comparatively short, experts find that the country has contradictory bankruptcy legislation, especially with respect to prioritizing claims (see box 2.2). Moreover, in Serbia and Montenegro, the bankruptcy procedure takes more than 7 years to achieve efficient results; the country is also characterized by poor observance of priority claims in paying creditors. Indeed, only in Bulgaria and Croatia is the observance of priority strict.

The overall number of enterprises that have entered bankruptcy or liquidation in SEE has been low because exit rules have been carried out in cumbersome and ineffective ways. As noted already, although Albania fares well on the indicators presented in table 2.2, the insolvency law enacted in 1995 proved detrimental to the bankruptcy procedure. As of May 2002, not a single case involving large-scale firms, particularly in proceedings involving state-owned enterprises, has been processed under the business-exit legislation. According to experts, judges

---

**Box 2.2 Challenges in Establishing a Working Bankruptcy Institution in Albania and Bosnia and Herzegovina**

In Bosnia and Herzegovina, if a company files for bankruptcy, it faces a lengthy court procedure that is conducted by a panel of three judges and is governed by strict rules denying the court the flexibility required for a speedy process that could save healthy parts of the firm and recover assets for creditors. In addition to the challenges concerning court procedures and the organization of the bankruptcy process, unique country-specific problems stem from the poor coordination between cantons and municipalities and from their different viewpoints with respect to their future in a unified economic space. The various levels of government continue to apply complex rules, which often duplicate or contradict one another. A case in point is the bankruptcy issue. Each of the entities of Bosnia and Herzegovina (the Federation of Bosnia and Herzegovina and Republika Srpska) has passed a separate bankruptcy law, which regulates the bankruptcy procedure only within the entity, not across the country.

The Albanian bankruptcy legislation is also problematic. The law is contradictory in places, particularly with respect to the priority of claims. The law on bankruptcy procedure requires the court to prepare a list of claims submitted by creditors, giving first priority to tax and other state obligations. However, the civil code, which was amended to reflect the enactment of a new law on securing charges, has a completely different list for ranking the creditors. According to the civil code, claims arising from purchase money security receive first priority, and claims made by secured creditors specifically mentioned in the code (other than those who have a purchase money security) receive seventh priority. How this contradiction will be managed in practice is not clear, although a new bankruptcy law was passed in October 2002 to iron out the differences.

In both countries, building consensus for a uniform policy and institutions is key to the introduction of new legislation to promote domestic and foreign investment. Effects thus far have been limited.

---

and lawyers do not understand the legal style of the new bankruptcy regulation; moreover, the law itself engages multiple—and often inconsistent—traditions and complicated procedures, which makes it difficult to interpret and enforce (Gupta, Kleinfeld, and Salinas 2002, p. 17).

The problems involved in carrying out bankruptcy proceedings in Bosnia and Herzegovina and Moldova[6] stem from the lack of a registrar for pledges; the lack of specialized bankruptcy courts; and the scarcity of well-trained judges, trustees, and lawyers who are capable of interpreting and enforcing the law. Furthermore, the bankruptcy regulation in Bosnia and Herzegovina falls entirely within the ambit of the entities and further complicates the implementation of exit regulation (see box 2.2).

Yet another source of problems in carrying out the intent of the law comes from the content of those laws. For example, the current federal bankruptcy law of Serbia and Montenegro is too constraining to provide adequate safeguards for creditors.[7] Priority measures include helping creditors foreclose on collateral outside formal bankruptcy proceedings, giving creditors (as opposed to judges) more power to oversee adminis-trators, and introducing incentive compensation to encourage adminis-trators to focus on maximizing creditor recoveries. As of fall 2003, a new bankruptcy law was being prepared in Serbia, although it was still not enacted.

In Croatia, the bankruptcy law is relatively well crafted, and yet the bankruptcy mechanism proceeds with a sluggish pace. The total of about 600 cases of bankruptcies processed per year is low compared with a pop-ulation of enterprises exceeding 60,000 (including de novo firms and for-mer state-owned enterprises) and is abnormally small compared with the total in other countries in transition (World Bank 2000).

Despite the difficulties in facilitating market exit, most of the SEE8 con-tinue to invest efforts to overcome the loopholes in existing regulations and to strengthen bankruptcy institutions. In October 2002, the Albanian government passed a new bankruptcy law in response to the uncertainty surrounding the ranking of creditors' claims and priorities (see box 2.2). The goal of the law was to foster the practical enforcement of the insol-vency law through special courts that have exclusive jurisdiction over insolvency proceedings. Amendments to the Croatian bankruptcy law, which were enacted in 2000, created problems involving the qualifi-cation requirements for trustees and the role of bankruptcy tribunals. In response to these challenges, the Croatian government enacted addition-al amendments to the law in July 2003 to make bankruptcy proceedings quicker and, thus, to help overcome the inadequate institutional capacity of the commercial court system to handle bankruptcies expeditiously.[8]

In FYR Macedonia, 2003 amendments to the bankruptcy law have improved creditor rights by simplifying and accelerating bankruptcy and collateral foreclosure proceedings and by closing loopholes that had allowed debtors to delay creditor actions.

Bulgaria and Romania have made several amendments to their insol-vency laws since that legislation was initially established. Although the legal framework was well advanced, significant shortfalls in the bank-ruptcy procedures arose in practice. For example, the bankruptcy process in Bulgaria used to take longer than a year. However, as of June 2003, amendments to the insolvency section of the commercial code have shortened the period for court-declared bankruptcy to 4 to 7 months. The amendments also present more detailed merger regulations. These changes enable a company to be considered insolvent when it has not performed within 60 days of the due date. The amendments also provide for the creation of regional legal chambers to deal with bankruptcy procedures (see EBRD 2003, p. 128). Streamlining bankruptcy court procedures and introducing short appeal deadlines should presumably help speed up the process.

A major change in the Romanian bankruptcy reform in 1998 put administrative duties related to bankrupt companies in the hands of private liquidation companies that had the business skill and knowledge to handle these cases efficiently. As a result, thousands of cases have been processed, and a field of 132 registered private liquidators has emerged (Gupta, Kleinfeld, and Salinas 2002).

In summary, the lack of well-functioning bankruptcy mechanisms throughout the region still appears to be a major impediment to improving the investment climate in SEE. Further reforms are needed in each of the SEE8 to address court and case management issues as well as to help inexperienced commercial judges, trustees, and receivers. Modernizing the existing commercial courts and designing a regulatory framework for bankruptcy trustees and administrators will strengthen the public's trust in the bankruptcy process and will facilitate the exit of unsound (illiquid and insolvent) firms so that resources are more efficiently used in the economy, thus permitting greater prospects for growth.

REFORMING THE TAX CODE

As pointed out above, soft budget constraints also are perpetuated through lax enforcement of taxation, selective tax exemptions for privileged enterprises, or both. Poor enforcement of tax rules discourages not only the government-shielded state enterprises but also the rest of the market participants from complying with the legislation. Moreover, selective tax enforcement that protects the state sector creates uncompetitive markets, disheartens entrepreneurship, and stimulates the shadow economy. Apart from hurting new entrants, soft budgets help unsound enterprises stay unrestructured and afloat, which bottles up resources.

As evidence from BEEPS1 and BEEPS2 and from the case studies shows, a culture of extensive tax evasion still pervades the region. To strengthen the collection of taxes and the enforcement of tax regulation, the SEE8 have launched fiscal reforms. Through these reforms, they intend not only to recover lost tax revenues but also to create a fair and competitive environment for all market participants. How far have they come in achieving this goal?

Tax reforms that are designed to simplify rate structures and treat market agents equally have been introduced throughout the region. For example, in Romania, two new laws that are related to enterprise taxation came into force in 2002: the value added tax (VAT) law, which established a 19 percent VAT rate, and the profit tax law, which enforced a standard 25 percent tax rate. Similarly, in Bulgaria, the corporate profit tax and municipality tax were consolidated at a 23.5 percent rate as of January 2003; this consolidation resulted in a major simplification of fiscal obligations for firms. In addition, the Bulgarian government intends to gradually decrease the corporate profit tax rate to 15 percent by 2005 (Stability Pact and OECD 2003, p. 20).

In FYR Macedonia, a VAT law was introduced in April 2000. The government simplified and reduced the personal income tax rate at the beginning of 2001 and reduced the VAT rate in 2003.[9] To attract investment to the country, the parliament adopted in July 2003 changes to the law on profit tax. Under the amendments, investments of up to €100,000 will be completely deductible from taxable profits, and investments above that threshold will be granted a 30 percent tax write-off.

The Serbian government has also introduced wide-ranging reforms to its tax system. Since 2001, the government has greatly reduced the number of taxes, lowered the tax rate on various goods and services, and widened the tax base by eliminating exemptions. The sales tax rate was unified at a rate of 17 percent, and preparations for the introduction of VAT in July 2004 are under way. The government in Montenegro has prepared a tax action plan, which is intended to broaden the effective tax base and to lower tax rates. Initial efforts to carry out this plan will focus on amendments to the turnover tax legislation. VAT was introduced in April 2003.

Similarly, tax reforms in Bosnia and Herzegovina have been designed to reduce high tax rates, to broaden the base for tax collection, and to put in place effective enforcement and deterrence mechanisms to reduce barriers to entry. The basic sales tax on goods is now the same in both entities (20 percent), but business tax rates have been reduced only in Republika Srpska. There are plans to introduce VAT at the state level by January 2005 and to set up a database that will identify each taxpayer with a unique number to monitor compliance.

In addition to the reforms discussed above, countries have also taken steps toward strengthening the administrative capacity of the tax agencies in the region. For example, FYR Macedonia, like the other former Yugoslav republics, established a treasury system to begin the transition away from the central payments systems inherited from the former Yugoslavia. The Payment Operation Offices are also in the process of being dismantled. Bosnia and Herzegovina closed its payment bureaus in January 2001 and replaced them with (a) giro-clearing arrangements with participating banks for smaller transactions and (b) a real-time gross settlements system for large transactions.[10]

In Bulgaria, the Council of Ministers created the National Revenue Agency in July 2002 to administer the collection of all public receivables. The agency will be fully functional by 2005. The Albanian government has invested efforts in strengthening tax and customs administration by decentralizing customs offices, improving the valuation system, elaborating reward-based performance schemes, and launching an independent tax-payer appeals commission.

Overall, though some progress has been made in addressing weaknesses in the competitive environment for business in SEE (as the detailed analysis in chapter 3 makes clear), significant challenges remain.

## Access to Regulated Infrastructure Utilities

Although the data in figure 2.1 suggest a major improvement in the perceptions that the businesses in SEE8 maintain with respect to the public infrastructure sector since 1999, the quality and efficiency of these services has remained rather weak across all countries in the region. Furthermore, as our case studies corroborate, poor delivery of infrastructure utility services has discouraged investors and limited the growth opportunities for the local businesses in SEE. In addition, public sector utilities often struggle to maintain resources when they are pressured by political entities to sell services below cost.

The quality of infrastructure in SEE varies at the country level. Figure 2.5 presents the aggregate picture of the perceptions held by the surveyed firms across the eight countries with respect to the infrastructure services in 1999 and 2002.

## Figure 2.5   Assessment of Quality of Infrastructure

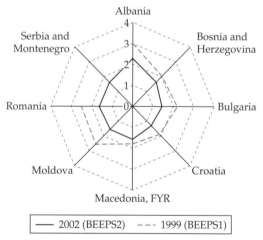

_Sources:_ EBRD and World Bank (1999, 2002).
_Note:_ The results for BEEPS2 are aggregated. To derive the measure of the quality of infrastructure in figure 2.5, we have used simple averages of the following indicators: telecommunications, electricity, transportation, and access to land. Indicators range from 1 to 4, with 4 representing the worst state of infrastructure quality.

Again, although figure 2.5 indicates an improvement between 1999 and 2002, firms participating in the case studies and the enterprise-level surveys indicate that the infrastructure in the SEE8 is still weak, especially in Albania. According to our overall business environment indicator (figure 2.1), Albanian enterprises complain substantially more than those in other countries of the region about poor infrastructure.

The SEE8 governments face several important challenges in terms of regulating and carrying out efforts to improve the quality of the infrastructure services in the region, challenges that chapter 4 tackles in more detail. Yet, country-specific and regional progress has been made in the telecommunication, energy, transportation and border crossing, and water sectors, as the following sections make evident.

TELECOMMUNICATIONS

Of the regulated utility services, the telecommunication sector has experienced the most dynamic transformation during the 1990s in SEE. The telecommunication sector has expanded primarily because competition (particularly in cellular and Internet services) has been introduced and because the dominant operators have been privatized. Four of the SEE8 have already privatized their telecommunication operators, and divestiture of the state ownership in the remaining countries is under way but still not completed. Here, we briefly review the experience of the SEE8 with the privatization of their national telecommunication firms.

In December 2000, a consortium led by Matáv (the dominant telecommunication operator in Hungary), which is 60 percent owned by Deutsche Telekom, won a tender for a 51 percent controlling stake of Makedonski Telekomunikacii (the telecommunication operator in FYR Macedonia), ahead of the OTE (Οργανισμός Τηλεπικοινωνιών της Ελλάδος of Greece) and Telekom Slovenija. Through an agreement reached in July 2001, Deutsche Telekom has taken majority ownership in Hrvatski Telekom, the dominant telecommunication operator in Croatia. In 1997, 49 percent of the fixed-line telecommunication company in Serbia, Telekom Srbija, was sold to a consortium led by the Italian Stet (29 percent) and the Greek OTE (20 percent), although the government of Serbia purchased back the 29 percent stake from Stet in January 2003.

Privatization of the Bulgarian fixed-line state telecommunications monopoly, Bulgarian Telecommunications Company, has been finalized, and in February 2004, Viva Ventures of Austria acquired 65 percent ownership. The Telecommunications Regulatory Authority, an independent body, was formed in 1998, but it has yet to show that it is capable of implementing regulations and is effectively independent.

In Bosnia and Herzegovina, more progress has been made in Republika Srpska, where the government committed to privatize the state-owned company by the end of 2004, than in the Federation of Bosnia and

Herzegovina. Several attempts to privatize the Albanian and Moldovan dominant operators have not been successful, and the countries were not able to attract strategic investors.

The eight countries also have made first steps toward intraregional cooperation in the information and communication technology field. Ministers of the SEE8 signed an agenda that launches plans for the development of an information society in the region.

Privatization of the state-owned telecommunication firms and demonopolization of the sector in SEE are essential for increasing the quality and accessibility of services. Abolishing the state monopoly and liberalizing the sector means that telecommunication subscribers have additional choices of operators and services at competitive prices. However, setting up and strengthening an independent regulator in each of the countries is key because that effort (a) establishes the institutional framework to formulate the rules of market conduct, (b) safeguards the benefits from competition, and (c) prevents the government from interfering in the industry.

ENERGY

Progress in privatizing electricity distribution and generation and in opening up the market to competition has proceeded at a sluggish pace and, generally, has varied by sector and by country. In addition, obsolete machinery and equipment, the low number of investments, the legacy of widespread expectations that energy should be provided at little or no cost, and a reform stalemate resulted in power shortages and in an inadequate energy supply policy throughout SEE. Only Bulgaria is a net exporter of energy among the SEE8. To overcome the supply challenges, the SEE8 established the South Eastern Europe Electricity Regulatory Forum initiative. The initiative is intended to provide a coordinated solution on a regional level, thereby setting the framework for a regional energy market (see chapter 4).

At the country level, the government in FYR Macedonia is struggling to jumpstart reforms in the sector. The state-owned electricity company still controls most of the energy sector and administratively sets most energy prices (see box 2.3). The government has launched initiatives to rehabilitate seven small hydroelectric power plants under revitalization, operation, and transfer projects. An independent regulator was established only in July 2003, thus delaying the modernization of the utilities and infrastructure sector. Despite the limited progress, major steps toward the unbundling and privatization of the energy sector are yet to be taken in FYR Macedonia (see box 2.3).

In Serbia and Montenegro, energy was one of the sectors worst affected by the Kosovo conflict in 1999. Since then, blackouts have been frequent and widespread, especially during the winter months, and the

Box 2.3 Energy Problems and Setbacks for Reform
in FYR Macedonia

The electric power company of FYR Macedonia (Elektrostopanstvo na
Makedonija or ESM) continues to struggle with its supply of electricity. In
the spring 2003, for example, ESM disrupted electricity for hours to whole
towns in the area of Kumanovo and Prilep mainly because of debts from
unpaid utility bills. ESM's bill-collection rate is below 10 percent, and the
company has arrears of approximately US$200 million (of which more
than 62 percent represents overdue payments of industrial consumers). To
tackle the energy problem, ESM announced that the government of FYR
Macedonia had signed an agreement with a foreign investment bank
(Meinl Bank of Vienna) to manage the restructuring of the state utility. To
meet the increasing needs of electric power, ESM is planning to construct
two new thermal power plants (coil fired and gas fired), upgrade six
hydropower plant facilities, and supply a new dispatching system to
monitor the electricity production. Although the state monopoly has
made some restructuring efforts, more fundamental changes have been
postponed.

The restructuring and modernization efforts will not bring an effective
solution to the energy troubles in FYR Macedonia if ESM continues to tol-
erate the arrears of industrial consumers and if the government allows
ESM to keep its monopoly position on the FYR Macedonian market. ESM
will not be attractive to foreign investors until it settles the problem of
unpaid bills. The unbundling of the firm into separate generation, distribution, and transition companies, followed by the privatization of the integrated monopoly, is key to liberalizing the sector and solving the local
energy problems.

*Source:* European Commission (2003c).

country has had to import electricity. Power facilities that were damaged
by the war need urgent repairs. Investment decisions are usually made at
the municipal or national government level with a strong bias toward
new infrastructure, disregarding maintenance and rehabilitation. Priorities for reform in the sector include (a) setting up a basic institutional regulatory and policy framework, (b) transferring ownership of assets fully
to the municipal level while developing planning and overall regulatory
responsibilities at the republic level, and (c) replacing the tariff formulas
with one that provides incentives for cost reduction (EBRD 2001a).

Similarly, the Albanian government has intensified its efforts to tackle its
poor energy supply services, focusing on regulatory reform. But progress
has been slow. It plans to restructure the state-owned energy company,
Korporata Elektro-energjetike Shqiptare (KESH), with management

assistance from the Italian company Enel. A reform strategy has been launched for the electricity sector that includes specific quantitative targets for improving the main indicators of KESH's performance. As part of the effort to combat electricity shortages, a two-tier tariff structure was adopted to reduce excessive demand for electricity for heating purposes and still protect the most vulnerable. Because of strong actions against electricity theft and increased penalties for nonpayment, KESH is gradually being brought back to profitability.[11] However, the privatization of KESH, originally intended for 2001, has been postponed. The government has developed an action plan for 2003–04 to tackle the problems in the power sector. It indicates, however, that even with significant measures being taken to curb illegal use of electricity and to reduce electricity demand, a subsidy of about US$35 million and a layoff of 40 percent of its employees are required to restructure the utility before privatizing it.[12]

In contrast, independent regulatory frameworks in the energy sector have been established through primary legislation in Bulgaria, Croatia, and Romania, and restructuring of utility services has been launched. The five energy laws approved by the Croatian parliament formalize the restructuring of Industrija Nafte (INA), the oil and gas company, and Hrvatska Elektroprivreda (HEP), the electric power company, as well as formalizing the establishment of the district heating enterprises in the country. In July 2003, the government approved the sale of 25 percent of INA plus one of INA's assets to the Hungarian company Magyar Országos Levéltár. Despite these positive developments in the sector, HEP still retains state monopoly and dominant status in the area of energy transmission and distribution. In addition, new entrants in the energy sector in Croatia find it particularly difficult to launch business operations because of cumbersome restrictions with respect to energy distribution. It takes 3 to 5 years for a new firm to obtain an operating license in the energy sector, whereas incumbent energy firms are granted the same licenses in 15 days.[13]

Power distribution companies in Bulgaria and Romania are in the process of privatization, too. For example, in March 2003, the Bulgarian Privatization Agency launched a two-stage competition for the privatization of two district heating distributors—Toplofikatsia Samokov and Toplofikatsia Lovech. Parallel to the privatization initiative of the two district heating companies, a competitive tender for the modernization of the heating supply network in Sofia and Pernik also is under way. The future contractor will be in charge of more than 1,350 substations for the district heating in Sofia. In Romania, the privatization process of the first four electricity distribution companies and the two gas distribution companies is ongoing. The experience with the divestiture of state ownership in the district heating and power distribution companies in Bulgaria and Romania, as well as their experience with labor restructuring, is likely to bring valuable lessons for the rest of the region.

## Box 2.4 Implementation Problems in Moldova

In June 1997, the government launched a Strategy for Energy Development as a first step in moving the sector toward better economic and financial management. In October 1997, the state monopoly Moldenergo was broken up into 16 separate entities, including 3 joint-stock combined heat and power generation companies, 5 joint-stock power distribution networks, and the transmission and dispatch company Moldtranselectro. Although Moldtranselectro still remains in state hands, three distribution companies have already been privatized, and the remaining generation and distribution companies are lined up for full privatization.

However, the new regulatory authority (which was set up in 1997) has experienced growing interference from the government and from the court system, particularly with respect to the implementation of tariff increases, which has caused delays to the development of the sector.

Privatizing energy providers and introducing market-driven incentives would improve the quality and supply of energy in the region. In Moldova, for example, the early 1990s were characterized by blackouts, widespread barter transactions, and nonpayment compliance, which hampered the hardening of budget constraints and introduction of financial discipline among energy consumers. After Moldova conducted a successful privatization of three power distributors with a strategic foreign investor, blackouts were rare and the collection rate of bills improved. However, problems of a different nature have emerged in Moldova (see box 2.4). The court system, which supported the government's postprivatization motion, questioned not only the commitment of the cabinet to market reforms but also the ability of the system to protect property rights and contracts.

TRANSPORTATION AND BORDER CROSSING

In its 2003 annual report on the stabilization and association process for South Eastern Europe, the European Commission suggested that, for the Balkans, "the only realistic and sustainable approach to transport investment needs is a transnational one" (European Commission 2003d, p. 13). Given the large amount of investment needed for modernizing and restructuring the transportation sector, the international donor community has focused on providing assistance in the rebuilding of the region after the conflicts of the 1990s. For example, 28 percent of the EU assistance to the western Balkans under the Community Assistance for Reconstruction, Development, and Stabilization scheme is, for 2000–2004, allocated to infrastructure projects, which constitute the first stage of the assistance process focusing on emergency operations and reconstruction. Yet intraregional and international efforts with a decisionmaking authority to support the development needs of the transportation sector in SEE are still small, except for the establishment of the pro-committees under the Southeast European Cooperative Initiative. The pro-committees are a working mechanism for identifying key measures in the transportation sector in SEE. They impose pressure on government institutions to implement reforms, and monitor the reform process (World Bank 2003b).

However, problems of a regulatory nature—for example, liberalizing road transit traffic, establishing technical standards for vehicles, and harmonizing documentation requirements and transit permits—are issues that need to be tackled on a national level in each of the SEE8. Moreover, the surveyed businesses in the region perceive the conduct of law enforcement officials and the operation of customs agencies as especially problematic because of the rigid and unpredictable application of rules and the widespread corruption (EBRD and World Bank 2002). Beyond the national peculiarities in overcoming customs and inspection obstacles, excessive waiting times and petty corruption at border crossing points have been constraining trade opportunities for the businesses in the region, as further discussed in chapter 4.

The international donor community and the governments of South Eastern Europe have recognized the impediments created by poor customs procedures and the need for a mix of institutional reforms, simplified procedures, improvements in information technology, and upgraded border crossing facilities to support regional cooperation.[14] In this vein, steps to modernize customs administration and simplify the bureaucratic burden of overregulation in the region have produced positive results.

The lack of transparency and the complexity of inspections, customs operations, and tax administration have also posed great constraints to business development. In Bosnia and Herzegovina, the problem is particularly acute because the legislature needs (a) to rationalize the multiple processes now in effect for business inspections and (b) to eliminate the overlap that occurs at different levels of government and among different types of inspections.

At the country level, the transportation authorities in SEE often face challenges related to regulatory issues involved in accommodating the needs and means of the transportation operators (World Bank 2003b). In addition, conflict in the region has damaged transportation infrastructure facilities, especially in Bosnia and Herzegovina and in Serbia and Montenegro. For example, the Bosnian railway system suffered severely during the war and has been in urgent need of rehabilitation. The public railway corporation (Bosansko-Hercegovacke Zljeznicke Javne Korporacije) will be the executing agency for a modernization project, EBRD's

Railways Recovery Project for Bosnia and Herzegovina (EBRD 2001b). Key covenants of the project stipulate that the two railway companies currently operating in the Federation of Bosnia and Herzegovina be consolidated into one company and that the railway companies operating after the consolidation (one in the Federation of Bosnia and Herzegovina and one in Republika Srpska) each prepare a new business plan and a labor restructuring plan.

Ports and water facilities throughout the region are also undergoing major restructuring efforts, but the process is hampered by controversies. In Croatia, for example, a court ruling has impeded the privatization of management and operation of the port of Rijeka, one of Croatia's most essential transportation links with the region. In Bulgaria, the privatization of shipyards and ports has been launched but has advanced at a sluggish pace. For example, in December 2003, the privatization of the Bulgarian Varna shipyard had almost been completed, but one of the conditions for the privatization of the shipyard had been to divest it from its current owner the Bulgarian Sea Fleet (Navibulgar). Navibulgar conducted a tender and selected Bulyard consortium, which is to take more than 75 percent of the shipyard. To complete the transaction, Navibulgar has to request the permission of the privatization agency, which is expected to be granted sometime in 2004.

The systemic recession, obsolete equipment, and poor maintenance of the shipyards and ports in SEE have made them deteriorate and assume heavy debt. Several of the governments in the region are seeking assistance from the international donor community to open ports to private operators through concessions, something that the new port law in Bulgaria, for example, makes possible.

WATER

Although the region has adequate water resources, challenges exist in the water sector of each of the eight countries. The problems vary by country, but the countries share some common deficiencies, including problems with water quality, access to piped water, sewerage service, intersectoral allocation, and wastewater treatment. All of these areas need major improvement (see box 2.5 for an overview of the problems in Albania). For example, approximately 25 percent of the population in the region has no access to piped water. In the rural areas, the problem is more acute; only 51 percent of the population receives piped water, and only 17 percent of the population has access to sewerage services.[15]

A recent study by the World Bank (2003c) assessed the consequences of poor water resource management. Its principal findings are that poor water resource management (a) leads to damage and loss of life from floods, droughts, landslides, and erosion; (b) imposes health risks; (c) damages

---

## Box 2.5  Water Challenges in Albania

Albania faces acute challenges related to watershed and flood management; water sanitation and irrigation and drainage; and management of lakes, wetlands, and coastal areas. The country also lags behind in creating a framework with broad stakeholder ownership and institutions for water services delivery. The government did not liberalize the national uniform water supply tariffs until July 1998, when it established the Utility Regulatory Commission, giving it powers to set tariffs and determine how they would be enforced. However, even then, the tariff for many local water utilities was well below the one requested by the utilities. The country continues to experience water problems not only because of outdated supply and sanitation systems but also because of sluggish progress with reforms. In Tirana, more than 50 percent of the water is drained because of leakages and illegal connections. In the urban areas, only about 40 percent of the people have sewerage connections and only about 80 percent have access to piped water. Although the privatization of the water sector has started, major efforts are needed to modernize and maintain the sector.

*Sources:* World Bank (2003c) and European Commission (2003a).

---

fisheries, tourism, and recreation industries and leads to loss of ecosystems; (d) threatens the well-being of local communities through poor service delivery of drinking water; (e) weakens intersectoral allocation of water supplies for irrigation, hydropower, municipal water supply, and ecosystem maintenance; and (f) brings about inadequate water policies, institutions, and pricing regimes that drain government budgets and lead to poor water resource management and service delivery.

All of the SEE8 are working toward improving the regulatory side of the water sector to increase accessibility and the efficiency of the water delivery while establishing a sound, market-oriented, institutional framework for the sector. The lack of sufficient investment for maintenance and modernization of the water infrastructure is a common and acute problem for every country in SEE. Although pricing reform and price adjustments have been initiated in the SEE8, institutional reforms for accountable public and private organization of the water sector are needed everywhere. Bulgaria and Romania, in line with their EU accession process, have adopted legislation governing water resources management, but both countries face serious problems in carrying out this legislation. At the conclusion of the Thessaloniki Summit of the European Council in June 19–23, 2003, the council recommended drawing up integrated water resource management plans for transboundary water bodies within the western Balkans.

## *Corporate Governance Incentives and Institutions*

To address the corporate governance needs in the SEE8, we look at four areas: restructuring and enterprise ownership, financial disclosure and transparency, minority shareholder rights, and access to finance.

RESTRUCTURING AND ENTERPRISE OWNERSHIP
The slow output recovery in the SEE8 reflects the pace of enterprise restructuring and privatization in the region as well as the new ownership and corporate governance structures that are emerging. Competing methods of privatization entail different anticipated outcomes with respect to control over the privatized enterprise and, in turn, "the likelihood of its extensive restructuring" (Bornstein 2001, p. 190). Djankov and Murrell (2002), in a recent empirical study, find that, across transition economies, outsider privatization is associated with larger restructuring gains than insider privatization. In the same study, they also demonstrate that the effect of privatization through sales to foreigners is on average 10 times as strong as sales to diffuse individual owners and that state ownership has the least effect on restructuring among all other types of ownership.

As table 2.3 reveals, the dominant method of privatization across the SEE8 has been the *management-employee buyout* (MEBO)—that is, the sale or giveaway of all or substantial ownership of a company to its managers and employees. For example, observers have estimated that in Romania, by the end of 1998, over a third of all industrial firms in the State Ownership Fund had undergone MEBO privatization, with average employee ownership of 65 percent and median employee ownership of 71 percent (Earle and Telegdy 2002, p. 8). In addition, MEBO participants were the largest owner group in one-fourth of the Romanian privatized firms, which makes the MEBO technique the most important tool of state ownership divestiture in the country.

**Table 2.3   Primary Methods of Privatization in SEE**

| Method of privatization | Direct sales | Vouchers | MEBOs |
|---|---|---|---|
| Albania | — | Secondary | Primary |
| Bosnia and Herzegovina | Secondary | Primary | — |
| Bulgaria | Primary | Secondary | — |
| Croatia | — | Secondary | Primary |
| Macedonia, FYR | Secondary | — | Primary |
| Moldova | Secondary | Primary | — |
| Romania | Secondary | — | Primary |
| Serbia and Montenegro | Secondary | Primary | — |

*Source:* EBRD (2002).
*Note:* The primary (secondary) methods of privatization are those that have been used most (second most) frequently since the start of transition.

## Figure 2.6   Largest Shareholder's Identity in Surveyed Firms, 2002

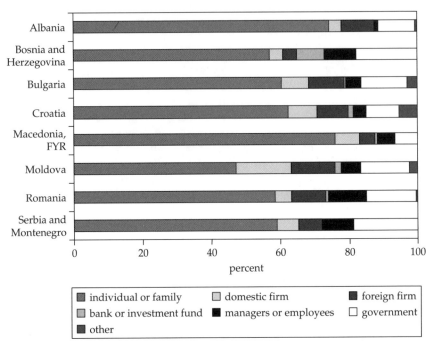

*Source:* EBRD and World Bank (2002).

BEEPS2 confirmed this finding on a cross-country basis. On average, in one-fifth of the surveyed enterprises in 2002, the largest shareholders were either the managers or the employees of the firm (see figure 2.6). According to BEEPS2, the highest proportions of insider-dominated governance structures are in Bosnia and Herzegovina and in Moldova, where 28.3 percent and 24.8 percent, respectively, of managers or employees of privatized enterprises have become the new owners of former state-owned companies. Because of the prevalence of MEBOs, enterprises in SEE are characterized by highly fragmented ownership, inadequate management skills, and insufficient fresh capital for restructuring and investment.

Another striking feature of enterprises in the region is the limited presence of foreign ownership. As presented in figure 2.6, for the region, on average approximately 8.4 percent of the surveyed firms in 2002 were foreign owned. However, in Bosnia and Herzegovina, FYR Macedonia, and Serbia and Montenegro, the share of foreign ventures among the surveyed enterprises was below the average for the region and stood at 4.0 percent, 4.6 percent, and 6.7 percent, respectively. In addition, institutional investors (such as privatization funds or commercial banks) and block investors are not popular types of shareholders in the region. However, they are gaining importance as key players, especially in privatization transactions that empower insiders. For example, the privatization experience of FYR Macedonia illustrates an interlocking relationship between commercial banks and enterprises. Privatizing the banking sector required the privatization of dozens of enterprises and resulted in fragmented ownership that tends to abuse credit rather than safeguard bank capital.

A 2003 OECD and Stability Pact white paper on corporate governance in SEE outlines three common features that characterize the emerging ownership structures in SEE. These features, which are also reflected in the results from BEEPS1 and BEEPS2, are as follows:

(i) Significant control by insiders and, more precisely, by managers who have secured control either through direct ownership or indirectly by de facto control over employee shares

(ii) The importance of retaining state ownership and control, especially in large firms and utilities that are to be privatized

(iii) The emergence of various forms of institutional investors, mainly former privatization funds that play a significant role in the ownership structure of enterprises (OECD, South East Corporate Governance Roundtable, 2003, pp. 64–65)

The experience of SEE with insider-dominated privatization techniques reveals that, as a whole, MEBOs have produced enterprises with weak corporate governance practices because the transformed enterprises have a rudimentary incentive structure. For example, the culture of "social capital" in the former republics of Yugoslavia gives the employees' assembly significant decisionmaking power in firms to be privatized. Details of the enterprise's privatization and the choice of future owners are left to the employees. This type of ownership transformation creates conditions that preserve overemployment, permit low management turnover, and limit the flow of new human capital in the firms. Consequently, little effective restructuring takes place.

Moreover, insiders' privatization deals often materialize through informal ties between politicians and industrial incumbents. These kinds of nontransparent relationships breed corruption and nepotism. In Croatia, for instance, the enterprise privatization program of the early 1990s combined partial sales to employees with tendering to politically related investors. The privatization attempt empowered incumbents without promoting the incentives for corporate restructuring and governance. In Romania, powerful insiders such as the labor unions not only influenced the choice of privatization tools but also blocked the divestiture of state firms.

Mass privatization has been another widespread privatization instrument in SEE. Vouchers were popular because the belief was that they could empower the population equally and quickly create new private owners of state firms. Generally, vouchers have been used extensively in countries where capital for direct investment is scarce and inaccessible to the public. In Bosnia and Herzegovina, Moldova, and Serbia and Montenegro, vouchers are the primary method of privatization, and in Albania, Bulgaria, and Croatia, they have been a secondary technique for divestiture.

However, the results of mass privatization techniques in SEE are disappointing. Not only is the pace of privatization slow (resulting in a low percentage of state assets being privatized), but also these techniques have failed to create market incentives in the firms with new owners. For example, in Romania, the first wave of the voucher privatization transformed only 8 percent of state assets, and the second one in 1995 proved to be excessively complicated, because the trading of vouchers and the formation of intermediaries were prohibited. The state retained a large ownership stake by offering only 60 percent of the shares in the firms for mass privatization.

Major setbacks affected voucher privatization in Bosnia and Herzegovina, too (see box 2.6). Although the privatization process began in 1997, ownership transformation has been only partly completed, primarily among SMEs in the country, as large and strategic enterprises are privatized very slowly. The regulations in both the Federation of Bosnia and

---

### Box 2.6  Institutional Hurdles to Privatization in Bosnia and Herzegovina

In Bosnia and Herzegovina, the privatization legislation created an entity-based scheme involving 12 privatization agencies: one for each of the two entities, the Federation of Bosnia and Herzegovina and Republika Srpska, and one for each of the 10 cantons. The key problem is that the agencies' powers often overlap or conflict because a firm with operations in more than one canton or a firm with strategic significance can fall within the purview of several cantonal agencies and the federal agency. This institutional and regulatory framework has enormous potential for corruption. It also has stimulated ethnic rivalry because entity governments were allowed to distribute disproportionate numbers of vouchers to war veterans, discriminating against citizens who had fled or had been removed from their homes during the war. Political obstruction was and still is more apparent in profitable state-owned enterprises that are enjoying either monopolies or particularly favorable market positions. The OECD assesses the potential sources of failure for the Bosnia and Herzegovina mass privatization techniques in the areas of "political uncertainties, public mistrust of vouchers, and a specific danger that privatization may become dominated by war profiteers and political insiders" (OECD 2000, p. 22)

Herzegovina and Republika Srpska have favored domestic holders of vouchers over foreign owners of cash, permitting the latter to acquire upto 30 percent of the shares with cash. Of the remainder, up to 55 percent of shares can be purchased with vouchers, up to 20 percent can be purchased with citizens' old hard-currency savings, and 15 percent is reserved for the entity. The high ratio of vouchers to cash leaves most newly privatized companies without sufficient working capital to function. In addition, a rule that allows voucher investors to appoint only two members to the board of directors effectively allows the entity (the Federation of Bosnia Herzegovina or Republika Srpska) to retain control over the privatized firm. For example, in the Republika Srpska, the state retains 30 percent of shares in all mass privatized firms. The state-controlled Pension and Disability Fund receives 10 percent of all shares, and the Restitution Fund gets another 5 percent. Most of the enterprises in Bosnia and Herzegovina still lack strategic owners.

Similarly, in Albania and Moldova, voucher privatization has been used extensively, especially in the housing, transportation, and retail trade sectors, but it has not transformed a significant share of state assets. The mass privatization programs in both countries proceeded slowly and transformed only a negligible amount of assets. In Albania, only 97 enterprises (or 12 percent of medium-size and large state-owned enterprises) were sold over five rounds from October 1995 through July 1996, and in Moldova, in two rounds, approximately 3 million Moldovans became shareholders in 225 firms by using their promotional bonds. Generally, voucher schemes of privatization across the region have failed to bring sound corporate governance mechanisms because they have caused ineffective corporate restructuring and a consequent decline in competitiveness.[16]

Enterprises that are controlled by insiders still dominate the structure of privatized firms in SEE. How does this corporate structure affect enterprise restructuring and private sector development in the region?

Insider control mirrors the poor corporate governance structure in SEE. The weak institutional framework for corporate governance, as well as the lack of financial transparency and disclosure, creates owners of corporate assets without also creating the proper incentives for restructuring and modernizing the newly privatized firms. When corporate governance structures and incentives (namely, the rules and institutions that determine the extent to which managers act in the best interest of shareholders) are weak, then firm performance suffers, and the incentives for opportunistic behavior and corruption strengthen. This pattern is especially true for firms with significant (or even complete) state ownership because in such cases, often, little effective separation between government and business has been established. In these firms, fundamental conflicts of interest are more likely to arise because of the tension between the decisions of managers—who are appointed by the government and, thus, are naturally more inclined to protect workers and delay the restructuring process—and the interests of shareholders. In addition, insiders rarely have the capital and know-how to bring their enterprises to the competitive edge of the market without using preferential treatment in their transactions.

This conflict of interests and objectives between shareholders and managers is also present in privately held firms with widely dispersed ownership. In firms with weak checks and balances (for example, firms with ineffective boards of directors or firms that lack independent financial audits), the shareholders cannot be assured that their interests are fully protected from those of the managers. Conversely, if (a) share ownership is closely held and the main shareholder plays an active role in management (insider control) and (b) there are weak internal and external disciplines on corporate performance (for example, a banking system that does not engender strong creditors' rights or require scrupulous payment of credit), then deleterious outcomes and economic distortions can arise. Unchecked insider control can lead to asset stripping, decapitalization, and corruption, all of which seriously hamper the restructuring process. This unchecked control can also create powerful interest groups against corporate governance reforms.

At the end of the 1990s, the SEE8, having a poor privatization record and fearing the dangerous implications of dispersed and insider ownership, started to abandon mass privatization and insider techniques and shifted their strategy toward direct sales of enterprises. In both Albania and Moldova, for example, the voucher privatization programs are phasing out, and both governments have started to rely on direct sale methods, especially for large industrial enterprises. The Albanian government's privatization strategy of 1998 provided for an auction-based sale of all remaining SMEs, allowing the sale of shares to either local or foreign investors. The SME privatization process proved to be difficult, however, and several SMEs that could not find private investors were liquidated.[17] The government of Romania started privatization in more than 1,500 state-owned enterprises in 1999, began the measures in another 700 in 2000, and continued the process in the following years, using case-by-case sales, pool sales, and sales by the State Ownership Fund.

The fate of the Bulgarian MEBO and mass privatization programs was similar. These methods were abandoned in 1998. Since then, the privatization of state-owned enterprises has been conducted primarily by means of direct sales. In March 2002, to improve transparency in the privatization process and eliminate potential sources of red tape, the Bulgarian government enacted major amendments to the privatization law. The amendments that FYR Macedonia made to its two key privatization laws in June 2000 had similar goals and outlawed nontransparent methods of privatization that would be conducted by means of direct negotiation with politically and socially sensitive enterprises.

In Romania, too, legislative changes were made to overcome the slow pace of large-scale privatization.[18] Yet a significant number of state-owned enterprises still remain under the Authority for Privatization and Management of State Assets, the main authority in charge of privatization in Romania. Among these enterprises are many unprofitable companies that are not suitable for privatization. However, the imposition of investment and employment conditions in the amendments to the privatization law—a move that allows companies to be sold for a nominal price, conditional on future investment commitments—has had positive results. In September and October of 2003, some ailing state-owned companies (including Aro, Tractorul, Siderurgica, and Petrotub) were sold to strategic foreign investors using this method. The Sidex privatization also benefited from these conditions.

Efforts to privatize and create incentive-based ownership structures have spurred further reforms in the rest of the SEE8. In Serbia, the parliament adopted a new law on privatization at the end of June 2001. The law specifies that at least 70 percent of shares in the state and socially owned assets ought to be sold to private investors.[19] However, the results of the privatization program in 2002 were mixed. Although most of the auctions for small and medium-sized companies were completed in 2002, auctions for socially owned enterprises continued into 2003, and the plan was to sell about half of those companies by the end of the year (EBRD 2003). The privatization of large companies has advanced slowly. In March 2003, the Serbian government enacted amendments to the privatization law that were designed to speed up sales, but only three deals to privatize large companies were finalized after those amendments—the sale of the major steel conglomerate Sartid in June 2003 and the sale of two tobacco companies in August 2003.[20] Other sales have been marred by allegations of irregularities.

Privatization efforts in Montenegro have also advanced, including the tender privatization of 15–20 large enterprises (with about 25,000 employees in total), a mass voucher privatization program for 240 medium-size companies, a batch sale privatization of 33 companies, and the liquidation of about 30 companies (World Bank 2001d). The largest privatization to date is the sale of the oil company Jugopetrol, approximately 54 percent of which was purchased in October 2002 by Hellenic Petroleum of Greece. Other privatization initiatives under way in 2003 include the privatization of the aluminum conglomerate Kombinat Aluminijuma Podgorica, a tender for the Niksic steel mill, and 11 tenders for hotels (EBRD 2003). The tenders for hotels, surprisingly, have attracted little interest from foreign investors.

FYR Macedonia dealt with large loss-making enterprises by restructuring 23 loss-making firms into more than 165 separate business units under a special restructuring program supported by the World Bank that began in 1995. In the first half of 1999, significant progress was made in dealing with these firms: 108 were privatized and 8 were put in bankruptcy. Under the World Bank's Second Financial and Enterprise Sector Adjustment Program (FESAL II), 24 companies were still awaiting sale or liquidation at mid-2003, and 8 of these were reported to have been sold by late August 2003. At the same time, the Privatization Agency relaunched the privatization program in an effort to restore momentum. A new privatization timetable was published for 22 loss-making enterprises, and in most cases, an adviser was appointed for the sale. In each case, the asset will be sold to the highest bidder, and bidders will not be required to commit either to making future investments or to retaining current employees. The government intends to complete the program, at which point the Privatization Agency will be closed down.

Although the SEE8 have stepped away from the insider ownership and dispersed ownership methods of privatization, the corporate governance elements of transparency and of accountability in exercising property rights are yet to emerge fully to drive market-oriented enterprise sector development and growth in the region—a key theme of chapter 5.

FINANCIAL DISCLOSURE AND TRANSPARENCY

One key reason for the failure of dispersed privatization efforts to establish effective corporate governance structures in the region is the inability of the SEE8 to implement financial transparency and disclosure requirements. Without institutions to ensure that transparent financial disclosure occurs, investors make uninformed decisions with respect to their prospective investments, and at the same time, shareholders and the public cannot assess the performance of the public companies or hold managers responsible for their actions.

The contours on figure 2.7 represent a combination of (a) the extent to which financial audits have been carried out and (b) the extent to which IAS have been adopted in the SEE8. The score is normalized on a scale from 1 (universally carried out) to 4 (poorly carried out). The data show not only that financial disclosure and transparency vary tremendously across the countries over the observed period but also that they have generally declined since 1999. For example, in 1999, the adoption of IAS was almost universal among the surveyed firms in Croatia and very high in Bosnia and Herzegovina, but it was much lower in Croatia in 2002 among surveyed firms. In interpreting these findings, however, one should bear in mind that the sample is skewed toward small enterprises, which in most countries are not legally obliged to adopt IAS or independent financial audits. Looking at a reduced sample of the larger firms that participated in

## Figure 2.7   Financial Disclosure and Transparency

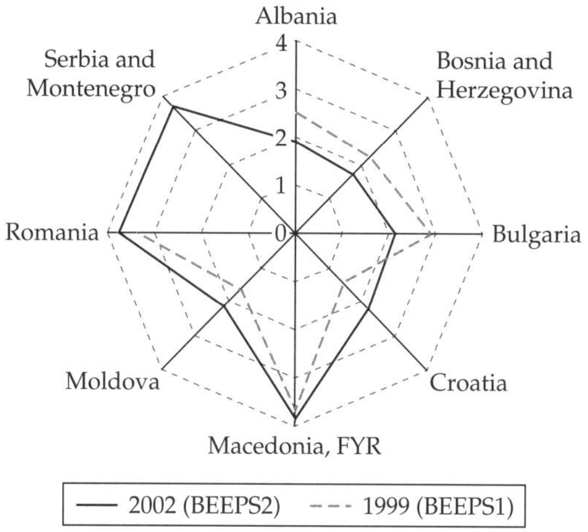

Sources: EBRD and World Bank (1999, 2002).
Note: Scores are normalized on a scale from 1 (universally carried out) to 4 (poorly carried out).

the survey, we find in chapter 5 a stronger pattern of adoption of IAS and financial audits in the SEE8.

It is important to keep in mind, however, that adoption of IAS is a necessary condition only for improved corporate governance: improvements in the use of financial information depend on having sufficient numbers of well-trained accountants and auditors—an unmet condition in many of these countries. In addition, as our enterprise-level case studies show, the external auditing process often does not provide independent, accurate, and complete information to the shareholders of a company, and the managers from the region rarely consider it a mechanism for obtaining independent expertise.

The limited disclosure of corporate information is a widespread characteristic of the region. Companies publish their corporate records under external pressure because most of the countries' legislation formally requires publicly held firms to disclose information. In practice, however, disclosure is not used to attract potential investors or generate economic interest; rather, it is used to fulfill a bureaucratic obligation, and in this sense, it undermines the notion of financial transparency of publicly held enterprises.

Because the region demonstrates these flaws in financial transparency, it appears that only a combination of external and internal controls can ensure effective corporate governance. Internal controls are important in minimizing the risk posed by ill-defined relationships among shareholders, managers, and stakeholders, whereas external controls are effective only if the institutions that regulate corporate governance are suited to the local business environment.

### MINORITY SHAREHOLDER RIGHTS

Enforcement of minority shareholder rights in firms with dispersed ownership structures is weak throughout the region. If the number of shareholders is large, especially in firms privatized through mass privatization, individual owners are often quite unaware of their rights and responsibilities. As a result, the diffused owners of these companies play a passive role in corporate governance because managers or major investors in the firms do not recognize them as true investors. Thus, there is limited recognition of small shareholders' rights and few incentives for such shareholders to exercise those rights.

When compared with international corporate governance standards, the legal framework in Albania, Bosnia and Herzegovina, Moldova, and Serbia and Montenegro fares poorly.[21] Often, the lack of legislation safeguarding minority shareholders has left these shareholders (who in fact often constitute most of the shareholders in a single company) unprotected from decisions made by state agencies. For example, in Albania, the company law does not afford minority shareholders protection in the event that another company makes a bid for fewer than all the shares of a widely held target company. Cumulative voting for directors does not exist. Although the law in Albania points out the directors' duty to perform their functions in good faith and their obligation to avoid self-dealing, in practice, these duties and obligations are often ignored. Similarly, in Serbia and Montenegro, the Federal Enterprise Law does not provide for a right of preemption over newly issued shares; an increase in share capital could be fully allocated to a third party. In Bosnia and Herzegovina, shareholders' rights to elect board members also are relatively weak. Furthermore, minority shareholders are neither protected with respect to stock repurchase rights nor provided with derivative suit rights.[22] In addition, they are not given cumulative voting rights.

To strengthen minority shareholders' rights and to foster ownership consolidation, FYR Macedonia adopted an initial set of amendments to its securities law in July 2000. The amendments provide for the transfer of shareholder books from companies to the new Central Securities Depository and Central Share Registry. The government also plans further amendments to strengthen insider trading rules, to fortify listing requirements, and to protect minority shareholders, but security of minority shareholder rights is still at issue.[23]

According to EBRD's legal assessment, which draws on the experience of lawyers working in the field, the Bulgarian, Croatian, and Romanian company laws compare reasonably well with international standards. In July 2003, amendments to the Croatian Company Law and the Law on Takeover Procedure of Joint-Stock Companies were enacted to strengthen minority shareholders' rights, to enable more transparent securities trade, to help joint-stock companies place their stocks on the stock markets, and to harmonize corporate governance practices with EU rules (World Bank 2001c). With the enactment of the Public Offering of Securities Act in 1999, Bulgaria took a substantial step forward in modernizing the country's corporate governance rules and, specifically, in reinforcing the minority shareholders' protection regime. Under the new act, for example, any shareholder of 5 percent or more can hold managers accountable for any action that adversely affects shareholders' interests within a year of its occurrence. In Romania, Ordinance 229 of 2000 sought to strengthen equitable treatment among shareholders. Although the ordinance has since been declared null, it drew attention to the importance of corporate governance. The government has pledged to issue new legislation to strengthen shareholder rights. Despite these developments, individual investors and entrepreneurs in the region still face difficulties in exercising property rights.

ACCESS TO FINANCE
Access to finance is another common bottleneck that businesses in SEE face. Among the SEE8 firms that participated in BEEPS1 in 1999, more than 54 percent indicated that financing was a major impediment to the development of their business (see figure 2.8). Although under BEEPS2 the total number of these firms decreased substantially in 2002, two-thirds

**Figure 2.8   Financing as an Obstacle to Enterprise Development**

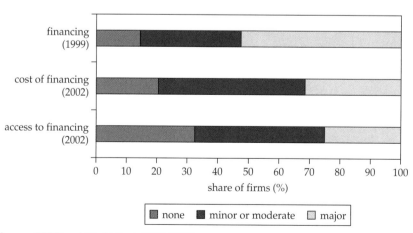

*Sources:* EBRD and World Bank (1999, 2002).

of the surveyed businesses in the region still viewed access to finance as an obstacle to business operations. Similarly, close to 80 percent of the firms indicated that the cost of obtaining financing presented a burden to their operations.

The results from the BEEPS1 and BEEPS2 are supported generically by aggregate data for the SEE8. The low levels of domestic credit provided to the private sector confirm the difficulties firms face. Table 2.4 shows these levels as a share of gross domestic product (GDP). In 2002, the levels were low in all countries except Croatia, and they were especially low in Albania (4.7 percent) and Serbia and Montenegro (8.4 percent).

The difficulties enterprises face accessing financial resources require policymakers to examine bank-enterprise relationships from the perspective of the efficacy of governance incentives. Uncertainty with respect to actual ownership and the lack of a clear title can prevent a business from obtaining financing at attractive terms because business assets cannot be used as collateral. Banks are discouraged from lending to enterprises in which they do not have shareholdings or another relationship (Berglof and Bolton 2002). As table 2.4 reports, at the end of 2002, domestic credit to the private sector as a share of GDP stood at 18 percent on average for the SEE8, a figure considerably lower than the 27 percent average for the five most advanced Central and East European economies. Croatia is an obvious outlier in the SEE8 group, with domestic credit to the private sector comprising 45 percent of output in 2002.

Institutional alternatives to bank-based financing in SEE are not well developed. The use of state insurance companies or other nonbank vehicles for financing has been almost negligible in the region. The equity capital market is relatively limited in size, and it mostly caters to the top corporations, which also have access to foreign sources of financing. The lack of long-term bank financing and other sources of financing has led to a situation in which corporate capital investment, outside of foreign investment, is mainly limited to internal earnings.

The lack of financing is not a problem only for capital investment; its effects also extend to trade financing and make it difficult for enterprises to maintain normal commercial operations. Despite the shortage of working capital from the banking system, few enterprises offer trade credit because credit tracking and dispute settlement mechanisms are underdeveloped.

Another obstacle blocking access to finance in SEE arises from inadequate mechanisms for tradability of vouchers on the secondary market. Underdeveloped stock markets constrain the ability of voucher holders to execute market transactions, which in turn creates an adverse perception of the value of the newly acquired ownership stakes in former state enterprises. The problem is especially acute in the countries that use mass privatization as the primary method of divestiture. The Tirana Stock

## Table 2.4  Domestic Credit to Private Sector and Stock Market Capitalization, 1993–2001

*(percentage of GDP)*

| Country or region | 1993 | 1994 | 1995 | 1996 | 1997 | 1998 | 1999 | 2000 | 2001 | 2002 |
|---|---|---|---|---|---|---|---|---|---|---|
| *Domestic credit to private sector* | | | | | | | | | | |
| Albania | — | 3.9 | 3.6 | 3.9 | 3.9 | 0.6 | 2.1 | 2.9 | 3.8 | 4.7 |
| Bosnia and Herzegovina | — | — | — | — | — | — | 8.9 | 7.4 | 9.5 | 12.0 |
| Bulgaria[a] | 3.7 | 3.8 | 21.1 | 35.3 | 12.3 | 12.2 | 14.0 | 11.6 | 14.6 | 18.0 |
| Croatia | 37.7 | 21.2 | 22.9 | 21.4 | 25.3 | 26.6 | 22.1 | 27.8 | 34.2 | 45.0 |
| Macedonia, FYR | 59.3 | 45.3 | 23.1 | 26.5 | 27.3 | 17.7 | 10.4 | 10.5 | 12.8 | 14.4 |
| Moldova[b] | 5.0 | 3.7 | 5.8 | 6.8 | 14.8 | 15.8 | 11.1 | 12.6 | 14.8 | 18.7 |
| Romania | 3.1 | 4.3 | 7.8 | 11.5 | 8.4 | 11.6 | 8.1 | 7.2 | 7.7 | 8.4 |
| Serbia and Montenegro | — | — | — | 9.2 | 10.8 | 11.2 | 9.8 | 7.6 | 5.6 | — |
| SEE8 average | 21.8 | 13.7 | 14.0 | 16.4 | 14.7 | 13.7 | 11.0 | 11.0 | 12.0 | 18.16 |
| CEE5 average[c] | 28.4 | 26.6 | 27.1 | 28.8 | 33.2 | 33.0 | 32.7 | 32.2 | 28.3 | 27.1 |
| *Stock market capitalization* | | | | | | | | | | |
| Albania | — | — | — | — | — | — | — | — | — | — |
| Bosnia and Herzegovina | — | — | — | — | — | — | — | — | — | — |
| Bulgaria | — | — | 0.5 | 0.2 | 0.0 | 7.4 | 5.8 | 4.8 | 3.7 | 4.3 |
| Croatia | — | 3.3 | 3.1 | 15.3 | 21.6 | 14.5 | 14.0 | 14.5 | 16.8 | 16.1 |
| Macedonia, FYR | — | — | — | 0.3 | 0.3 | 0.2 | 0.2 | 0.2 | 1.3 | 4.8 |
| Moldova[d] | — | — | — | — | — | — | 32.3 | 27.2 | 22.3 | 24.9 |
| Romania[e] | — | 0.0 | 0.4 | 0.2 | 2.0 | 3.0 | 2.9 | 3.4 | 5.8 | 10.2 |
| Serbia and Montenegro | — | — | — | — | — | — | — | — | — | — |

*Source:* EBRD (2003).

*Note:* — = not available.

a. Credit expansion in Bulgaria in 1995 and 1996 was followed by a banking crisis in 1997, which greatly reduced the stock of credit to the enterprise sector.

b. The figures comprise credits to individuals and enterprises, excluding credits to banks and the Moldovan government.

c. The CEE5 are Czech Republic, Hungary, Poland, Slovakia, and Slovenia.

d. Data from survey of Moldovan stock exchange, including government securities. Data from IFC give a figure of 4.56 percent of GDP for listed companies in 1997.

e. Data include listings on the Bucharest Stock Exchange and the over-the-counter market, the Romanian Association of Securities Dealers Quotation.

Exchange, for example, was established in 1996, but it is still not operating.[24] In addition, the capital market in Albania is in its early stage of development and involves negligible trading. Delays in the mass privatization resulted in only a small number of initial public offerings, despite the fact that, since 1998, the number of the listings has slightly increased.

In the rest of the SEE8, stock exchanges are also unable to mobilize the sufficient level of financing that is sought by the firms. Stock exchanges are thin and illiquid, with trade concentrated in a small number of firms and with very low levels of stock market capitalization (see table 2.4). Indeed, the market does not attract many new investors, and stocks are traded between existing stakeholders and brokers. Many listed companies are neither trusted nor traded, which also reflects investors' passivity and low turnover. For example, in 2000, market capitalization of the Bucharest Stock Exchange (BSE) was US$363.2 million, while the turnover was only US$86.2 million. Only 114 companies were listed on the BSE as of the end of 2000 (Gupta, Kleinfeld, and Salinas 2002). Trade on the stock exchanges in Croatia, Serbia, FYR Macedonia, and Moldova has been even slower. As previously mentioned, the lack of transparency because of poor accounting and auditing standards in the listed companies alienates potential investors.

Some countries are actively strengthening their corporate governance institutions. For example, in Croatia, amendments to the Law on Securities Issuance and Trade were enacted in early 2003 to harmonize the law with proposals and instructions of the International Organization of Securities Commissions as well as with the EU directives. Thus, the law now enables the Croatia Security and Exchange Committee to impose substantial penalties on securities dealers who violate investors' rights, thereby allowing more effective oversight of brokerage houses. Other benefits of the new legislation include stronger disclosure requirements and new rules for depositories. Romania is also making an effort to improve legislation pertaining to the supervision of capital markets, despite the inefficiencies of the agencies created to monitor the stock exchanges (Gupta, Kleinfeld, and Salinas 2002).

The low volumes of traded shares, capitalization, and liquidity are likely influenced by the fact that the region's stock exchanges were created in response to the dispersed methods of privatization and were intended to serve as privatization devices in the initial distribution and trading of shares. This fact has led to a notable tendency in the region: increased concentration of ownership achieved by delisting companies from the stock exchange, especially in the postprivatization phase. Experts assess the trend as derived from "the excessive ownership dispersion that results from voucher privatization, and more generally and fundamentally from the inability or great difficulty for minority investors to have their rights respected" (OECD, South East Corporate Governance Roundtable 2003,

p. 65). This tendency to consolidate ownership and abandon the status of being publicly listed is especially popular among SMEs. SMEs cannot effectively access outside capital through the local stock exchanges, but they accrue administration and legal costs by being listed. Furthermore, the legal organization of a joint-stock company is not appropriate for them (OECD, South East Corporate Governance Roundtable 2003).

Poor regulation of the capital and stock markets as well as weak corporate governance incentives—especially with respect to small shareholders—have made dispersed ownership a less attractive structure for divestiture of the state sector. The expected restructuring and reorganization do not materialize easily in an environment of small, unmotivated owners and inexperienced managers of investment funds. Restrictions on secondary share trading and a lack of investment funds and other mechanisms to consolidate shares in the hands of strategic investors hamper efforts to overcome the disadvantages of weak corporate governance in the region.

## Commercial Disputes and Contract Enforcement

Problems with commercial disputes and contract enforcement are endemic to the SEE8. The business environment in most countries is characterized by difficulties with protecting property and contract rights, corruption, an ineffective court system, a lack of security, and an ineffective means of resolving business disputes.

### DIFFICULTIES WITH UPHOLDING PROPERTY AND CONTRACT RIGHTS AND COMBATING CORRUPTION

Results from BEEPS1 and BEEPS2 reveal that, on average, the business community perceives the judiciary and court systems in SEE as among the worst public providers of services in the region. (Other public providers included infrastructure providers, educational providers, the police, parliament, and the central bank.) In countries where the courts and other legal institutions cannot be relied on to uphold the law and, in particular, to enforce contracts, corruption extends to the court system. The courts are perceived as weak and subject to political influence, which makes the resolution of commercial disputes and litigation lengthy and subject to uncertainty. These institutional weaknesses within the legal environment lead foreign investors and companies trading with SEE8 firms to avoid local courts to every extent possible.

Yet, as will be discussed later in this chapter, the effectiveness of the judiciary systems in the region has improved slightly since 1999. This observation is reflected not only in the results of BEEPS1 and BEEPS2 but also in the experts' assessment of the legal environment of the region

(EBRD 2002; Heritage Foundation 2003; Kaufmann, Kraay, and Mastruzzi 2003). Observers saw that the 2002 indicators of legal effectiveness throughout the region had made a considerable leap forward, particularly in Albania and Bosnia and Herzegovina, but have revised downward their assessments of the extensiveness of the commercial laws in Bulgaria, Croatia, and FYR Macedonia, as shown in table 2.5.

**Table 2.5   Control of Corruption, Protection of Property Rights, Legal Effectiveness, and Legal Extensiveness in the SEE8**

| | Control of corruption[a] | | Protection of property rights[b] | | Legal effectiveness[c] | | Legal extensiveness[c] | |
|---|---|---|---|---|---|---|---|---|
| Country | 2002 | 1998 | 2003 | 1999 | 2002 | 1999 | 2002 | 1999 |
| Albania | 23.2 | 9.8 | Low | Low | 3.00 | 1.66 | 3.00 | 2.00 |
| Bosnia and Herzegovina | 34.5 | 45.4 | Very low | Very low | 3.00 | 1.00 | 3.00 | 2.00 |
| Bulgaria | 52.6 | 39.9 | Moderate | Moderate | 4.00 | 3.67 | 3.67 | 4.00 |
| Croatia | 63.9 | 46.4 | Low | Low | 3.30 | 2.67 | 3.30 | 4.00 |
| Macedonia, FYR | 29.4 | 48.1 | Low | — | 3.67 | 3.67 | 3.30 | 3.67 |
| Moldova | — | — | Moderate | Moderate | 3.67 | 3.00 | 3.67 | 3.67 |
| Romania | 45.4 | 44.3 | Low | Low | 4.00 | 3.67 | 3.67 | 3.30 |
| Serbia and Montenegro | 26.3 | 8.2 | Low | — | 3.00 | — | 3.00 | — |

*Sources:* For control of corruption, Kaufmann, Kraay, and Mastruzzi (2003). For protection of property rights, Heritage Foundation (2003). For legal effectiveness and legal extensiveness, EBRD (2002).

*Note:* — = not available.

a. Percentile rank indicates the percentage of countries worldwide that rate below the selected country (subject to margin of error). For more information, see Kaufmann, Kraay, and Mastruzzi (2003).

b. Rankings are defined as follows: *Very high*—private property is guaranteed by the government, the court system efficiently enforces contracts, the justice system punishes those who unlawfully confiscate private property, corruption is nearly nonexistent, and expropriation is unlikely. *High*—private property is guaranteed by the government, the court system suffers delays and is not always strict in enforcing contracts, corruption is possible but rare, and expropriation is unlikely. *Moderate*—the court system is inefficient and subject to delays, corruption may be present, the judiciary may be influenced by other branches of government, and expropriation is possible but rare. *Low*—property ownership is weakly protected, the court system is inefficient, corruption is present, the judiciary is influenced by other branches of government, and expropriation is possible. *Very low*—private property is outlawed or not protected, almost all property belongs to the state, the country is in such chaos (as might be caused by an ongoing war) that property protection is nonexistent, the judiciary is so corrupt that property is not effectively protected, and expropriation is frequent.

c. The indexes of legal effectiveness and extensiveness refer to commercial laws (pledge, bankruptcy, and company legislation) only. Indicators range from 1 (limited in scope, unclear, and contradictory) to 4 (comprehensive, clear, and readily ascertainable). See EBRD (2002).

As table 2.5 shows, on average, the region has a lower score on the legal extensiveness indicator than on the legal effectiveness one.[25] This finding suggests that the legal rules in the areas of pledges, bankruptcy, and company law may be reasonably clear, but as their experience with the laws grows, lawyers continue to identify problems and gaps in these commercial laws. That the commercial legal frameworks of the SEE8 need further improvement is reflected in the countries' weak scores in protection of property rights (also presented in table 2.5). Although implementation of existing laws appears adequate (as per the legal effectiveness scores in table 2.5), there is room for improvement, particularly as the commercial legal framework continues to be expanded and advanced.

Except in Bulgaria and Moldova, experts consider the protection of private property rights as being low in the region—and very low in the case of Bosnia and Herzegovina (see table 2.5). None of the SEE8 has improved its ranking since 1999 on the protection of property rights index. Although recent reforms are beginning to increase public awareness of corruption, particularly in Bulgaria and Croatia, the control of corruption index still reflects high levels of corruption in the region. In fact, since 1998, Bosnia and Herzegovina and FYR Macedonia have ranked lower on the control of corruption index. A weak institutional environment, which is characterized by rent-seeking and illicit behavior among officials, ineffective protection of property rights and contracts, and lax enforcement of the law, has created grounds for corruption in SEE.

The ratings in table 2.5 reflect the imminent need to fight corruption and reform the legal and judicial system in the region. Government and cross-national initiatives are under way. A major anticorruption initiative that was launched in 1999 under the auspices of the Stability Pact is attempting to identify the main areas of corruption in the regions and to recommend measures to combat the problem. In addition, another international effort—the Southeast European Legal Development Initiative—was established to create a regionwide institutional framework for fighting corruption.

Anticorruption programs and surveys are also under way on the national level throughout the region. In Bulgaria, for example, the government has launched a comprehensive and outreaching anticorruption program, which is supported by active public-private partnerships, research and analytical work, and surveys to identify the most acute areas of corruption and to develop mechanisms to combat it (see box 2.7).

In Croatia, important anticorruption measures are being taken that involve civil society, nongovernmental organizations, trade unions, and judges' associations. The Ministry of Justice appointed a high representative in 2001, prepared legislation for establishing an Office for Anticorruption and Combat against Organized Crime, and drafted a National Anticorruption Program.

---

## Box 2.7   Combating Corruption in Bulgaria through Public-Private Partnerships

Coalition 2000 is one of the most prominent examples of a private-public partnership in the area of anticorruption in SEE. Coalition 2000 was established in 1997 by Bulgarian nongovernmental organizations to create a cooperative platform of public and private institutions. It is an all-inclusive platform combining the input and efforts of various stakeholders irrespective of their political or institutional affiliations. The partnership has developed a Corruption Monitoring System (CMS) to serve as a special tool for diagnosing corruption. Using a set of corruption indexes, the CMS also provides regular, comprehensive summaries of public attitudes and behavior related to corruption. The methodology is based on a model of corrupt behavior (defined as a type of interaction between actors) that consists of four main elements: preconditions, practical interaction, action results, and future expectations. Corruption indexes are grouped respectively in the following categories: attitudes toward corruption, corrupt practices, assessment of the spread of corruption, and corruption expectations.

Coalition 2000 also has completed a best practices initiative on a local level. The initiative was implemented in three programs from April 1999 to December 2000. The initial program focused on Transparency of Local Authorities, the second on Open Municipalities, and the third on Civil Society against Corruption. Under these programs, nongovernmental organizations, managers, experts from municipal and district institutions, journalists, and others have made joint efforts to fight the red tape that often shields corruption. The anticorruption initiative promotes participation by civil society in applying mechanisms of civil control over the state, especially with respect to carrying out the National Anticorruption Strategy for Bulgaria for the period 2001–04. The Civil Society against Corruption program supports public awareness activities and anticorruption coalitions at the local and national levels that are based on a partnership between nongovernmental organizations and state and municipal authorities in the framework of the Anticorruption Action Plan of Coalition 2000.

The experience of Coalition 2000 demonstrates that a determined citizenry can demand better government and turn the tables on those who are corrupt.

*Sources:* Anticorruption Coordination Commission (2004) and Center for International Private Enterprise (2001).

---

To fight corruption, the government of Bosnia and Herzegovina has launched an antifraud and anti–tax avoidance strategy. The financial police of the Federation of Bosnia and Herzegovina, which are supported by the Antifraud Department, have largely concentrated on investigating corruption and financial crimes. Through their efforts, high-profile cases of corruption have been brought to court, and 12 officials have been removed for corruption and abuse of office. The Republika Srpska's financial police have been less successful in fighting corruption, however. No official has been dismissed, nor has the entity brought any major corruption case to court. However, important changes were made in June 2000, when the law on judicial service amended the rules governing the appointment of judges and prosecutors in Republika Srpska and set higher salaries in both entities as a hedge against bribery and corruption. The Office of the High Representative has also set up the Independent Judicial Commission, an advisory body of foreign and domestic legal experts to advise and supervise the implementation of legal and judicial reforms. Although these measures have marginally enhanced the independence of judges, the system is still vulnerable to political influence. Moreover, implementation efforts are still lagging, and contracts are often violated. Legal remedies are difficult to find, and even court cases resulting from breach of contract can take years to be resolved.

Apart from widespread corruption problems in SEE, the causes of a relatively weak rule of law include an undertrained and understaffed judiciary that lacks proper resources to effectively enforce enacted legislation. For example, in Albania, the constitution of November 1998—along with the Law on Judicial Organization of 1999 (which introduced minimum academic standards for new judges and a gradual application of these standards for existing judges) and the Anticorruption Action Plan of June 1998 (an initiative supported by the World Bank's Judicial and Public Administration Reform Project)—provided a clear foundation for judicial independence. Implementation problems continue to occur, however, partly because so many new laws have been enacted so quickly that the Albanian government lacks the institutional capacity to carry out and swiftly enforce the new measures.

Throughout the region, the courts are overloaded with cases, and they lack basic levels of information technology. Judges are poorly trained and are not well remunerated, which creates additional incentives for corruption.

Even in countries such as Serbia and Montenegro with a strong tradition of commercial law litigation, judges do not enjoy the confidence of the business community because of their excessive legalistic (rather than practical) approach to resolving disputes.[26] In addition, commercial laws are numerous, excessively detailed, and not well drafted. Consequently, uncertain and unpredictable bureaucratic interpretations have become the norm. Excessive discretion is exercised in carrying out administrative procedures, particularly in cases dealing with the delivery of utility and other public services.

Combating corruption and establishing a well-functioning judiciary (one that approaches Western European standards) in all of the SEE8 will require decades because small steps forward have been followed by setbacks.[27] Stability and economic growth in the region depend on building strong public support for standards of integrity, exposure of corruption, and advocacy reforms.

EFFECTIVENESS OF THE COURT SYSTEM
An important dimension of the dispute resolution regime is the extent to which the legal system can be relied on to uphold contract and property rights in resolving business disputes. The institutional environment in which the enterprises exist is a key determinant of the way firms are structured and operate. Enterprises need a business environment with some degree of policy predictability. Failure to consistently and transparently enforce the law and regulations weakens general respect for them and the institutions that govern them. Across the region, a substantial proportion of enterprises consider regulations and their application to be inconsistent and unpredictable. The available evidence suggests that, over time, the lack of consistency and predictability has been tilting against private sector start-ups.

Figure 2.9 presents the cross-country rankings from BEEPS1 and BEEPS2 of the effectiveness of the judiciary in the eight countries by aggregating the following attributes of the judiciary: fairness, honesty,

**Figure 2.9    Aggregate Effectiveness of the Judiciary**

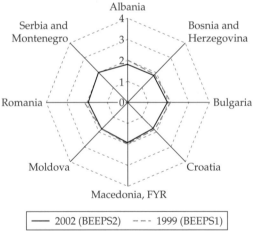

*Sources:* EBRD and World Bank (1999, 2002).
*Note:* Firm managers were asked the following question: "How often do you associate the following description with the court system in resolving business disputes: fair and impartial; honest and uncorrupt; quick; affordable; and able to enforce its decisions?" A higher value of the indicator indicates a lower rating on a 1–4 scale (with 1 representing a "very good" assessment and 4 a "very bad" assessment).

speed, consistency, and enforcement. As detailed analysis in chapter 6 demonstrates, the surveyed enterprises complain about the slowness of the procedures in all eight countries, but they perceive the court system as even more unable to enforce its decisions effectively and honestly. In the case of Albania, for instance, estimates suggest that fewer than 10 percent of civil judgments are effectively enforced. Fairness in legal judgment is perceived as more problematic in Romania and Serbia and Montenegro than anywhere else in the region. Of all the countries in the region, Serbia and Montenegro has the court system least trusted by the surveyed firms to settle business disputes and protect property rights.

Nonetheless, BEEPS1 and BEEPS2 indicate that, compared with the findings in 1999, the perceptions of the business community in 2002 do show a small (though not statistically significant) overall improvement in the effectiveness of the judiciary. Participating businesses in the survey assess the legal environment in 2002 slightly more favorably, especially on attributes such as fairness, honesty, and affordability. These findings suggest that governments' efforts to strengthen the institutional framework for protection of property rights and contracts are having an effect. The Croatian government, for example, has adopted a reform program to address the problems of the country's inefficient court system. The program involves modernizing all commercial courts with the goal to (a) improve compliance with economic and financial legislation, (b) reduce the case backlog in the largest commercial court in Zagreb and other pilot courts by 2003, and (c) speed up bankruptcy proceedings and shorten the time needed for case processing. Because of an ongoing pilot program, fast-track bankruptcy proceedings are expected to be introduced in a number of commercial courts.

SECURITY AND ENFORCEMENT OF PROPERTY RIGHTS
The uncertainty about the security of property rights and institutional arrangements for their enforcement in SEE is particularly acute in issues such as land titling and registration. In all the countries under study, it is not uncommon for several parties to claim to be the legitimate owner of disputed land. Unclearly defined property rights usually stem from the lack of accurate and consistent records in land registries and the cadastre, from conflicting and inconsistent efforts to carry out land-use regulation, and from unnecessary delays and overcomplication of administrative procedures as well as the intensive intermediary nature of those procedures (see box 2.8). The lack of formalized property rights prevents the use of dormant assets and their transformation into financial capital.

Major difficulties in acquiring state-owned land, agricultural land, and larger plots in general exist throughout the region. For example, in Serbia, most urban land is state owned, but according to the existing land

## Box 2.8 Land Reform in Romania: Identifying and Tackling the Problems

In Romania, land acquisition and registration rules vary depending on the type of land. Four types exist: private, state-owned, authority-owned, and free zone land.

According to a Foreign Investment Advisory Services (FIAS) study on adminstrative barriers, the major problems in land acquisition are as follows: (a) land is regulated on the local level, and each municipality has its own procedures; (b) identification of the real owners is difficult because 70 percent of the issued land titles end up in litigation; (c) so far, restitution has been made only for agricultural land outside city borders; (d) there is no legal obligation to register land, so cadastre records are incomplete; and (e) there is a lack of sufficient coordination between local courts (which register the titles) and cadastres (which keep the records). Although a single land registration system, with only one land book, was established in 1999, the unification process has been slow. Registration is done at the local level with little coordination among the cities. FIAS's recommendations are directed toward removing the legal and procedural difficulties, completing the unification of land registration, and introducing a system to resolve land claims quickly and effectively.

*Source:* FIAS (2000).

regime, state-owned land cannot be acquired (FIAS 2001b). In addition, the land books in Serbia are outdated and incomplete. As a result, land titles are often not registered, and parcels are missing from the cadastre, which leads to further delays and complications in the transfer of ownership of private land.

Insecurity of land tenure and rights limits the use and value of property in business transactions. In Bosnia and Herzegovina, for example, the court process for repossessing assets is too long, allowing owners to strip all assets of value from the property or enterprise in question. The complicated and obsolescent system of land registry poses significant problems that, together with the unresolved problems of clear ownership and the inadequate regulations governing collateral, severely restrict access to working capital.

New firms in Albania and FYR Macedonia perceive very weak security of contracts and property rights. These perceptions are based in part on excessively broad legal interpretations of the principle of expropriation for public purpose, which covers construction of gas and oil pipelines, construction of electricity generation and distribution facilities, preservation of cultural heritage, maintenance of public order and national security, and construction of public housing blocks. The reform efforts in the region are directed at overcoming the hurdles of the process through strengthening the institutional framework and introducing viable restitution policy and land laws. Initiatives to reform and modernize the cadastre system as well as to advance restitution policy reforms are under way in all countries in the region.

To overcome the deficiencies in the enforcement of property rights and contracts, the FYR Macedonia has eased collateral constraints and established a system of national registries. The newly created Central Register Organization is now responsible for development and maintenance of movable and immovable collateral registers as well as a central legal entities database. Although the state still needs to resolve claims on land under the 1998 Land Restitution Law, a new rural land-use law was enacted that introduces a basis for secure property and tenancy rights. However, a workable title registry is not yet in place, which continues to make land titling difficult.

RESOLUTION OF BUSINESS DISPUTES

Establishing a formal system that secures and defines property rights fosters the resolution of commercial disputes. The countries in the region are working actively toward improving enforcement of commercial dispute resolutions—although with varying degrees of success. Progress is slow, especially in the absence of effective appeals mechanisms, which makes resolution of business disputes obsolete.

The introduction of mechanisms for alternative dispute resolution (ADR)—a variety of methods for resolving disputes using out-of-court procedures such as mediation, arbitration, or both—is gaining popularity in SEE. Although ratifying the major international conventions in all the SEE8 is an important and necessary step toward the use of ADR, harmonizing the national laws and establishing suitable institutions for out-of-court settlement of disputes requires more than the mere ratification of the international rules in this area. In fact, ADR needs to complement judicial reform in the region and must be used to foster efficiency in dispute resolution.

In this vein, for example, the government of Serbia and Montenegro is currently working on a law to further modernize and expand the scope of arbitration. Independent centers for ADR have been established throughout the region. And yet, in all the SEE8, arbitration is not a commonly used tool for dispute resolution and remains largely underdeveloped. Given the cumbersome procedures for resolving disputes through the court system, ADR may gain importance and provide a viable alternative to enduring the delays, inaccessibility, expenses, and unsatisfactory outcomes of the formal legal system.

# Conclusion: The Unresolved Institutional Problems in South Eastern Europe

South Eastern Europe has made solid progress in establishing an appropriate institutional environment for the formation and functioning of private enterprises. Initiatives include the passage of company and commercial laws, laws on collateral and secured lending, and bankruptcy laws. However, substantial challenges still remain throughout the region. Although most of the SEE8 have adopted policies to foster enterprise restructuring and privatization of assets, more decisive institutional solutions are needed to create conditions for a business environment that favors competition, respects property rights, protects creditors, and treats equally all participants in the market. Advancing these "second generation" reforms would encourage investment (both domestic and foreign) into productive ventures and would promote sustainable growth in the region. Developing these market institutions in the eight countries is not only critical to creating an investment-friendly policy framework but also necessary for their integration with Western Europe.

The main messages of this chapter highlight the deficiencies in the development of the four market institutions that are explored in detail in the subsequent chapters: competition and barriers to entry and exit, regulated infrastructure utilities, corporate ownership, and resolution of business disputes. First, most of the countries have adopted policies directed to remove administrative barriers (for example, streamlining business licensing and registration procedures). In many of the countries, however, failure to implement the improved registration or licensing requirements in a predictable manner and failure to interpret laws and regulations consistently has led to discrimination among different types of investors and, thus, to deficiencies and corruption. More important, few of the countries have strengthened the fundamental market institutions that protect firms from anticompetitive structures and conduct; although some of the countries have sound competition laws, the use of these instruments to reduce economic barriers to entry is almost universally neglected. Furthermore, key legislation has yet to be implemented to facilitate the restructuring or liquidation of large loss-making enterprises.

Second, countries are in the process of overcoming the severe infrastructure bottlenecks caused by the conflict and inadequate maintenance that have characterized the region—though to different extents, depending on the country and sector. However, the development of predictable and transparent regulatory frameworks that would ensure users' access to competitively priced, high-quality services and that would engender investment in the utility sectors (and, generally, in infrastructure) is lagging in all countries. Indeed, the inefficient pricing and cross-subsidies embedded in many of these sectors stifle incentives for attracting investors and privatizing utilities.

Third, the governments of the SEE8 have shifted away from insider techniques of state ownership divestiture and have increasingly relied on more transparent methods of privatization. However, although some countries have adopted international accounting standards and have introduced independent financial audits for enterprises, most are still in the process of doing so. In addition, adoption of these instruments needs to be supplemented with the training of managers who can properly interpret and use the improved financial information to engender improved enterprise performance. At the same time, in most countries, enforcement of commercial legislation is still ineffective in protecting minority shareholders and in imposing the needed discipline of financial disclosure and transactional transparency. As a result, there are weak checks and balances on managerial performance.

Fourth, the legal frameworks help ensure the protection of property rights and the enforcement of contracts in all countries. But the functioning of the associated institutions is limited by lengthy procedures, by the lack of qualified and independent judges, and by weak enforcement mechanisms. Alternative out-of-court administrative channels for dispute resolution—such as the use of arbitration—are underdeveloped in all eight countries. In addition, inefficient registration systems for land and property rights present another source of dispute and a further barrier to investment in most of South Eastern Europe.

# Endnotes

1. This improvement might be interpreted as a strong evidence of the similarities of the SEE8. However, it depends crucially on the level of aggregation of the indicators and hides a substantial variation in each single subcomponent, as our more detailed analysis will show.

2. Throughout the region, the ownership transformation process for most medium-size and small enterprises has been completed in just a few years. Conversely, the large-scale transformation of ownership has lagged substantially across the region, except in Bulgaria (EBRD 2002).

3. Most of the self-employed in Romania are in agriculture, operating small, family farms.

4. The budgets of both entities rely to a considerable extent on fines from inspections. Inspectors have the right to shut down a company or to seize goods. Companies are also vulnerable to inspectors discovering fictitious violations of nonexistent regulations or to political opponents who make them targets. For more detailed information, see FIAS (2001a) and Stability Pact and OECD (2003).

5. These initiatives follow the recommendations of the FIAS (2001a). See also Stability Pact and OECD (2003).

6. Moldova adopted bankruptcy regulations in November 2001 that went into effect as in January 2002.

7. The information on Serbia and Montenegro in this and subsequent sections is largely based on World Bank (2001a).

8. A thorough description is contained in World Bank (2001b).

9. In March 2003, the government of FYR Macedonia adopted draft changes to the VAT law. Under the amendments, the general VAT rate will be reduced from 19 percent to 18 percent, but the tax base will be expanded because the 5 percent rate for most of the preferential products and services will be abolished.

10. These payment bureaus handled all transfers within the country, collected taxes, and reported on tax payments. They had the power to decide who was to be paid and when, as well as the power to divert tax funds to political parties and other nongovernmental institutions. Under the new system, the tax authorities are directly responsible for collecting taxes. For additional information, see also the country assessment for Bosnia and Herzegovina in EBRD (2001c).

11. For more information on KESH, see box 4.3 in chapter 4.

12. In addition, the budget would have to provide subsidies amounting to US$9 million to the budgetary and nonbudgetary entities (primarily the water and mining companies). Subsidy levels from 2002 are projected to fall by 25 percent annually. See also Albanian Ministry of Finance (2001).

13. The Directive on the Periods of Operating Licenses regulates the issue of licenses in the energy sector. See Stability Pact (2003a).

14. See, for example, the home page of the Trade and Transport Facilitation in Southeast Europe Program at http://www.seerecon.org/RegionalInitiatives/TTFSE.

15. For detailed assessment of the water resource management in the Balkans, see World Bank (2003c).

16. The Czech experience with voucher privatization is particularly telling, as are cases from the Russian Federation. See, for example, Shleifer and Vishny (1997).

17. A comprehensive review of the privatization program is provided by Hashi and Xhillari (1999).

18. The Romanian legislature created several mechanisms for easing the process, including the following: (a) arrears as of December 2001 would be written off for companies that were to be privatized; (b) creditor utilities would have 90 days to decide on writing off company debts, rescheduling them, or converting them into shares; (c) regardless of the prices sought by the state, the firms would be sold at any price offered, including a nominal price of, for example, €1.

19. Employees and other eligible citizens can retain up to 30 percent of the shares, depending on the pace of the firm's privatization.

20. The privatization law amendments include measures to help ensure that company insiders cannot block a sale indefinitely and that existing owners and

managers cannot artificially raise the cost to buyers through social programs and redundancy packages (see EBRD 2003, p. 188).

21. The information on corporate governance legislation in this and other sections is based on information provided by the EBRD Legal Transition Team.

22. *Derivative suit rights* are actions brought by a shareholder on behalf of a corporation to protect the company's legal rights.

23. These planned amendments are supported by FESAL 2000.

24. In March 2002, the Tirana Stock Exchange was registered as a joint-stock company with a single owner, the Ministry of Finance. As of December 2003, the stock exchange was still preparing the legal and administrative framework necessary for the start of operations.

25. For an extensive discussion on the EBRD legal surveys, see Ramasastry (2002).

26. There are 16 commercial courts in Serbia and Montenegro (including one in Kosovo).

27. For instance, in Albania, 2 years after the government made the decision to establish a new institution, the Judicial Inspectors' Office, it is still debating the role of this new institution.

# References

Albanian Council of Ministers. 2001. "Strategy on Growth and Poverty Reduction." Tirana.

Albanian Ministry of Finance. 2001. "Medium-Term Expenditure Framework." Tirana. Processed.

Anticorruption Coordination Commission. 2004. "Anticorruption.bg." Sofia. Available online at http://www.anticorruption.bg/index_eng. php.

Berglof, Erik, and Patrick Bolton. 2002. "The Great Divide and Beyond: Financial Architecture in Transition." *Journal of Economic Perspectives* 16(1):77–100.

Bornstein, Morris. 2001. "Post-Privatisation Enterprise Restructuring." *Post-Communist Economies* 13(1):189–203.

Center for International Private Enterprise. 2001. "Coalition 2000: A Public-Private Partnership." Washington, D.C. Available online at http://www.cipe.org/programs/corruption/c2000.htm.

Djankov, Simeon, and Peter Murrell. 2002. "Enterprise Restructuring in Transition: A Quantitative Survey." *Journal of Economic Literature* 40(3): 739–92.

Earle, John S., and Almos Telegdy. 2002. "Privatization Methods and Productivity Effects in Romanian Industrial Enterprises." W. E. Upjohn Institute Staff Working Paper 02-81. W. E Upjohn Institute for Employment Research, Kalamazoo, Mich. Available online at http://ssrn.com/abstract=292825.

EBRD (European Bank for Reconstruction and Development). 2001a. *Belgrade Municipal Infrastructure Reconstruction Programme Project.* London.

———. 2001b. *Railways Recovery Project for Bosnia and Herzegovina.* London.

———. 2001c. *Transition Report 2001: Energy in Transition.* London.

———. 2002. *Transition Report 2002: Agriculture and Rural Transition.* London.

———. 2003. *Transition Report 2003: Integration and Regional Cooperation.* London.

EBRD and World Bank. 1999. *Business Environment and Enterprise Performance Survey* (BEEPS1). London and Washington, D.C. Data available online at http://info.worldbank.org/governance/beeps.

———. 2002. *Business Environment and Enterprise Performance Survey* (BEEPS2). London and Washington, D.C. Data available online at http://info.worldbank.org/governance/beeps2002.

European Commission. 2003a. "Albania: Stabilisation and Association Report 2003." Commission Staff Working Paper. Brussels. Available at online at http://europa.eu.int/comm/external_relations/see/sap/rep2/com03_339_en.pdf.

———. 2003b. "European Charter for Small Enterprises." Brussels. Available online at http://europa.eu.int/comm/enterprise/enterprise_policy/charter.

———. 2003c. "Former Yugoslav Republic of Macedonia: Stabilisation and Association Report 2003." Commission Staff Working Paper. Brussels. Available online at http://europa.eu.int/comm/external_relations/see/sap/rep2/com03_342_en.pdf.

———. 2003d. "Report from the Commission: The Stabilisation and Association Process for South East Europe. Second Annual Report."

Brussels. Available online at http://europa.eu.int/comm/ external_relations/see/sap/rep2/com03_139_en.pdf.

FIAS (Foreign Investment Advisory Services). 2000. *Romania Administrative Barriers*. Washington, D.C.

———. 2001a. *Bosnia and Herzegovina Commercial Legal Framework and Administrative Barriers to Investment*. Washington, D.C.

———. 2001b. *The Climate for FDI: Serbia*. Washington, D.C.

Gupta, Pooman, Rachel Kleinfeld, and Gonzalo Salinas. 2002. *Legal and Judicial Reform in Europe and Central Asia*. Washington, D.C.: World Bank.

Hashi, Iraj, and Lindita Xhillari. 1999. "Privatization and Transition in Albania." *Post-Communist Economies* 11(1):99–125.

Heritage Foundation. 2003. "Index of Economic Freedoms Database." Available on line at http://www.heritage.org.

Kaufmann, Daniel, Aart Kraay, and Massimo Mastruzzi. 2003. "Governance Matters III: Governance Indicators for 1996–2002." Policy Research Working Paper 3106. World Bank, Washington, D.C.

OECD (Organisation for Economic Co-operation and Development). 2000. *Country Fact Sheets: A Summary of the Current State of the Investment and Business Environment and Key Policy Reform Priorities in South East Europe*. Paris. Available online at http://www.investment-compact.org/pdf/CFSxpress.pdf.

OECD, South East Corporate Governance Roundtable. 2003. *White Paper on Corporate Governance in South East Europe*. Paris. Available online at http://www.investmentcompact.org/pdf/CGWhitePaper.pdf.

Ramasastry, Anita. 2002. "What Local Lawyers Think: A Retrospective on the EBRD's Legal Indicator Surveys." *Law in Transition* (Autumn): 14–30

Shleifer, Andrei, and Robert W. Vishny. 1997. "A Survey of Corporate Governance." *Journal of Finance* 52(2):737–83.

Stability Pact. 2003a. "National Measures Providing Exceptions to National Treatment in South East European Countries: Regional

Overview." Submitted to the Investment Compact Project Team Meeting, Bucharest, October 13. Available online at http://www. investmentcompact.org/pdf/9thPTMtgNTOverview.pdf.

————. 2003b. "Regional Network of Foreign Investor Organisations: Summary Note on Role and Terms of Reference of the Network." Available online at http://www.investmentcompact.org/pdf/ 9thPTMtgRegionalFIC.pdf.

————. 2003c. *Summary Report: Ministerial Conference on "Pushing Ahead with Reform: Removing Obstacles to FDI in SEE."* Available online at http://www.investmentcompact.org/pdf/Min2003Summary.pdf.

Stability Pact and OECD (Organisation for Economic Co-operation and Development). 2003. "Progress in Policy Reform in South East Europe: Monitoring Instruments." 3rd ed. Paris. Available online at http:// www.investmentcompact.org/pdf/MONITORING_2003.pdf.

World Bank. 2000. *Croatia: A Policy Agenda for Reform and Growth.* Washington, D.C.

————. 2001a. *Breaking with the Past: The Path to Stability and Growth. Volume 1: The Economic, Social, and Institutional Reform Agenda.* Washington, D.C. Available online at http://www.seerecon.org/ serbiamontenegro/documents/ertp/.

————. 2001b. *Croatia: Country Assistance Strategy Progress Report.* Washington, D.C.

————. 2001c. "President's Report on the World Bank Structural Adjustment Loan to Croatia." World Bank Report P7490-HR, October. Washington, D.C.

————. 2001d. *World Bank Country Economic Memorandum on Serbia and Montenegro.* Washington, D.C.

————. 2003a. Doing Business database. Washington, D.C. Available online at http://rru.worldbank.org/DoingBusiness/.

————. 2003b. "Trade, Energy, and Infrastructure in South Eastern Europe: Concept Note for World Bank Strategy Study." Washington, D.C.

————. 2003c. *Water Resources Management in South Eastern Europe.* World Bank, Washington, D.C.

# 3
# Competition in South Eastern Europe

Developing and strengthening institutions that engender vigorous inter-enterprise competition is essential to improving the investment climate and accelerating sustainable growth in South Eastern Europe (SEE). Along with key institutional reforms in three areas—greater financial transparency, accountability, and protection of property rights; more effective mechanisms to settle commercial disputes; and improved access of businesses to better quality and efficiently priced infrastructure services[1]—a more competitive business environment in SEE will help capitalize on the economic reform progress made to date and further enhance peace and stability in the region.

The European Union's trade-opening measures of 2001 have helped improve South Eastern European firms' access to Western European markets, and intraregional trade liberalization is also high on the policy agendas of South Eastern European authorities (World Bank 2003). However, in the absence of institutional reforms that propagate robust "behind-the-border" competition within and among countries in the region—by facilitating the entry of new firms, restructuring of noncompetitive businesses, and reorganizing or liquidating commercially nonviable firms that take up "economic space"—such trade opportunities will not be effectively realized.[2]

As discussed in chapter 1, most South Eastern European countries have chronically high rates of unemployment and low rates of job creation, which reflect and exacerbate the persistently high poverty rates in the region. The experience of many other transition economies is that institutional reforms that enhance enterprise competition—even reforms that provide opportunities for credible threats of entry by new competitors—discipline inefficient businesses to restructure and improve performance. Although there may be short-term social costs from greater enterprise competition and restructuring, particularly if social safety nets are inadequately developed,[3] there is abundant evidence that, in the medium term, increased business rivalry and the presence of new entrants, including small and medium-size enterprises (SMEs), are the main engines of job creation, growth, and prosperity.

This chapter assesses the incentives and constraints on competition in the eight South Eastern European countries (SEE8) that are the focus of this study and recommends policies for reform. In developing policy recommendations, the study relies on both at the aggregated level—through firm-level quantitative surveys (the two European Bank for Reconstruction and Development [EBRD]–World Bank Business Environment and Enterprise Performance Surveys, BEEPS1 of 1999 and BEEPS2 of 2002)—and at a disaggregated level—focusing on certain industry sectors through the 40 qualitative business case studies developed in the field. The chapter illuminates salient cross-country differences in the nature of competition across the eight economies and shows how South Eastern European firms both respond to and shape these differences. The chapter also highlights the evolution of cross-country changes in enterprise competition over time, focusing on changes between 1998/99 and 2002 (the two periods covered by BEEPS1 and BEEPS2). The aspirations of the South Eastern European authorities and investors (both domestic and foreign) necessitate progress beyond such narrow issues as administrative barriers to firm registration and licensing. To that end, the chapter focuses on the fundamental determinants of competition. A thorough diagnosis of basic market institutions and their effect on competition is essential for the design of "second generation" medium-term structural policy reforms.

In brief, our analysis concludes that many industrial firms in SEE are, in differing degrees, effectively immune to robust competitive market forces, not only because of administrative impediments, but also, more importantly, because of more entrenched institutional and structural ones. These impediments are especially found at the local level, where in many sectors horizontal and vertical market power is possessed by incumbent firms, some of which enjoy protection from both appreciable barriers to exit as well as high barriers to entry by new rivals. There is an apparent trend, however, that over the period under examination, competitive pressures within individual countries and the region as a whole are modestly increasing. The competition may be due to economywide structural reforms, including those in competition policy, and because of greater exposure of SEE8 firms to the international marketplace. Still, progress is considerably uneven among the countries, necessitating an extensive and ambitious set of reforms.

With respect to policy recommendations, we conclude that certain competition-enhancing reforms will apply to all the SEE8. However, given the economic (and political and social) heterogeneity of the SEE8, in some countries, where the transition is more complex, more fundamental institution-building and policy changes are required. A general policy theme that emerges from the contemporary history of these countries—where geographic boundaries are widely at variance with more natural economic boundaries—is the need to strike a balance, over the medium term, between policies that reduce anticompetitive structural conditions (such as through horizontal or vertical divestiture) and those that allow for sufficient economies of scale and scope.

Conversely, policies and institutions that impede entry of new private-sector competitors should be reformed in the short run. Indeed, even if excessive horizontal and vertical structural dominance remains, facilitating free entry and exit can help make such markets contestable and can provide strong pressures to compel competitive performance from incumbents. At the country level, it is equally important in the short run to fortify rules-based institutional frameworks for implementing and enforcing competition policy with a view to reducing discretion, increasing transparency and predictability, and enhancing incentives for accountability. In the medium term, a case may be made for coordination of competition policy across the region, a likely outcome of European Union (EU) accession.

This chapter is organized as follows. We first assess the prospects for interenterprise competition within and among the SEE8 by examining the extent of the development of private sector businesses in the region over the past decade as well as the attributes of that development. We then analyze the competitive nature of industry in the region by assessing the horizontal and vertical dimensions of South Eastern European markets. The next section concentrates on the nature and extent of barriers to entry and exit in the SEE8 and assesses both the structural and behavioral sources of such barriers. Finally, we examine the relationship between competition, firm growth, and performance of SEE8 businesses before concluding with policy recommendations.

## Development of the Private Sector and Prospects for Competition in SEE

International experience shows that in the transition economies the existence of a substantial private sector is generally a prerequisite for the operation of competitive market forces (see, for example, Djankov and Murrell 2002). The emergence of private sector businesses in the SEE8 economies has been one of the hallmarks of the countries' enterprise reform programs since the transition period began. Table 3.1 examines the pattern of the development of the private sector among the SEE8. As of 2002 (the latest year for which comparable data are available) most of the countries had private sectors whose output values contributed to at least 50 percent of national gross domestic product (GDP). For the region as a whole, the average share of GDP accounted for by the private sector was approximately 58 percent. There is, however, considerable variation across the countries: Albania and Bulgaria have private sector shares of GDP of

**Table 3.1    Private Sector Share of GDP in the SEE8**
*(percent)*

| Country | 1993 | 1998 | 2002 |
|---|---|---|---|
| Albania | 40.0 | 75.0 | 75.0 |
| Bosnia and Herzegovina | — | 35.0 | 45.0 |
| Bulgaria | 35.0 | 65.0 | 75.0 |
| Croatia | 30.0 | 55.0 | 60.0 |
| Macedonia, FYR | 35.0 | 55.0 | 60.0 |
| Moldova | 15.0 | 50.0 | 50.0 |
| Romania | 35.0 | 60.0 | 65.0 |
| Serbia and Montenegro | — | — | 45.0 |
| SEE8 average | 30.0 | 57.0 | 59.4 |

*Source:* EBRD (2003).
*Note:* — = not available.

75 percent, while private sector businesses in Bosnia and Herzegovina and in Serbia and Montenegro contribute only 45 percent of GDP.

The pattern of development of the private sector in SEE has also varied over time. Table 3.1 indicates that, although there was a substantial increase in private sector development in the early to mid-1990s, since 1998 the trend has slowed considerably.

Many of the current SEE8 private sector firms had their origins in the privatization of state-owned or "socially owned" enterprises. However, unlike the transition economies of the Russian Federation or the Czech Republic, which engaged in mass privatization early in transition, the scale and rapidity of privatization in SEE have generally been more modest. Thus, as the individual company case studies and the BEEPS data illustrate, a significant proportion of the number of private sector firms in SEE were established either de novo; as new private subsidiaries (or affiliates) of formerly state-owned enterprises; or as new private foreign joint ventures and not through the privatization process (see table 3.2).[4] In interpreting the BEEPS data, however, it is important to keep in mind that the sample of firms covered by the survey was deliberately slanted toward small- and medium-size firms. In other words, the BEEPS data do not portray a representative sample of the population of firms in the countries.[5]

Table 3.2 indicates that the smallest proportion of de novo firms exists in Bosnia and Herzegovina and in Moldova. The table also shows that in 2002, on average, the smallest proportion of current private sector firms that have their genesis in privatization existed in Albania and Serbia and Montenegro. Conversely, privatization was a more significant origin for present-day private sector firms in Bosnia and Herzegovina, Bulgaria, and Moldova. Other BEEPS data indicate that for the surveyed firms the privatizations took place earliest in Croatia and Albania, peaking in

## Table 3.2    Origin of Private Sector Firms in the SEE8, 2002
*(percent)*

| Country | Privatized state-owned enterprises | De novo enterprise | Nonprivatized firms Private subsidiary of former state-owned enterprise | Joint venture | Other private firm |
|---------|---------|---------|---------|---------|---------|
| Albania | 8.78 | 84.46 | 0 | 3.38 | 3.38 |
| Bosnia and Herzegovina | 25.79 | 67.92 | 2.52 | 3.77 | 0 |
| Bulgaria | 19.71 | 74.52 | 1.92 | 3.37 | 0.48 |
| Croatia | 16.89 | 70.95 | 2.03 | 4.05 | 6.08 |
| Macedonia, FYR | 14.11 | 80.37 | 3.68 | 1.84 | 0.00 |
| Moldova | 23.97 | 67.81 | 0.68 | 6.85 | 0.68 |
| Romania | 15.28 | 77.78 | 2.78 | 1.85 | 2.31 |
| Serbia and Montenegro | 13.07 | 82.91 | 0.50 | 2.31 | 1.01 |
| SEE8 average | 17.20 | 75.84 | 1.76 | 3.43 | 1.74 |

*Sources:* EBRD and World Bank (1999, 2002).

## Table 3.3    Average Annual Sales Revenues of Privatized and De Novo Private Firms by Country, 2001

| Country | Privatized state-owned enterprises (US$) | De novo private enterprises (US$) | Ratio of privatized to de novo enterprises |
|---------|---------|---------|---------|
| Albania | 477,800 | 314,010 | 1.5 |
| Bosnia and Herzegovina | 3,293,570 | 536,200 | 6.2 |
| Bulgaria | 11,225,170 | 531,900 | 21.1 |
| Croatia | 5,673,080 | 1,088,900 | 5.2 |
| Macedonia, FYR | 4,586,360 | 179,760 | 25.5 |
| Moldova | 705,040 | 161,720 | 4.4 |
| Romania | 2,126,300 | 596,270 | 3.6 |
| Serbia and Montenegro | 3,640,090 | 579,370 | 6.3 |
| SEE8 average | 31,727,410 | 3,988,130 | 8.0 |

*Source:* EBRD and World Bank (2002).

1994–95, whereas such privatizations occurred more recently for current private sector firms in Bosnia and Herzegovina, Bulgaria, and Serbia and Montenegro, with the bulk taking place between 1998 and 2001.

Table 3.3 presents data on the relative size of privatized versus de novo private firms in the SEE8, as measured by average 2001 sales revenues. As might be expected, privatized businesses are larger than their de novo

BUILDING MARKET INSTITUTIONS IN SOUTH EASTERN EUROPE

counterparts in all countries. The region shows the average size differential as considerable, with privatized firms being eight times larger than de novo firms. There is, however, considerable variation across countries. The greatest differences in size are in FYR Macedonia and Bulgaria, where privatized firms are more than 20 times larger than de novo firms. In contrast, there is an almost negligible size differential among these private sector firms in Albania.

Table 3.4 examines the origin of private firms in the SEE8 across sectors. The manufacturing sector accounts for the greatest proportion of firms

**Table 3.4  Origin of Private Sector Firms in the SEE8, by Sector, 2002**
*(percent)*

| Sector (share of sector in total survey sample) | Privatized state-owned enterprise | De novo enterprise | Private subsidiary of former state-owned enterprise | Joint venture | Other private firm |
|---|---|---|---|---|---|
| | | | *Nonprivatized firms* | | |
| Mining and quarrying (2.0 percent) | 2.95 | 0.28 | 0.00 | 2.17 | 4.35 |
| Construction (9.7 percent) | 9.70 | 7.48 | 16.00 | 2.14 | 13.04 |
| Manufacturing (30.3 percent) | 41.35 | 25.19 | 24.00 | 41.3 | 21.74 |
| Transportation, storage, and communications (7.4 percent) | 7.59 | 6.06 | 4.00 | 15.22 | 4.35 |
| Wholesale and retail trade, motor vehicle repair, and personal and household goods (30.8 percent) | 22.78 | 39.20 | 40.00 | 30.43 | 21.74 |
| Real estate, rentals, and business services (5.1 percent) | 3.38 | 9.19 | 0.00 | 4.35 | 8.7 |
| Hotels and restaurants (9.0 percent) | 8.86 | 6.63 | 12.00 | 4.35 | 13.04 |
| Other services (5.3 percent) | 3.38 | 5.97 | 4.00 | 0.00 | 13.04 |

*Source:* EBRD and World Bank (2002).

that became private through the privatization process. The wholesale and retail trade sector accounts for the largest proportion of private firms that were started de novo. The mining and the transportation, storage, and communication sectors have the smallest proportion of de novo private firms; these sectors typically have higher barriers to entry—a topic we will discuss in detail below.

## Structural Conditions for Competition in SEE: Horizontal and Vertical Elements

Generally, the industrial sectors that many of the SEE8 inherited were not competitively structured. They were often characterized by plants and firms that were disproportionately larger than actual market demand, hence resulting in diseconomies of scale and scope. The distorted industrial structure had resulted from central planning's emphasis on heavy industrialization at the expense of services. Socialist objectives dictated that businesses produce goods that did not always accord with market preferences. Production decisions were often dictated by state orders or military needs rather than by supply and demand. Additionally, the central planning system actively promoted economic autarky and self-sufficiency for some locales, and extreme regional specialization for some sectors as part of a national assembly-of-components production schema.

After a decade of reform and the substantial privatization of the relatively large state-owned enterprises, plus the complementary establishment of relatively numerous (but smaller) private firms, the results of the business case studies indicate that the private sector in SEE8 industries may still be insufficient to induce commensurate competitively structured markets and the competitive conduct of business operations (box 3.1). Other transition countries' experience suggests such an outcome may be due to weak incentives in the South Eastern European countries' market institutions and policy frameworks. These incentives have produced little restructuring of large state-owned firms and have engendered insufficient restructuring of privatized firms (especially if privatization led to distorted insider control). Furthermore, institutional and policy impediments have allowed firms that were dominant in their sectors to operate unchecked in a largely noncompetitive market structure and have permitted inefficient businesses to continue operations without any consequences of competitive discipline.

As reflected in the case studies, enterprise development in the SEE8 has been a competitively weak process. It has given rise to an industrial landscape characterized, in some cases, by dominant firms with large market shares, markets exhibiting "horizontal dominance" of either high

---

## Box 3.1   Is Ownership Change Enough?

A relatively large firm in the construction sector, interviewed for the case studies, is typical of many of today's privatized businesses in SEE. The firm was established in 1952. Six years ago the company was privatized through a management-employee buyout. Currently, it is an insider-controlled joint-stock company that is 100 percent privately owned. The annual turnover of the firm is between US$100 million and US$150 million in revenues. Currently, it employs 3,200 people. In the mid-1990s, it had 7,400 employees. The firm's major customers are still state-owned enterprises and other public or government entities, which account for approximately 60 percent of the company's sales revenues. Although the bulk of the business is in industrial and infrastructure construction (such as roads, tunnels, bridges, dams, and sewerage systems), the firm also builds residential apartments in a vertically integrated fashion. The firm buys or leases the land, builds the apartments, and then sells the residential units. It only competes with four other construction firms in the country. It also has contracts in neighboring countries, which account for about 25 percent of its sales revenues. The firm's largest overdue receivables are with the government, at both the central and local levels. Often these accounts are settled through barter.

---

seller or high buyer concentration, and enterprises exhibiting a high degree of vertical integration or exclusive buyer-seller relationships. It has also yielded a business environment that continues to be characterized by "duplication of facilities," artificially located industries, and geographic market segmentation.

Sufficiently concentrated horizontal and vertical market structures, reflected by businesses with few competitors and dominant market shares, engender not only market power but also welfare costs to an economy. These include (a) incentives for price collusion (whether tacit or explicit) and higher consumer prices; (b) reduced output; (c) diminished quality in products and service; (d) frozen, commercially unsound, vertical transactional relationships and the stifled participation of new suppliers and distributors; and (e) opportunities for rent seeking and corruption.

Certainly, sizable horizontal and vertical integration can create real economic efficiencies. In certain industries the technology fundamental to the production process naturally gives rise to (horizontal) economies of scale and scope, and unit costs decline as output expands to meet market demand. In such industries it is unlikely that multiple businesses can all attain the minimum efficient scale to be commercially viable. It is, therefore, economically efficient to have only a few large, multiplant firms (horizontal integration) brought about through investment or mergers and acquisitions. But though there may well be significant scale economies in certain segments of an economy's infrastructure or utility sectors, in most manufacturing sectors worldwide, scale economies are unlikely to be as pronounced relative to market demand. Thus there is little economic justification for dominant firms or heavily horizontally concentrated markets.

By the same token there can be vertical economies of scale and scope and a savings in transactions costs in combining successive stages of production under one corporate roof. The classic case of continuous steel-casting is well known. It would be economically inefficient to have three separate firms heating iron ore, rolling it into ingots, and then finishing the ingots into steel products. Most manufacturing processes, however, allow economic efficiencies only up to a point. Indeed, in many manufacturing sectors throughout the world it is often cheaper for a firm to buy inputs (or sell outputs) on the open market or through arm's-length contracts rather than to produce them internally through ownership of the stages of production (vertical integration). Of course, in many transition economies, pronounced commercial (and often political economy) risks associated with market transactions—for example, because effectively enforceable contracts are nascent or because corruption is present— can be strong incentives for vertical integration.

Thus, as we turn to review the data on horizontal and vertical features of the SEE8 markets, it should be noted that there are instances of tradeoffs between efficiency and anticompetitive market power of concentrated horizontal and vertical market structures. On the other hand, when markets exhibiting concentrated horizontal and vertical structures are also characterized by the presence of high entry and exit barriers (examined later in this chapter), such tradeoffs are more limited and the prospects for competition are much lower. In such cases, incumbent firms enjoying market power or operating inefficiently are protected from external discipline and thus are effectively immune to competition. The consequences include the aforementioned welfare costs as well as the following: (a) constraints on rechanneling enterprise assets and preventing workers from engaging in more productive ways, thus reducing the flexibility and resiliency of the economy; (b) diminished incentives for businesses to fully exploit economies of scale and scope, except in expelling rivals through predatory price reductions; (c) stifled incentives for geographic market segmentation and constraints on interregional trade among the SEE8; (d) diminished incentives for innovation and managerial improvements; (e) and reduced new investment from domestic and foreign sources.

## Horizontal Dimensions of the South Eastern European Market Structure

### NUMBER OF COMPETITORS

As elsewhere, businesses in SEE face a different number of competitors depending on their ownership, on the sector in which they operate, and on specific country attributes. This observation is well documented by the case studies (see box 3.2). The BEEPS data also shed light on these elements in the region's competitive environment, including how they have changed over time.

Figure 3.1 shows that, in all the SEE8 combined, the surveyed de novo private firms face a greater number of competitors than do privatized businesses or state-owned enterprises. It also indicates that this pattern

---

### Box 3.2  Variation in Number of Competitors

The different sectors covered by the case studies revealed variations in the number of competitors firms face. In part, this variation was a function of the sector or the circumstances of the country itself. Most often, however, ownership type seemed to matter significantly. An examination of the textile sector across the eight countries makes the point quite clearly.

In Bosnia and Herzegovina, one of the interviewed companies, a state-owned textile firm, was the largest employer in its town. It was founded in the late 1970s. Although it used to sell its fabric throughout all of former Yugoslavia, its production has declined dramatically since the early 1990s—it is currently operating at only 15 percent of capacity. The company sells 100 percent of its specialized final product and faces no effective domestic competitors. In the nonspecialized fabric it has about a 30 percent share of the domestic market.

A fairly successful de novo private textile firm in Serbia and Montenegro, which was founded in the early 1990s, has a small in-house production and design unit of about 15 workers. It farms out much of its assembly operations to other firms, but virtually all of its product line is sold through its own retail stores. It extensively uses branding in advertising. Competition is much more intense at the retail level, especially for products that must compete with cheaper imports.

A privatized Croatian textile firm, which dates back to the late 1950s and was privatized in 1993, faces several competitors in the domestic market that import higher-end fabric or garments mostly from European countries and lower-end products from Turkey and China. Maintaining cash flow from and keeping receivables current with Croatian customers has been difficult for this firm. Foreign customers, however, tend to keep current. The result has been a shift toward the export market, which now accounts for 60 percent of the firm's sales revenues.

# Figure 3.1    Number of Competitors by Ownership Type, 1999 and 2002

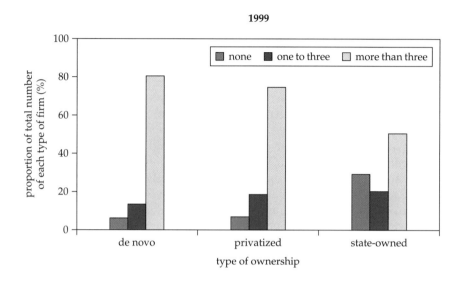

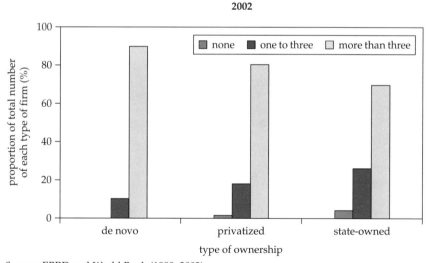

*Sources:* EBRD and World Bank (1999, 2002).

has not changed between 1999 and 2002. On the other hand, the BEEPS data show that all the surveyed firms have faced a modestly greater number of competitors over this period, suggesting, all other things being equal, the evolution of a more competitive business environment in the region. These data also show that, on average in 2002, approximately

15 percent of the surveyed firms indicated they faced three or fewer competitors, whereas 85 percent indicated they competed with four or more firms. However, in interpreting these findings, one must bear in mind that the sample design of the BEEPS is highly skewed toward smaller firms. Thus, the survey respondents will indicate a larger number of competitors than is representative of the actual population of firms in these economies.

The variation across the SEE8 in the number of competitors firms faced in 1999 and 2002 is depicted in Figure 3.2. Although in all the countries there was a general increase between 1999 and 2002, FYR Macedonia, at both the start and end of the period, had the greatest proportion of firms reporting that they faced four or more competitors. In 2002, Albania and Moldova had the largest proportion of firms indicating they faced no competitors (3 percent and 2 percent, respectively), and Romania and Albania had the largest proportion of firms indicating three or fewer competitors (18 percent and 15 percent, respectively). Overall, surveyed firms in Albania, Moldova, and Romania indicated the least increase in competition between 1999 and 2002.

Table 3.5 shows the differences across industry sectors for all the SEE8 in the number of competitors indicated by the surveyed firms in 2002. Not surprisingly, the sectors in which the surveyed firms indicated the fewest number of competitors were the infrastructure-related sectors— transport, storage, and communications. In these sectors, where state ownership is greatest, approximately 25 percent of the firms indicated they faced three or fewer competitors. The sectors in which the firms most often indicated that they faced four or more competitors were the construction, trade, and business services.

## Table 3.5   Number of Competitors by Sector, 2002
*(% of firms)*

| Sector | No competitors | 1–3 competitors | 4 or more competitors |
|---|---|---|---|
| Mining | 0 | 18.75 | 81.25 |
| Construction | 0 | 8.96 | 91.04 |
| Manufacturing | 0.70 | 20.00 | 79.30 |
| Transportation, storage, and communications | 4.65 | 20.16 | 75.19 |
| Trade | 0 | 9.37 | 90.63 |
| Business services | 0.75 | 9.02 | 90.23 |
| Hotels and restaurants | 0 | 11.97 | 88.03 |
| Other | 2.75 | 13.76 | 83.49 |

*Source:* EBRD and World Bank (2002).

# Figure 3.2    Number of Competitors by Country, 1999 and 2002

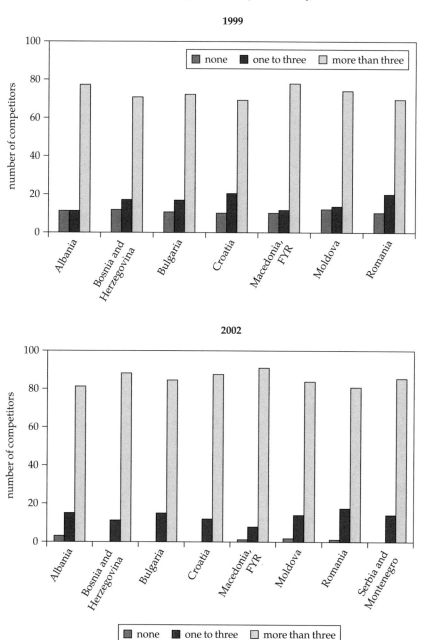

*Sources:* EBRD and World Bank (1999, 2002).

Statistical tests using the BEEPS data for 2002 of the bilateral relationship between the indicated number of competitors and the firm's characteristics indicate some statistically significant correlations. As shown in table A.3.2 in the annex, there is a statistically significant positive relationship between the indicated number of competitors an SEE8 firm faces and the likelihood the firm is de novo private (as opposed to being a privatized or remaining a state-owned business). There is also a statistically significant negative correlation between the indicated number of competitors and (a) firm size, measured by number of employees or sales revenue; (b) market share; (c) extent of horizontal integration, as measured by number of establishments or plants under common ownership (discussed below); and (d) amount of subsidies received as a percentage of sales revenues.

MARKET SHARE
The case studies suggest that, in general, there is significant variation in the market share attained by SEE8 firms. This variation appears to be associated with the number of competitors a firm faces. Moreover, many of the attributes that are associated with firms that have a relatively limited number of competitors also are associated with firms that have attained high or dominant shares in the markets in which they produce. The converse is also true.

Approximately 42 percent of the businesses surveyed under the BEEPS indicated market shares greater than 5 percent, and 58 percent indicated market shares of 5 percent or less. The large proportion of firms reporting small market shares is not surprising, given that the BEEPS concentrated on the smaller firms in the region. However, it is critical to note that the BEEPS market share data do not correct for the relevant geographic boundary of the specific product or sector in question. The survey instrument implicitly assumes all products trade in a national market, even though trade may be limited to local markets for certain products (such as bricks) but may be international for others (such as textiles). Thus, the available data on market share should be seen as an approximation of the real economic span of a firm's horizontal control over a market.[6] With that caveat in mind, the BEEPS data do still show important differences in firms' market shares by country, by business ownership, and by sector.

Table 3.6 presents data from 2002 for the surveyed firms with market shares greater than 5 percent. On average in the SEE8, firms have attained approximately 30 percent of the share of their markets. Romanian firms enjoy the highest market share, averaging about 45 percent, whereas Croatian firms' average market share is about 22 percent—about one-half the size of their counterparts in Romania.

Table 3.6 demonstrates a clear pattern among ownership types. Greater state involvement results in greater dominance of the firm. State-owned

**Table 3.6  Market Share by Country and by Ownership Type, 2002**
*(percent)*

| Ownership type | Albania | Bosnia and Herzegovina | Bulgaria | Croatia | Macedonia, FYR | Moldova | Romania | Serbia and Montenegro | SEE8 |
|---|---|---|---|---|---|---|---|---|---|
| State-owned | 53.77 | 35.60 | 44.88 | 34.50 | 39.00 | 40.63 | 61.06 | 30.95 | 42.95 |
| Privatized | 23.00 | 22.71 | 25.87 | 17.92 | 36.94 | 42.28 | 31.89 | 29.65 | 29.07 |
| De novo | 20.34 | 28.33 | 35.96 | 19.71 | 21.08 | 23.45 | 39.00 | 27.52 | 25.93 |
| Total | 26.22 | 28.01 | 34.78 | 21.93 | 25.97 | 31.97 | 44.84 | 28.62 | 29.94 |

*Source:* EBRD and World Bank (2002).
*Note:* Covers only surveyed firms indicating market shares greater than 5 percent.

enterprises hold the greatest market shares, with an average of 43 percent for the region. Within the region, Romanian and state-owned enterprises in Romania and Serbia and Montenegro register the largest and smallest market shares (61 percent and 31 percent), respectively. Privatized firms exhibit smaller market shares, with a regional average of 29 percent. Moldovan privatized firms exhibit the largest average market shares of 42 percent, whereas Croatian privatized firms registered the smallest, 18 percent. De novo private firms have the smallest market shares, with a regional average of 26 percent. The average Romanian de novo private firm registers the largest market share of 39 percent, and the average Croatian de novo firm registers the smallest market share of 20 percent.

Market shares of SEE8 firms also vary significantly by sector. Table 3.7 shows that the firms in infrastructure sectors (transportation, storage, and communications) have the largest market shares—about 42 percent on average for the region. There is, however, great variance across the countries within those sectors. For example, surveyed infrastructure firms in Croatia have on average significantly smaller market shares than do their counterparts in Romania. Still, this finding is consistent with our earlier finding that firms face relatively fewer competitors in the infrastructure sectors, because in those sectors underlying technologies and high fixed costs produce large economies of scale. Conversely, in the hotel and restaurant sector and the trade sector, where competition is greater and economies of scale are small, market shares are low and, furthermore, there is much smaller cross-country variance within those sectors. In general, looking across sectors and countries, Romania, Bulgaria, and Moldova are distinguishable as having the most dominant firms in the survey sample.

The statistical tests using the 2002 BEEPS data of the bivariate relationship between market share and the firm's characteristics indicate some important statistically significant correlations (see table A.3.2 in the annex). There is a statistically significant negative relationship between the size of a firm's market share and (a) the likelihood that the firm is a de novo private enterprise (rather than a privatized or state-owned enterprise), (b) the firm's indicated number of competitors, and (c) the likelihood that the firm is in the services rather than the manufacturing sector. On the other hand, market share has a statistically significant positive relationship with (a) size, measured by sales revenue or by number of employees; (b) extent of vertical integration (discussed later in this chapter); (c) extent of horizontal integration, (d) subsidies received as a percentage of sales (also discussed below), and (e) technological prowess, measured by spending on research and development (R&D) as a percentage of sales.

**Table 3.7 Market Share by Sector and by Country, 2002**
(*percent*)

| Sector | Albania | Bosnia and Herzegovina | Bulgaria | Croatia | Macedonia, FYR | Moldova | Romania | Serbia and Montenegro | SEE8 |
|---|---|---|---|---|---|---|---|---|---|
| Mining | | 30.00 | 15.00 | 22.00 | 20.00 | | | 52.50 | 31.23 |
| Construction | 17.75 | 13.40 | 12.67 | 23.83 | 20.83 | 52.50 | 32.86 | 25.71 | 23.41 |
| Manufacturing | 22.19 | 33.33 | 40.67 | 23.00 | 33.11 | 34.86 | 43.50 | 26.32 | 32.11 |
| Transportation, storage, and communications | 45.20 | 25.00 | 32.67 | 17.67 | 50.00 | 52.86 | 58.00 | 29.00 | 41.89 |
| Trade | 18.65 | 23.64 | 29.72 | 20.56 | 21.15 | 17.60 | 35.91 | 26.36 | 23.27 |
| Business services | 35.00 | 20.00 | 41.67 | 18.43 | 33.67 | 28.67 | 40.80 | 44.00 | 33.11 |
| Hotels and restaurants | 12.67 | 19.00 | 40.50 | 27.50 | 14.89 | 26.00 | 25.00 | 16.67 | 19.86 |
| Other | 44.00 | 36.17 | 45.40 | 36.67 | 32.00 | 35.56 | 90.00 | 21.67 | 39.97 |
| Total | 25.60 | 28.01 | 35.58 | 22.03 | 25.97 | 31.81 | 44.33 | 28.05 | 29.71 |

*Source:* EBRD and World Bank (2002).
*Note:* Covers only surveyed firms indicating market shares greater than 5 percent. Empty cell indicates no firms surveyed in that sector.

## Table 3.8    Horizontal Integration: Number of Establishments under Single Firm Ownership, 2002

| Ownership type | Average number of establishments |
|---|---|
| State-owned | 5.72 |
| Privatized | 4.74 |
| De novo | 2.17 |

Source: EBRD and World Bank (2002).

HORIZONTAL INTEGRATION

The effect of horizontal dominance on competition can also depend on the number of production facilities generating similar outputs under the common ownership and control of each firm. All other things being equal, the more extensive the horizontal integration attained by a firm, either within a single geographic market or across geographic markets, the greater its ability to exercise control over market outcomes.

Table 3.8 depicts the varying extent of horizontal integration across ownership categories among the surveyed firms in SEE. On average, the horizontal integration of state-owned firms is greater than that of privatized or de novo private firms; indeed, the extent of state-owned enterprises' horizontal integration is more than two and a half times that of de novo private firms.

Table 3.9 shows that horizontal integration also varies significantly across the SEE8 and across sectors (although somewhat less so than ownership categories). Surveyed firms in Albania exhibit the least horizontal integration, whereas firms in Serbia and Montenegro exhibit the most extensive—about three times greater than Albanian firms. Across sectors, infrastructure firms stand out as the most horizontally integrated, and hotels and restaurants, the least: a finding entirely consistent with the other aspects of our analysis. On a bivariate basis, there is a statistically significant positive correlation between horizontal integration and firm size, measured either by number of employees or by sales (table A.3.2 in the annex). Interestingly, there is also a statistically significant positive correlation between horizontal integration and a firm's capital productivity. As other variables were not taken into account, this finding is not conclusive. However, it does suggest economies of scope might arise from such integration.

CUSTOMER CHARACTERISTICS

Assessing the characteristics of industrial firms' domestic customers sheds light on an important aspect in the way interenterprise competition is mediated in SEE. In this regard, the 2002 BEEPS focuses on (a) the size of the customer and (b) whether the customer is a governmental entity.

# Table 3.9 Horizontal Integration: Number of Establishments under Single Firm Ownership by Sector and by Country, 2002

| Sector | Albania | Bosnia and Herzegovina | Bulgaria | Croatia | Macedonia, FYR | Moldova | Romania | Serbia and Montenegro | SEE8 |
|---|---|---|---|---|---|---|---|---|---|
| Mining | | 2.00 | 4.00 | 1.33 | 3.50 | | | 1.75 | 2.47 |
| Construction | 1.05 | 3.50 | 2.74 | 1.50 | 3.69 | 1.20 | 1.63 | 4.39 | 2.40 |
| Manufacturing | 1.34 | 2.78 | 4.71 | 1.76 | 1.57 | 2.18 | 4.16 | 4.19 | 2.97 |
| Transportation, storage, communications | 2.21 | 2.50 | 2.92 | 3.20 | 3.00 | 2.73 | 7.45 | 9.05 | 4.53 |
| Trade | 1.64 | 1.89 | 4.52 | 3.92 | 1.68 | 1.81 | 2.29 | 8.11 | 3.44 |
| Business services | 1.11 | 1.29 | 2.14 | 2.46 | 1.09 | 2.67 | 3.88 | 5.44 | 3.03 |
| Hotels and restaurants | 1.00 | 1.40 | 1.14 | 2.10 | 1.50 | 1.78 | 2.12 | 5.33 | 2.12 |
| Other | 1.33 | 1.75 | 2.11 | 1.70 | 1.00 | 1.23 | 1.44 | 7.67 | 2.55 |
| Total | 1.44 | 2.30 | 3.59 | 2.64 | 1.86 | 1.90 | 3.33 | 6.22 | 3.11 |

Source: EBRD and World Bank (2002).
Note: Empty cells indicate no firms surveyed in that sector.

**Table 3.10    Share of Revenue Earned from Sales to Customers of Different Size by Firms of Different Ownership Type, 2002**

| Ownership type | Large customers[a] | Small customers |
|---|---|---|
| State-owned | 18.4 | 54.9 |
| Privatized | 21.3 | 60.8 |
| De novo | 12.8 | 68.8 |

Source: EBRD and World Bank (2002).
a. Large customers are defined as having more than 250 employees.

For the region as a whole, the surveyed firms indicated that, on average, 15 percent of sales are to customers that are large businesses (those with 250 or more employees) and 66 percent of sales are to customers that are small businesses, individuals, and so forth. The result is not surprising given the small-firm bias in the sample design of the survey. There is considerable cross-country variation, however. Albanian firms registered the smallest proportion of sales to large customers (about 4 percent), and Croatian firms the greatest (about 23 percent). Moldovan firms indicated the largest proportion of sales to small customers (about 84 percent), whereas the smallest proportion of sales to small customers was indicated by firms in Serbia and Montenegro and Bosnia and Herzegovina (both approximately 50 percent). A more striking pattern emerges in comparing proportion of sales to customers of different size by firms of varying ownership type. As depicted in table 3.10, both privatized and state-owned firms earn a significantly greater proportion of their sales revenues from large firms than do de novo private firms. The converse is true with respect to the proportion of sales to small customers: de novo private firms earn a significantly greater proportion of their sales revenue from small customers than do state-owned enterprises and privatized firms.

Further, on average for the overall SEE region, about 5 percent of all the surveyed firms' combined sales revenues are earned from government entities. There is, of course, variation across the countries and across ownership types. Although the average Albanian firm earns about 16 percent of sales revenues from transactions with government, the average firm from FYR Macedonia or Romania earns approximately 3 percent of sales revenues from government purchases. Figure 3.3 shows a clear trend of the heavy reliance by state-owned enterprises on sales to government in comparison with the case with de novo private firms (except in FYR Macedonia). On average state-owned enterprises' sales revenues from government transactions are about 12 percent, whereas such transactions account for less than 4 percent of de novo firms' sales, a difference by a factor of four.

## Figure 3.3    Sales to Governmental Entities by Ownership Type and by Country, 2002

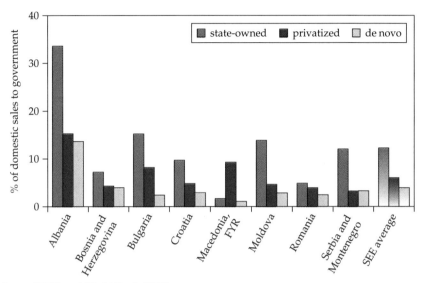

*Source:* EBRD and World Bank (2002).

HORIZONTAL EXPANSION AND INTERNATIONAL EXPOSURE

The extent to which SEE8 businesses have expanded into or are exposed to competition from rivals in international markets is a critical issue in assessing the competitiveness of the firms and domestic markets of the eight countries as well as the competitiveness of the region overall. International exposure may be through (a) direct or portfolio investment, licensing agreements, or other forms of partnerships and/or (b) exports. On the first score, the BEEPS assessed whether an SEE8 firm had any holdings or operations outside its home country. Figure 3.4 shows that on average for the region, 14 percent of the firms had such holdings or operations. Across the eight countries, a greater proportion of firms based in FYR Macedonia indicated that they had holdings or operations abroad than firms in any other country. Albania had the smallest proportion of firms with international exposure.

The second factor, export intensity patterns, both across countries and across sectors, is shown in tables 3.11 and 3.12. On a regional basis, export receipts of the surveyed SEE8 firms represent about 13 percent of their total sales revenues, on average. The average Bulgarian firm indicated the greatest proportion of sales revenues from exports—almost 16 percent—whereas the average firm in Serbia and Montenegro reported the lowest

## Figure 3.4    Firms with Holdings or Operations outside Their Home Countries, 2002

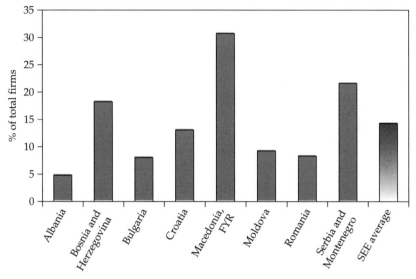

*Source:* EBRD and World Bank (2002).

## Table 3.11    Export Intensity by Country, 2002

| Country | Export receipts as a percentage of sales revenue |
| --- | --- |
| Albania | 14.8 |
| Bosnia and Herzegovina | 10.6 |
| Bulgaria | 15.7 |
| Croatia | 12.4 |
| Macedonia, FYR | 14.1 |
| Moldova | 15.5 |
| Romania | 11.8 |
| Serbia and Montenegro | 6.8 |
| SEE8 average | 12.5 |

*Source:* EBRD and World Bank (2002).

export intensity—roughly 7 percent of sales revenues. Across sectors, the survey data indicate that construction firms—which, as our case studies reveal (see box 3.3), tend to concentrate on their domestic markets (especially public procurement contracts)—derive the least proportion of sales revenues from exports (about 3 percent). In contrast, the contribution of

## Table 3.12    Export Intensity by Sector, 2002

| Sector | Export receipts as a % of sales revenue |
|---|---|
| Mining | 21.3 |
| Construction | 3.1 |
| Manufacturing | 22.5 |
| Transportation, storage, and communications | 19.7 |
| Trade | 7.3 |
| Business services | 6.7 |
| Hotels and restaurants | 11.6 |
| Other | 4.7 |

*Source:* EBRD and World Bank (2002).

---

### Box 3.3  The "Home-Grown" Construction Sector in SEE

Most of the sales of construction firms in SEE are concentrated in the domestic market and, in some cases, the municipal market, in which they are located. Bidding on government and (to a lesser extent) private contracts with neighboring or more distant countries is increasingly attempted but is not always successful. During the case studies, firms complained that they are subject to discrimination as foreign firms and that preference is shown to local companies, especially in the case of public procurement contracts. Consequently, home governments have sought to help their domestic firms win public contracts abroad through political suasion.

In general, however, the construction firms that served as case studies find home government contracts quite attractive—some companies do more than 70 percent of their business with the government. However, the "competitive" selection process is not always transparent, and often the government agencies do not pay promptly, necessitating litigation. Some firms note that to be successful in the domestic public procurement construction business, they must be politically well connected. In some cases, ministries ask for pro bono construction, design or engineering advice, which the firms readily give in order to build goodwill.

A few construction firms concentrate on winning construction contracts from domestic private companies or foreign private multinational subsidiaries located in the local market; complaints about lack of transparency in the contracting process are voiced here as well, but these complaints are more muted than in the case of domestic public procurement contracts. Some of these firms are interested in pursuing government contracts, but without a public procurement law in place, they are reluctant to do so.

## Table 3.13   Proportion of Firms Having New Export Destinations, 1998–2002

| Country | % of firms that made exports to new countries since 1998 |
|---|---|
| Albania | 11.2 |
| Bosnia and Herzegovina | 16.6 |
| Bulgaria | 25.2 |
| Croatia | 20.0 |
| Macedonia, FYR | 20.2 |
| Moldova | 50.8 |
| Romania | 32.6 |
| Serbia and Montenegro | 12.4 |
| SEE8 average | 20.2 |

Source: EBRD and World Bank (2002).

export receipts to sales revenue is greatest for manufacturing firms (almost 23 percent).

Finally, table 3.13. depicts international horizontal expansion as shown by the percentage of SEE8 firms that exported to new markets between 1998 and 2002. On average, 20 percent of the firms in the region indicated that they exported to new markets during the period. Moldova had the largest proportion of firms indicating new export destinations (about 51 percent), whereas Albania registered the smallest proportion (about 11 percent).

PERCEIVED MARKET POWER: PRICE AND SALES SENSITIVITY, MARKET SHARE, AND NUMBER OF COMPETITORS

Firms that achieve sufficient market dominance as a result of facing fewer competitors and attaining appreciable market share should, all other things being equal, have greater discretion in price setting. Consequently, the sensitivity of such firms in changing output—and in expected sales—in response to changes in prices should be less than that of firms facing a greater number of competitors but exhibiting large market shares. Box 3.4 illustrates the point with an example of price wars in one of the sectors in which the case studies were carried out.

Tables 3.14 and 3.15, both based on BEEPS2 data, present interesting data on SEE8 firms' perceptions of their market power. The survey posed a hypothetical question to the respondents about how their firms' sales would be affected by a 10 percent increase in the market price of their principal output. Across the SEE8, on average, a significantly smaller proportion of Moldovan firms, relative to the other eight countries, indicated that their sales would not decrease. Bulgaria registered the largest

---

## Box 3.4 Market Dominance and Anticompetitive Pricing in SEE

The market structure in a sector represented in the case studies is best characterized as a core of a few large, dominant firms and a competitive fringe of more numerous small- and medium-sized firms. The combined market share of the three dominant firms—which are either privatized or de novo private enterprises—is approximately 45 percent. About seven other firms—all of medium size, mostly state-owned enterprises but also some private businesses—have a combined market share of 15 to 20 percent. The remaining share of the market comprises many small private firms.

One of the private medium-size firms, which is affiliated with a major local bank, has been an aggressive marketer and has tried to break into the dominant core. Its market share in 2001 was 2.6 percent, but a year later its share had increased to 4.5 percent. The senior manager of this firm voiced great concern that his company was suffering from "unfair competition." In particular, pricing behavior in this market is often predatory, with the dominant firms lowering prices to try to drive out competitors. The result has been frequent price wars.

One of the price wars was so destructive to the involved firms' bottom lines that this senior manager invited the two other chief executive officers over for lunch. In a discussion that lasted almost 5 hours, they agreed to fix prices on certain key products. One of the participants agreed to stop selling at a lower price for 2 months, another for 4 months, and the third for 1 month. Because they had the same or similar suppliers, they also agreed on markup margins. The margins were fixed at 25 to 30 percent for one firm, 22 to 23 percent for another, and 13 to 18 percent for the third. It is likely that the participants accepted the pricing deal in part because they were seeking credits from the firm affiliated with the bank. After 4 months, the predatory pricing resumed.

---

proportion of firms that perceived losing all their sales to rivals, although the proportion of Moldovan firms was only slightly smaller. This finding suggests that Moldovan firms—and to a lesser extent Bulgarian firms—perceive themselves as relatively less able to exercise market power than surveyed firms in the other countries. At the other end of the spectrum, firms in Serbia and Montenegro, and to a lesser extent, firms in Romania, perceive themselves as relatively better able to exercise market power.

Across firm ownership categories, a greater proportion of state-owned enterprises clearly perceive themselves as being able to exercise greater market power than do privatized or de novo private firms. Interestingly,

## Table 3.14    Expected Sales Change after a 10 Percent Price Increase, by Country, 2002
*(percent)*

| Country | Sales would not decrease | All sales would accrue to rivals |
|---|---|---|
| Albania | 13.0 | 29.0 |
| Bosnia and Herzegovina | 13.4 | 29.1 |
| Bulgaria | 16.1 | 38.8 |
| Croatia | 16.7 | 23.1 |
| Macedonia, FYR | 16.0 | 28.4 |
| Moldova | 8.6 | 37.4 |
| Romania | 25.5 | 26.3 |
| Serbia and Montenegro | 24.4 | 18.8 |
| SEE8 average | 17.5 | 28.6 |

*Source:* EBRD and World Bank (2002).
*Note:* Table shows the percentage of surveyed firms indicating that sales would not decrease or that all sales would accrue to rivals. Percentages do not sum to 100 because intermediate outcomes are not shown.

## Table 3.15    Expected Sales Change after a 10 Percent Price Increase, by Ownership Type, 2002
*(percent)*

| Ownership type | Sales would not decrease | All sales would accrue to rivals |
|---|---|---|
| State-owned | 23.6 | 23.6 |
| Privatized | 12.7 | 30.9 |
| De novo | 17.6 | 29.3 |

*Source:* EBRD and World Bank (2002).
*Note:* Table shows the percentage of surveyed firms indicating that sales would not decrease or that all sales would accrue to rivals. Percentages do not sum to 100 because intermediate outcomes are not shown.

the proportion of de novo private firms that perceive themselves as being able to exercise market power is larger than the proportion of privatized businesses that do so.

Figures 3.5 and 3.6 deepen the analysis by examining how such perceptions of market power in fact relate to a firm's market share and the number of competitors it faces. The results are consistent with the hypothesis articulated above. In figure 3.5, there is a clear inverse relationship between the size of market share and the degree to which a firm's conduct would result in a loss of sales in the event of a 10 percent increase in market prices (its *sales sensitivity*). Figure 3.6 yields the same conclusion but is based on the number of competitors faced by the firm.

**Figure 3.5   Expected Sales Sensitivity after a 10 Percent Price Increase, by Firm Market Share, 2002**

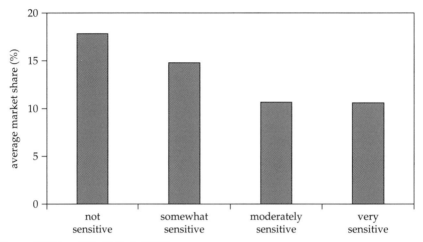

*Source:* EBRD and World Bank (2002).

**Figure 3.6   Expected Sales Sensitivity after a 10 Percent Price Increase, by Number of Competitors, 2002**

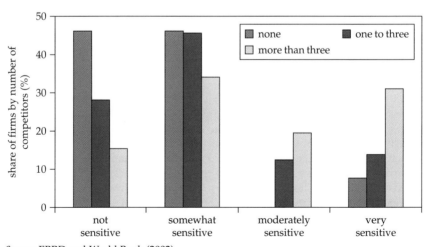

*Source:* EBRD and World Bank (2002).

## Vertical Dimensions of the South Eastern European Market Structure

EXTENT OF VERTICAL UPSTREAM AND DOWNSTREAM INTEGRATION

Our case studies suggest that the degree of vertical integration by SEE8 firms—whether *upstream* (producing inputs internally rather than purchasing them from unrelated parties) or *downstream* (distributing or selling outputs directly to end users rather than through an intermediary)—varies across sectors, across firms of different ownership types, and across countries. Box 3.5 illustrates these differences in the case of vertical upstream integration.

The BEEPS data shed light on differences among firms in terms of vertical downstream integration (see table 3.16). The data show that for the

---

**Box 3.5  Vertical Integration in the South Eastern European Food Processing and Retailing Sector**

A number of firms in the food processing and retail sector in SEE are both vertically integrated upstream to the food growing or supply portion of the market and vertically integrated downstream to distribution and retail sales. Typical of this pattern is a de novo private firm interviewed during the case studies that started out as a small retail salami and cheese business. The firm started in 1992 as a small retail shop selling salami and cheese. A family outfit, the firm was run by the founder and his wife. At the time, the founder was a sports teacher, but he decided to go into business with an initial investment of US$1,000. In 1993, he managed to expand his retail store, and two and a half years later, he started a small factory for sausages. In 2000, he opened a second factory. Today the firm has two factories for salami, its own distribution network, 10 warehouses, and 14 retail shops. A third factory for salami was scheduled to open in 2003. In the spring of 2002, the firm purchased land and some fish-lakes. Breeding and selling fish proved to be quite lucrative, so the firm also began to raise its own cows, sheep, and pigs. A milk factory was set to open in 2003. The average sales per day equal 45 tons of processed meat. Today there are 1,400 employees, and since the early 1990s, the company has significantly increased production, employees, and profits. It not only sells its produce through its own retail outlets but also supplies its products to supermarkets. In all, it has 3,750 clients and issues some 1,200 invoices per day. The structure of the client-base is about 17 percent supermarkets; 35 percent direct distributors, including the firm's own retail shops; and 50 percent independent warehouses. Turnover for the first half of 2002 was US$38 million.

## Table 3.16  Downstream Integration by Country, by Sector, and by Ownership Type, 2002

*(average percentage of an enterprise's sales made to parent firm or affiliated subsidiary)*

| Country | Average share (%) | Sector | Average share (%) | Ownership type | Average share (%) |
|---|---|---|---|---|---|
| Albania | 3.8 | Mining | 7.3 | State-owned | 10.8 |
| Bosnia and | 28.2 | Construction | 7.6 | Privatized | 7.6 |
| Herzegovina | | Manufacturing | 13.5 | De novo | 11.7 |
| Bulgaria | 2.7 | Transportation, | 11.5 | | |
| Croatia | 4.5 | storage, and | | | |
| Macedonia, FYR | 22.7 | communications | | | |
| Moldova | 2.1 | Trade | 11.6 | | |
| Romania | 2.3 | Business | 10.4 | | |
| Serbia and | 23.3 | services | | | |
| Montenegro | | Hotels and | 5.6 | | |
| SEE8 average | 11.0 | restaurants | | | |
| | | Other | 7.8 | | |

*Source:* EBRD and World Bank (2002).

region as a whole, on average about 11 percent of the surveyed firms' sales transactions are conducted internally or are made to related parties. However, the case studies suggest a higher level for upstream integration. By country, downstream integration is lowest for firms in Bulgaria, Moldova, and Romania, and it is highest for firms in Bosnia and Herzegovina, FYR Macedonia, and Serbia and Montenegro. As might be expected, manufacturing firms appear to exhibit the greatest degree of downstream integration, whereas hotels and restaurants register the least. A curious finding is that, although state-owned enterprises indicate a greater degree of downstream integration than their privatized counterparts, de novo private firms indicate a degree of downstream integration that is even higher than that of state-owned enterprises. In part, this finding may be a statistical artifact insofar as the category of de novo firms includes joint venture enterprises.

### STRUCTURAL CONDITIONS FOR COMPETITION IN UPSTREAM AND DOWNSTREAM TRANSACTIONS

About two-thirds of the SEE8 firms covered by the BEEPS2 indicated that on average they had at least four suppliers for their "main material inputs." Although this finding may suggest that the average firm in the entire South Eastern European region enjoys structurally competitive

**Figure 3.7    Number of Material Input Suppliers by
Country, 2002**

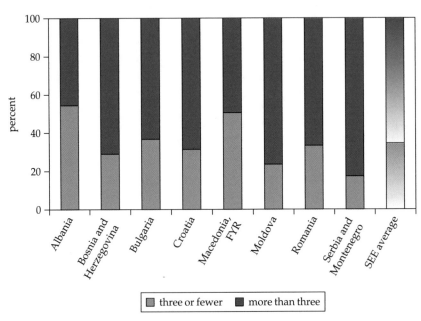

*Source:* EBRD and World Bank (2002).

upstream markets, no conclusion is possible without knowing the size distribution of the firm's market shares and the number of a firm's suppliers.

A more informative picture emerges by looking at the competitive structure of supply markets across countries, across ownership types, and across
sectors. Figure 3.7 indicates that the proportion of surveyed Albanian and
FYR Macedonian firms that buy inputs in relatively less competitive supply markets is greater than that of surveyed firms in Moldova and Serbia
and Montenegro. In Figure 3.8, the BEEPS data indicate that there is a
clear trend across the region of proportionately more de novo private
firms, versus privatized or state-owned firms, buying their inputs in markets with more suppliers. This finding suggests that, all other things being
equal, new business start-ups are most able to benefit from upstream
competition. Across sectors, there is great variation in the number of input
suppliers. The construction sector registers the greatest proportion of
firms with at least four suppliers (81 percent), and the business sector
indicates the smallest proportion with at least four suppliers (45 percent).

BEEPS2 also contains significant data on the competitive structure of
firms' downstream markets. Table 3.17 shows that, in the case of surveyed

## Figure 3.8 Firms with More Than Three Material Input Suppliers, by Ownership Type and by Country, 2002

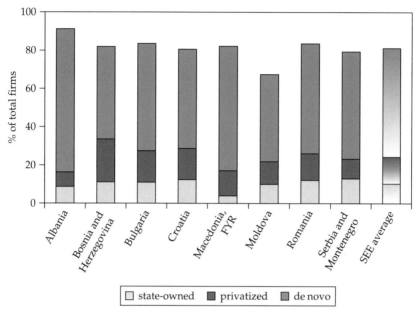

□ state-owned  ■ privatized  ■ de novo

*Source:* EBRD and World Bank (2002).

## Table 3.17 Size Distribution of Downstream Sales by Country and Ownership Type, 2001–02

*(average share of enterprises' sales to their three largest customers)*

| Country | Average share (%) | Ownership type | Average share (%) |
|---|---|---|---|
| Albania | 59 | State-owned | 51.4 |
| Bosnia and | 57 | Privatized | 57.4 |
| Herzegovina | | De novo | 49.1 |
| Bulgaria | 49 | | |
| Croatia | 60 | | |
| Macedonia, FYR | 63 | | |
| Moldova | 37 | | |
| Romania | 44 | | |
| Serbia and | 46 | | |
| Montenegro | | | |
| SEE8 average | 52 | | |

*Source:* EBRD and World Bank (2002).
*Note:* Table only covers firms that sell more than 20 percent of their output to their three largest customers.

firms that sold more than 20 percent of their output to their three largest customers, on average such firms sold slightly more than half of their output to those customers. Firms in FYR Macedonia and Croatia indicated the most concentrated downstream market structure, whereas Moldovan firms indicated the least concentrated downstream market structure. Across ownership categories, although de novo private and state-owned firms indicated approximately the same proportion of downstream sales to their three largest customers—close to the regional average—privatized firms indicated a more concentrated downstream market structure.

TENURE OF VERTICAL RELATIONSHIPS

Another perspective on the competitiveness of vertical market structure is provided by the tenure of the relationships between the firm and (a) the suppliers of its principal inputs and (b) the distributors and customers of its principal outputs. Notwithstanding the risk factors inherent in such transactions—which are likely to be appreciable, especially in transition economies—one might expect greater fluidity in firms' relationships with suppliers in more competitive supply markets. Figure 3.9 indicates that, on average, slightly over 80 percent of the firms in the region maintained

**Figure 3.9    Tenure of Supply Relationships: Firms with at Least 20 percent of Material Inputs from Suppliers Maintained for at Least 3 Years, 2002**

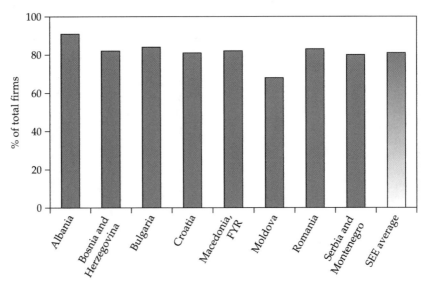

*Source:* EBRD and World Bank (2002).

the same suppliers for 3 or more years for at least 20 percent of their material inputs. Although there is not a great deal of cross-country variance, Moldova indicated the smallest proportion (68 percent) and Albania the largest proportion (91 percent) of firms with those attributes. This finding suggests that, all other things being equal, Moldovan firms tend to have a relatively short tenure of supply relationships, and Albanian firms tend to have a relatively long one.

Interestingly, with respect to differences across ownership types, the survey data indicate that for the overall region, a smaller proportion of state-owned enterprises (74 percent), relative to both privatized and de novo private firms (both 83 percent), maintain the same suppliers for 3 or more years for at least 20 percent of their material inputs.

On the output side, as depicted in table 3.18, the proportion of enterprises in the region that on average sold at least 20 percent of their output to the same distributors or customers for 3 or more years is 62 percent—appreciably below the counterpart upstream attribute just discussed. There is also more cross-country variation. Yet, once again the survey concluded that Moldova has the smallest proportion of firms indicating such a tenured—but this time, downstream—relationship. By the same token, Albania registered a large proportion of surveyed firms indicating this result. However, the proportion of surveyed Croatian firms indicating such a tenured downstream relationship is the largest.

Across ownership categories, the results on the downstream portion of the market contrast with those of the upstream portion. This time state-owned enterprises registered the largest proportion of firms maintaining a relationship of at least 3 years with the same parties for the distribution or

**Table 3.18  Tenure of Distribution and Sales Relationships, 2002**
*(average share of enterprises that sold at least 20 percent of output to the same distributors and customers for 3 or more years)*

| Country | Average share (%) | Ownership type | Average share (%) |
|---|---|---|---|
| Albania | 70 | State-owned | 65 |
| Bosnia and | 59 | Privatized | 64 |
| Herzegovina | | De novo | 61 |
| Bulgaria | 65 | | |
| Croatia | 77 | | |
| Macedonia, FYR | 63 | | |
| Moldova | 47 | | |
| Romania | 62 | | |
| Serbia and | 55 | | |
| Montenegro | | | |
| SEE8 average | 62 | | |

*Source:* EBRD and World Bank (2002).

sale of at least 20 percent of the firms' outputs. Moreover, the proportion of state-owned enterprises indicating that they met this criterion was larger than that of privatized firms, which, in turn, was larger than that of de novo private firms. In view of the above findings, all other things being equal, this result suggests that, although privatized or private firms shop around for distributors and customers more than state-owned enterprises, state-owned enterprises tend to shop around more when purchasing inputs.

USE OF IMPORTED INPUTS
Another dimension of the competitiveness of vertical market structure is the extent to which firms purchase inputs from domestic sources instead of international ones. Firms in SEE rely to varying degrees on imported inputs (see figure 3.10). For the region as a whole, imports account on average for about 38 percent of total input purchases. Surveyed firms in Albania indicate the largest portion of input imports—about 51 percent of total purchased inputs. But the import content of total input purchases by firms in Bosnia and Herzegovina, Croatia, FYR Macedonia, and Serbia and Montenegro is also substantial—all above 40 percent. In contrast, Romania, and to a lesser extent Bulgaria, purchase the vast majority of their inputs from domestic suppliers—79 percent and 72 percent, respectively.

**Figure 3.10   Reliance on Imported Inputs, 2002**

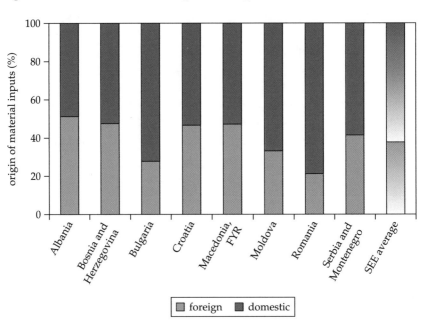

*Source:* EBRD and World Bank (2002).

PERCEIVED UPSTREAM MARKET POWER

Finally, a key issue regarding the competitiveness of South Eastern European vertical market structures is the extent to which firms perceive that they can exercise market power vis-à-vis their suppliers. Once again, the BEEPS instrument asked the SEE8 firms how they would respond to a 10 percent price increase charged by their suppliers. Table 3.19 describes the results. On a regionwide basis, on average, though 19 percent of the firms would not alter their input purchases with their incumbent suppliers, a larger portion—28 percent—would switch to purchase all of the input from an alternative supplier. Across countries, Moldova's surveyed firms indicated that they would be most sensitive to such a price change. Moldova (with FYR Macedonia) had the smallest proportion of firms that would continue purchases with existing suppliers and the second largest proportion of firms that would switch completely to a new supplier. Firms in Bulgaria were somewhat less sensitive. In contrast, Romanian firms indicated that they would be the least sensitive to such a price change.

Across ownership types, the surveyed state-owned enterprises indicated that they would be the most sensitive to the change in input prices. In contrast, de novo private firms indicated they would be the least sensitive to such a change.

**Table 3.19 Expected Input Purchase Change after a 10 Percent Price Increase, by Country and Ownership, 2002**
*(percent)*

| Country | Input purchases would not decrease from existing supplier | All input purchases would be made with an alternative supplier | Ownership type | Input purchases would not decrease from existing supplier | All input purchases would be made with an alternative supplier |
|---|---|---|---|---|---|
| Albania | 23 | 23 | State-owned | 18 | 34 |
| Bosnia and Herzegovina | 16 | 23 | Privatized | 18 | 29 |
| | | | De novo | 20 | 27 |
| Bulgaria | 18 | 36 | | | |
| Croatia | 16 | 32 | | | |
| Macedonia, FYR | 12 | 24 | | | |
| Moldova | 12 | 34 | | | |
| Romania | 28 | 25 | | | |
| Serbia and Montenegro | 24 | 24 | | | |
| SEE8 average | 19 | 28 | | | |

*Source:* EBRD and World Bank (2002).
*Note:* Table shows the percentage of surveyed firms indicating the two outcomes. Percentages do not sum to 100 because intermediate outcomes are not shown.

## Assessment of Entry and Exit Barriers

The benefits a firm accrues by exploiting anticompetitive horizontal and vertical elements of market structure are not sustainable. Such exploitation is usually reflected in excessive profits or in excessive costs incurred from inefficient conduct (perhaps in the form of "gold-plating" or the payment of high salaries to senior management). The exercise of market power can be sustained only to the extent that (a) business rivals are restrained from entry to the market or (b) claimants of the firm (banks, shareholders, tax collectors, and so forth) cannot effectively demand changes that render a more efficient use of the firm's resources (such as changes in senior management, restructuring of operations, or liquidation of assets).

Over the past decade, as the SEE8 proceeded to move to a market system, case studies show that in some instances various types of entry barriers, especially economic and institutional factors, have helped insulate incumbent dominant firms from new competitors. At the same time, inefficient, value-subtracting firms have been protected from market exit or competitive restructuring through soft budget constraints (weak fiscal and financial discipline such as tax or loan payment forbearance). These firms are being propped up through subsidies by political economy interests (see box 3.6). Before examining these entry and exit barriers in greater detail, let us first assess the extent of fluidity in enterprise turnover and restructuring in the region.

## *Business Turnover and Restructuring in South Eastern Europe*

Table 3.20 shows data on changes in the number of registered firms and full-time employees in the industrial sector in the SEE8 economies between 1999 and 2002. For the region overall, there was, on average, a 35 percent increase in the number of registered firms (with all countries indicating an increase) and a 6 percent decrease in the number of full-time employees (with all countries registering a decrease). Even though these data on firm registration may include (a) re-registered firms and (b) registered firms that are inactive, the rough picture that emerges is one of modest restructuring of existing firms—as reflected in the employment turnover numbers—and perhaps substantial creation of smaller firms.

Table 3.21 explores this proposition in more detail by focusing on turnover in the number of active firms (rather than registered firms) and by comparing firms of different sizes. Again, there are potential cross-country inconsistencies in these data, as, for instance, not all countries define an *active firm* in the same way. Still, these data suggest a sizable increase (12 percent) in the number of active small firms, on average, for

---

## Box 3.6  Weak Financial Discipline Delays the Exit of Loss-Makers and Distorts the Use of Capital

One case study concerns a firm that was founded in 1937 as an iron and steel foundry and machine shop. In 1945, it became a state-owned company, and it is still state owned today. In 1965, the factory was restructured, and its manufacturing capabilities were brought to 4,000 metric tons per year. In 1978, its manufacturing capabilities reached 8,500 metric tons per year. In 1983, because of a modernization effort, the factory's manufacturing capabilities reached 12,000 metric tons per year.

Currently, however, the firm operates at only 20 percent of its capacity. Total employees have been reduced to 420 from 1,380 in the early 1990s. Management believes that the company still carries an excess of 150 to 200 workers on its payroll. The firm is the largest employer in the area, and it faces only two other competitors in the country. Its chief executive officer (CEO) has expressed concern that many social burdens that should fall on the state are being carried out by the firm.

However, the state has been useful on several occasions. Several years ago, for example, the firm was being charged what it thought were excessively high land-use and property taxes by the local authorities. The CEO wrote a letter to the government proposing the company pay only a portion of those taxes and that the portion be tied to the capacity utilization of the plants. The government supported the proposal, and the taxes were reduced accordingly.

The management board of the firm consists of five people, all members of political parties. No financial audits are performed on the firm's accounts because the enterprise is a strategic state-owned enterprise. The company's debts are to other state enterprises, the state budget, and one commercial bank. The CEO acknowledged that, if the firm were to pay off all its loans, "We would be bankrupt. We would need to give up 1 month of production to repay the loans and would stop paying budget contributions, wages, etc. Once we explained this situation to our creditor [the bank], they agreed to allow us to continue to defer loan payments." In another example, in the winter of 2001 the company was 1 month late paying for electricity, and the CEO wrote to the electric utility indicating that if the electrical company stopped the power supply, the enterprise would shut down. He advised in the letter that the utility check with the prime minister before cutting off the supply. As a result, the utility was not cut, and the firm paid its power bill late.

---

the SEE8; a very modest increase (3 percent) in the number of active medium-size firms; and a modest decrease (6 percent) in the number of active large firms. In each size category, there are instances of two countries that exhibit reverse trends to the SEE8 average. Overall the pattern suggests that, though there was modest restructuring of existing firms

## Table 3.20    Turnover of Number of Registered Firms and of Full-Time Employees in South Eastern European Industry, 1999 and 2002

| Country | Number of registered firms in industry | | Total number of full-time employees in industrial firms | |
|---|---|---|---|---|
| | 2002[a] | 1999 | 2002[b] | 1999 |
| Albania | 10,195 | 9,302 | 53,965 | 55,068 |
| Bosnia and Herzegovina | 14,491 | 12,334 | 216,993 | 227,930 |
| Bulgaria | 72,359 | 64,372 | 812,963 | 891,164 |
| Croatia | 31,415 | 29,410 | 325,600 | 346,776 |
| Macedonia, FYR | 24,536 | 15,585 | 185,774 | 199,010 |
| Moldova | 13,992 | 11,597 | 143,068 | 154,765 |
| Romania | 57,753 | — | 2,210,000 | 2,300,000 |
| Serbia[c] | — | — | 678,758 | 725,401 |
| SEE8 average | 32,106 | 23,767 | 578,390 | 612,514 |

Sources: Official statistics and World Bank staff estimates.
Note: — = not available. Industry includes mining, manufacturing, and construction.
a. Data for Albania, Bosnia and Herzegovina, Bulgaria, and Romania are for 2001.
b. Data for Albania, Bosnia and Herzegovina, Bulgaria, FYR Macedonia, and Romania are for 2001; data for Croatia are for 2000.
c. Data do not include Montenegro.

(a small increase in medium-size firms and a small decrease in large firms), the entry that occurred in the SEE8 was overwhelmingly by small firms. This picture is generally consistent with the findings of other recent studies of enterprise restructuring in Central and Eastern Europe (see, for example, World Bank 2002).

## Constraints on New Entrants

Economists distinguish between two different types of entry barriers: those that are economic in nature (these barriers are principally determined by technology or underlying market forces) and those that are institutionally determined, policy driven, or administratively induced. The need for policy intervention to deal with economic barriers generally arises only when such barriers are chronically high or in markets where there is already significant horizontal or vertical dominance. Intervention is best decided on a case-by-case basis. For institutionally determined entry barriers, the case for policy intervention is more clear cut.

### ECONOMIC BARRIERS TO ENTRY

In certain industries, the technology fundamental to the production process naturally gives rise to economies of scale, in which unit costs

Table 3.21    Turnover of Number of Active Firms in South
Eastern European Industry by Size, 1999 and 2002

| Country | Total number of active small firms | | Total number of active medium-size firms | | Total number of active large firms | |
|---|---|---|---|---|---|---|
| | 2002[a] | 1999[b] | 2002[a] | 1999[b] | 2002[a] | 1999[b] |
| Albania | 32,616 | 33,029 | 1,697 | 1,448 | 1,208 | 1,202 |
| Bosnia and Herzegovina | — | — | — | — | — | — |
| Bulgaria | 43,867 | 23,128 | 1,775 | 1,695 | 527 | 563 |
| Croatia | 56,173 | 57,323 | 2,044 | 2,075 | 556 | 574 |
| Macedonia, FYR | 54,320 | 52,222 | 533 | 532 | 510 | 473 |
| Moldova[c] | 15,320 | 12,086 | 1,308 | 1,559 | — | — |
| Romania[d] | 44,532 | 39,860 | 10,579 | 10,163 | 2,642 | 2,846 |
| Serbia[e] | 44,131 | 42,010 | 1,226 | 1,218 | 2,029 | 2,304 |
| SEE8 average | 41,566 | 37,090 | 2,737 | 2,670 | 1,245 | 1,327 |

Sources: Official statistics and World Bank staff estimates.
Note: — = not available. Industry includes mining, manufacturing, and construction.
Unless otherwise noted, small firms are those with 49 employees or fewer, medium-size firms are those with between 50 and 249 employees, and large firms are those with 250 or more employees.
a. Data for Albania, Bulgaria, FYR Macedonia, Romania, and Serbia are for 2001. Data for Croatia are for 2000.
b. Data for FYR Macedonia are for 2000.
c. Data for medium-size firms also include large firms.
d. Data do not include Montenegro. Data include all active economic and social units, including regies autonomies (large state-owned enterprises).
e. Estimates are as of June 2002. Small firms are those with 49 employees or fewer, medium-size firms are those with between 50 and 100 employees, and large firms are those with more than 100 employees.

decline as output expands to meet market demand. In such industries, those scale economies are a barrier to entry because it is unlikely that multiple businesses can all attain the minimum efficient scale to be commercially viable. As noted earlier, there may be significant scale economies in certain segments of the infrastructure sectors in the SEE8. However, in most of the industrial sector in the region and worldwide, scale economies are unlikely to be as pronounced relative to market demand, and thus, absent other types of constraints, such economic barriers to entry are likely to be relatively modest.

When incumbent firms enjoy brand loyalty among consumers, product differentiation becomes an entry barrier. Potential rivals must then invest heavily in advertising to become commercially viable. As in many other transition countries, brand loyalty among the products of firms in the SEE8 was not strong at the beginning of the transition and, thus, was

---

**Box 3.7  Brand Loyalty as a Barrier to Entry: The Case
of Food Processing and Retailing**

Of all the sectors covered by the case studies, firms in food processing and
retailing rely most heavily on marketing, advertising, and brand loyalty to
increase and maintain market share. In virtually all of the eight countries,
this sector tends to be dominated by three to five firms that are largely
supermarkets. Weekly advertising by the firms is extensive, including use
of sales, discounts, and coupons. While competition is mediated largely by
pricing among the dominant firms, smaller firms and potential entrants
have difficulty reaching a higher level of market penetration as customers
have developed loyalties to the large incumbents. The incumbents have
built name recognition not only through advertising, but also through uniformity in store layouts, issuance of store credit cards, and consistency in
product quality. The heavy investment newcomers must make to challenge
the incumbents has kept entry modest. Generally, when there is entry, it is
in the form of horizontal expansion across neighboring countries and often
involves foreign joint venture investors.

---

not a potent constraint on entry. In the past decade, advertising and marketing have become more sophisticated, and product differentiation can
well be used as an entry barrier (see box 3.7 for an illustration from the
case studies).

The advantages that accrue from innovation can also prevent new
entry. Much depends on the embedded technological prowess of firms
and whether the country has a patent system in place to protect and reinforce that capability by granting exclusive production and marketing
rights. As in most transition economies to date, there is no effective patent-
ing system in the SEE8 economies. Thus, technological innovation may be
only a modest impediment to entry in these countries' industrial sectors.

Finally, natural resource endowment may act as an entry barrier. During an industry's development, firms that are first to locate and exploit
such deposits will have a strategic market advantage over those seeking
entry later (unless new resource deposits are discovered or the initial
firms decide to license access rights). Mining or petroleum firms may be
able to exploit this type of barrier to entry.

INSTITUTIONAL, POLICY-BASED, AND ADMINISTRATIVE BARRIERS TO ENTRY

Evidence from the case studies and from the BEEPS suggests several
institutional, policy-based, or administrative factors that constrain the
entry and growth of new firms in the SEE8. The BEEPS asked respondents to rank in terms of severity the importance of a variety of such factors. A summary of the results is contained in table 3.22.

## Table 3.22    Comparative Severity of Potential Barriers to the Operation and Growth of Businesses in the SEE8, 2002
*(percentage of responses)*

| Barrier | No obstacle | Minor obstacle | Moderate obstacle | Major obstacle |
|---|---|---|---|---|
| Access to financing (such as collateral required or financing unavailable from banks) | 32.62 | 17.42 | 24.85 | 25.11 |
| Cost of financing (such as interest rates and charges) | 20.56 | 20.62 | 27.20 | 31.63 |
| Access to telecommunications | 66.73 | 18.00 | 8.50 | 6.77 |
| Access to electricity | 59.64 | 18.23 | 10.75 | 11.37 |
| Access to transportation | 63.08 | 18.46 | 10.58 | 7.88 |
| Access to land | 68.35 | 15.18 | 9.93 | 6.53 |
| Tax rates | 17.39 | 15.59 | 31.61 | 35.41 |
| Tax administration | 27.55 | 22.48 | 26.47 | 23.50 |
| Customs and trade regulations | 42.54 | 19.99 | 20.45 | 17.03 |
| Business licensing and permits | 38.35 | 21.69 | 23.94 | 16.02 |
| Labor regulations | 53.09 | 25.23 | 14.80 | 6.89 |
| Skills and education of available workers | 48.99 | 24.37 | 17.28 | 9.37 |
| Economic policy uncertainty | 12.68 | 14.08 | 26.89 | 46.35 |
| Macroeconomic instability (inflation or exchange rate problems) | 16.12 | 15.93 | 24.87 | 43.08 |
| Functioning of the judiciary | 28.40 | 25.18 | 24.98 | 21.44 |
| Corruption | 28.26 | 19.32 | 23.10 | 29.32 |
| Street crime, theft, and disorder | 42.11 | 24.95 | 16.44 | 16.50 |
| Organized crime | 47.11 | 18.05 | 15.97 | 18.86 |
| Anticompetitive practices of other producers | 27.98 | 21.37 | 24.78 | 25.87 |
| Contract violations by customers and suppliers | 31.26 | 24.22 | 24.92 | 19.60 |
| Title or leasing of land | 66.83 | 15.77 | 10.01 | 7.39 |
| Overall average | 39.98 | 19.82 | 19.92 | 20.28 |

*Source:* EBRD and World Bank (2002).

Table 3.22 suggests several insights, bearing in mind that the BEEPS measures firm managers' perceptions of the business environment rather than making a factual assessment of business conditions based on firms' actions and decisions (the methodology used in the case studies). First, generic economic policy uncertainty—unanticipated or unilateral changes in the rules of the game—and macroeconomic instability are seen as the most pernicious obstacles to business development and operations in SEE. This finding is important because it means that governments in the region can, in fact, proactively carry out policy reforms to reduce barriers to entry. Moreover it suggests that there are important constraints on investment that are economywide (probably even regionwide) in nature and are not rooted solely in the natural underlying technology or economic character-istics of a specific sector. Second, the data in table 3.22 suggest that other key entry barriers are (a) high tax rates, (b) high financing costs, (c) cor-ruption, and (d) anticompetitive practices of other businesses. Those bar-riers are generally institutionally or policy driven.[7] Finally, the data lend less credence to the conventional wisdom that administrative barriers are the major impediments to business development. Access to land, titling or leasing of land, business licensing and permits, and tax administration are not perceived by SEE8 businesses as major impediments. This finding is consistent with recent microeconomic studies of barriers to investment in other transition countries (see, for example, Broadman 2002).

Figure 3.11 and table 3.23 systematically illustrate how perceived key entry barriers vary across the eight countries. Using the BEEPS ranking of severity for obstacles, surveyed firms in Bulgaria and Moldova indicated a greater severity in financial cost and economic policy uncertainty than did firms in the other six countries. Albanian, Moldovan, and Romanian firms ranked macroeconomic instability as a more severe barrier than their counterparts in the other five countries. Firms in Albania ranked both corruption and anticompetitive practices as more problematic than did firms in any of the other surveyed countries. Finally, Moldovan firms complained more about high tax rates than firms in the other countries. Overall, the picture that emerges is one in which Moldovan firms are more adversely affected by entry obstacles than the other countries, fol-lowed closely by firms in Albania. Barriers in Bulgaria and Romania are comparably less severe but are still appreciable.

Dealing with corruption and obtaining business licenses and permits are perhaps the most often cited barriers in the literature on transition economies. Let us look in greater detail, by firm ownership and by coun-try, at these barriers to assess the variance in their incidence. Figure 3.12 depicts the "bribe tax" or direct costs to firms from corruption for 2002 according to BEEPS2. The data show clearly that de novo private firms are burdened by the heaviest bribe tax, followed by privatized firms and then state-owned enterprises. Comparing these data with those from BEEPS1, we find this pattern has been roughly maintained over the

## Figure 3.11   Key Barriers to Entry in SEE, 2002

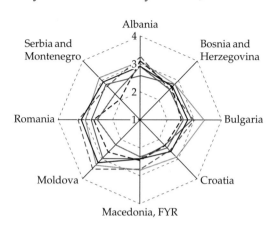

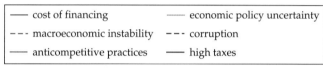

| | cost of financing | | economic policy uncertainty |
|---|---|---|---|
| - - - | macroeconomic instability | - - - | corruption |
| | anticompetitive practices | | high taxes |

*Source:* EBRD and World Bank (2002).
*Note:* Survey respondents ranked each category on a scale 1 to 4, with 1 representing no obstacle and 4 representing a major obstacle.

## Table 3.23   Key Barriers to Entry in SEE, 2002

| Country | Cost of financing | Economic policy uncertainty | Macroeconomic instability | Corruption | Anticompetitive practices | High taxes |
|---|---|---|---|---|---|---|
| Albania | 2.59 | 3.12 | 3.28 | 3.10 | 2.91 | 2.92 |
| Bosnia and Herzegovina | 2.79 | 2.82 | 2.52 | 2.65 | 2.52 | 2.67 |
| Bulgaria | 2.88 | 3.34 | 2.96 | 2.53 | 2.59 | 2.76 |
| Croatia | 2.27 | 2.87 | 2.53 | 2.29 | 2.40 | 2.62 |
| Macedonia, FYR | 2.38 | 2.79 | 2.77 | 2.45 | 2.34 | 2.41 |
| Moldova | 2.95 | 3.30 | 3.48 | 2.65 | 2.25 | 3.19 |
| Romania | 2.80 | 3.03 | 3.29 | 2.70 | 2.56 | 3.17 |
| Serbia and Montenegro | 2.78 | 3.14 | 2.71 | 2.02 | 2.30 | 2.92 |

*Source:* EBRD and World Bank (2002).
*Note:* Survey respondents ranked each category on a scale 1 to 4, with 1 representing no obstacle and 4 representing a major obstacle.

1999–2002 period. Among the sample of firms that indicate that they paid such a tax in 2002, the average amount paid in all ownership categories was above 3.5 percent of the firms' sales revenues.

Table 3.24 shows the cross-country disparity in the incidence of barriers emanating from the business licensing and permitting process. (For

**Figure 3.12    Average "Bribe Tax" Paid in SEE, by Firm Ownership, 2002**

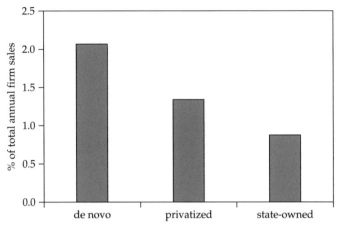

*Source:* EBRD and World Bank (2002).

**Table 3.24    Incidence of the Burden of Business Licensing and Permitting in SEE, 2002**

| Country | No obstacle | Major obstacle |
|---|---|---|
| Albania | 42.5 | 22.9 |
| Bosnia and Herzegovina | 42.3 | 11.9 |
| Bulgaria | 44.5 | 15.1 |
| Croatia | 38.0 | 9.2 |
| Macedonia, FYR | 34.8 | 17.4 |
| Moldova | 24.0 | 22.2 |
| Romania | 34.2 | 23.2 |
| Serbia and Montenegro | 44.0 | 7.8 |

*Source:* EBRD and World Bank (2002).
*Note:* Table shows the average percentage of surveyed firms responding in this category. Percentages do not sum to 100 because intermediate outcomes are not shown.

simplicity, we include only the two extreme measures of obstacles.) The surveyed firms in Albania, Moldova, and Romania registered the greatest severity of business licensing and permitting barriers, with more than 20 percent of the respondents in those countries indicating such barriers were major obstacles. In contrast, the largest proportions (approximately 45 percent) of surveyed firms indicating that these barriers were not obstacles to business operations and growth were in Bulgaria and Serbia and Montenegro.

## Barriers to Exit

In any economy, to create space for new entrants and to rechannel productive assets away from inefficient firms to new ventures that expand
employment and create new products, governments must ensure that exit
barriers are low. This action calls for hard budget constraints to engender
improved corporate competitiveness from viable firms and to expose
firms that are no longer commercially viable. The case studies show that
in many of the SEE8, budget constraints are soft and barriers to exit are,
in some cases, appreciable. The BEEPS data also shed light on the number
of business exits and the softness of budget constraints in SEE—with
respect to plant closures, subsidies, and tax arrears.

PLANT CLOSURES

The BEEPS survey asked respondents two questions: had they (a) opened
at least one plant and (b) closed at least one plant between 1998 and 2002?
The extent to which surveyed businesses indicated they closed at least
one plant during this period is set out in table 3.25 by country, by sector,
and by firm ownership. We also show the percentage of firms with net
closures. On average for the region, 11 percent of the firms indicated that
they closed at least one plant during this period—a rather low share by
international standards, given that many SEE8 firms are not commercially
viable. Indeed, on a net basis, about 9 percent of the firms indicated opening at least one plant.

Across the eight countries, Croatia registered the largest proportion of
firms indicating plant closures. Albania and FYR Macedonia recorded the
smallest proportions. On a net basis, however, only Albanian firms indicated plant closures; Romania and Serbia and Montenegro registered
firms with the greatest percentage of net plant openings. Looking at sectoral variation, we find that the infrastructure sector (transportation, storage, and communications) had the largest percentage of firms reporting
plant closures and had very few new plant openings on a net basis. The
mining sector had the second largest percentage of firms indicating plant
closures and also reported net closures. Across ownership types, there is
a clear and consistent pattern: state-owned enterprises reported the greatest proportion of plant closures and also registered closures on a net
basis. In contrast, de novo private firms had the smallest proportion of
plant closures and, in fact, indicated the largest share of plant openings
on a net basis.

SUBSIDIES FROM GOVERNMENT

The BEEPS2 data suggest that there is great variation in subsidies
received by respondent firms from all levels of government (national,

**Table 3.25  Extent of Plant Closure by Country, by Sector, and by Ownership Type, 1998–2002**
*(percent)*

| Country | Percentage of firms indicating closure | Sector | Percentage of firms indicating closure | Ownership type | Percentage of firms indicating closure |
|---|---|---|---|---|---|
| Albania | 3.6 (+1.8) | Mining | 17.7 (+0.1) | State-owned | 20.6 (+3.2) |
| Bosnia and Herzegovina | 9.0 (−6.8) | Construction | 6.8 (−15.9) | Privatized | 17.3 (−5.4) |
| Bulgaria | 10.0 (−4.4) | Manufacturing | 12.0 (−13.3) | De novo | 7.6 (−12.9) |
| Croatia | 15.6 (−10.9) | Transportation, storage, and communications | 18.3 (−1.6) | | |
| | | Trade | 12.7 (−7.0) | | |
| Macedonia, FYR | 3.5 (−11.2) | Business services | 6.8 (−6.7) | | |
| Moldova | 8.4 (−9.2) | Hotels and restaurants | 7.8 (−6.9) | | |
| Romania | 15.3 (−15.7) | Other | 6.4 (−10.3) | | |
| Serbia and Montenegro | 12.3 (−14.0) | | | | |
| SEE8 average | 11.2 (−9.3) | | | | |

*Source:* EBRD and World Bank (2002).
*Note:* Table shows the percentage of surveyed firms indicating that they closed at least one plant between 1998 and 2002. Numbers in parentheses show the percentage of firms indicating net plant closures; therefore, a minus sign indicates net plant openings.

regional, and local). For all of the SEE8 combined, the average surveyed
firm indicated that it received subsidies from the national government
amounting to 9.5 percent of sales revenues and subsidies from regional
and local governments equaling 17.7 percent of sales revenues (the percentages are annual averages for 1998–2002). Thus, the survey suggests
that, on average, subsidies received from local and regional governments
are almost twice as large as those received from the national government.
According to the survey respondents, the average amount of total government subsidies (that is, the sum of local, regional, and national subsidies) as a proportion of sales revenues is greatest in Croatia (43 percent),
followed by Moldova (29 percent). Surveyed firms in Albania responded
that they receive the lowest amount of subsidies as a percentage of sales
revenues (9 percent).

Figures 3.13 and 3.14 depict how total government subsidies as a percent of average annual sales revenues between 1998 and 2002 vary across
the SEE8 by firm ownership and by sector. For the region, state-owned
enterprises received the greatest amount of subsidies as a proportion of
sales revenues, followed by privatized firms and then by de novo private
firms. This pattern is consistent across all countries except FYR Macedonia

**Figure 3.13   Government Subsidies by Firm Ownership
Type, 2002**

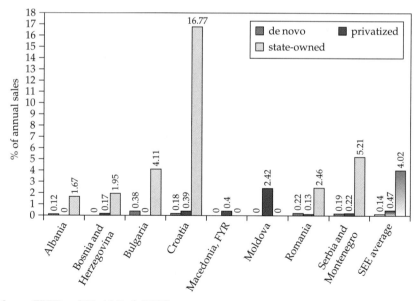

Source: EBRD and World Bank (2002).
Note: Figure shows total government subsidies as a percentage of average annual sales revenues for 1998–2002.

## Figure 3.14    Government Subsidies by Sector, 2002

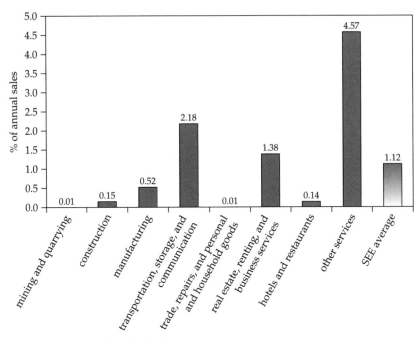

*Source:* EBRD and World Bank (2002).
*Note:* Figure shows total government subsidies as a percentage of average annual sales revenues for 1998–2002.

and Moldova (where privatized firms received the largest share of subsidies as a percentage of sales revenues). Across sectors, the largest recipients of subsidies were firms in the services and infrastructure sectors. Firms in the trade, mining, and hotel and restaurant sectors were the smallest recipients of subsidies.

TAX ARREARS TO GOVERNMENT
As discussed in chapter 2, the government's forbearance on tax payment also contributes to soft budget constraints and provides disincentives for restructuring or bankruptcy of otherwise value-subtracting or insolvent firms. Table 3.26 contains BEEPS data on tax arrears by country, sector, and firm ownership type (*arrears* is defined as payments at least 90 days overdue). For the surveyed firms, the regional average level of tax arrears is 12 percent of sales revenues, which is not an insignificant amount. Across countries, Albania and Romania stand out as having the highest amount of tax arrears per sales revenues, 14 percent and 20 percent,

**Table 3.26   Extent of Tax Arrears to Government by Country, by Sector, and by Ownership Type, 2002**

| Country | Annual average (%) | Sector | Annual average (%) | Ownership type | Annual average (%) |
|---|---|---|---|---|---|
| Albania | 14.0 | Mining | 10.0 | State-owned | 14.7 |
| Bosnia and | 7.8 | Construction | 12.3 | Privatized | 9.1 |
| Herzegovina | | Manufacturing | 11.5 | De novo | 12.9 |
| Bulgaria | 11.0 | Transportation, | 12.3 | | |
| Croatia | 8.1 | storage, and | | | |
| Macedonia, | 8.0 | communications | | | |
| FYR | | Trade | 13.6 | | |
| Moldova | 5.3 | Business services | 12.4 | | |
| Romania | 19.7 | Hotels and restaurants | 6.6 | | |
| Serbia and | 10.4 | Other | 13.5 | | |
| Montenegro | | | | | |
| SEE8 average | 12.0 | | | | |

*Source:* EBRD and World Bank (2002).
*Note: Arrears* are defined as payments at least 90 days overdue to government.

respectively. Moldovan firms indicated the lowest level of tax arrears (5 percent). With one exception, there is much less variation across sectors, with average tax arrears between 10 and 14 percent of sales revenues. The hotels and restaurants sector's average tax arrears, however, amounted to 7 percent of sales revenues. The survey on the incidence of tax arrears by firm ownership type reveals a curious finding: although state-owned enterprises in the SEE8 indicated that they have the highest incidence of tax arrears among ownership groups—almost 15 percent of sales revenues—de novo private firms indicated tax arrears at approximately 13 percent of sales revenues, a figure that is not significantly lower.

# Business Performance and Competition

To assess the competitive performance of firms within SEE, we consider several dimensions across countries, across sectors, and across firm ownership types. We also assess how these performance indicators have changed over time. We then examine profitability, a key element of business performance and econometrically analyze the importance of key factors that determine the observed differentials in firm profitability in the SEE8. In so doing, we evaluate how the competitiveness of market structure accounts for variance in profitability among firms.

## Business Performance Differences across Countries, Sectors, and Firm Ownership Types

BUSINESS PERFORMANCE ACROSS THE SEE8

Figures 3.15 and 3.16 depict average annual changes in sales revenues, exports, employment, investment in fixed assets, and profit margins (measured by the difference between a business's domestic sales price and its operating costs) among the South Eastern European firms participating in the BEEPS.[8] For the period 1995–98, the firms in these countries performed in a generally consistent manner, except that Bulgarian firms, on average, had a lower profit margin for 1998, firms in Bulgaria and Croatia had larger amounts invested in fixed assets, and employment and sales growth in Bosnia and Herzegovina were above average (figure 3.15).

In the more recent period, 1998–2001, however, there has been considerably less uniformity among the countries in almost all performance dimensions except for 2001 average profit margins (figure 3.16). Employment growth jumped in Albania and Moldova, while firms in Albania,

**Figure 3.15 Annual Changes in Sales Revenues, Exports, Employment, Investments in Fixed Assets, and Profit Margins, by Country, 1995–98**
*(percent)*

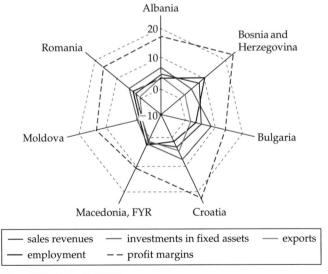

Source: EBRD and World Bank (1999).
Note: Profit margins pertain only to 1998.

**Figure 3.16 Annual Changes in Sales Revenues, Exports, Employment, Investments in Fixed Assets, and Profit Margins, by Country, 1998–2001**
*(percent)*

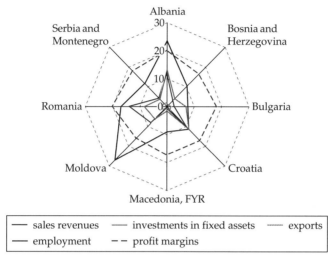

*Source:* EBRD and World Bank (2002).
*Note:* Profit margins pertain only to 2001.

Croatia, and Romania exhibited sizable spurts in sales revenues. Albania and Croatia also experienced above-average growth in investments in fixed assets. Compared with 1995–1998, growth in exports indicated by the surveyed firms diminished significantly in 1998–2001.

CROSS-SECTORAL CHANGES IN BUSINESS PERFORMANCE
Figures 3.17 and 3.18 show performance comparisons across sectors.[9] In 1995–98, growth in investments in fixed assets was particularly high in the various service sectors and in transportation and manufacturing (figure 3.17). Generally, firms indicated high growth rates of employment in these same sectors in the later period (figure 3.18). In fact, there was a general surge in employment in 1998–2001, a key difference from the earlier period. Although the firms in the service sectors and, to a lesser extent, power generation, registered significantly higher profit margins than those in other sectors in 1998, there was more uniformity in profit margins across sectors in 2001. Compared with 1995–98, growth in exports indicated by the firms diminished significantly in 1998–2001.

**Figure 3.17    Annual Changes in Sales Revenues, Exports, Employment, Investments in Fixed Assets, and Profit Margins, by Sector, 1995–98**
*(percent)*

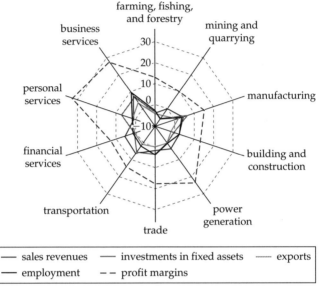

*Source:* EBRD and World Bank (1999).
*Note:* Profit margins pertain only to 1998.

PERFORMANCE ACROSS OWNERSHIP TYPES

Figures 3.19 and 3.20 illustrate that, for almost all the dimensions of performance, the variation across firm ownership types is striking. As expected, the surveyed de novo private firms indicated that they outperformed privatized and state-owned enterprises in all dimensions in 1995–98 (figure 3.19). Curiously, while growth in investments in fixed assets and the profit margins between state-owned enterprises and privatized firms were not significantly different for this period, state-owned enterprises indicated more rapid growth in sales revenues and employment than did privatized firms. In contrast, privatized firms indicated more rapid export growth.

In 1998–2001, again, de novo private firms generally outperformed the two other ownership types (figure 3.20). However, performance differences between privatized firms and state-owned enterprises narrowed considerably along all dimensions. The gap in employment growth rates between de novo private firms and privatized and state-owned firms considerably widened, but the margin in employment growth indicated by state-owned enterprises increased relative to the 1995–98 period.

**Figure 3.18 Annual Changes in Sales Revenues, Exports, Employment, Investments in Fixed Assets, and Profit Margins, by Sector, 1998–2001**
*(percent)*

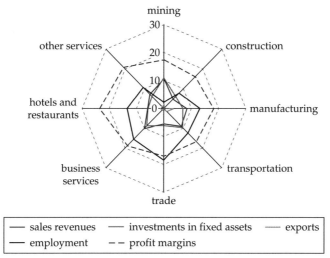

*Source:* EBRD and World Bank (2002).
*Note:* Profit margins pertain only to 2001.

**Figure 3.19 Annual Changes in Sales Revenues, Exports, Employment, Investments in Fixed Assets, and Profit Margins, by Ownership, 1995–98**
*(percent)*

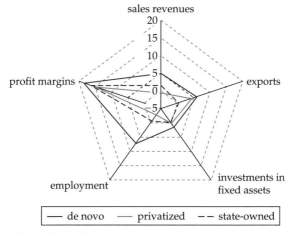

*Source:* EBRD and World Bank (1999).
*Note:* Profit margin pertains only to 1998.

**Figure 3.20    Annual Changes in Sales Revenues, Exports, Employment, Investments in Fixed Assets, and Profit Margins, by Ownership, 1998–2001**
*(percent)*

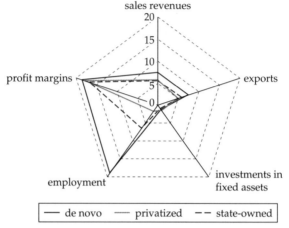

Source: EBRD and World Bank (2002).
Note: Profit margins pertain only to 2001.

## Analysis of the Relationship between Firm Profitability and Market Competitiveness

DISPERSION OF FIRM-LEVEL PROFITABILITY

To begin our analysis of profitability among businesses in SEE, we examine the frequency distribution of corporate profitability by country, by sector, and by firm ownership type. The measure of profitability we use is the ratio of reported profits to sales revenues in 2001, as indicated by each firm covered by the BEEPS.[10] The ratio is measured as a categorical variable in the survey, as described in the key to the set of profitability-distribution histograms in figure 3.21.

Figure 3.21 offers several important insights. First, in all eight countries, there are loss-making firms; the greatest shares of those firms are in Bosnia and Herzegovina (about 11 percent), Bulgaria (about 8 percent), and Croatia (about 4 percent). Moreover, a substantial share of surveyed firms in virtually all the countries (except Romania and Albania) indicated that their profits were zero. Together with the number of firms that indicated losses, this finding shows that business conditions can be difficult for some of the surveyed firms. In every country, the profitability category that contains the greatest proportion of firms indicating a positive profit-to-sales ratio is the 1 to 10 percent range. The distribution of firms in the profitability categories above 10 percent varies significantly among the countries. Some exhibit a relatively smooth downward distribution (for example, Albania, Croatia, Romania, and Serbia and Montenegro), whereas others exhibit a more uneven pattern.

Across most sectors, there is a bit more uniformity in the distribution of firm profitability than across countries. However, the mining and the hotel and restaurant sectors are notable. In the mining sector, a significant proportion of the surveyed firms indicated relatively high profitability, and those indicating negative or zero profits constituted an almost equal proportion. In the hotel and restaurant sector, there is not only a significant share of firms indicating 1 to 10 percent profitability, but also an almost equal share indicating 11 to 20 percent profitability.

In the distribution of profitability across firm ownership types, lossmakers and those earning zero profits are most heavily represented in the

## Figure 3.21 Distribution of Profit-to-Sales Ratio by Country, by Sector, and by Ownership Type

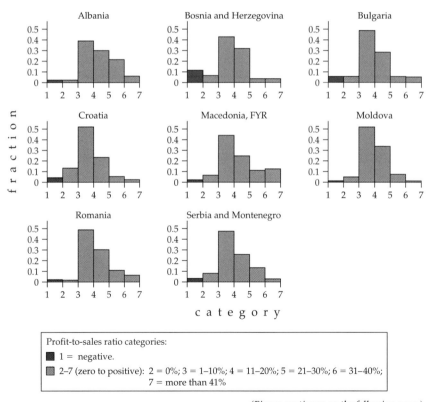

Profit-to-sales ratio categories:

■ 1 = negative.

▨ 2–7 (zero to positive): 2 = 0%; 3 = 1–10%; 4 = 11–20%; 5 = 21–30%; 6 = 31–40%; 7 = more than 41%

*(Figure continues on the following page.)*

## Figure 3.21    (continued)

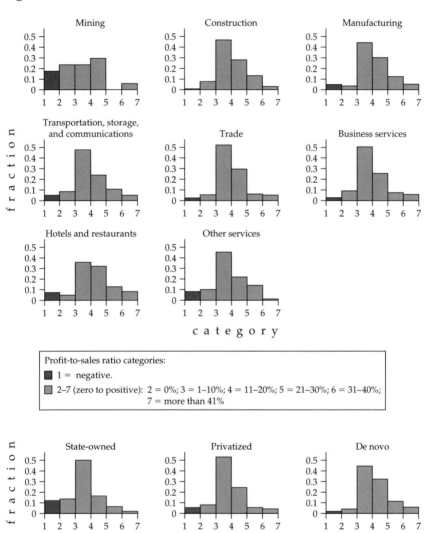

*Source:* EBRD and World Bank (2002).

state-owned enterprise category. Privatized firms have the next largest proportion of firms in those two categories. Beyond that, the distribution of profitability for all ownership types has a declining distribution as profitability rises. De novo private firms exhibit the smoothest downward distribution in this respect.

DETERMINANTS OF FIRM PROFITABILITY
The literature on industrial organization suggests a formulaic model of a set of variables that determine differentials in observed firm profitability. Empirical application of the model can provide insights into the extent to which, when we control for other factors, higher levels of observed profitability are associated with elements of market structure and firm conduct that reflect the potential to exercise market power.[11] Equation 3.1, which draws on this literature, describes the broad components of the basic model we use, which is designed to assess these relationships on a cross-country basis and to account for the economic and institutional features characteristic of transition economies, including the SEE8:

(3.1)   Profitability = f   (horizontal market dominance, extent of
                            integration, barriers to entry, barriers to exit,
                            firm size, ownership type, sector, country-
                            specific characteristics)

Using the firm-level BEEPS data, which cover approximately 1,600 firms across the eight countries, we econometrically estimate several variants of the basic model in which we construct specific variables to represent the broadly defined factors in equation 3.1. In particular, the models we estimate are variants of equation 3.2:

(3.2)   Profit-to-sales ratio = f   (market share, horizontal integration,
                                    vertical integration, ratio of advertising
                                    expenditures to sales, ratio of R&D
                                    expenditures to sales, ratio of total fiscal
                                    subsidies received to sales, number of
                                    employees, sales revenues, ownership cat-
                                    egory, sector category, country location)

Table A.3.1 in the annex to this chapter presents descriptive statistics for the core variables we use (as well as other variables that were constructed and tried in different variants). Generally, the data are for 2001.

Before estimating the multivariate models, we performed simple bivariate correlations between the variables. The complete results of those statistical correlations are contained in table A.3.2 in the annex. In general, the results show statistically significant bivariate correlations between profitability and many of the variables of interest. The results also indicate that there are statistically significant bivariate correlations among the variables that are being posited as the determinants of profitability.

Of course, neither set of results can be interpreted to suggest causal relationships; by their nature, bivariate correlations do not take into account any other factors that may explain differences in the value of a variable. Nonetheless, they do indicate that the basic model we have posited may well be appropriate. They also indicate, however, that because of the correlations among the determinant variables, discerning the statistical effect of a particular variable on profitability may be difficult, due to the collinearity among some of the variables will bias the estimates of their individual explanatory power.[12]

Table 3.27 shows simple multivariate regression results for four variants of equation 3.2.[13] (We estimate both linear and nonlinear natural logarithm forms.) Although the models explain only approximately 10 percent of the variation in profits as a percentage of sales, the results for some of the individual variables are surprisingly strong. In all cases, the estimated coefficient on market share is positive and statistically significant, thus suggesting that, for this sample of South Eastern European businesses, the greater a firm's horizontal dominance in the market, the greater its ability to exercise market power and increase its profits, all other things being equal. Specifically, market share appears to be a robust determinant of profitability after controlling for firm size (whether measured by number of employees or by total sales revenues) and the extent of horizontal integration. Neither firm size nor horizontal integration, however, appears to play a statistically significant role in explaining the firms' indicated profits independent of market share or the other included variables.

The estimated positive and statistically significant coefficients on vertical integration and R&D expenditures as a percentage of sales—as a proxy for technological prowess—also suggest that these factors are important elements of market structure that account for differentials in profitability among the sample of SEE8 firms. In contrast, product differentiation or brand loyalty—as proxied by advertising expenditures as a percentage of sales—does not appear to play a statistically significant role in explaining firms' indicated profits. The estimated coefficients on subsidies—a proxy for hardness of budget constraints—are statistically significant in the nonlinear models. Their negative sign suggests that firms that receive greater levels of subsidies (that is, those that face softer budget constraints) tend to be the less profitable, although the direction of this relationship is not easily discernible from these variables or these models.[14]

The estimated coefficients on the ownership variables are statistically significant and have the expected positive signs. They suggest that de novo private firms register a higher profitability rate than privatized

## Table 3.27   Estimated Determinants of Profitability: Multivariate Ordinary Least Squares Regressions

| | (1)<br>Profit-to-<br>sales ratio | (2)<br>Profit-to-<br>sales ratio | (3)<br>Natural<br>logarithm of<br>profit-to-<br>sales ratio | (4)<br>Natural<br>logarithm of<br>profit-to-<br>sales ratio |
|---|---|---|---|---|
| Constant | 3.3 | 3.302 | 1.129 | 1.111 |
| | (25.06)*** | (22.19)*** | (23.48)*** | (26.95)*** |
| Bosnia and | -0.654 | -0.705 | -0.254 | -0.228 |
| Herzegovina | (4.91)*** | (4.54)*** | (5.20)*** | (5.47)*** |
| Bulgaria | -0.387 | -0.463 | -0.163 | -0.133 |
| | (3.40)*** | (3.55)*** | (3.97)*** | (3.74)*** |
| Croatia | -0.502 | -0.603 | -0.194 | -0.15 |
| | (3.84)*** | (3.95)*** | (4.04)*** | (3.66)*** |
| Macedonia, FYR | -0.267 | -0.431 | -0.137 | -0.1 |
| | (2.08)** | (2.59)*** | (2.61)*** | (2.50)** |
| Moldova | -0.382 | -0.572 | -0.15 | -0.093 |
| | (3.09)*** | (4.05)*** | (3.37)*** | (2.40)** |
| Romania | -0.206 | -0.27 | -0.076 | -0.058 |
| | (1.83)* | (2.10)** | (1.89)* | (1.65)* |
| Serbia and | -0.429 | -0.67 | -0.183 | -0.123 |
| Montenegro | (3.63)*** | (4.02)*** | (3.50)*** | (3.33)*** |
| Employees | 0.005 | | | 0.015 |
| | (0.07) | | | (0.61) |
| Sales revenue | | -0.003 | -0.0003 | |
| (US$ millions, 2001) | | (0.72) | (0.25) | |
| Privatized | 0.271 | 0.298 | 0.122 | 0.113 |
| | (2.46)** | (2.38)** | (3.09)*** | (3.27)*** |
| De novo | 0.625 | 0.606 | 0.216 | 0.223 |
| | (6.61)*** | (5.66)*** | (6.44)*** | (7.52)*** |
| Services | -0.071 | | -0.016 | -0.019 |
| | (1.14) | | (0.69) | (0.98) |
| Vertical integration | 0.003 | 0.006 | 0.002 | 0.001 |
| | (3.01)*** | (3.39)*** | (3.59)*** | (3.14)*** |
| Horizontal integration | -0.001 | 0.008 | 0.002 | -0.001 |
| | (0.35) | (1.48) | (1.04) | (1.13) |
| Subsidies | -0.007 | -0.01 | -0.003 | -0.003 |
| | (1.26) | (1.60) | (1.69)* | (1.85)* |
| Market share | 0.005 | 0.005 | 0.001 | 0.001 |
| | (2.93)*** | (2.53)** | (2.43)** | (2.85)*** |
| Advertising | 0.006 | 0.002 | 0.001 | 0.003 |
| | (1.07) | (0.31) | (0.54) | (1.49) |
| R&D | 0.019 | 0.023 | 0.006 | 0.005 |
| | (3.16)*** | (3.29)*** | (2.73)*** | (2.71)*** |
| Observations | 1337 | 885 | 885 | 1337 |
| R-squared | 0.09 | 0.11 | 0.13 | 0.10 |

Source: Author's estimates using data from EBRD and World Bank (2002).
Note: Absolute value of t-statistics in parentheses.
* significant at 10 percent; ** significant at 5 percent; *** significant at 1 percent.

businesses, which, in turn, register higher profitability rates than state-owned enterprises. However, sector category does not appear to play a statistically significant role in explaining the differences in indicated profitability among this sample of firms independent of the other included variables. Interestingly, the results suggest that there are country-specific factors that explain the variance in firm profitability across the region. In other words, there is intercountry variation in the overall determinants of firm profitability.

## Policies to Enhance Competition in South Eastern Europe

*Need for a Two-Pronged Reform Approach*

The emergence of the private sector in the SEE8, although variable across both the countries and the different sectors and still very much in an evolutionary phase, creates the prospects for increased interenterprise competition in the region. Yet incentives for robust competition in SEE generally remain weak, partly because the countries have not yet undertaken or completed sufficient fundamental, economywide institutional and structural reforms that are integral to market economies. Certainly, as these economywide reforms mature and budget constraints continue to harden—thus ensuring that the prices firms pay for inputs and charge for outputs are in cash, timely, and free of subsidies—the inefficient, large incumbent enterprises will likely decline in importance. Proactive policies—both basic economywide institutional and structural reforms as well as competition policy reforms—are needed in SEE to both foster the horizontal and vertical restructuring of such incumbent firms and to facilitate the entry of new businesses.

Indeed, this two-pronged approach provides a roadmap for reform that encourages greater interenterprise competition in the region. The portion of the reform program that focuses on incumbents would include a stronger institutional competition policy to enforce de-monopolization and disintegration of dominant firms. It would prohibit mergers and acquisitions that reduce the number of sellers and increase structural dominance. It would penalize restrictive business practices, such as collusion, price fixing, and predatory pricing to drive out competitors and deter entrants. Finally, it would protect consumers from unfair trade and false advertising practices. Worldwide, effective implementation of such competition policies has proved difficult. Implementing these policies is particularly challenging in transition economies, especially in those that have also undergone civil strife. Despite the improvements already made in the competition policy regimes of the SEE8 (see chapter 2) and the additional reforms that are suggested below, implementation of reforms in the incumbent firms will take some time. The slow pace of reform is dictated by the significant political economy and social costs that large restructurings entail, especially when potent vested interests are challenged or transition costs for workers are perceived to be large.

The other main component of the reform program for greater competition is reducing structural, institutional, policy, and administrative barriers to entry. This effort can be completed sooner. New entrants increase pressure on privatized companies and on the remaining state-owned enterprise; indeed, they increase pressure on de novo private firms as well. Even when incumbent firms have attained dominance, facilitating entry (or facilitating credible threats of entry) can help instill competitive performance, especially in markets in which sunk costs are relatively small and newcomers can exit relatively cheaply should demand soften. Improving the conditions for entry can thus help make otherwise structurally dominant markets contestable. Entrants are also a source of market expansion and economic growth. They create employment, not only by developing new businesses, but also by providing the absorption capacity as restructured firms shed redundant or underused labor and other resources.

New entrants engender other benefits. They offer modern management techniques and entrepreneurial skills, they usually use new plant and equipment technologies, and they increasingly employ incentive structures that provide for market-oriented corporate governance practices. Reducing entry barriers through greater openness to imports and foreign direct investment (FDI) is especially critical. Yet, though liberalization toward imports and FDI can be the primary tool of competition policy in small open economies, for the larger transition economies, including some of those in SEE, trade and FDI policy reform must be coupled with other policies to enhance structural competition within the domestic market. In fact, empirical evidence bears this observation out even in the tradable sectors. The effect of import competition is significantly muted without competitively structured distribution networks, because distribution services are location specific. Thus, trade and FDI become segmented by geography and transportation costs. Overall, there is accumulating evidence in many transition economies—from small open economies such as the Baltic states to large heterogeneous economies such as China and Russia—that the policy emphasis should be on encouraging entry.[15] This finding is instructive for the eight economies of SEE.

## Reform of the SEE8 Competition Policy Regimes

As we have suggested, greater interenterprise competition in SEE will be achieved, not only from deeper basic structural and institutional reforms, but also from more effective implementation of competition policies.

Chapter 2 indicated that the eight economies, like many Eastern European and former Soviet countries, have modeled (or are modeling) their competition statutes on those found in industrial market economies, including the European Union and the United States. In addition, like most Eastern European and former Soviet countries, the SEE8 have tried to encourage new entry through programs that provide financial support for the development of SMEs. However, SEE8 economies have paid less attention to formulating systematic policies that remove structural, institutional, and policy barriers to entry. Furthermore, they have generally made only modest efforts to confront dominant (and often politically important) firms that are in a position to exercise market power or firms that should exit the market.

Table 3.28 systematically assesses and compares implementation of competition policy in the eight countries between 1997 and 2002 (as part of an assessment of a larger group of approximately 27 transition countries). Although such rankings are affected by subjective judgments and perceptions and, thus, are imperfect, they do convey the relative magnitude of the development of competition policy regimes in the countries.

The data in the table suggest a number of insights. First, all of the SEE8 have made only limited progress in developing and implementing competition policies during the 1997–2002 period. Second, the data also suggest that, though most of the countries either improved their implementation records slightly or maintained the same level, the effectiveness

## Table 3.28   Ranking Effectiveness of Competition Policy Implementation in SEE

| Country | 2002 | 1997 |
|---|---|---|
| Albania | 2− | 2 |
| Bosnia and Herzegovina | 1 | — |
| Bulgaria | 2+ | 2 |
| Croatia | 2+ | 2 |
| Macedonia, FYR | 2 | 1 |
| Moldova | 2 | 2 |
| Romania | 2+ | 2 |
| Serbia and Montenegro | 1 | — |

*Sources:* EBRD (1997, 2002).
*Note:* — = not available; 1 = no competition legislation and institutions; 2 = competition policy legislation and institutions set up; some reduction of entry restrictions or enforcement action on dominant firms; 3 = some enforcement actions to reduce abuse of market power and to promote a competitive environment, including breakups of dominant conglomerates; substantial reduction of entry restrictions; 4 = significant enforcement actions to reduce abuse of market power and to promote a competitive environment; and 4+ = standards and performance typical of advanced industrial economies; effective enforcement of competition policy; unrestricted entry to most markets.

of Albania's implementation actually declined. Finally, the table suggests that Bulgaria, Croatia, and Romania have the most effective regimes when compared with the other countries.

## Principles for a Reform Agenda

The general experience of the SEE8 in developing competitive policies parallels that of most transition countries. Competition policy has focused more on deterring anticompetitive conduct (for example, through establishing price controls) than on dealing with imperfections in market structure. It is not surprising that progress has been slow. Establishing an effective requisite policy regime can involve institution building, public administration reform, training of government personnel in specialized skills, and, most importantly, creating the political will to take on vested interests and rent seekers. Countries that have made progress in implementing competition policy—especially industrial economies such as the EU member states and the United States—have emphasized (a) dismantling excessive horizontal and vertical dominance; (b) implementing clearly defined and widely publicized pro-competitive merger guidelines to prevent anticompetitive mergers; (c) establishing credible and sizable sanctions against collusion and price fixing; (d) reducing significantly the structural, institutional, and policy-induced impediments to new entry; and (e) bolstering rules-based competition policy agencies with effective enforcement authority, ample resources, and a well-trained staff.

Like many transition economies, the SEE8 generally have given special attention to SMEs. Although there is little economic rationale for policy to favor a particular business ownership form or size, at a minimum a policy of neutrality is called for. Thus, a reorientation of the countries' policy regimes is needed to reduce the bias against SMEs and to eliminate barriers to entry. Conversely, in the SEE8, where market failures are often pronounced, SMEs generate singular positive externalities that can address some market failures. As noted earlier, because of their size and their ability to easily fill market niches, SMEs offer a source of flexibility in business development. Flexibility is especially needed in the transition process, in which experimentation is critical. Evidence from a number of transition countries suggests that, whereas initially SMEs tend to occupy the retail or services sectors, over time they can become significant players in manufacturing. Also, SMEs represent employment outlets for a rational downsizing of state-owned enterprises; thus, they increase stability. Finally, growth in the SME sector is characterized less in terms of expansion of incumbent firms (which is typical for growth in the large-firm sector) and more in terms of de novo entry and the introduction of new products and processes.

It is on these grounds that a regime's financial support of SME development can be justified. However, such a regime should have limited objectives, be transitory, and be implemented transparently with minimal opportunities for rent seeking and corruption. It should also be seen as a supplement to other structural reform policies that eliminate barriers to entry and deal with the anticompetitive conduct and structure of incumbent firms. The regime should also promote reform and development of a commercial banking sector. International experience is replete with cautionary examples of promotional programs for small business that often create new bureaucracies that outlive their use.

## Policy Recommendations

### MAKE STRUCTURALLY DOMINANT MARKETS CONTESTABLE FOR NEW ENTRANTS

The case studies and survey data suggest that one area of emphasis in competition policy in SEE should be on dealing with horizontal and vertical structural market imperfections in incumbent industrial firms. Redressing the situation would create economic space for new entrants. The markets with significant concentration and structural dominance should receive priority attention and resources; other markets can be dealt with subsequently.

Moreover, the SEE8 should direct resources at preventing further horizontal and vertical consolidation in markets where concentration and structural dominance are already excessive. In this regard, they should develop more explicit and well-defined merger guidelines that establish general policy parameters for distinguishing between pro-competitive and anti-competitive mergers. These guidelines should be based on similar guidelines used in industrial countries such as the EU member states and the United States. Public announcement of the guidelines is critical to maximize transparency, credibility, and predictability of the policy for mergers and acquisition so that a "market for corporate control" is not hindered (see below). Merger applicants should know ex ante that they must prove that a merger will enhance efficiency and not result in a significant loss of competition. However, a balance must be achieved between, on the one hand, prohibiting excessive enterprise integration and subsequent exercise of market power and, on the other, fostering sufficient integration that permits the technical economies of scale and scope.

### FOSTER PROACTIVE COMPETITIVE RESTRUCTURING OR EXIT OF VALUE-SUBTRACTING INCUMBENTS

In the SEE8, as in other transition economies, relatively little policy emphasis has been directed toward the restructuring, reorganization, bankruptcy or—where necessary—liquidation of insolvent firms. The concerns about the potential social costs of such actions are understandable. Yet with adequate social safety nets in place, such costs can be substantially reduced. International experience provides important lessons about the benefits of hardening budget constraints to engender improved corporate competitiveness from viable firms and to expose firms that are no longer commercially viable. Indeed, viewed from the broader structural reform perspective, the bankruptcy process engenders important benefits. It allows the rechanneling of productive assets to new ventures so that employment can be expanded and new products can be created. Significantly, facilitating the bankruptcy process should not be seen as the sole purview of the government; on the contrary, the main focus should be on strengthening the legal rights of creditors. Hence, the SEE8 must accelerate reform of their banking systems to create one in which banks can make credit, lending, and debt-collection decisions scrupulously on the basis of commercial and risk criteria. Exacting external discipline from firms in the real sector will go far in fostering the competitive restructuring of industry in SEE.

STRENGTHEN RULES-BASED COMPETITION POLICY INSTITUTIONS
Experience in SEE shows that if a competition policy regime is poorly implemented (that is, as a new source of discretionary authority), it may be distorted into an industry promotion regime that selects certain sectors for preferential treatment. Although competition laws in SEE are, for the most part, beginning to approximate international standards, the institutional incentive framework and infrastructure for their implementation remain weak and discretionary. The dominant role of local governments in promoting industrial policy may be the barrier to successful competitive policy. Several remedial steps can be taken. The SEE8 governments should review, at the highest levels, the mission of their current competition policy agencies and should consult international experts to develop recommendations that strengthen their rules-based incentive structures. These agencies can be institutionally strengthened if they are matched with their counterparts in member countries of the Organisation for Economic Co-operation and Development to carry out a series of appraisals on sector competitiveness.

INTRODUCE PROMOTIONAL POLICIES FOR SMES
Support for SMEs is critical in engendering new entry and competition in the region. However, in some countries, current preferences (such as tax concessions) for SMEs are creating widespread distortions by encouraging firms to remain at relatively small levels so that they may enjoy such benefits. Existing firms that are below the minimum efficient scale should

be encouraged to integrate. SME preferences may be considered along a sliding and less graduated scale. However, systems of targeted SME support through subsidized lines of credit can be counterproductive. In the long run, such regimes may undermine market-based reforms of the banking sector and the commercial intermediation role of banks (see chapter 5). The credit lines in some of the countries can breed corruption, particularly in the context of weak property rights. Nongovernmental support programs (sponsored by commercial banks or international donors) can assist by (a) providing equity participation in venture capital and investment funds, (b) funding local banks that provide commercially based credit to SMEs, and (c) cofinancing SME projects with local banks.

ESTABLISH INDEPENDENT MONITORING SYSTEMS AS A CHECK
ON REFORM IMPLEMENTATION
International experience suggests that a reform program to reduce institutional barriers to business operations and growth is most effective when there is independent public monitoring of the program's implementation with strong support at the highest political levels. A specialized unit should be entrusted to monitor and oversee reforms. There should also be widely publicized and anonymous feedback channels that enterprises can use to report violations. For example, monitoring mechanisms in the area of business inspections could include (a) quarterly public reporting by inspection or supervisory agencies, (b) introduction of inspection logs at enterprises and organizations, and (c) establishment of coordinating boards to organize inspection activities (these boards would monitor and sum up the results of all inspections and maintain a database of them).

STRENGTHEN "BEHIND-THE-BORDER" COMPETITION REFORMS TO FACILITATE
REGIONAL TRADE AND FOREIGN DIRECT INVESTMENT
While all but two of the SEE8 (Bosnia and Herzegovina and Serbia and Montenegro) are members of the World Trade Organization, more progress is needed on liberalizing tariff and other nontariff barriers on imported goods and services in the region (see World Bank 2003). Especially important in enhancing trade flows are the "behind-the-border" competition policy reforms that we have analyzed. For example, greater competition in the internal distribution networks within one of the eight countries will facilitate cross-border trade flows, from countries outside the region and among the SEE8 themselves, where discriminatory and preferential arrangements hinder neighborhood trade. Furthermore, to facilitate cross-border flows of FDI, the SEE8 governments should also continue to

align their FDI policy regimes with international best practice in the following ways: (a) national treatment for foreign investors; (b) binding international arbitration for investor-state disputes; (c) substantial reduction in restricted sectors and limitations on FDI in other sectors; (d) freedom for profit remittances; (e) expropriation only for a bona fide public purpose and with prompt, adequate compensation; and (f) an absence of trade-related investment measures. Again, this effort will help encourage FDI not only from countries outside the region, but among the SEE8 themselves.

COMPETE FOR REFORM PROGRESS IN THE REGION

Documenting the progress of competition policy reform among the SEE8 could help create pressure for more effective implementation in the region as a whole. Comparable information on the incidence of policy-based barriers to entry and expansion (such as the average number of days and cost to acquire a specific license or register a new business) would identify countries with a more favorable investment climate to investors domiciled in the region as well as to foreign investors. Such benchmarks of reform, if appropriately disseminated, could allow local enterprises to advocate for more rapid reforms in areas in which their governments are resisting change. They could also permit governments to implement further reform so that the countries can attract more investment and, hence, greater employment and growth. In response to the conclusions of the European Council meeting held in Lisbon in March 2000, the European Commission has launched a "Benchmarking Scoreboard" to include indicators on constraints in starting new enterprises and the average time and costs involved in setting up a company. The intention is to provide an assessment of relative effort, performance, and progress in EU member states and the community as a whole vis-à-vis a number of other countries. This effort will allow member states to act on the basis of shared learning and good practices. In order to jumpstart this type of virtuous reform competition among South Eastern European countries, governments could play an important role in proposing appropriate metrics and a simple survey methodology to assess progress in reform.

ENHANCE PUBLIC EDUCATION EFFORTS TO FOSTER
A CULTURE OF COMPETITION

As part of their competition advocacy mandate, SEE8 governments should undertake public relations and educational initiatives aimed at ensuring that consumers and enterprises, especially start-ups, are aware of the importance of the competitive process and the objectives and content of competition law.

# Statistical Annex

## Table A.3.1 Summary Statistics of BEEPS Data on the SEE8

| Variable | Mean | Minimum | Maximum | Standard Deviation | Number of Observations | Notes |
|---|---|---|---|---|---|---|
| Number of employees (thousands) | 0.14 | 0.002 | 5.5 | 0.43 | 1,625 | |
| Number of competitors | 2.8 | 1.000 | 3 | 0.38 | 1,591 | 1: none, 2: 1–3, 3: 4 or more |
| Market share | 13.3 | 2.500 | 100 | 20.3 | 1,510 | |
| Share of domestic sales to parent company | 10.4 | 0.000 | 100 | 27.6 | 1,638 | |
| Number of establishments | 3.1 | 1.000 | 99 | 8.7 | 1,638 | |
| Subsidies (as a % of annual sales) | 0.75 | 0.000 | 100 | 5.9 | 1,591 | |
| Advertising and marketing (as a % of average annual sales) | 2.7 | 0.000 | 50 | 5.1 | 1,638 | |
| Utilization | 80.5 | 15.000 | 100 | 19.8 | 1,573 | |
| R&D (as a % of average annual sales) | 1.8 | 0.000 | 70 | 5.1 | 1,638 | |
| Price-cost margin | 18.1 | 1.000 | 80 | 10.02 | 1,403 | |
| Capital productivity | 24.6 | 0.008 | 2,300 | 127.9 | 786 | |
| Labor productivity | 16.6 | 0.167 | 200 | 20.8 | 1,047 | |
| Ownership type | 1.6 | 0.000 | 2 | 0.724 | 1,583 | 0: state owned, 1: privatized, 2: de novo |
| Sales revenue (US$ millions) | 1.9 | 0.001 | 250 | 9.9 | 1,051 | |
| Sector | 1.6 | 1.000 | 2 | 0.5 | 1,638 | 1: industry, 2: services |
| Gross profit-to-total sales ratio | 3.5 | 1 | 7 | 1.1 | 1,541 | 1: negative, 2: 0 percent, 3: 1–10 percent, 4: 11–20 percent, 5: 21–30 percent, 6: 31–40 percent, 7: more than 40 percent |

Source: EBRD and World Bank (2002).

## Table A.3.2 Bivariate Correlations of BEEPS Data on the SEE8

| | Number of employees (thousands) | Number of competitors | Market share | Share of domestic sales to parent company | Number of establishments | Subsidies (% of annual sales) | Advertising expenses (% of average annual sales) | Utilization | R&D (% of average annual sales) | Price-cost margin | Capital productivity | Labor productivity | Ownership type | Sales revenue (US$ millions) | Sector | Gross profit-to-total sales ratio |
|---|---|---|---|---|---|---|---|---|---|---|---|---|---|---|---|---|
| Number of employees (thousands) | 1<br>1,625 | | | | | | | | | | | | | | | |
| Number of competitors | -0.2457*<br>0<br>1,579 | 1<br>1,591 | | | | | | | | | | | | | | |
| Market share | 0.2966*<br>0<br>1,499 | -0.4761*<br>0<br>1,509 | 1<br>1,510 | | | | | | | | | | | | | |
| Share of domestic sales to parent company | 0.0057<br>0.8194<br>1,625 | 0.0363<br>0.148<br>1,591 | 0.0457***<br>0.076<br>1,510 | 1<br>1,638 | | | | | | | | | | | | |
| Number of establishments | 0.4059*<br>0<br>1,625 | -0.0929*<br>0.0002<br>1,591 | 0.1229*<br>0<br>1,510 | 0.0403<br>0.1029<br>1,638 | 1<br>1,638 | | | | | | | | | | | |
| Subsidies (% of annual sales) | 0.0790*<br>0.0017<br>1,579 | -0.0711*<br>0.0052<br>1,545 | 0.0841*<br>0.0013<br>1,468 | 0.0365<br>0.1451<br>1,591 | 0.0068<br>0.785<br>1,591 | 1<br>1,591 | | | | | | | | | | |
| Advertising and marketing (% of average annual sales) | 0.0069<br>0.7804<br>1,625 | 0.0101<br>0.6868<br>1,591 | 0.0378<br>0.1418<br>1,510 | 0.0075<br>0.7605<br>1,638 | 0.036<br>0.1448<br>1,638 | 0.0014<br>0.9559<br>1,591 | 1<br>1,638 | | | | | | | | | |
| Utilization | -0.0175<br>0.4887<br>1,565 | -0.0174<br>0.4964<br>1,527 | -0.0037<br>0.8875<br>1,450 | 0.1102*<br>0<br>1,573 | 0.0267<br>0.2903<br>1,573 | -0.0022<br>0.9327<br>1,534 | 0.0428***<br>0.0896<br>1,573 | 1<br>1,573 | | | | | | | | |

(Table continues on the following page.)

# Table A.3.2 (continued)

| | Number of employees (thousands) | Number of competitors | Market share | Share of domestic sales to parent company | Number of establishments | Subsidies (% of annual sales) | Advertising expenses (% of average annual sales) | Utilization | R&D (% of average annual sales) | Price-cost margin | Capital productivity | Labor productivity | Ownership type | Sales revenue (US$ millions) | Sector | Gross profit-to-total sales ratio |
|---|---|---|---|---|---|---|---|---|---|---|---|---|---|---|---|---|
| R&D (% of average annual sales) | 0.0855* 0.0006 1,625 | -0.0638** 0.0109 1,591 | 0.0701* 0.0064 1,510 | -0.0223 0.3678 1,638 | 0.0389 0.1155 1,638 | 0.0052 0.8346 1,591 | 0.1825* 0 1,638 | 0.0044 0.8613 1,573 | 1 1,638 | | | | | | | |
| Price-cost margin | 0.0052 0.8477 1,392 | -0.0215 0.4262 1,372 | 0.0712* 0.0098 1,315 | -0.0218 0.4136 1,403 | -0.01 0.708 1,403 | 0.0038 0.8876 1,376 | 0.0738* 0.0057 1,403 | 0.0356 0.1884 1,365 | 0.0378 0.1567 1,403 | 1 1,403 | | | | | | |
| Capital productivity | 0.052 0.146 783 | 0.0434 0.2327 758 | 0.0119 0.7482 727 | -0.0261 0.4658 786 | 0.1038* 0.0036 786 | 0.0415 0.2483 775 | -0.0128 0.7199 786 | 0.0941* 0.0095 759 | -0.0093 0.7946 786 | -0.0241 0.5224 706 | 1 786 | | | | | |
| Labor productivity | -0.0449 0.1465 1,047 | 0.0002 0.9959 1,010 | 0.0208 0.5189 968 | 0.0498 0.107 1,047 | 0.0404 0.1919 1,047 | -0.0515*** 0.0983 1,030 | 0.0772** 0.0124 1,047 | 0.0989* 0.0016 1,018 | 0.0134 0.6656 1,047 | -0.0385 0.2417 928 | 0.0474 0.1849 783 | 1 1,047 | | | | |
| Ownership type | -0.3442* 0 1,571 | 0.2255* 0 1,539 | -0.2529* 0 1,460 | 0.0269 0.285 1,583 | -0.1585* 0 1,583 | -0.2186* 0 1,536 | 0.0547* 0.0296 1,583 | 0.1142* 0 1,519 | -0.0589** 0.0192 1,583 | 0.0591** 0.0295 1,356 | -0.0052 0.8861 757 | 0.1085* 0.0006 1,009 | 1 1,583 | | | |
| Sales revenue (US$ millions) | 0.5838* 0.0000 1,047 | -0.2091* 0.0000 1,014 | 0.2212* 0.0000 971 | 0.0451 0.1442 1,051 | 0.4259* 0.0000 1,051 | 0.0002 0.9959 1,034 | -0.0025 0.9367 1,051 | -0.0213 0.4971 1,021 | 0.0198 0.5220 1,051 | -0.0139 0.6729 931 | 0.025 0.4846 786 | 0.1632* 0.0000 1,047 | -0.1852* 0.0000 1,013 | 1 1,051 | | |
| Sector | -0.1144* 0 1,625 | 0.063** 0.012 1,591 | -0.1089* 0 1,510 | -0.0214 0.3873 1,638 | 0.0249 0.3143 1,638 | 0.0423*** 0.0915 1,591 | 0.0752* 0.0023 1,638 | 0.0723* 0.0041 1,573 | -0.0778* 0.0016 1,638 | 0.0346 0.195 1,403 | 0.0852* 0.0168 786 | 0.1152* 0.0002 1,047 | 0.0806* 0.0013 1,583 | -0.0527*** 0.0875 1,051 | 1 1,638 | |
| Gross profit-to-total sales ratio | -0.0629** 0.0139 1,532 | 0.0002 0.993 1,499 | 0.0325 0.2198 1,430 | 0.0683* 0.0073 1,541 | -0.0301 0.2369 1,541 | -0.0691* 0.0075 1,499 | 0.0659* 0.0096 1,541 | 0.1467* 0 1,489 | 0.0638* 0.0122 1,541 | 0.3554* 0 1,338 | 0.0071 0.8455 757 | 0.0149 0.6368 1,003 | 0.2313* 0 1,488 | -0.0232 0.463 1,005 | -0.034 0.1821 1,541 | 1 1,541 |

Source: EBRD and World Bank (2002).
*significant at 10 percent; **significant at 5 percent; ***significant at 1 percent.

# Endnotes

1. This chapter focuses on competition in the noninfrastructure sectors—largely manufacturing, mining, construction, and services—of the South Eastern European economies.

2. Of course, reforms that bring about greater international trade and investment and reforms that enhance structural competition are mutually reinforcing, as discussed in more detail later in this chapter.

3. A companion World Bank study is under way examining reforms in social protection in SEE.

4. In addition to assessing the relative *number* of firms, we examine the average sales revenue by ownership category to get a sense of the relative *size* of these different private sector firm types. Unfortunately, data do not exist to assess the relative value added to the national economy by firms of different ownership forms. However, later in the chapter we compare performance across ownership categories (among other traits).

5. For a description of the BEEPS sample study design, see the EBRD (2002) and chapter 1 of this book.

6. For products that economically trade in *local* markets, using market share data defined on the assumption that the relevant geographic market is *national* in scope, market shares will be biased downward; for products that economically trade *internationally*, the indicated market shares will be biased upward.

7. We should note that, in business surveys worldwide, virtually all firms complain about high tax rates. Yet many case studies of firms do not find that tax rates rank high enough to be serious barriers to investment decisions. Therefore, it is unclear if participants simply see a survey as a forum to air their tax complaints.

8. Only seven South Eastern European countries were covered in BEEPS1.

9. The sectoral breakdown for BEEPS1, which asked questions on performance in the 1995–98 period, is not strictly the same as that used in BEEPS2.

10. In the BEEPS data, the profit-to-sales ratio is a better measure of profitability than the profit margin measure. The latter measures the difference between sales price and operational costs only. Also, fewer firms replied to the question about profit margin than to the profit-to-sales ratio question. Finally, only in the profit-to-sales ratio question were firms able to note whether they had losses; hence that measure yields a more accurate profile of performance than would a profit distribution truncated at zero.

11. The literature is vast. For a sampling, see Waldman and Jensen (2001) and Scherer and Ross (1990).

12. The problem of multicollinearity is common in models of this type, and certain corrective procedures can be undertaken to reduce its effect and the biased estimates it produces.

13. As noted in table 3.27, ordinary least squares regressions are used. This simple procedure does not correct for potential bias that may be present in the model

specification and the variables used in the BEEPS. However, in light of the rough quality of the survey data, more sophisticated procedures are difficult to justify.

14. That is, the direction of the relationship between profitability and subsidies may be two-way, which would call for a more sophisticated estimation procedure.

15. With regard to China's enterprise reform program, see, for example, Broadman (2001a). For Russia, see, for example, Broadman (2000). For a comparison of China's and Russia's approach to enterprise reform, see Broadman (2001b).

# References

Broadman, Harry. 2000. "Reducing Structural Dominance and Entry Barriers in Russian Industry." *Review of Industrial Organization* 2: 155–75.

———. 2001a. "The Business(es) of the Chinese State." *World Economy* 24(7): 849–75.

———. 2001b. "Lessons from Corporatization and Corporate Governance Reform in Russia and China." Paper presented at the Asian Development Bank International Conference on Corporate Reform, Hanoi, Vietnam, October 2001. Available online at http://papers.ssrn.com/sol3/papers.cfm?abstract_id=292599.

———, ed. 2002. *Unleashing Russia's Business Potential: Lessons from the Regions for Building Market Institutions.* Washington, D.C.: World Bank.

Djankov, Simeon, and Peter Murrell. 2002. "Enterprise Restructuring in Transition: A Quantitative Survey." *Journal of Economic Literature* 40(3):739–92.

EBRD (European Bank for Reconstruction and Development). 1997. *Transition Report 1997: Enterprise Performance and Growth.* London.

———. 2002. *Transition Report 2002: Agriculture and Rural Transition.* London.

———. 2003. *Transition Report 2003: Integration and Regional Cooperation.* London.

EBRD and World Bank. 1999. *Business Environment and Enterprise Performance Survey* (BEEPS1). London and Washington, D.C. Data available online at http://info.worldbank.org/governance/beeps.

———. 2002. *Business Environment and Enterprise Performance Survey* (BEEPS2). London and Washington, D.C. Data available online at http://info.worldbank.org/governance/beeps2002.

Scherer, Frederick M., and David Ross. 1990. *Industrial Market Structure and Economic Performance*, 3rd ed. New York: Houghton-Mifflin.

Waldman, Don E., and Elizabeth J. Jensen. 2001. *Industrial Organization: Theory and Practice*, 2nd ed. Reading, Mass.: Addison-Wesley.

World Bank. 2002. *Transition: The First Ten Years: Analysis and Lessons for Eastern Europe and the Former Soviet Union.* Washington, D.C.

———. 2003. *Trade Policies and Institutions in the Countries of SEE in the EU Stabilization and Association Process.* Washington, D.C.

# 4
# Access to Regulated
# Infrastructure Utilities

The current regulations and their enforcement across the eight South Eastern European countries (SEE8) that are the focus of this study do not appear to reflect recent international trends toward rules that increasingly support competition, the unbundling of services, and more open entry and exit. The SEE8 need to create appropriate incentives for innovation both by service providers and by business users. Thus, clear priorities for these governments are to break up monopolies, to privatize the existing infrastructure networks, and to introduce competitive forces where "natural" monopoly conditions no longer exist. Regulation should be restricted to those areas where competition alone is not likely to generate desirable outcomes.

Ensuring the appropriateness of the regulatory rules matters enormously. Achieving this goal will remove one significant obstacle to the development and expansion of business as well as to regional trade and integration. Barriers related to infrastructure are particularly relevant for the SEE8 because those countries are in the process of overcoming the severe infrastructure bottlenecks caused by conflict and by inadequate maintenance. Developing predictable and transparent regulatory frameworks would ensure users' access to competitively priced, high-quality services and would engender investment in the infrastructure sectors.

This chapter discusses the state of regulated infrastructure utilities in the SEE8. Using evidence from two *Business Environment and Enterprise Performance Survey* (BEEPS) reports (EBRD and World Bank 1999, 2002) and from case studies, we discuss the assessment by the enterprises of the accessibility and quality of infrastructure service. We then explore the relevance of broader regulatory reforms, including private sector involvement and independence of rulemaking. Next, we analyze the role of infrastructure development in fostering investment in the real sector and in fostering regional integration. We thus explore the links between the providing of infrastructure services at more competitive terms and greater competitiveness in the real sector (particularly among intensive users of infrastructure sectors). Finally, we present some policy recommendations.

## Tariffs, Access, and Quality of Service across Countries

To better understand the extent to which infrastructure represents a significant obstacle to the development and growth of enterprises, we must consider the current condition of provision of infrastructure services themselves, related to terms of access, tariffs, and quality.

### Infrastructure as Barriers to Entry

Uneven access to infrastructure services can act as a powerful barrier to entry for all enterprises, but particularly for smaller ones, which are more vulnerable to anticompetitive practices that are in many cases related to the uneven delivery of infrastructure services. Complaints by business users to competition and regulatory agencies about the price and quality of the infrastructure services, as well as about discriminatory access, are well documented. In turn, there have also been several cases of anticompetitive acts by dominant infrastructure service providers toward smaller alternative providers. Thus, clear evidence exists of the lack of a competitive environment in the providing of infrastructure services. Some of the SEE8 competition and regulatory authorities have been handling an increasing number of complaints. Over the past few years, some of the top fines imposed by the competition agencies related to severe abuse of dominant position by infrastructure providers at the expenses of smaller providers and business and residential users.[1]

The results of the European Bank for Reconstruction and Development (EBRD) and World Bank *Business Environment and Enterprise Performance Surveys* (BEEPS1 and BEEPS2, carried out in 1999 in 2002, respectively) allow us to analyze the assessment of infrastructure services in terms of quality and responsiveness to enterprises' needs, both across time and across countries. As reported in chapters 2 and 3, one of the key messages arising from a comparison of data across time is that enterprise perceptions have significantly improved over time in all of the SEE8. With the notable exceptions of Albania and the former Yugoslav Republic of Macedonia, where progress appears to be minor, the countries report a major improvement in infrastructure services (see figure 2.5 in chapter 2). This improvement also reflects the success of the major reconstruction efforts under the concerted efforts of the Stability Pact. Despite such progress, however, Albania remains the country where infrastructure is the most problematic barrier to entry and expansion. Official data confirm the progress across the main infrastructure sectors according to some performance indicators,

## Table 4.1    Infrastructure Performance Indicators

| | Telecommunication fixed-line penetration[a] | | Railway productivity[b] | | Electricity tariff[c] (%) | |
|---|---|---|---|---|---|---|
| | 1999 | 2002 | 1999 | 2002 | 1999 | 2002 |
| Albania | 3.7 | 5.5 | 32.1 | 39.8 | 3.5 | 3.8 |
| Bosnia and Herzegovina | 9.6 | 12 | 153.7 | 267.2 | 5.1 | 6.2 |
| Bulgaria | 34.2 | 37.5 | 65.3 | 65.9 | 2.8 | 3.7 |
| Croatia | 36.5 | 38.8 | 52.9 | 78.1 | 6.8 | 9.8 |
| Serbia and Montenegro | 21.4 | 23.3 | 25.1 | 45.1 | — | 2.9 |
| Macedonia, FYR | 23.4 | 26.4 | 66.7 | 59.2 | 3.3 | 4.7 |
| Moldova | 12.7 | 14.6 | 15.6 | 27.5 | 4.4 | 5.6 |
| Romania | 16.7 | 18.4 | 46.0 | 50.4 | 4.7 | 5.1 |

Source: EBRD (2003).
Note: — = not available.
a. Number of main lines per 100 inhabitants.
b. Derived from the ratio between the number of traffic units (passengers/kilometer + freight tone/kilometer) and the total number of railway employees.
c. Average retail tariff in U.S. cents per kilowatt-hour.

including telecommunication fixed-line penetration rates, railway productivity, and electricity tariffs (see table 4.1).

As discussed in chapter 2, on the one hand, there has been some progress in the telecommunication sector, although a number of countries, including Albania and Bosnia and Herzegovina, still lag behind. On the other hand, Bulgaria and Croatia are reaching penetration rates close to 40 percent, which compare very favorably with the average rate in Central Eastern European economies. Railway productivity is also recording quite remarkable progress in countries that have been implementing major restructuring projects over the past few years (for example, Bosnia and Herzegovina). In the power sector, tariff reforms can be especially challenging because they encounter strong political resistance and because, for a full cost recovery, steep price increases are required. On the one hand, Albania, Bulgaria, and Serbia and Montenegro still have very low tariffs. On the other hand, prices in Croatia have been increasing substantially, reaching a level comparable with those found in the Central Eastern European countries.

The BEEPS2 allows us to disentangle the different perception of enterprises across each of the infrastructure sectors, including telecommunication, electricity, and transportation, as represented in figure 4.1.

For the overall region, the power sector is perceived as having the most severe barriers to entry and expansion of enterprises, followed by the

## Figure 4.1     Infrastructure-Related Barriers by Sectors

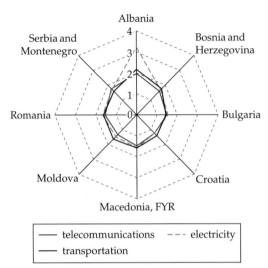

Source: EBRD and World Bank (2002).
Note: Ratings range from 0 (indicating the lowest obstacle) to 4 (indicating the highest obstacle).

transportation and telecommunication sectors. The overall result is driven by Albania (together with Bulgaria and Romania), where electricity is perceived as the most relevant obstacle to business entry and expansion. This finding is a result of an electricity crisis that has been affecting the country since 2000. Not surprisingly, differences in perception across the infrastructure sectors are also greatest in Albania.

For many other countries—Bosnia and Herzegovina, Croatia, FYR Macedonia, and Moldova—transportation is considered the most relevant infrastructure-related barrier to entry. In most of these countries, the road network has been disrupted by war and also suffers from severe underinvestment. In addition, alternative modes of transportation still need substantial restructuring.

Finally, for Serbia and Montenegro, telecommunication represents the most relevant barrier to entry and expansion. This situation is undoubtedly related to the highly politicized and criticized privatization of the telecommunication operator under the Slobodan Milosevic era.

### Infrastructure as Barriers to Exit

Before analyzing in more detail how access to infrastructure services affects enterprises across other dimensions such as ownership, size, and location, let us explore whether access to infrastructure is a relevant

## Figure 4.2   Infrastructure-Related Arrears

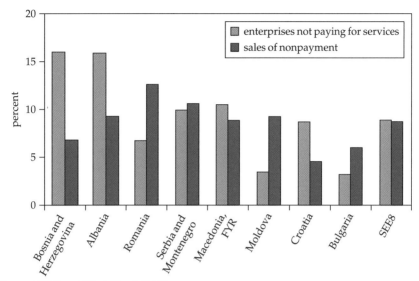

*Source:* EBRD and World Bank (2002).

source of exit barriers. For more details about the concept of barriers to exit, see chapter 3. Here, we explore only the extent to which nonpayment of utility bills represents a relevant source of enterprises arrears, both in economywide terms (such as percentage of enterprises not paying for infrastructure services) and in terms of severity of the arrears problems for enterprises (such as percentage of sales).

Figure 4.2 provides strong evidence of problems of arrears, which affect almost 10 percent of enterprises and account for approximately 10 percent of enterprises' sales. The region is also characterized by significant cross-country variations. Moreover, the countries where the problem is the most widespread (in terms of percentage of enterprises in the economy characterized by arrears) are not always the ones for which utility arrears account for the highest value in terms of percentage of sales. The highest percentages of enterprises with utility arrears are the western Balkan states—particularly Albania and Bosnia and Herzegovina. The lowest percentages are in Bulgaria and (surprisingly) Moldova. The most serious problems of utility arrears in terms of percentage of sales are in Moldova, Romania, and Serbia and Montenegro; the less serious problems are in Bosnia and Herzegovina, Bulgaria, and Croatia.

Figure 4.3 reports the percentage of enterprises affected by arrears across the different ownership classes. It presents strong evidence of how

## Figure 4.3    Infrastructure-Related Arrears across Ownership Classes

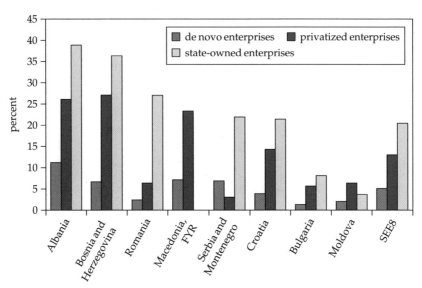

*Source:* EBRD and World Bank (2002).

privatized and state-owned enterprises are by far the greatest beneficiaries of soft budget constraints for all countries. It also confirms in this context the presence of an uneven playing field tilted against start-ups. Indeed, 13 percent and 20 percent of privatized and state-owned enterprises, respectively, are not paying infrastructure providers on time, compared with only 5 percent of de novo enterprises. The uneven playing field across different ownership classes also emerges quite strongly from the case studies (box 4.1).

To illustrate the extent to which intra-infrastructure utility arrears are reinforced, we report the case of Moldova. The main debtors of Union Fenosa, which owns three of the Moldovan electricity distribution companies, include Apa-Canal (the water company) and Termocom (the heating company). Apa-Canal and Termocom are, in turn, suffering from nonpayment of water and heat bills by consumers of all categories—mainly state-owned enterprises, but also private ones. It should be noted that disconnection of electrical power is technically easy and can be carried out without the consumer's presence. The same does not hold true for disconnection of water and heat supply. Hence, Apa-Canal and Termocom have become in arrears to Union Fenosa. In turn, the electricity distribution companies raised tariffs. Business and residential consumers tend to prioritize payment of electricity bills over payment of

---

**Box 4.1 Uneven Playing Field in the Energy Sector**

The most recurrent problems related to utilities' arrears are in the energy sector. Many of the enterprises interviewed for the case studies, particularly those that were energy-intensive users such as the metal-producing enterprises, complained that electricity providers face collection problems from major loss-making enterprises, especially those in the state-owned sector. However, the electricity providers never stop supplying electricity or change the terms of the supply to these companies. Instead, the electricity providers apply discriminatory rules to private sector enterprises, often interrupting services or changing arbitrarily the terms of the contract.

Some private enterprises in FYR Macedonia reported that they had experienced business disputes with the electricity company related to violations of the service agreement. According to the reports, the electricity company raised its prices yet lowered the quality of service by supplying lower voltage (especially during the very cold winters). These violations often forced the energy-intensive enterprises to stop production. After failed attempts to resolve the disputes through bilateral negotiations, the disputes were finally resolved through the courts by the conclusion of a new agreement.

An enterprise in Bosnia and Herzegovina that decided to generate its own heat was reluctant to sell the electricity it produced to the municipality in which it was resident because the municipality would not be capable of collecting payments from its customers on time. Hence, the enterprise felt that the municipality would have difficulty making its own payments.

Finally, enterprises in Albania—the country characterized by the highest percentage of state-owned enterprises not paying their utility bills (close to 40 percent)—identify the interference of politics in soft agreements between the electricity provider and the state-owned managers as the key source of the severe problems that led to the electricity crisis in that country (see also box 4.3).

---

water and heat bills, thereby reinforcing a vicious circle of nonpayment at the expense of the water and heating companies.

Similar arrears problems affect Moldovagas, the country's natural gas provider. One of its main debtors—Chisinau Glass Works—owes Moldovagas an amount corresponding to one and one-half years of consumption of natural gas. The debt accumulation peaked when Chisinau Glass Works changed ownership and was assigned to the government administration. According to reports, Chisinau Glass Works has a huge amount of unsold goods in stock, but the disconnection of gas supply to the enterprise (which operates on an uninterrupted production cycle) would so disrupt Chisinau's furnaces (which have a capacity of 840 metric tons) that the factory would have to be shut down.

The problems are worsened by officials of the city of Chisinau, who are reluctant to increase water and heat tariffs. This lack of action is driving the water and heat providers close to insolvency. Only in December 2002, after a long debate, did the city's administration approve tariff increases for residential users of water and heat. These increases were accompanied by tariff reductions for economic entities. However, in anticipation of a local election in spring 2003, the Chisinau City Council rescinded the tariff increases.

Official data also confirm the extent of arrears problems in the energy sector. Cash collection (that is, the percentage of total cash collected) averages only 67.5 percent, and commercial losses (defined as nonbilled consumption) average only 20 percent, as shown in table 4.2. This situation affects the real sector. Cash collection is particularly low for industrial consumers, and consequently, incentives for industrial restructuring are limited.

The problem of payment discipline in the power sector is reinforced by severe underpricing. Under central planning, power tariffs were low relative to long-run costs, and there was a tendency to consume power beyond what was actually required to meet production and consumption needs. This situation was sustainable given the existence of implicit and explicit subsidies in the form of low primary energy prices and budgetary transfers to the power industry. The inability of budget-constrained governments to increase support—coupled with their failure to increase tariffs to cost-recovery levels—has undermined the financial viability of the power sector throughout the region. The extent of underpricing in the power sector is illustrated in table 4.3. The optimal pricing rule that is applied to transition economies, where demand is stagnant and excess capacity often exists, sets the optimal price somewhere

### Table 4.2    Power Cash Collection and Commercial Losses, 2002

| Country | Cash collection (%) | Commercial losses (%) |
|---|---|---|
| Albania | 71 | 37 |
| Bosnia and Herzegovina | 86 | 25 |
| Bulgaria | 95 | 10 |
| Croatia | 100 | 5 |
| Macedonia, FYR | 75 | — |
| Moldova | 90 | 35 |
| Romania | 95 | 5 |
| Serbia and Montenegro | 85 | 20 |

Source: EBRD (2003).
Note: — = not available.

## Table 4.3 Power Tariffs in the SEE8, 2002

| Country | Residential tariff (%) | Industrial tariff (%) |
|---|---|---|
| Albania | 3.5 | 3.2 |
| Bosnia and Herzegovina | 5.7 | 6.2 |
| Bulgaria | 3.7 | 3.9 |
| Croatia | 7.3 | 6.7 |
| Macedonia, FYR | 4.7 | 4.7 |
| Moldova | 5.6 | — |
| Romania | 4.2 | 3.9 |
| Serbia and Montenegro | 3.9 | 3.9 |

Source: EBRD (2003).
Note: — = not available.

between marginal operating cost and long-run marginal cost (LRMC). The price could be expected to rise above marginal operating cost and toward LRMC as demand picks up and investments are undertaken. If the LRMC is equal to US$0.08 per kilowatt-hour,[2] then the mean ratio of residential tariffs to LRMC across the countries is 4.4, a low figure by Western standards. In addition to the widespread problem of under-pricing, the difference in prices among consumer groups can also be problematic. Across all the SEE8, with the notable exceptions of Albania, Croatia, and Romania, industrial tariffs are higher than or equal to residential tariffs. This situation contrasts sharply with that in Western Europe, where industrial tariffs are on average two-thirds of the price charged to households, reflecting the relative costs of supplying these two customer categories.

Moreover, the case studies also show that prices do not yet reflect energy use (see box 4.2). Our analysis thus far led us to identify the main challenges facing the utility sectors in terms of barriers to entry and exit. These challenges are to increase prices, to reduce the cross-subsidies between customer categories, and to improve payments discipline. Meeting them will also reduce the governments' utility liabilities (particularly in the energy sector), which, in turn, will reduce budgetary and external debt pressures. Investments will also become economically viable on a nonsovereign basis if the challenges are met. Financing will become available for new power- and heat-generating stations and for upgrading of transmission and distribution networks, which will result in declining losses and improvements in system security. Industry will have incentives to improve energy efficiency and to move away from energy-intensive production methods. In designing tariff increases and broader tariff reforms, countries must take into account the issue of affordability. It is crucial to consider adequately the social effects of tariff

---

### Box 4.2    Utility Pricing

Case studies for Bosnia and Herzegovina, the country for which the percentage difference between industrial and residential users is the highest
(about 50 percent), reveal that users must pay a fixed sum for electricity.
This sum is based on a fixed number of kilowatt-hours, which they must
pay for regardless of the amount of electricity they actually consume.
Enterprises normally use only a small percentage (ranging from one-third
to one-half) of the electricity that they pay for. However, if an enterprise
should consume more than the fixed number of kilowatt-hours, then each
additional kilowatt-hour is charged at a much higher rate.

Also, enterprises in Bulgaria complain that, because of lack of metering,
they are not able to get a discount for electricity used in off-peak hours.
Although some Bulgarian enterprises have requested that the power company establish a separate meter for off-peak consumption, they are still
waiting for a response.

Even in countries such as Croatia where pricing reforms are at an
advanced stage, enterprises complain about not being given the opportunity to negotiate prices. Croatian enterprises find the rate of electricity high and rising as a result of the monopoly power of Hrvatska
Elektroprivreda, the country's electricity provider. The quality of the service is satisfactory, but in many cases, enterprises are forced to operate
only at night because of the high price of electricity during the day. As a
result, the capacity of such energy-intensive enterprises has decreased
tremendously (as much as six times).

---

increases on consumers and to ensure that an appropriate social
protection system is in place to mitigate the impact on the socially vulnerable consumers.[3]

## Access to and Reliability of Infrastructure Services

Let us now turn to quantitative measure of access to and reliability (or
quality) of infrastructure services across countries. Figure 4.4 reports the
average number of days needed to get connected to main fixed telecommunication lines and electricity services. According to the sample of
surveyed enterprises in 2002, waiting times for fixed-line telecommunication for the overall South Eastern European region are more than three
times higher than those for electricity, averaging 13 days and 4 days,
respectively. The regional averages hide significant cross-country variations and the presence of outliers. Surveyed firms in Albania and Serbia
and Montenegro represent the two main outliers respectively for

## Figure 4.4    Waiting Times for Infrastructure Services

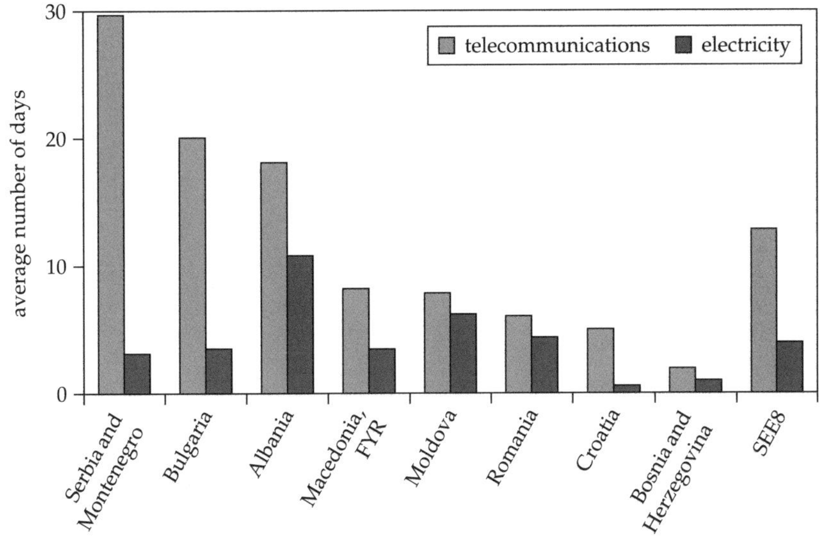

Source: EBRD and World Bank (2002).

telecommunication and for electricity services, with waiting times equal to 10 and 30 days, respectively.

Evidence from the case studies in Bulgaria indicates that even getting service hookups for telecommunication, electricity, or gas supplies often requires side payments to the utilities and the regulators. Some enterprises have resorted to stealing service from neighboring firms or renting space within existing firms' warehouses just to be able to get utility service. Albanian enterprises report that fixed telecommunication lines are often stolen or someone illegally connects to the lines. When enterprises call the main telephone provider to repair a line, the technician comes immediately, because making repairs is a way to generate revenue. However, it is extremely difficult to get new telephone lines, even by paying bribes. One interviewed Albanian enterprise filed an application for 40 telephone lines in one of its buildings and has not received an answer for more than a year. To tackle the problem of access to utility services, a combination of secondary legislation and investment is required. With respect to secondary legislation, connection targets can be included in the conditions for licensing the utilities, and investment to increase network capacity should be pursued in places where it is significantly constrained. Access to infrastructure utilities can also increase if tariffs are raised. Thus, utilities will have incentives to connect additional customers because this expansion yields a source of additional revenues.

## Figure 4.5    Outages for Infrastructure Services

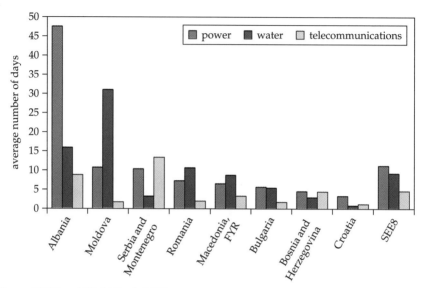

*Source:* EBRD and World Bank (2002).

At the same time, the quality of infrastructure service is poor. Figure 4.5 reports the average number of days in 2001 when enterprises experienced major utilities outages. The figure covers power outages, insufficient water supply, and unavailable mainline telecommunication services. Across the region, power outages stand out as a major problem. Power outages average more than 11 days per year, followed by water outages (9 days) and telecommunication outages (5 days). These figures show that telecommunication services, though characterized by higher waiting times, are on average more reliable. The opposite holds for electricity services. The three countries most affected on average by utility outages—Albania, Moldova, and Serbia and Montenegro—are affected by problems in different utilities sectors. In the case of Albania, the electricity sector is the most unreliable because of the electricity crisis affecting the country, which is discussed in more detail in box 4.3.

Case studies confirm the extent of disruption caused by the electricity crisis. For example, one of the interviewed companies in Albania reported that, in the winter months of January and February 2002, the plant was out of power for 1.5 months; the total outage time was 3 months in 2001. In contrast, Moldova is the country characterized by the highest water outages because it lacks an institutional framework for water resource management and experiences underinvestment aggravated by underpricing, as noted earlier.

## Box 4.3    Electricity Crisis in Albania

Albania has been facing a severe electricity crisis since the summer of 2000, as a result of the chronic failure to curb illegal use of electricity, the severe extent of arrears (deriving from unpaid bills), and the deteriorating hydrological conditions on the predominantly hydropower-based system. Losses of power transmission and distribution experienced by the dominant energy provider, Korporata Elektro-energjetike Shqiptare (KESH), equaled 43.4 percent of the electricity KESH supplied to the grid. About 20 percent of these losses were attributed to theft. KESH's collection ratio was as low as 61.5 percent. Electricity was sold at an average price per kilowatt-hour that was less than the import price (including tax).

In 2000, KESH succeeded to earn an after-tax profit, but only because it received a subsidy of US$25 million from the government for the purchase of imported electricity. In 2001, with steeply increased electricity imports and a proportionally lower import subsidy, KESH incurred substantial losses. In late 2000, the government developed a 2-year action plan to tackle the critical issues. The plan included reducing electricity losses, improving collection, and reducing demand. Efforts to carry out the plan were successful in the first years, as shown by the end of 2002 power losses, which were reduced to 30 percent, and bill collection, which improved to 84.5 percent, both above the targeted levels. The action plan has been updated for 2003–04 with a renewed emphasis on eliminating illegal connections in specific areas that have been identified (about 30,000), enforcing the penal code related to theft of electricity through prosecution of 5,000 cases, and installing meters. The action plan also includes new incentive schemes linked to financial performance objectives for KESH's employees and increased efforts to strengthen the regulatory agency, to unbundle KESH, to establish rules for a new commercial energy market (following a single-buyer model), and to eventually privatize the power sector, beginning with its distribution components and then with its generation components.

This privatization sequencing is the best solution to reduce nontechnical power losses and improve the quality and reliability of the power supply. The projections in the new action plan show a decrease in demand from 6,395 gigawatt-hours (including 994 gigawatt-hours of load shedding) in 2001 to 5,585 gigawatt-hours (with zero load shedding) in 2005. This reduction in demand is expected because part of the unpaid demand will disappear. It will permit the import subsidy to fall to zero by the end of 2004. Associated fiscal benefits include the use of those budgetary resources for other critical needs, such as mitigating the impact on the poor of higher tariffs. The reduction in load shedding would bring large benefits in terms of improved quality of the services and avoided need for backup generators for businesses. Preliminary results relative to the first half of 2003 show that KESH has met its tariff collection target, collecting about 93 percent of the bills and reducing the reported losses and theft from the network to about 37 percent of production.

Serbia and Montenegro suffers from its lack of available telecommunication fixed lines, most likely because of severe underinvestment in the sector after the highly politicized and criticized privatization of the dominant operator. Enterprises in the country reported that the quality of electricity was also a constant problem for them, especially in the winter months. One enterprise reported the need to stop production when blackouts occur for 2–4 days in a row. However, the situation in Serbia and Montenegro is increasingly improving, with only limited blackouts reported in 2002.

Croatia exhibits the least disruption across all the infrastructure sectors. Surprisingly, the surveyed enterprises in Bosnia and Herzegovina reported low utility outages, although all enterprises that were interviewed there complained particularly about the quality of electricity and the frequency of blackouts. However, access and quality of the electricity services in Bosnia and Herzegovina are moving forward with the adoption of sectoral reforms.

## Infrastructure's Access and Quality across Different Enterprises' Characteristics

Let us now analyze how the access to and the quality and reliability of infrastructure services vary across enterprises within each country according to kinds of ownerships, enterprise sizes, and location types. We conduct this analysis sector by sector, starting with the telecommunication sector and continuing with the power and water sectors. The chosen measure of unevenness with respect to ownership is the differential percentage of the indicator as reported by de novo enterprises and state-owned enterprises. With respect to size, we calculate the differential percentage of the indicator as reported by small enterprises and large enterprises. Finally, the chosen measure of unevenness with respect to location is the differential percentage of the indicator as reported by enterprises located in the capital and those located in less densely populated cities.

### The Telecommunication Sector

Figure 4.6 reports strong evidence that telecommunication services have uneven access among surveyed enterprises, particularly with respect to ownership and size across all countries. Surveyed state-owned firms wait on average 4 days, whereas de novo enterprises report getting connections in 16 days. The difference with respect to size across the surveyed firms, though smaller, is still relevant; large enterprises get

## Figure 4.6    Unevenness of Waiting Times for Telecommunication Services

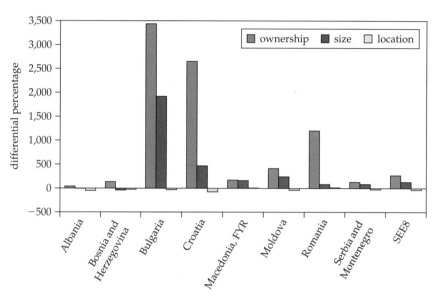

Source: EBRD and World Bank (2002).

connected in approximately 1 week, whereas small enterprises have to wait twice as long.

Bulgaria and Croatia stand out clearly as outliers. In Bulgaria, one of the countries characterized by the highest waiting time for telecommunication access, de novo enterprises that were surveyed waited on average approximately 1 month, whereas state-owned enterprises were connected on average in less than 1 day. Unevenness also affects countries with low waiting times. In Croatia, the country characterized by one of the lowest waiting times, the difference is also relevant, with surveyed de novo enterprises waiting approximately 1 week and state-owned counterparts being connected in approximately 6 hours. Albania and Serbia and Montenegro, the countries characterized by the lowest unevenness, are also the only two countries for which state-owned enterprises wait considerably longer than the regional average to get connected to telecommunication services. In both countries, surveyed state-owned enterprises wait on average for almost 2 weeks, and the regional average is 4 days.

Bigger size, regardless of ownership, is also significantly associated with lower waiting times. Larger enterprises have much more bargaining power with telecommunication providers because they represent the providers' biggest source of revenues. Surveyed enterprises located

## Figure 4.7    Unevenness in Outages for Telecommunication Services

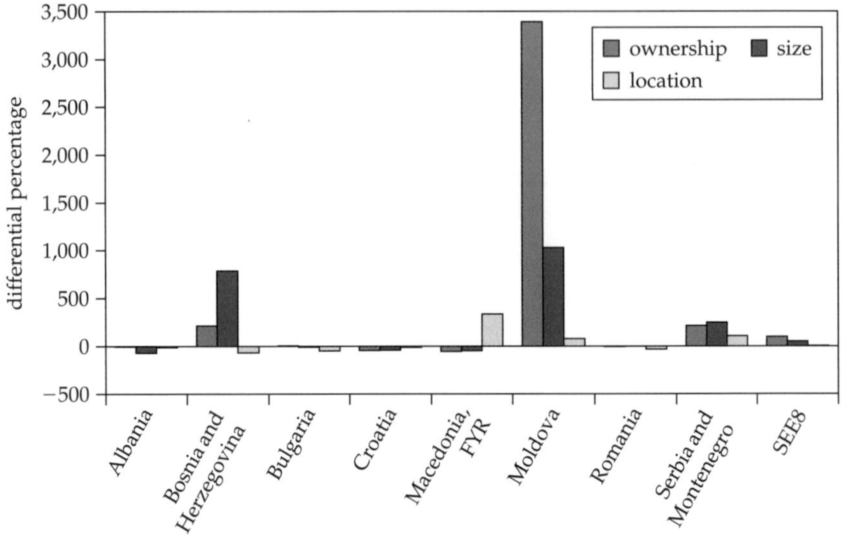

Source: EBRD and World Bank (2002).

outside of the capital do not seem to suffer delays in waiting times. Indeed, except in FYR Macedonia and Romania, the waiting time is lower for surveyed enterprises that are located outside their country's capital, most likely because of the congestion of the networks in the capital city.

The quality of telecommunication services does not differ as dramatically as access does across the three selected enterprise characteristics of ownership, size, and location. Again, consistent with the analysis carried out for access, ownership and size create more differences than location, as shown by figure 4.7. For the surveyed firms in the SEE8, telecommunication outages total almost 6 days per year for de novo enterprises and total fewer than 3 days per year for state-owned enterprises. The outlier is Moldova, where the great percentage difference is driven by the low outages times for state-owned enterprises (the lowest for the region, amounting to only a couple of hours per year). Among the surveyed firms, larger enterprises appear to be less subject to outages than smaller ones, particularly in Bosnia and Herzegovina, Moldova, and Serbia and Montenegro. Finally, although no evidence of an uneven playing field was found for location across the whole region, a strong uneven playing field was found in FYR Macedonia and Serbia and Montenegro. In FYR Macedonia, surveyed enterprises located outside the capital are disconnected from the main telecommunication line for almost 6 days per year, compared with 1 day per year for enterprises located in the capital. In Serbia and Montene-gro, enterprises located outside the capital are subject to almost 18 days of outages per year, more than twice the number of days of outages (8 days) for enterprises located in the capital.

## The Power Sector

Let us now consider the power sector. Figure 4.8 shows strong evidence of unevenness of access to electricity services, particularly with respect to ownership and size across all countries, with countries such as Croatia and Moldova standing out clearly as outliers. Unevenness affects coun-tries with both high and low waiting times. In Croatia, the country char-acterized by the lowest waiting times, the difference is relevant; surveyed de novo enterprises wait approximately 14 hours, whereas surveyed state-owned enterprises are connected in approximately 2 hours. In Moldova, one of the countries with the highest waiting time for electrici-ty, surveyed de novo enterprises wait on average approximately 8 days, whereas state-owned enterprises are connected on average in less than 1 day.

Size, regardless of ownership, is also significantly associated to lower waiting times, most likely because larger enterprises have more bargaining

## Figure 4.8    Unevenness of Waiting Times for Power Services

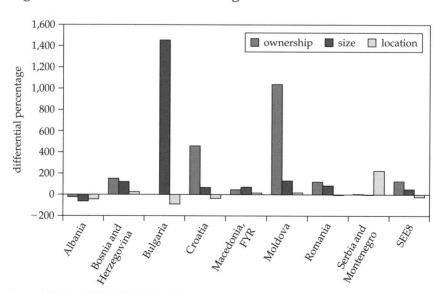

*Source:* EBRD and World Bank (2002).

## Figure 4.9    Unevenness in Outages for Power Services

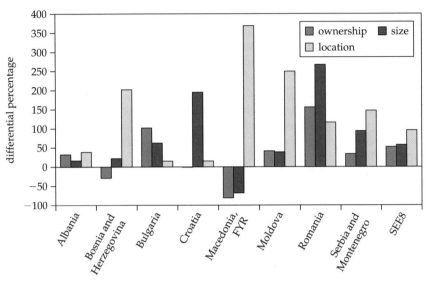

Source: EBRD and World Bank (2002).

power with electricity providers. In Bulgaria, surveyed large enterprises are connected in approximately 6 hours, whereas smaller enterprises have to wait more than 4 days. Location outside the capital does
not seem to pose delays in waiting times. Indeed, except in Serbia and
Montenegro, the waiting time is lower for enterprises that are located
outside the capital.

In contrast to the telecommunication sector, outages in the power sector
are much more frequent for less densely populated areas (see figure 4.9).
For the overall region, the survey found that enterprises located outside
the capital are subject to more than 13 days of power outages, almost twice
as much as for enterprises located in the capital (which are disconnected
for fewer than 7 days).

Surveyed enterprises outside the capital are particularly discriminated
against in Bosnia and Herzegovina, FYR Macedonia, and Moldova. Location is less of a problem in countries such as Croatia and Romania. In
Croatia and Romania, the main unevenness derives from the size of
enterprises, most likely because larger enterprises face this challenge by
building their own generators. Ownership is one of the lowest sources of
unevenness for all countries, with the notable exception of Bulgaria,
which shows the highest percentage difference between surveyed de
novo and state-owned enterprises (amounting to 100 percent). Albania

Figure 4.10   Unevenness in Outages for Water Services

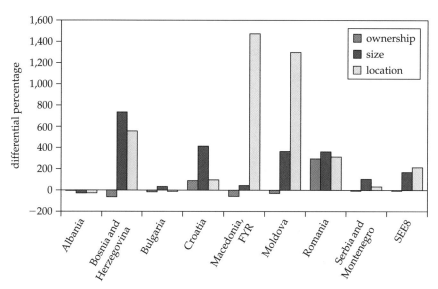

*Source:* EBRD and World Bank (2002).

displays one of the most even playing fields because the electricity crisis hit all enterprises.

## The Water Sector

Very much in line with the power sector, outages in the water sector are much more frequent for less densely populated areas, as figure 4.10 shows. For the overall region, surveyed enterprises located outside the capital are subject to 12 days of water outages, more than three times the number for enterprises located in the capital (which are disconnected for less than 4 days). Enterprises outside the capital are particularly discriminated against in Bosnia and Herzegovina, FYR Macedonia, and Moldova, the same countries that also suffered most in terms of power outages. An enterprise's size is also a major source of unevenness across most of the countries, particularly Bosnia and Herzegovina, Croatia, Moldova, and Romania.

In addition, the divide between urban and rural areas in terms of basic access to water is strongly reinforced by official data, which is reported in figure 4.11. In urban areas across the countries, on average more than 90 percent of the population is connected to water services; for rural areas, the average drops to slightly more than 50 percent.

In summary, the evidence of key infrastructure problems shows that the SEE8 are still in the process of overcoming the severe infrastructure

## Figure 4.11 Urban and Rural Access to Water Services

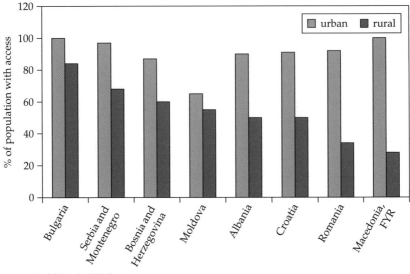

*Source:* World Bank (2003).

bottlenecks caused by conflicts and inadequate maintenance. However, problems vary substantially depending on country and sector contexts. Problems range from major structural difficulties (such as those underlying the electricity crisis in Albania) to complaints related to high prices and inadequate quality (for example, those in Croatia).

## Private Sector Involvement and Independence of Rulemaking

Having identified the key infrastructure problems in the SEE8, we will now consider how best to address them. Broad regulatory reforms, including private sector involvement and independence of rulemaking, are needed in the countries.

### Private Sector Delivery of Utility Services

Some of the arguments for private ownership of utility services—for example, the need to access capital to meet growing demand and improve quality of service—are even stronger for South Eastern Europe (SEE) than for other regions. And the discipline provided by private ownership is even more needed. The scale of losses and noncollection in some of the utility sectors (particularly the energy sector, as we have shown earlier in the chapter) is very high. Moreover, losses and noncollection are simply inconsistent with good management and protection of customers and would not be tolerated under private ownership.

There are powerful reasons for accelerating private sector involvement in utility services when payment discipline is low. A private firm that is owned or managed by a foreign strategic investor will have a stronger incentive to enforce payment discipline. That investor will also have the technical knowledge and financing required for essential remetering programs, computerization of billing, and other measures that can help improve payment performance. The definition and enforcement of customer service standards should be an integral part of pricing decisions. Customers will perceive as one-sided efforts to enforce payment discipline if they are not accompanied by improvements in quality of supply and services. Such perceptions tend to discredit privatization, particularly in the period immediately following privatization. Experience to date suggests that, in cases in which the private sector has entered power distribution, payment collection has gone up. Moldova has experienced major improvements in payment discipline. Case study evidence indicates that most enterprises in Moldova that have switched from a public infrastructure service provider to a private one perceived a substantial improvement in service (see box 4.4).

In many cases, privatization of *strategic companies* (those enjoying a monopolistic position or playing a key economic role) has proven to be difficult. Such firms operate in many sectors: telecommunications, media, postal services, public transportation, airport administration and air traffic control, energy, and gas and oil. These assets have been kept in public ownership for several reasons, including political parties' interests and management opposition. Finally, the opposition might come from governmental bodies (at the central, state, and local levels) and from other players involved in the privatization process (and in the regulation of network industries) that might have different interests and views on the privatization process or methods.

Moreover, SEE presents special challenges common to transition countries. State and public enterprise budgets can be manipulated; regulation can be distorted and perverted; corruption is widespread; and product, labor, capital, and financial markets often work imperfectly with considerable risk of tunneling.[4] In addition, many different privatization methods (including a variety of voucher schemes, various forms of insider privatization, auctions, and direct sale to a strategic outside investor) have been used, and ample evidence shows that the modalities of the initial privatization can have a lasting influence on the performance of the privatized industry. The original privatization methods interact in a complex way with product-market, factor-market, and financial-market structures (including the markets for corporate control and for managerial

---

### Box 4.4  Effect of Privatization on Infrastructure Business Users

In Moldova, the overall assessment by surveyed enterprises of infrastructure services is negative. However, an exception applies to electricity after the privatization of the key distribution companies. Before privatization, the quality of electricity was considered low in terms of stability of voltage and frequency. One of the interviewed managers estimated that the company was subject to approximately 4,000 power cuts per year. After privatization, power interruptions decreased to only 140 per year. The reported energy savings at all levels are assessed as significant.

In countries where privatization has not yet been undertaken, intensive users of power services have resorted to installing their own generators at extra cost. In Albania, three of the five interviewed companies have their own power generators because the electricity supply and quality are not reliable. Operating their own generators is expensive (roughly three times more expensive than using the electricity provider) because the price of fuel is higher, but according to the general managers of these enterprises, they have no other alternative when faced with the monopoly status of the electricity company. Other complaints reported in Albania, as well as in other countries, refer to the fact that the power company does not provide discounts for major users, nor does it cover losses of income from blackouts or lower quality. Loss of income from blackouts prompted enterprises in the food retail industry in Bosnia and Herzegovina and Romania to buy generators for their stores.

---

skills) to produce economic success or failure. For more details on the subject, see chapters 2 and 5, which analyze the implications of privatization methods on corporate governance.

To successfully enhance efficiency, privatization requires a number of complementary institutional changes, including restructuring to create scope for competition, to enhance the commercial viability of the privatized utility, or both. The privatization of network utilities has proven to be an effective means of attracting private investors and, significantly, a way of attracting foreign direct investment (FDI), particularly when privatization has occurred by selecting a strategic investor through open international auctions. In general, informed external investors with a strategic share have turned out to possess both stronger incentives and greater ability to identify and bring in appropriate agents with industry-specific knowledge and the necessary financing. Privatization through sale to strategic outsiders has promoted higher corporate governance standards. Such companies are less likely to be stripped by their owners, and they have a better financial structure and show improved performance when compared to companies that are not privatized.[5]

Telecommunication privatization has typically involved selling controlling stakes to a Western operating company, usually in exchange for a large upfront payment plus obligations to update and expand the network and services. This approach allows national governments lacking the managerial and financial resources to import the needed capital and expertise to implement the major technological and service upgrades. Subsequently, the government plans to sell some or all of its residual holdings through initial public offerings, thereby helping to jumpstart development of the national stock market and to spread ownership of the firms' equity as broadly as possible throughout the citizenry, something that has not yet been tried in the region.

Table 4.4 shows the privatization efforts made to date. The countries not shown in table 4.4 are paying the price of waiting too long to privatize. The business environment in the telecommunication sector has grown adverse, and many Western strategic investors are reluctant to invest further. In fact, in some cases, Western investors are even withdrawing their presence from the region.

After a controversial process that started in April 2002, the Bulgarian government has finalized in February 2004 the sale of a 65 percent share of the Bulgarian Telecommunications Company (BTC) to a financial consortium that is headed by the Austrian Viva Ventures, an arm of the U.S.-British equity house Advent International. In October 2002, Viva Ventures was named preferred buyer, but the deal was suspended when

**Table 4.4   Telecommunication Privatization in the SEE8**

| Country | Year | Buyer | Amount | % of ownership |
|---|---|---|---|---|
| Bulgaria | 2004 | Viva Ventures (Austria) | €230,000,000 | 65 |
| Croatia | 1999 | Deutsche Telekom (Germany) | US$850,000,000 | 35 |
|  | 2001 | Deutsche Telekom (Germany) | US$465,000,000 | 16 |
| Macedonia, FYR | 2000 | Matav (Hungary) | US$363,000,000 | 51 |
| Romania | 1998 | OTE (Οργανισμός Τηλεπικοινωνιών της Ελλάδος) (Greece) | US$695,000,000 | 35 |
| Serbia and Montenegro | 1997 | Stet (Italy), OTE (Greece) | US$909,000,000 | 49 |
|  | 2002 | Stet (Italy) | (offer withdrawn) | (offer withdrawn) |

*Source:* Information updated from Buiter and Vagliasindi (2003).

a rival Turkish group came forward. In July 2003, a five-judge panel of the Supreme Administrative Court of Bulgaria confirmed a previous decision by a three-judge panel to revoke the decision. Finally, the price for the 65 percent stake of the BTC capital was increased from €210 million to €230 million; the investment schedule was accelerated, with the bulk of investments planned for the first 3 years; and the number of the intended layoffs was reduced by 2,000.

Some progress has been made in Republika Srpska, one of the two country entities of Bosnia and Herzegovina. A sound preprivatization policy has been adopted for Telekom Srpske, which includes tariff rebalancing and a commitment to fully privatize the company by end of 2004.

The Albanian government relaunched the sale of a majority (51–76 percent) stake in the Albanian telecommunications provider, Albtelecom, in April 2003 after a number of previous attempts failed to produce a serious buyer. By including a Global System for Mobile Communications (GSM) license together with Albtelecom's fixed services, the government hopes to make Albtelecom more appealing to a strategic investor. A third GSM operator would operate alongside the leading operator, Albanian Mobile Communications, which is owned by the Greek telecommunication company OTE, and the second operator, Vodafone.

Moldova has failed three times to privatize its main operator, Moldtelecom, one of the few state-owned enterprises that consistently earns a profit. The first attempt took place in 1997, when OTE offered US$47 million for a 40 percent stake. The second tender was scheduled for 2000 but was canceled because of unfavorable market conditions. The final attempt was made in June 2002, when a tender was announced with a target price of US$100 million. By the first deadline at the beginning of August 2003, only two bidders had applied to the tender, and one was disqualified for failing to meet the requirements. Unofficial sources revealed that the second bidder had offered US$20 million for a 51 percent stake and had made a US$10 million investment commitment. Hoping to attract more bidders, the government extended the deadline until the end of August 2003 and then again until the end of September 2003. No other offers were made, however.

Privatization in the electricity sector can be designed in ways that encourage payment discipline through appropriate sequencing. A private firm owned or managed by a foreign strategic investor will have a stronger incentive to enforce payment discipline. Experience to date suggests that, when the private sector has entered power distribution, major improvements in payment discipline arise. Improvements in efficiency also result from private participation and may, in turn, reduce the price increases necessary to ensure the viability of the power sector. The introduction of the private sector can also help mobilize financing and increase the possibility of further investments in the sector.

In March 2000, Union Fenosa privatized three of the five distribution electricity companies in Moldova. The Bulgarian government plans to sell a majority stake in seven regional electricity distribution companies. The privatization of the first two Romanian electricity distribution companies, Electrica Banat and Electrica Dobrogea, was launched in January 2003. In March 2003, the Romanian government selected an adviser for the privatization of two other electricity distributors.

For the other countries, restructuring is under way, but it has not always been fully successful. The World Bank, with contributions from the EBRD and the European Investment Bank, led a major program for investment in the power sector in Bosnia and Herzegovina. The program, known as Power III, is suffering delays because the authorities have failed to carry out the necessary reforms. Both country entities (the Federation of Bosnia and Herzegovina and Republika Srpska) have adopted action plans for restructuring, unbundling, and privatizing the sector. Independent audits of the three integrated electricity companies, published in March 2003, highlighted problems of fraud, mismanagement, and conflicts of interest in all three companies.

Progress in the restructuring of the electric power company of FYR Macedonia, Elektrostopanstvo na Makedonija (ESM), has also been slow. The privatization of ESM power utility is expected to start by the end of 2004. In accordance with the restructuring plan approved at the start of 2004, electricity production activities of ESM should be separated from transmission and distribution, which will enable the privatization of some units. ESM would retain state control over power transmission and distribution, but foreign investors would be allowed to enter the energy sector by establishing new production capacities. Restructuring of the energy users (particularly of public-owned companies), as discussed in chapters 3 and 5, might also help improve payment discipline by removing at the enterprise level one of the most important sources of soft budget constraints.

In the railway sector, the first steps toward privatization entail separating operation and infrastructure. In Bulgaria and Romania, separation of operation and infrastructure has been implemented, and private operators are permitted to operate rolling stock. In 2003, Croatia adopted a new railway law, which brings its railway legislation in line with European Union (EU) directives. Features of the new law include the separation of infrastructure from operations and the establishment of an office of the railway regulator. The restructuring process in FYR Macedonia is supported by an action plan, which was developed in consultation with the World Bank, that requires labor restructuring and separating operations from infrastructure. In Bosnia and Herzegovina, the railway company is developing its business plan and is in the process of jumpstarting labor restructuring, with support from the EBRD.

In summary, only some of the SEE8 seized opportunities for privatization and have attracted and maintained FDI. Delays in privatization have, in some cases, been caused by failure to attract strategic investors (as in the case of telecommunication companies in both Albania and Bulgaria). A reduced interest on the part of investors in infrastructure sectors such as telecommunications has not helped. As documented by Harris (2003), investment flows generated to finance infrastructure projects in developing countries have fallen dramatically from a peak of US$128 billion in 1997 to less than half of that level (approximately US$60 billion). Telecommunications and electricity were the two sectors characterized by both the biggest growth and the biggest decline in investment.

The challenges ahead include tackling regulatory problems such as enforcement of payment discipline and removal of inefficient pricing and cross-subsidies, which are embedded in many of the infrastructure sectors. These problems stifle incentives for attracting investors and privatizing utilities. Also needed is the establishment of a stable and predictable regulatory framework through independent agencies, which is discussed in the next section.

## Independence of Rulemaking

The specific regulatory regime that is adopted for the privatized network utilities encompasses several forms of regulation. The establishment of an independent regulator is a key regulatory challenge vital for the settling of market disputes as well as policy and other regulatory issues. If the regulator is not independent, then the government is still able to interfere, even if the network utility is privatized. Even with an independent regulator, however, the difficult challenge facing the national government is to endow that entity with technically competent people and give those people the authority and budget needed to implement the entity's mandate effectively.

Network industries are typically capital intensive, and the needed investment is sector specific; that is, it cannot be easily reallocated and can be viewed as "sunk." Consequently, a fair return on capital is guaranteed only if the private investment plan for the utility is successfully carried out over a sufficiently long time horizon that permits the private owner to recoup the sunk investment. A precondition is a stable regulatory framework. The investor makes its decisions on the basis of a country's announced regulatory policy and the credibility of that policy. Insecurity, lack of transparency, and predictability represent critical problems that could potentially deter investment. A regulatory risk premium is required to attract private financing into the sector. In transition economies, the importance of legal and institutional frameworks has been often underestimated. Even in the more industrial SEE8 countries,

## Table 4.5    Independent Regulators in the SEE8

| Country | Electricity | Telecommunication |
|---------|-------------|-------------------|
| Albania | 1996 | 1998 |
| Bosnia and Herzegovina | Planned | Planned |
| Bulgaria | 1999 | 2002 |
| Croatia | 1997 | 2000 |
| Macedonia, FYR | 2003 | 2000 |
| Moldova | 1997 | 2000 |
| Romania | 1998 | 2002 |
| Serbia and Montenegro | Planned | Planned |

Source: EBRD (2003).

the appropriate legislative and regulatory framework, as well as the institutions to implement that framework, is not always in place.

Institutional reforms are needed that support private investment through a system of credible and effective regulation. As reported in table 4.5, the SEE8 have set up independent regulatory agencies relatively recently, and even when these agencies have been established, business and residential users generally lack awareness of their existence and their effectiveness. In particular, no public consultation process has been put in place, and to date, infrastructure end users have had only limited involvement in contributing to improved regulation.

One of the most difficult challenges that transition economies face is the establishment of credible regulatory mechanisms. These economies lack several prerequisites, including a well-functioning legal system that provides protections against state or regulatory confiscation of private property, the norms and underlying laws necessary to carry out effective delegation of authority, good contract laws and mechanisms for resolving contract disputes (as discussed in chapter 6), and sound administrative procedures to make the regulatory process transparent and to provide legal protections from regulatory abuse through effective judicial review. Moreover, as the experience of industrial countries shows, the process of developing credible regulatory mechanisms and establishing strong and independent agencies takes time. In several instances, the SEE8 have failed to implement regulatory reforms because government interference has led to the overturning of pricing decisions.

Nevertheless, strong evidence shows that countries where an independent regulator has been established generate better performance indicators related to access and reliability of the utility services (see figure 4.12). SEE8 countries that have established an independent regulator in the electricity sector generally have waiting times of 7 days as compared with a waiting time almost four times longer (equal to 27 days) for countries with no independent regulator. Similarly, countries with an independent

## Figure 4.12    Effect of an Independent Regulator on Performance Indicators

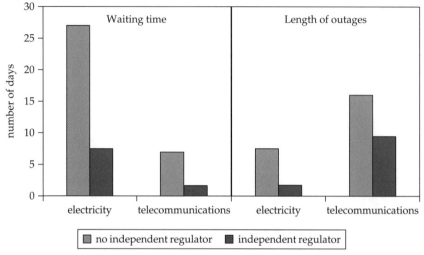

*Source:* EBRD and World Bank (2002).

## Table 4.6    Infrastructure Transition Indicators

| | Telecommunication | | Power | | Railways | | Roads | | Water | |
|---|---|---|---|---|---|---|---|---|---|---|
| | *1999* | *2002* | *1999* | *2002* | *1999* | *2002* | *1999* | *2002* | *1999* | *2002* |
| Albania | 1 | 3+ | 2 | 2+ | 2 | 2 | 2 | 2 | 1 | 1 |
| Bosnia and Herzegovina | 1 | 3+ | 2 | 3 | 2 | 3 | 2 | 2 | 1 | 1 |
| Bulgaria | 3 | 3 | 3 | 3+ | 3 | 3 | 2+ | 2+ | 2 | 3 |
| Croatia | 3 | 3+ | 2+ | 3 | 2+ | 2+ | 2+ | 2+ | 3 | 3+ |
| Serbia and Montenegro | 2 | 2 | 2 | 2 | na | 2+ | 2− | 2+ | 2− | 2 |
| Macedonia, FYR | 2 | 2 | 2 | 2+ | 2 | 2 | 2+ | 2+ | 1 | 2 |
| Moldova | 2+ | 2+ | 3 | 3+ | 2 | 2 | 2 | 2 | 2 | 2 |
| Romania | 3 | 3 | 3− | 3 | 4 | 4 | 2+ | 3 | 2+ | 3 |

*Source:* EBRD (2003).
*Note:* Rankings span from 1 (little reform) to 4+ (standard and performance typical of advanced countries).

regulator in the telecommunication sector have much lower waiting times (fewer than 2 days) as compared with a wait of more than 7 days in the remaining countries.[6]

Governments are making efforts at reform. Table 4.6 presents some indicators of the progress that countries have made in implementing legal and regulatory reforms for each of the utility sectors. Not surprisingly, the telecommunication sector has been the most dynamic and presents the highest score, reflecting efforts by governments to introduce a legal framework consistent with EU directives. However, efforts related to tariff rebalancing and cost-oriented interconnection rules still lag. In addition, little has been done in the power sector to implement secondary legislation, particularly with respect to network and end-user tariffs. In the transportation sector, transportation departments (for example, road agencies at the federal level) or transportation companies (for example, railways at the federal level or urban transport companies at the local level) have been established in most cases, but these units still lack the institutional strength to plan, select, and bring about the capital expenditures they require to meet their infrastructure needs. For road investments and for most urban transportation services, revenues depend, to a large extent, on the central budget or municipal subsidies. The local nature of water services argues for placing primary responsibilities at the local government level. Some countries have decentralized most of the regulatory functions to the local government. However, most of these countries still need regulators to scrutinize the cost of service providers, and, consequently, they need regulators with a degree of financial, economic, and administrative expertise and independence. Notable exceptions are the two EU accession countries (Bulgaria and Romania) and Croatia, which is the leader in the water sector.

In the absence of competition, regulation is needed to provide incentives for efficient production and allocation, so that benefits can be passed on to consumers. However, regulation cannot replicate all the pressures of the market, and expecting it to do so would be unrealistic. Competition has brought dramatic change to the developing countries. Companies now discover and provide what customers want. For instance, industrial customers have secured customized metering and billing arrangements.

For the newly established regulatory agencies, two key tasks requiring decisions are establishing pricing rules and providing adequate incentives for efficiency. The optimal choice among alternative regulatory mechanisms (rate-of-return regulation or price-cap regulation) depends on a variety of country and sector characteristics, including the quality of cost accounting and auditing systems, the availability of economic and technical expertise, the institutional checks and balances, and the investment requirements of the regulated sectors. Fixed rate-of-return or cost-plus contracts offer no incentives to firms to reduce costs because any variation in cost is appropriated by the regulator (and through the regulator, by the government). A fixed-price contract induces the right amount of effort because the regulated firm appropriates any reduction in cost. The enterprise is the residual claimant for cost savings. In light of the scarce technical expertise and severe informational problems in the region, enterprises must set up clear regulatory goals and simplify administrative procedures as much as possible. The need for these efforts does not suggest, however, that enterprises should settle for a second-best method of intervention. Evidence has shown that a strong incentive-based pricing formula does not necessarily demand more informational or administrative expertise than a cost-plus regime (Bartle 2003). The role of the regulator can be limited to impose floors on prices to protect against predation and impose ceilings on prices to protect against monopolistic behavior. These floors and ceilings should be based on an economic analysis of costs or on appropriate international benchmarks.

In the United Kingdom, retail price caps have been used only on a temporary basis for a number of reasons (see, for example, Vagliasindi 2003a). First, price controls limited the scope within which competitors could offer price cuts. Second, repeatedly tightening controls in this way could severely reduce customers' incentive to search out alternative offers from the market. Finally, the approach could suggest to customers that price regulation was an important and permanent element of a competitive market. Insofar as the approach induced more customers to stay with the incumbent, that entity would build up a constituency that was dependent on it. Such consideration led the U.K. regulators to gradually relax and remove retail price controls. Even in the United Kingdom, price regulation has been kept for wholesale pricing (for example, interconnection rates in the telecommunication sector and transmission and distribution in the power sector).

One of the most critical bottlenecks constraining entry is the market power exercised by infrastructure service providers and the regulatory regime governing their service offerings. In the key infrastructure services (electricity, district heating, natural gas, railways, and telecommunications), state-dominated monopolies still play a major role. In purchasing these kinds of infrastructure services, manufacturing firms, particularly new, smaller ones, confront little, if any, price competition or few opportunities to choose among suppliers. Opportunities to choose among alternative suppliers are extremely limited, and switching suppliers is quite costly in most of the infrastructure sectors, with the notable exception of telecommunications. In this context, regulation is needed to support competition. The establishment of a regional electricity market (as discussed in more detail in box 4.9) will open the electricity markets so eligible customers can access alternative suppliers.

Important regulations are needed to ensure the emergence of effective competition by providing third-party access to the incumbent's network. Interconnection is critical in providing efficient investment and effective competition. If the regulator fails to understand interconnection, distorted market-entry signals, invalidated investments, and the abuse of dominant positions will result, to the detriment of consumers. Hence, those operators with the ability to abuse their market power should be subject to special rules (ex ante regulation) to ensure that they do not abuse their dominance. These rules should include a requirement for the operator to meet all reasonable demands for interconnection services from other network operators (for example, transparent and cost-based interconnection, unbundling of interconnection charges, nondiscrimination, and publication of interconnection offers, including terms and conditions of contracts and prices). From a public policy viewpoint, the resulting interconnection price needs to be economically efficient, to guarantee fair recovery of costs for all operators, and to provide the right entry signals.

The challenges ahead for the SEE8 include the development of predictable and transparent regulatory frameworks. Progress in this dimension will encourage investment in the infrastructure sectors, with spillover effects for the rest of the economy and regional integration. The next section discusses this issue.

## Role of Infrastructure Development in Fostering Investment in the Real Sector and in Regional Integration

The ability to provide better infrastructure services could offer tremendous opportunities to reduce costs, increase revenues, or both. Downstream innovation (particularly in the user-intensive sectors of infrastructure services) is constrained by the lack of innovation at the upstream level (for example, delivery of enhanced infrastructure services). First, the following analysis will focus on two infrastructure sectors (telecommunications and transportation) and their effect on intensive users (software companies and export-import enterprises, respectively). Second, the analysis will explore the benefits of a regional electricity market and water resource management.

### Links between the New Economy and Telecommunication Infrastructure

Better telecommunication services allow companies to reach customers, suppliers, and partners. Figure 4.13 shows the proportion of surveyed enterprises that regularly use the traditional and the more advanced telecommunication services in their interactions with clients and suppliers. On average, more than 90 percent of enterprises use both traditional fixed-line services and cellular services in these interactions. Internet use as a means of communication is significantly lagging behind, with slightly more than 50 percent of surveyed enterprises using it regularly. Albania, the country characterized by the lowest use of fixed-line services, has created effective competition in the cellular segment of the market, and mobile services have overturned fixed-line services. Nevertheless, the poor condition of the telecommunication network is hindering the diffusion of

## Figure 4.13    Business Use of Telecommunication Services

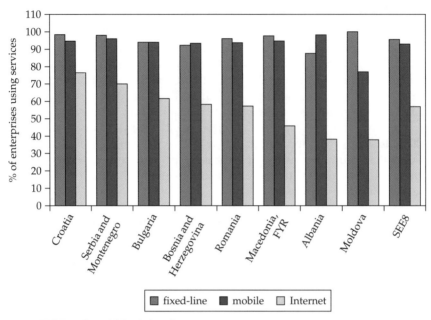

*Source:* EBRD and World Bank (2002).

Internet communication: after Moldova, Albania has one of the lowest proportions of enterprises that use e-mail.

A comparison of figure 4.13, showing telecommunication use by business users (distinguished by fixed-line, mobile, and Internet), with figure 4.14, showing the official data of telecommunication penetration rates (per 100 inhabitants), reveals an interesting point. From the comparison, it appears that, in reality, mobile penetration is still lagging in the SEE8 for both business and residential users. The notable exceptions are Albania and Croatia, which are, respectively, the country with the lowest and the country with the highest fixed-line penetration. The remarkable increase in mobile penetration in Albania is documented in box 4.5. Also worth noticing is the low diffusion of Internet service across all countries in the region.

We will now analyze the effect of increased investment and innovation on the operating environment of downstream intensive business users. In particular, we will consider the effect that enhanced telecommunication services such as Internet and other data transmission services have on intensive business users such as software companies. SEE's highly educated labor force and cheap wages promise to make the region a competitive base in Europe for knowledge-based industries, including

## Figure 4.14 Telecommunication Development

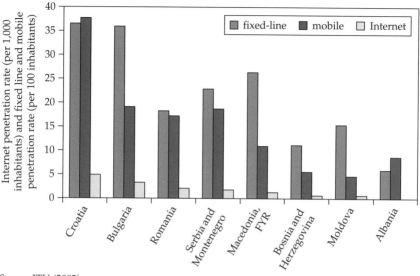

*Source:* ITU (2002).

## Box 4.5 Establishing a Competitive Mobile Market

Mobile penetration into transition economies has witnessed explosive growth in the recent years. The mobile penetration levels of some of the transition countries are close to Western European penetration levels. At the top of the league is Slovenia, with an 86.6 percent mobile penetration rate at the end of 2002, closely followed by the Czech Republic, Hungary, and Slovakia, all of which have penetration rates of well over 50 percent. Mobile penetration in Bulgaria and Romania at the end of 2002 stood at approximately 30 percent and reached 48 percent in Croatia.

Although hindered in part by a lower level of disposable income in the countries, growth in the mobile sector was also hampered at first by a lack of competition. However, by 2003, at least two mobile operators were operating in Bulgaria, Croatia, and Romania (which already had four mobile operators). In Croatia, the mobile arm of the incumbent is, by a narrow margin, the largest mobile operator, whereas in Bulgaria and Romania, neither of the incumbent operators holds a leading market position; indeed, the mobile arms of the incumbents in both cases are the smallest and least successful operators. Large foreign players such as Orange in Romania hold the largest market shares through a combination of low-cost, prepaid offers, backed by extensive marketing and branding activity as well as by national distribution networks.

*(Box continues on the next page.)*

## Box 4.5 (continued)

Mobile subscribers in FYR Macedonia grew by 66.7 percent between the end of 2001 and the end of 2002, and the country had a penetration rate of 18.3 percent by that time. The market appears ready to continue its healthy growth, particularly as the second GSM license holder has yet to launch services. So far, foot-dragging from incumbent MakTel's mobile unit, Mobimak, over the signing of interconnection agreements has prevented services being launched. In May 2003, MakTel finally signed an interconnection agreement with the holder of the second GSM license, MTS Cosmofon (OTE's Macedonian mobile arm) to finally launch its GSM services and bring to an end the monopoly that incumbent MakTel has held to date in the mobile sector. However, in FYR Macedonia, Mobimak has the advantage of an established market presence, thanks to having held a monopoly until now, and it already has a substantial subscriber base.

Competition is heating up in the Serbian market. Serbia's Telekom Srbija, which includes both mobile and fixed-line divisions, has been growing steadily. The mobile division—Mobile Telephony of Serbia—has boomed. It enjoyed a subscriber growth of 115.4 percent from the end of 2001 to the end of 2002 to reach 1.4 million subscribers. Mobile Telephony's subscriber growth brings it almost level with the market leader, MobTel, which has 1.5 million subscribers and a mobile penetration rate of almost 26 percent. A recent new telecommunication law passed by the Serbian parliament could be the catalyst in a drive to sell off Telekom Srbija, an effort that has been singled out as a priority by the government. Additionally, the government also recently outlined plans to launch a tender for a third GSM license. Although the plans did not give a fixed date, the tender forms part of the government's future strategy for the telecommunication industry, which it aims to realize over the next 3 years. However, although privatization could certainly bring with it much-needed revenues, it is also likely to bring disputes as everyone tries to gain a slice of Telekom Srbija's more money-spinning mobile division, Mobile Telephony of Serbia, at the expense of its less-appealing fixed-line division. OTE, which already owns a 20 percent equity investment in Telekom Srbija, has been in talks with the Serbian government to negotiate the acquisition of a stake in the mobile division. As a contingency plan to make sure it secures a mobile interest in Serbia, OTE has been in talks with the slightly larger mobile operator, MobTel. MobTel's ownership is also something of a gray area; the Serbian state is currently in a dispute with the Karic family, which (indirectly) owns a 51 percent share of MobTel. The family claims it holds a 49 percent stake in MobTel, but the state disagrees, and the matter has gone to court. No tender to sell off a further stake in the operator can take place until this dispute is resolved.

In Albania, the arrival of Vodafone in the market alongside Albanian Mobile Communications has provided a significant boost to subscriber

(*Box continues on the next page.*)

> **Box 4.5 (continued)**
>
> numbers. Vodafone launched services in the third quarter of 2001. Just
> 3 months later, at the end of 2001, its prepaid services had proved so pop-
> ular that it had gained 118,567 subscribers, helping to increase penetration
> to more than 25 percent by the end of 2002. This accomplishment is
> notable in a country whose 2002 per capita gross domestic product was
> among the lowest in the region. Subscriber bases are made up almost
> entirely of prepaid subscriptions (99 percent of Vodafone's Albanian sub-
> scribers at the end of 2002 were prepaid) and are attracted by an increas-
> ing number of cheap, prepaid offers, particularly as mobile can be bought
> and used immediately whereas fixed-line operators are still battling to
> overcome waiting lists.

software design businesses, translation services, and call centers. As documented in chapter 1, the countries of SEE8, unlike Central Eastern
Europe's successful transition economies, have attracted little foreign
investment. This fact has been attributed largely to the high degree of
political risk associated with the region, resulting from wars, sanctions,
and international isolation. However, with the region now more politically secure, new opportunities appear. The SEE8 would require a different approach to economic development than that taken by transition
countries in Central Eastern Europe. Two main factors prevent SEE from
mimicking the strategy of Central Eastern Europe. First, remaining political risk deters investors from projects requiring significant initial outlay
and "sunk" costs. Second, obstacles such as trade barriers and weak or
damaged infrastructure hinder the transportation of goods in SEE.

The population in SEE has a good overall education base, and some
countries also have developed specialization in particular skills. In
Bulgaria, the mathematics and informatics department is the most popular choice at Sofia's main university. People in the countries of former
Yugoslavia tend to be highly skilled in foreign languages. In addition,
wage levels remain low, particularly in Bulgaria, FYR Macedonia,
Romania, and Serbia and Montenegro, thus further boosting the comparative advantage of South Eastern European labor.

A number of sectors might thus flourish in the Balkan states over the
coming years. Entrepreneurs and investors have already spotted the
potential of the information technology (IT) industry in the region, and
several software design companies are operating there. One example in
Bulgaria is Rila Solutions, an Internet and wireless consultancy that
employs local staff members and has clients in the United States and
Western Europe. Large units are being established to offer translation services to companies based outside the region. For example, the Bulgarian
firm All Data Processing employs a body of translators to select, summarize,

translate, and code news material from more than 10,000 sources; Reuters distributes the finished product as part of its services.

These countries, building on the strong foreign language skills among their citizens, could establish call centers that use local employees to provide services or after-sales assistance to the customers of companies based elsewhere. Invoicing and payment collection are two activities that could, in some cases, straightforwardly be contracted out to SEE8 firms. In addition, multinational corporations are increasingly seeking to contract out research and development activities rather than maintaining expensive, in-house research teams. This trend is particularly evident in the financial sector, where a number of investment banks rely on locally based research units to produce the analysis, which they then provide to their clients. However, this trend might also become an attractive option for pharmaceuticals and telecommunication companies.

In the case studies that focused on the software sector, enterprises in Albania, Bosnia and Herzegovina, and Moldova have complained of serious problems resulting from an old telecommunication network. The quality of services is poor, and a lack of choice in providers keeps prices artificially high. Currently, these enterprises can use the Internet only for ordering and not for selling. Problems such as these are aggravated in Moldova by a temporary ban on competition to provide Internet services and by the lack of legislation on e-commerce. For software companies in Bosnia and Herzegovina, competition is also effectively delayed because switching from one Internet service provider (ISP) to another ISP may take 4 weeks.

Also, in the region's most industrial countries such as Bulgaria, the Web page of a company is the main marketing tool. Bulgarian dealers can order over the Internet, but their customers cannot. Within businesses, 90 percent of correspondence with foreign partners is by means of e-mail, but actual transactions are not conducted in this way. In 2003, a Bulgarian software company that was interviewed in the study has changed Internet providers three times. The quality, and mainly the speed, has improved tremendously. A Romanian software company told us that its policy is to encourage customers to buy directly from the distributors that have their own e-sales. A major problem is that the company cannot use credit cards online and needs to go through a German company (which charges a 15 percent commission) to provide this service to its customers. In Serbia and Montenegro, a software company that was interviewed in the study started an e-commerce site in October 2001. That site now accounts for about 1.2 percent of its total sales.

In many cases, both business and government officials are concerned about brain drain. Figure 4.15 shows the percentage of managers, professionals, and skilled workers within surveyed enterprises who

**Figure 4.15   Brain Drain**

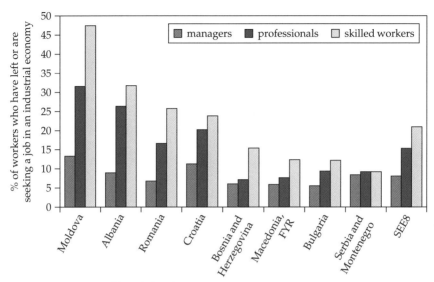

*Source:* EBRD and World Bank (2002).

have left for or are seeking a job in an industrial economy. Preventing leakage of human capital may be hardest in areas that are still scarred by conflict (such as Bosnia and Herzegovina) or that are perceived as having poor prospects (such as Moldova and, to a lesser extent, Albania). In fact, the brain drain phenomenon affects most the poorest countries—Albania and Moldova—where more than 30 percent and almost half of the surveyed enterprises, respectively, have been affected. But some of the region's wealthier countries such as Croatia and Romania also show an above-average brain drain.

The SEE8 may see benefits from this brain drain effect as they become locked into a process of integration with the European Union. The threat of losing labor to richer markets may create incentives for greater domestic investment in education. Also, remittances from migrants have been significant across the SEE8. In Albania, remittances in some years have been higher than the level of total exports in goods and services, taking on a proportion that may well offset the short-term effects of human capital loss, if not the reduction in long-term growth potential. In such areas, migration policies need to monitor outward flows of human capital, boost domestic educational investment, create more opportunities for the highly skilled within domestic labor markets, and encourage the remigration of expatriates. Moreover, Internet technologies raise the possibility of brain circulation without physical relocation, because of the increased flexibility of working online.

Of all the countries, Bulgaria has been the most successful so far at exploiting its potential as a knowledge economy, and it is already gaining a reputation for that capacity. However, greater action by the SEE8 is essential if this strategy for economic development is to succeed. Supportive policies are needed in three areas: (a) creating a more flexible labor market, (b) improving IT and telecommunication infrastructure, and (c) investing in education and training. Labor-intensive industries such as these rely on cheap labor costs and flexible labor markets to attract investment. The Romanian government in 2003 directly targeted the IT sector by exempting software companies from paying some categories of taxes on the salaries of programmers; that move should also have productive effects.

Internet access, which is highly important to maintaining a technologically competent labor force, is still limited in the SEE8. Many potential customers are thought to be deterred by the high costs currently associated with dial-up Internet access, which, in turn, reflects the monopolies that national telecommunication firms retain over fixed-line networks. Liberalization is gradually taking place and should be strongly supported to make markets more competitive. The Bulgarian and Romanian postliberalization environment in 2003 has brought a number of interesting developments, including cross-sector convergence. The advantage of railway or power companies offering telecommunication services is that they already have a backbone on which to run their own fiber-optic network. Thus, such companies can avoid the need to lease capacity from the incumbent. A number of ISPs and mobile operators have already launched (or are lining up to launch) postliberalization voice services. This option enables operators to provide a more attractive service package, particularly to the corporate sector. Any increase in digital subscriber line (DSL) rollouts by incumbents is likely to encourage cable television operators to increase their high-speed rollouts. Meanwhile, these DSL rollouts will enable providers to offer broadband Internet access, and more ISPs are likely to make dial-up prices more competitive.

How competition fares will hinge on a number of factors. First, having a transparent regulatory body will be crucial to promoting competition and the rollout of new technologies. The regulator, which is vital for settling market disputes and policy issues, must be able to operate as an independent legal body.

Second, because leasing access from the incumbent's networks can prove costly and difficult, accessing an alternative network can be beneficial, especially given the slow pace of local loop unbundling (LLU).

Third, a degree of consolidation among the smaller players will be inevitable, leaving only the most serious players and possibly prompting mergers among the smaller, less financially viable operators.

Within a liberalized environment, the survival of a new player also depends, paradoxically, on its harmonious cooperation with its fiercest competitor, the incumbent, which, for its part, may not be at all happy to relinquish its hold on the market. Across the European Union, local loop unbundling has proven a significant regulatory obstacle. LLU (allowing competitors to access the "last mile," or the stretch from the local exchange to the customer) would be a key driver in increasing DSL services in the region, but LLU has yet to be implemented in the SEE8. In countries throughout Europe, former incumbents have used various techniques to delay providing their rivals with network access. A number of Europe's incumbents, including Deutsche Telekom and France Telecom, have been criticized for their slow LLU practices.

Therefore, an instant rush of competition should not be expected in the SEE8, although in time, LLU should help the competitive climate, provided that the regulators can act decisively in resolving any disputes that arise, including foot-dragging by incumbents. The introduction of carrier selection, carrier preselection, number portability, and nationwide renumbering—all prerequisites for a liberalized market—have represented major investments for incumbents. The state of liberalization of the telecommunication sector across the SEE8 is summarized in box 4.6.

It is also essential that national governments invest heavily in education to maintain high general standards. Yet many countries, particularly those that formed former Yugoslavia, have reduced spending on education in recent years in response to tight fiscal conditions, thus jeopardizing one of the region's prime assets. In addition, because many IT companies are small, they face the start-up costs associated with small and medium-size enterprises in the region. To address this problem, Bulgaria will be establishing an investment fund dedicated to promoting small high-tech enterprises. The level of success will depend on national governments not only recognizing the opportunity but also responding with policies to liberalize the labor market and invest in the telecommunication infrastructure.

## Linkages between Transportation Infrastructure and Import-Export Problems

An adequate transportation infrastructure is crucial for developing regional trade. This point is particularly true for the SEE8. All countries in the region (except Romania) are small, and some of them are landlocked (Bosnia and Herzegovina and FYR Macedonia). The police and customs agencies are often mentioned as the main constraints hindering trade both because of their corruption and because of their unpredictable application of rules. This section addresses the extent to which import-export firms have been constrained by inadequate transportation infrastructure (including delays because of customs or preshipment inspection processes).

## Box 4.6 Telecommunication Liberalization in the SEE8

As of January 2003, the fixed-line sector was officially liberalized in Bulgaria and Romania. In July 2003, the Bulgarian Communications Regulation Commission (CRC) issued three alternative fixed-line licenses to private operators, thereby providing competition to incumbent BTC. Two 20-year licenses to offer fixed-line services have been awarded: one to Orbitel, which already offers Internet services, and the other to Netplus, an Internet service provider. A 15-year license has been awarded to Globaltech, a telecommunication service and software provider. Globaltech is also the Bulgarian arm of U.S.-based Global Communication Technologies.

In addition, the gas monopoly Bulgargas announced plans to use its existing copper cable network, which runs alongside the company's gas pipeline network, to set up cable network extensions to populated areas. The company's service will primarily target the corporate sector. Full competition is likely to be hindered initially by the speed of interconnection negotiations, particularly if BTC feels its new competitors are undercutting it. The low level of digitalization will also prove a hindrance to the overall development of a competitive market, and this problem is unlikely to be resolved without further investment in BTC. The role of the CRC (established in February 2002) will be to emphasize the importance of settling market disputes as well as policy issues and other regulatory questions.

The Romanian telecommunication market was officially liberalized at the beginning of 2003. So far, the Romanian Communication Regulatory Authority (Autoritatea Nationala de Reglementare in Comunicatii or ANRC) has granted numbering licenses to 30 companies that are authorized to provide telephone services and has allotted more than 27 million numbers. Licenses were granted to a combination of mobile operators and data providers, attracting interest from existing Romanian operators such as cable operator Astral and from international providers such as Equant. One license each was awarded to leading mobile operator Mobifon, international data provider Equant, wireless broadband provider AccessNET, and alternative telecommunication company and cable operator Astral Telecom. The alternative telecommunication company and domestic broadcaster, Reþeua Societãþii Naþionale de Radiocomunicaþii, was awarded the remaining two licenses. Mobifon, Equant, and AccessNET International each already hold a national point-multipoint license in Romania for 82 municipalities, while Astral Telecom holds a license for 14 localities. The new licenses will enable companies to offer alternative voice and data services to existing services provided by incumbent RomTelecom.

Currently, fixed-line penetration in Romania is low (approximately 18 percent at the end of 2002). RomTelecom's network modernization has been slow, and a number of rural areas still have no fixed-line service.

*(Box continues on the next page.)*

## Box 4.6 (continued)

Through fixed-wireless, point-multipoint services, companies will be able to offer competing voice and data services to those of RomTelecom, possibly even bypassing its networks altogether. Alternative providers are likely to target the more lucrative corporate sector, whose data needs are not necessarily being met by RomTelecom. RomTelecom offers a fairly limited range of data services, and by means of fixed-wireless, point-multipoint networks, competing operators will be able to target enterprises with a full package of telecommunication services, including data transmission. A number of alternative operators are lining up to launch—or, indeed, have already launched—competing telecommunication services and are planning to either use RomTelecom's network or seek an alternative network, such as a fixed-wireless or cable network, through which to offer services.

In February 2003, Căile Ferate Române, the railway operator, launched an international fixed-line service to private individuals. International calls could be made using prepaid cards, and the services were available in major railway stations across the country. Transelectrica, the power utility, also hopes to extend its network nationwide, but it will require a foreign partner to finance such an expansion.

In March 2003, Societatea Nationala de Radiocomunicatii, the national radio and television broadcasting company, gained a license to provide electronic communications and announced its intention to commence by offering prepaid international and long-distance services using Voice over Internet Protocol. PCNet, the Romanian ISP, also gained a license in March 2003 to provide electronic communications and announced a similar intention.

In Croatia, the government has prolonged Hrvatski Telekom's monopoly on the local loop until 2005. Nevertheless, the government seems keen to see another player enter the fixed-line sector and plans to grant one or more licenses to companies who can meet certain criteria. Hungary's PanTel was said to have been in talks in March 2003 with Croatian and foreign partners concerning a possible bid for the second fixed-line concession. VIPNet, the Croatian arm of leading Austrian mobile operator Mobilkom, is poised to enter the Croatian fixed-line sector. VIPNet will be offering fixed-line services in Croatia, despite what is felt to be an expensive price for the license: €5.8 million. VIPNet already offers mobile services in Croatia, and the company realized a 28 percent growth in mobile subscriber numbers at the end of 2002 to reach 1.1 million subscribers. Offering fixed-line services will enable VIPNet to offer subscribers a full-service package. VIPNet could also benefit from having an already established brand name within the mobile sector.

Of the other countries, only the Albanian telecommunication market was liberalized at the beginning of 2003. Nevertheless, Albtelecom remains the sole operator of local long-distance and international telecommunication services.

## Figure 4.16    Customs and Trade Regulation Barriers

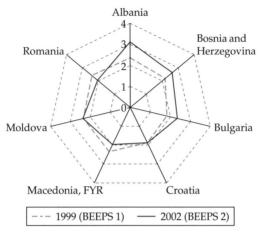

Sources: EBRD and World Bank (1999, 2002).
Note: Ratings range from 0 (indicating the lowest obstacle) to 4 (indicating the highest obstacle).

Figure 4.16 reports for each country the average rating of customs and trade regulation as a problematic factor for the surveyed businesses' operation and growth for 1999 and 2002. Ratings range from 1 (if the factor is not considered an obstacle) to 4 (where the factor is considered a major obstacle). Serbia and Montenegro was not included in the 1999 survey, so no comparison across time is possible for that country. With the notable exception of Romania and FYR Macedonia, where some progress has been registered, the obstacles determined by customs and trade regulation for all other countries have worsened.

Evidence from the case studies suggests that Albania has become the country that is worst affected. To address these barriers, several Albanian enterprises decided to employ a number of full-time employees to deal with customs clearance. One of the companies has also hired an agency that specializes in speeding up the customs procedures at the port. This strategy has considerably reduced the time to clear goods. Before, clearing used to take 2 weeks, but now, it usually takes approximately 3 days. Another company reports that, if bribes are paid, then the process to have a truck cleared will take only 2 hours. Otherwise, the truck can stay for as long as a week. Another inconvenience is that, because a payment is required for each time a truck is loaded or unloaded at the border, customs officials often make trucks load and unload many times. Irregularities committed by the customs officials have led one of the enterprises to officially complain. As a result, one customs official was suspended from work for 15 days and was fined.

## Figure 4.17    Export-Related Delays

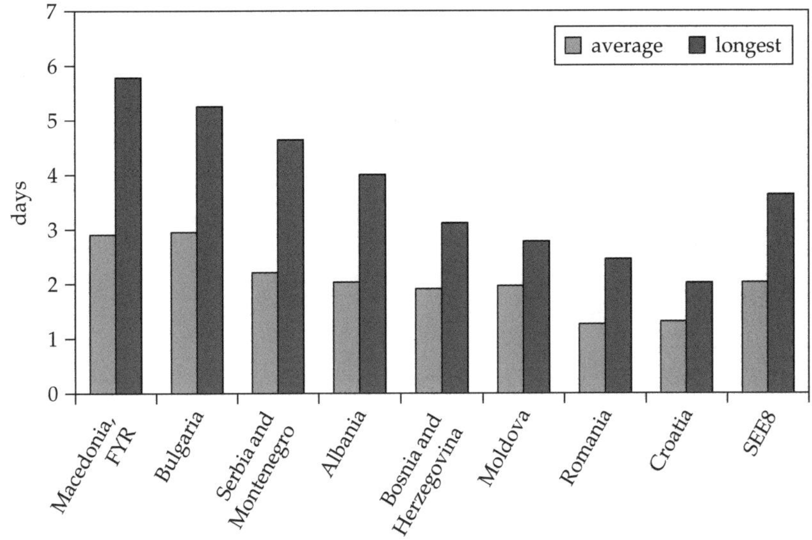

Source: EBRD and World Bank (2002).

Figure 4.17, which is based on the sample of surveyed firms, shows the average number of days and longest number of days that it took to export goods in 2001. Time is measured from arrival at the point of exit (port, airport) until the time that customs was cleared. Overall, the average was 2 days, but the process could last for 4 days. Countries above the average include Albania, Bulgaria, FYR Macedonia, and Serbia and Montenegro. Croatia and Romania had the most efficient process, and surveyed firms also perceived customs and trade regulation in those countries as less problematic.

Figure 4.18 reports the average number of days and longest number of days that it took to import goods in 2001. Time is measured from arrival at the point of entry (port, airport) until the time the surveyed firms cleared customs. In this case, both times are longer than the times reported in figure 4.17 for exports. Overall, importing goods takes on average almost 4 days, though the process can take as long as 1 week.

Serbia and Montenegro is the country most affected by import-related delays. This fact is not only confirmed by our case studies but is also prolifically documented in the international press. Cumbersome inspection procedures and paperwork characterize the 6-day-long wait at the Serbia-Montenegro border. A representative from one of the interviewed Serbian enterprises told us, "If you are lucky, you wait 2–3 days at the

## Figure 4.18   Import-Related Delays

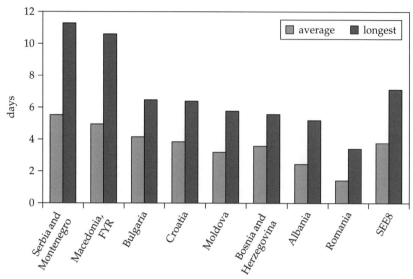

*Source:* EBRD and World Bank (2002).

border, but often trucks stay there for as long as 10 or more days." In addition, border control takes samples from the freight, and firms have no way of controlling the quantity of the goods taken as samples. Inspection and customs clearing usually take 7 days. Before 2001, bribes were regular. But under a new law, there is no stealing, and the processing and clearance of goods at the border is much quicker.

One indicator of efficiency—revenue per staff person—corroborates the importance of removing these obstacles to trade (see figure 4.19). Worth noting is how much more efficient customs authorities are in Romania and Croatia. Moldova and Serbia and Montenegro are at the bottom of the list. In the case of Moldova, the introduction of preshipment inspection has given rise to increasing concerns in the business community (see box 4.7).

Finally, evidence from the case studies reveals that transportation and trade have been constrained by problems in the use of rail services (characterized by inappropriate scheduling and mismatches of shipments) and by expensive road transportation. One of the Bulgarian enterprises that uses railway services complained about rates that were higher for freight than for passengers. The railway company requires advance payments for freight so that it can finance the rest of its services (in other words, it effectively cross-subsidizes its passenger services). The Bulgarian enterprise is concerned that, if the railway company loses its biggest customer (in the steelwork field), then the burden will be placed on the smaller industrial clients like itself.

**Figure 4.19    Ratios of Revenue Collected per Staff Person**

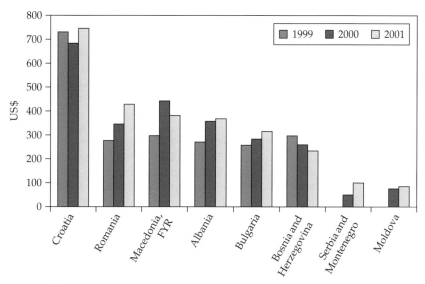

*Source:* TTFSE (2003).

Enterprises in Moldova also mainly rely on railways, which are the least expensive means of transportation. They face substantial delays of the freight delivery, which occur because the railways have no scheduled times for freight transportation as they do for passenger trains. One company interviewed commonly waits 5–10 days before receiving inputs, delivering products, or both. In some cases, additional delays may occur because of problems with customs officials or with the police. These delays cause serious problems in planning delivery and production schedules. To mitigate these problems, the company interviewed considered transporting its products by road instead. Because of the additional cost involved, however, road transportation was not a viable substitute.

Some enterprises in Albania and Bosnia and Herzegovina have resorted to using the trucks of freight-forwarding companies. This arrangement is considered simpler and cheaper. Rail transport is too slow, and enterprises' suppliers and customers are also reluctant to use rail because they need to reload at the train stations. Trucks are more flexible; they are able to travel to remote places and can deliver to several destinations on one trip.

## The Benefits of a Regional Energy Market

This section will analyze the benefits of establishing a regional trade market for energy. When resource endowments across countries within a region are heterogeneous, then the potential exists for substantial cost

## Box 4.7 Preshipment Inspection in Moldova

Preshipment inspections—which were introduced as a requirement of the International Monetary Fund under the Poverty Reduction and Growth Facility—have been the subject of intense debate among government officials and businesses. According to the legislation, an inspection company should inspect the incoming goods under import contracts when their value exceeds US$3,000 per contract. The inspection fee equals 0.8 percent of the value of the goods, but may not be less than US$235 for each freight. The growing concerns of the business community led the constitutional court of Moldova to declare the law on preshipment inspections unconstitutional at the end of September 2002. In June 2003, the government approved a new variant of the law on preshipment inspections. The government of Moldova will determine the company to conduct preshipment inspections and will ratify all documents (rules of inspection and the method for calculating a payment for rendered services) necessary to process them. The new law clarifies a combination of measures that are carried out to achieve quality surveillance and to confirm the quantity (amount) and price of the imported goods. It is designed to improve customs control, to increase the receipts to the budget from duties on import, and to create conditions that protect consumers.

Complaints from interviewed enterprises dealt with problems from preshipment inspections that were made under the initial rules, which were later declared unconstitutional. Long delays and additional costs led to substantial losses for these enterprises, Companies also did not understand the rationale behind the inspections, because the private company charged with implementing them did not check the quality and quantity of goods. Since that time, the problem has been gradually resolved. One problem pointed out by the enterprises remains relevant: other neighboring countries either do not impose such inspections or their process for carrying them out is smoother. Hence, suppliers have a strong incentive to switch to companies located in other countries to avoid the extra complications.

reductions through trade. At the same time, without domestic tariff adjustments, the benefits from regional trade will remain unrealized because cash flows within the regional trading system will be insufficient to cover import costs. The benefits from regional trade in energy are particularly large in regions where countries have noncoincidental peak demand, in which case trade opportunities for a given installed capacity increase. In addition, costs associated with reserve capacity—the capacity to meet unexpected upswings in demand or to compensate for units that are unexpectedly unable to supply—are lower in an integrated system.

With respect to technical capacity for regional trading, investments would be required in the areas of (a) transmission networking and

(b) installation of metering and data communication equipment. The costs associated with these investments are small relative to the associated benefits (in terms of cost reductions associated with trade). In addition, investments in institutional capacity would be required if a market were to work. A prerequisite for any power market is a grid code, without which system integrity is jeopardized. In a regional market context, ideally, a regional grid code should be established. At a minimum, national grid codes within in a regional market should be mutually consistent. Coordination might be achieved here through a regional regulators association, possibly supported by international financial institutions (IFIs), bilateral donors, or both.

A second prerequisite for any market is a transmission tariff method that reflects costs. In a regional context, questions arise over how system operators in transit countries should be compensated for transmission costs that occur because of international trade. Charging mechanisms here should be cost based—that is, based on the underlying flows of electricity—as opposed, for example, to distance based or based on the number of countries between trading parties. Mechanisms should be in place for coordinating investments in a regional context, given that these investments may be both substitutes and complements (for example, a transmission investment that strengthens links between countries might substitute for a generation investment in an importing country and might complement a generation investment in an exporting country). These mechanisms should enable the exchange of information and permit cooperation between governments.

Until these mechanisms are in place, coordination can be achieved through harmonization of regulatory rules by national regulators. Box 4.8 reports the steps agreed to by the SEE8 for the creation of a regional energy trade market.

## The Regional Dimension of Water Resource Management

Poor management of water resources is also at the root of several regional problems, including the recent drought. However, better management of water requires cooperation between countries with sometimes difficult past relationships. Bosnia and Herzegovina, Croatia, and Serbia and Montenegro have better access to water than the southern countries. The southern countries—particularly Bulgaria and FYR Macedonia— have far lower levels of available water and have experienced a decline in precipitation over the past 30 years. Agricultural demand for water is high in Albania, FYR Macedonia, and Romania, whereas Croatia needs little water for this purpose. Some countries, particularly Albania, Bosnia and Herzegovina, and Croatia, rely heavily on water to serve hydroelectric power stations. Water management is particularly critical for Albania, which regularly faces power shortages in the winter and lacks the funds

## Box 4.8 Regional Energy Market

The international community's support for SEE within the energy sector has gradually shifted from emergency support and efforts to address reconstruction needs to a more coordinated and long-term approach from a regional perspective. With the South Eastern Europe Electricity Regulatory Forum initiative, the European Commission has proposed a coherent vision with respect to the development of a competitive regional energy market in SEE. It has set the basis for the region's electricity standards to catch up, in the medium to long term, with the standards of the European Union. This initiative proposes that countries open their national electricity markets by 2005. This regional market will be based on the principles of the European Commission's Electricity Directive (96/92) and the relevant secondary legislation. The intended result will be that the electricity systems and companies of the region will participate fully in the internal electricity market of the European Union.

The benefits of the process are potentially great and include increased reliability in electricity supply; lower operating costs; reduced needs for additional capacity investments, especially in generation; improved opportunities for intra- and interregional trade, including peak load by hydroproducers in the region; and lower prices for the end-customers. However, the challenges entailed in the transition to the new systems are considerable. They include adopting numerous new laws and regulations; setting up independent regulatory agencies; training personnel; and introducing new business concepts and practices, stranded assets, and protection of poorest customers.

Under a memorandum of understanding, which was signed in Athens in 2002, all SEE8 countries, together with Turkey, have committed to undertake steps toward opening their energy markets. These steps include adopting energy strategies; setting up independent regulators; unbundling industry; and developing grid codes, cross-border transmission pricing and congestion management principles, and trading and commercial codes. Markets for eligible customers are expected to be open by 2007.

The European Commission and the Stability Pact for South Eastern Europe convened an informal donors' coordination meeting in Prague in July 2002. As a consequence of that meeting, a strategy paper was prepared, which lists the various actions required to achieve the objectives of the memorandum of understanding and presents a functioning complementarity of the different technical assistance programs.

So far, the World Bank together with other IFIs (including EBRD) is working with the European Union and donors to support the development of the regional energy market. Kreditanstalt für Wiederaufbau (KfW), the U.S. Agency for International Development (USAID), and the Canadian

*(Box continues on the next page.)*

---

**Box 4.8 (continued)**

International Development Agency (CIDA) are active in the region, and they are particularly important for the process:

- KfW is working on a review of regional demand, regional installed capacity, and regional trade. An appreciation of the likely gains from trade is necessary to allow infrastructure prioritization and appropriate agreement on regulatory functions and priorities.
- USAID's South East Cooperation Initiative will continue the projects on teleinformation and regional transmission planning. A new initiative is also under way with respect to regional transmission planning that will examine the role of hydropower systems. Support will also be provided to improve information exchange and encourage peer review visits.
- CIDA is working on specific transfer of the knowledge needed for operating a regional energy market to national power sector leaders. Thus, these leaders will be able to contribute effectively to the development of the market. Toward this end, a series of workshops on options for a regional energy market are already scheduled.

Given the number of initiatives in this region and the number of donors present in the energy sector (in particular, the power sector) of the countries of SEE, coordination between the interested players and between the various initiatives is clearly needed to ensure complementarity between projects and to avoid duplication of scarce donor resources.

---

for energy imports; domestic electricity generation in 2002, the lowest in 10 years, met only 58 percent of total consumption.

Because most river basins are shared by several countries, water-related problems tend to be felt in the region as a whole, even when the initial cause is localized. The whole region has suffered from drought in recent years. Ironically, floods also present a significant risk, which is felt by all countries. Romania's unsafe dams and mine facilities amplify the risk to that country's population. Floods have become much less predictable, making it more difficult to prepare for them. In addition, infrastructure to deal with floods has generally fallen into disrepair during the transition period.

Use of regional rivers for transporting of goods has been frequently disrupted in recent years by war, particularly by the North American Treaty Organization's bombing of Serbia in 1999. However, international initiatives to clear the Danube are under way, and traffic is beginning to normalize.

Sewerage services are available in 84 percent of the region's urban areas but in only 17 percent of its rural areas. The wastewater that goes untreated is a major pollutant of surface and groundwater sources. In addition, the region suffers from pollution by farms and industry upstream: The runoff from more chemical-intensive German agriculture is a significant source of pollution of the Danube.

Cooperation between South Eastern European states is essential to tackling these problems. Although the immediate aftermath of war proved to be nonconducive to cooperation, several recent initiatives sponsored by international organizations have encouraged the countries to work together on improving the management of various water resources (see box 4.9). Several initiatives by international organizations have created durable structures for regional cooperation over water management in the Balkans. However, far greater investment is needed to reduce the region's current vulnerability to water-related problems.

---

**Box 4.9     Regional Cooperation in Water Management**

In December 2002, representatives of Bosnia and Herzegovina, Croatia, Slovenia, and what is now Serbia and Montenegro signed an agreement to cooperate on management of the Sava river basin. The Sava catches water from 60 percent to 70 percent of the four countries' landmass and provides more than 80 percent of total available water. The Stability Pact for South Eastern Europe, known as the Sava Initiative, was established in June 2001 to bring the four countries together through a forum for discussion. A working group established two priorities: clearing the river for navigation and cooperating to prevent floods. The initiative culminated in 2002 with an agreement that established a framework for future planning and a recommendation that working groups be formed (a) to predict the environmental effect of economic development in the area and (b) to seek more efficient ways of using water resources for hydroelectricity.

In May 2002, 13 countries from the Danube river basin adopted a declaration establishing the Danube Cooperation Process. The Stability Pact first promoted the concept in 2001. Austria and Romania, with the support of the European Commission, subsequently led the way in turning the informal political initiative into a more concrete set of goals, although they insisted that the project not lead to new bureaucratic structures. For the goal of ensuring sustainable development in the region, the areas of cooperation include the economic sectors, especially transportation, navigation, and tourism (including agrotourism and ecotourism); culture, including the promotion of each country's culture and the common cultural ties of the Danube region; and subregional cooperation, including the promotion of initiatives and projects such as developing the potential of the already existing Euro-regions of the Danube and establishing new Euro-regions or different forms of cross-border and regional cooperation.

Since 1996, Albania and FYR Macedonia have been cooperating on the Lake Ohrid conservation project, which is intended to protect the lake's biodiversity. A bilateral management board monitors the environmental resources and manages sewage treatment and the water supply system. The World Bank financed the initial project, but the establishment of clear management structures has helped mobilize investment from other sources to fund various improvements in services.

# Policy Recommendations

A number of policy recommendations can be made with respect to infrastructure in the SEE8.

## *Establish a Sound Sequencing of Infrastructure Reforms*

Experience in infrastructure reforms and widespread private participation in infrastructure around the world suggest that the introduction of the private sector in a well-regulated and liberalized environment results in lower prices and better quality of services. Empirical studies have been undertaken at both the country and enterprise levels. Cross-country evidence generally indicates that the combination of privatization and broader regulatory reforms is associated with significant improvements in the performance of the utilities sector on any of a range of indicators, whereas privatization on its own has only limited effect (see Boylaud and Nicoletti 2000; Ros 1999). The ideal sequencing is, first, to set in place the regulatory framework and then to privatize utilities and use privatization to design the most appropriate market structure.

## *Promote Further Private Sector Involvement, Including Needed Steps toward Commercialization, Restructuring, and Ultimately, Privatization of the Key Utility Sectors*

The method of privatization is also crucial. If possible, it is preferable to involve strategic investors to maximize privatization revenues, to secure financing for necessary investments, and to strengthen incentives for improved efficiency. In the case of the electricity sector, when payment discipline is a problem, distribution should not be privatized after generation. Privatizing generation when cash collection is low will likely attract a low sales price, which may not support necessary investments. This low sales price could also lead to increasing political objections to privatization.

It is also crucial to undertake as early as possible the restructuring necessary to attract private sector participation. Restructuring should lead to significant operational efficiencies and should make the utility companies more attractive to potential investors. In light of the difficult market circumstances, which are characterized by a significantly reduced global interest from investors in the infrastructure sector, the key challenge is how to fill the still-large financing gap. The SEE8 face an enormous need for investment to rehabilitate and upgrade their infrastructure. For instance, estimates project that approximately US$15 billion will be required for the power sector over the next 10 years. The role that IFIs can play in this context is paramount.

## Establish an Independent, Transparent, and Publicly Accountable Regulatory Oversight Process

This recommendation entails strengthening not only the independence of the newly created sectoral regulatory agencies but also the financial base to ensure that the agencies have the necessary resources to operate. At the same time, independence needs to be balanced by accountability. A cost-benefit analysis is recommended to monitor and assess regulatory effects.

## Strengthen and Ensure Appropriate Coordination for the Institutions

With the creation of an independent sector regulatory agency, the competition authorities would no longer be responsible for tariff-setting processes and supervision. Technical and pricing regulation would be the responsibility of the specialized agency. Nevertheless, the competition authorities could play a more forceful role (a) in determining the appropriate scope of the regulatory authority and the appropriate structure of the infrastructure markets, and (b) in controlling anticompetitive conduct by dominant enterprises.

The Stability Pact's review of competition law and policy in SEE reports that informal and formal collaboration between independent infrastructure sectoral regulators and competition authorities has not yet been realized (OECD 2003). The problem, in many cases, hinges also on a lack of competition culture, including inadequate understanding of the benefits of competition and insufficient awareness of not only competition policy but also the body that should enforce competition rules and forcefully advocate for competition.

## Create a Competitive Environment

Important regulations have been established to ensure the emergence of effective competition by providing access to the incumbent's network. Those operators with the ability to abuse their market power should be subject to special rules (ex ante regulation) to ensure that they do not abuse their dominance. The EU directives for the telecommunication, energy, and transport sectors require the establishment of fair, transparent, and nondiscriminatory terms of access. The prospect of EU accession is expected to exert a very forceful incentive, particularly with respect to the telecommunication sector, as documented in box 4.10.

## Box 4.10 How Does EU Enlargement Affect Telecommunication Industries?

The wave of countries applying to gain EU membership in 2007 includes Bulgaria, Croatia (as of February 2003 when it submitted a bid to attain candidate status), and Romania. Once a country has gained candidate status, it must begin adopting the *acquis*. This requirement is supported by the European Union's "preaccession strategy," which is designed to help the candidate countries prepare for their future membership by aligning with the *acquis* (that is, the set of treaty obligations and legislation to which all member states must adhere) before accession, and it includes measures to help candidates monitor and assess progress toward meeting accession requirements. Crucially, the preaccession strategy also includes financial assistance, which is provided by the PHARE program. PHARE initially stood for Poland/Hungary Aid for the Reconstruction of the Economy, but as the programs purpose grew, the acronym was discarded. The PHARE program provides for assistance in institution building, together with assistance in associated investment and infrastructure development. PHARE support for institution building helps the candidates strengthen their capacity to implement the *acquis*.

Monitoring of candidate countries draws attention to areas that need to be addressed. For example, at the end of 2002, the European Union singled out Bulgaria's need to strengthen the regulatory capacity of its telecommunication industry and to focus on the designation of significant market power status. In Romania, the telecommunication market made rapid progress to fulfill its required *acquis* in a short space of time. By November 2002, the country was able to provisionally close the telecommunication chapter of its EU negotiations, and because the market was officially opened at the beginning of 2003, a huge number of operators (approximately 1,000 by May 2003) have gained certificates that allow them to provide electronic communication services.

The carrot of EU membership also influences the other countries in the region. For Bosnia and Herzegovina, FYR Macedonia, and Serbia and Montenegro, the prospect of closer integration with the European Union has fueled a government drive to improve the investment climate and draw in more foreign investors. Related to the telecommunication sector in Serbia and Montenegro, one significant example of this dynamic can be found in the recent passage of an EU-standard telecommunication law, which covers areas crucial to the development of a competitive market (for example, the establishment of an independent regulator). The telecommunication bill underscores the government's commitment to building a sound investment climate.

The prospect of EU accession is likely to mean that the region's industries will continue to grow and attract the interest of foreign investors. Not

*(Box continues on the next page.)*

---

**Box 4.10 (continued)**

only will the investment climate within the telecommunication sector be more stable, but also a shift will occur in the regional investment climate as perceived financial and investment risks continue to diminish. This shift, too, will ensure further growth and opportunity for the mobile and other telecommunication sectors.

---

## Developing Alternative Solutions, Including Cross-Sectoral and Regional Approaches

The SEE8 face significant constraints to infrastructure regulatory reforms stemming from their market size, their lack of sector-specific regulatory expertise, and the credibility of their national governments in establishing a regulatory environment. Hence, considering alternative solutions—such as adopting a cross-sectoral approach (as opposed to a sectoral regulatory approach), adopting a regional approach to regulation (as opposed to a national approach), and adopting "regulation by contract"—is worthwhile.

One question the SEE8 face is whether to adopt sector-specific regulatory offices or whether to adopt a multisectoral office. The United Kingdom opted for the first option, whereas the United States adopted a system of public utility commissions, with each commission typically covering several industries within a single state. U.K. regulators, as individual office-holders, have been more proactive than a panel of commissioners would have been and can more easily be held accountable for their decisions.

In the SEE8, a panel of commissioners might be less vulnerable to influences and might weaken the link with particular governments or ministers. Such a panel might increase stability, but it might be less effective in taking action. In the United Kingdom, it has been helpful for each regulator to focus on the most relevant issues within each industry and to learn from other regulators' experiences. Some have argued that a single commission covering several industries can make the best use of scarce regulatory expertise. Also, in the future, as utilities become more intertwined, a single body regulating all of them may have a greater advantage. This approach contains a major caveat, however; because of the very different market structure, ranging from telecommunications (the most competitive) to water utilities (the least competitive), the regulatory approaches, skills, and procedures required for each of these sectors can be very different.

The creation of regional regulatory authorities can offer a pragmatic solution to the problem of limited domestic regulatory capacity. Regional authorities could advance domestic regulatory reforms, enhance regulatory credibility, and help countries overcome their commitment problems. As discussed previously in this chapter, a prerequisite to the creation of a regional trade market is the coordination of regulatory rules that can be achieved only through strong exchange of information and cooperation between governments.

Finally, in addition to the cross-sectoral and regional approaches to address the constraints of regulatory expertise, an alternative approach could be "regulation by contract," an arrangement that facilitates privatization through a contract between the government and the privatized utility in the initial period and through tariff setting by the regulator in the later period. If the initial period is defined broadly enough, such an arrangement can enable privatization even in a country with a nascent regulatory agency. It provides stability and predictability of rules to the operator and establishes precedents for the regulator.

## Endnotes

1. For more evidence, see Vagliasindi (2001).

2. This amount roughly equals the LRMC for residential consumption in the United States.

3. The EBRD financed a study titled "Power Sector Affordability in South East Europe" (IPA Energy Consulting 2003), which highlighted the key challenges and possible remedies, including "lifeline" tariffs and targeted subsidies.

4. *Tunneling* is the transfer of assets and profits out of their controlling stakeholders.

5. For other details on the challenges facing network utilities privatization and the experience of European Union accession countries, see Buiter and Vagliasindi (2003).

6. The link between the establishment of an independent regulator in a sector and better performance indicators is robust to the introduction of enterprise and country level controls (see Vagliasindi 2003b).

## References

Bartle, Ian, ed. 2003. *The U.K. Model of Utility Regulation: A 20th Anniversary Collection to Mark the "Littlechild Report."* Bath, U.K.: University of Bath.

Boylaud, Olivier, and Giuseppe Nicoletti. 2000. "Regulation, Market Structure, and Performance in Telecommunications." Economics Department Working Paper 237. Organisation for Economic Co-operation and Development, Paris.

Buiter, Willem, and Maria Vagliasindi. 2003. "The Case of Privatization for Network Utilities." In Gertrude Tumpel-Gugerell and Peter Mooslechner, eds., *Structural Challenges for Europe*. Cheltenham, U.K.: Edward Elgar.

EBRD (European Bank for Reconstruction and Development). 2003. *Transition Report 2003: Integration and Regional Cooperation*. London.

EBRD and World Bank. 1999. *Business Environment and Enterprise Performance Survey* (BEEPS1). London and Washington, D.C. Data available online at http://info.worldbank.org/governance/beeps.

————. 2002 *Business Environment and Enterprise Performance Survey* (BEEPS2). London and Washington, D.C. Data available online at http://info.worldbank.org/governance/beeps2002.

Harris, Clive. 2003. *Private Participation in Infrastructure: Trends in Developing Countries*. Washington, D.C.: World Bank.

IPA Energy Consulting. 2003. *Power Sector Affordability in South East Europe*. Final report for the European Bank for Reconstruction and Development. Available online at http://www.ipaenergy.co.uk/seeurope/mainpage.htm.

ITU (International Telecommunication Union). 2002. *World Telecommunication Report*. Geneva.

OECD (Organisation for Economic Co-operation and Development). 2003. *Competition Law and Policy in South East Europe*. Paris.

Ros, Agustin. 1999. "Does Ownership or Competition Matter?: The Effect of Telecommunications Reform on Network Expansion and Efficiency." *Journal of Regulatory Economics* 15:62–92.

TTFSE (Trade and Transport in Southeast Europe Program). 2003. *TTFSE Indicator Workbook*. Available online at http://www.seerecon.org/ttfse/ttfse-indicators.htm.

Vagliasindi, Maria 2001. "Competition Policy across Transition Economies." *Revue d'Economie Financière* (Special Issue):215–50.

————. 2003a. "Regulatory Challenges: Lessons from the UK Model for Transition Countries." In Ian Bartle, ed., *The U.K. Model of Utility*

*Regulation: A 20th Anniversary Collection to Mark the "Littlechild Report."* Bath, U.K.: University of Bath.

————. 2003b. "The Role of Investment and Regulatory Reforms in the Development of Infrastructure across Transition Economies." European Bank for Reconstruction and Development, London. Processed.

World Bank. 2003. *Water Resources Management in South Eastern Europe.* Washington, D.C. Available online at http://lnweb18.worldbank.org/ ECA/ECSSD.nsf/ECADocbyUnid/8FF7BE53619B4DA685256D1D006 A06D8?Opendocument.

# 5

# Corporate Ownership, Financial Transparency, and Access to Finance

## Introduction

The private ownership of productive assets that characterizes capitalism relies on an institutional foundation nonexistent in the immediate post-communist systems. In particular, capitalist systems provide for legal protections that allow the pooling of capital with controlled risk for investors and a potentially important new source of financing for productive entities. Building those systems, however, requires reforms much deeper than stroke-of-the-pen passage of laws. Investor confidence—indeed fundamental fairness—requires corporate transparency and accountability. In the West, systems that have been in existence for centuries are yet to be perfected, a fact made clear by the wave of governance and accounting scandals that have occupied the headlines in recent years. The relative infancy of the systems in transition countries poses an even greater challenge.

This chapter uses the case studies of firms that were undertaken in each of the SEE8 (the eight countries that are the subject of this study) in the summer of 2002 and the data from the 2002 EBRD and World Bank *Business Environment and Enterprise Performance Survey* (BEEPS2) to examine the elements of the basic paradigm of corporate governance and access to finance, as well as the impact that both have on investment and growth in the region.[1] Certain core aspects of corporate governance have been the subject of a great deal of attention since the early days of the transition—namely, the basic questions of company law, legal forms of organization, and maintenance of minority shareholder rights (see Mesnard 2001). The essence of how legal provisions influence the incentives of managers and owners in the postsocialist world is much better understood now than a decade ago. This chapter will, for this reason, not dwell on these aspects of corporate governance but will focus instead on issues of financial transparency and accountability.

As described in chapter 2, in many countries of South Eastern Europe (SEE), the principal method of privatizing firms was the management-employee buyout (MEBO), a system that left ownership primarily in the hands of insiders. The reliance on insider-centered privatization schemes left a legacy of fragmented ownership, limited incentives to restructure, and in most cases no new infusion of capital for the enterprises. In some instances, the resulting ownership structures led to fundamental conflicts of interest. In the former Yugoslav Republic of Macedonia, interlocking ownership between banks and enterprises is reported to lead to misuse of available credit. In the countries of the former Yugoslavia, the tradition of self-management similarly led to powerful domination by employees, an effect that persists today, making fundamental restructuring and retrenchment of the enterprises more difficult. In some cases, privatization to insiders also facilitated the nontransparent award of state assets to the well connected. The informal ties between politicians and the new enterprise owners presented the fundamental conflict of interest—politicians had an incentive to use their powers for the benefit of certain enterprises, rather than for the whole of society, whereas enterprises tended to make decisions based on political, rather than profit-maximizing, criteria. Although insider privatizations are no longer the norm in some of the countries of SEE, the legacy of past decisions lingers.

The disposition of the bloated state-owned enterprises that epitomized central planning has coincided with the emergence of new firms that have provided the engine for employment, income generation, and growth in many countries. New firms and revitalized old firms alike require financing for their activities. Although the public trading of shares of corporatized enterprises potentially provides an avenue for the largest firms to raise equity capital, such firms still require day-to-day working capital. For medium-size and small companies, financing options are even more limited, and providers of debt financing require some assurances that their funds will be repaid. Systems that support financial transparency and accountability help provide peace of mind for creditors.

At first blush, the relationship between financial transparency and performance seems straightforward: Firms with more transparent finances should have an easier time securing financing for their activities and should ultimately grow faster. Indeed, cross-country research has found that, in countries with strong, well-enforced disclosure requirements, costs of capital are lower (Hall and Leuz 2003). Across the countries of SEE this pattern also seems to hold. Two rudimentary indicators of financial transparency—the degree to which firms believe that they adhere to International Accounting Standards (IAS) and the degree to which they claim to use external audits—are useful for explaining variation in growth at the country level. As we discuss in the next section, in some

## Figure 5.1 Financial Transparency, as Reported by Firms, and GDP Growth

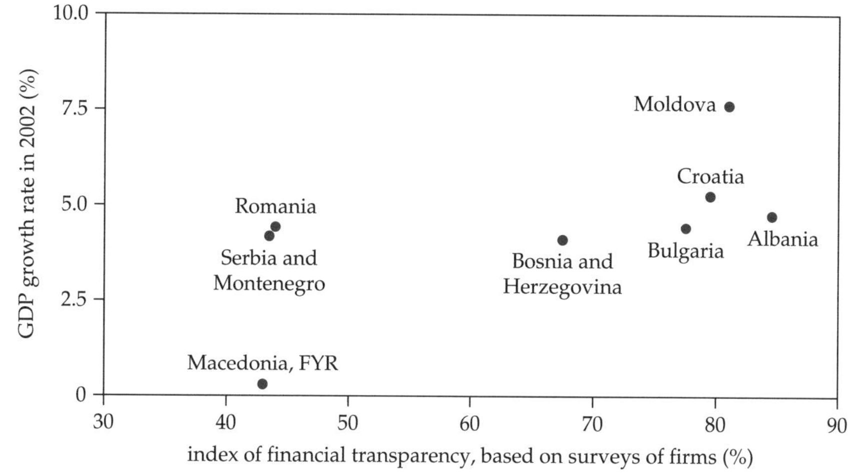

Source: EBRD and World Bank (2002).
Note: The index of financial transparency is the simple average of the percentage of firms saying that they use IAS and external audits.

cases such perceptions may represent wishful thinking, but they never-theless are useful for the variation in practices they reveal.

Figure 5.1 shows the average penetration of IAS and external audits, as reported by firms in each country in BEEPS2, mapped against the average gross domestic product (GDP) growth rate in each country in 2002, the same year as the survey. Of course, economic growth is complex, and no pretense is made that firms' perceptions of adherence to certain accounting and auditing practices provide the sole impetus to growth. Yet the positive partial relationship between these rudimentary indicators of reform and economic performance suggests the usefulness of this element of reform. Although the positive relationship evident in figure 5.1 is encouraging in the sense that it shows that patterns that hold in the rest of the world also hold in SEE, the chart begs further questions. Why is there so much varia-tion in the reported levels of financial transparency across the countries of SEE? How are firms within a country rewarded for their efforts at improv-ing financial transparency? How does financial transparency translate into improved financing opportunities for the firms themselves?

We will first discuss the forms of ownership of firms in the sample and then present the degree of transparency and accountability evident in the way the firms present their financial statements. Next, we will examine the financial modalities used by firms for their sales and purchases and the means by which they finance their activities. Finally, we will explore the link between institutions of financial transparency and firm-level investment and growth and make some summary policy recommendations flowing from the analysis.

## Forms of Ownership

One of the key features of early transition reform strategies—and one that persists today in some countries—is the privatization of state-owned enterprises. The motivation for the push toward privatization came, in part, from the desire to give the population a stake in the new system and thereby reduce the probability of backsliding on early reforms. But there was also a very real economic imperative founded on the idea that ownership matters. Specifically, private owners would be more likely than politicians to push enterprise managers to maximize profits. The politicians' motivation, for example, to maintain employment levels at all costs and to direct production toward certain buyers at submarket prices could lead to inefficiencies, soft budgets, and passive management. Privatizing state-owned assets was envisioned as a way to bring managerial incentives in line with market demands. A large body of research has confirmed that, by and large, private ownership leads to greater enterprise restructuring (Djankov and Murrell 2002).

In designing programs for the privatization of state assets, reformers were quickly confronted with conflicting goals—speed, revenue, fairness, and transparency are not all achieved by the same methods of privatization. Another goal, getting ownership into the hands of effective owners, also proved crucial. Empirical research has confirmed, for example, that concentrated ownership is associated with better firm performance (Frydman and others 1999).

As discussed in chapter 2, privatization has proceeded more slowly in SEE than elsewhere in Europe. In some cases, war (as in Bosnia and Herzegovina, Croatia, and Serbia and Montenegro) or political financial crises (as in Albania) have contributed to the slowness. In other cases (as in Romania), powerful unions have at times resisted privatization of industrial enterprises, and key enterprises remain under the control of the state.

The overall extent of privatization in SEE varies. Although it is difficult to compile an objective indicator of progress toward privatization, the European Bank for Reconstruction and Development (EBRD 2002) provides a subjective measure that helps illustrate the variations (see figure 5.2). Every country has progressed further in privatizing small enterprises than in the more politically sensitive privatization of large enterprises. In countries where privatization has progressed more slowly, the continued presence of the state in the affairs of enterprises leads to the mixed-up incentives that characterized the former system, as described in the case study of one firm in Bosnia and Herzegovina (see box 5.1).

## Figure 5.2    Privatization, Enterprise Restructuring, and Governance

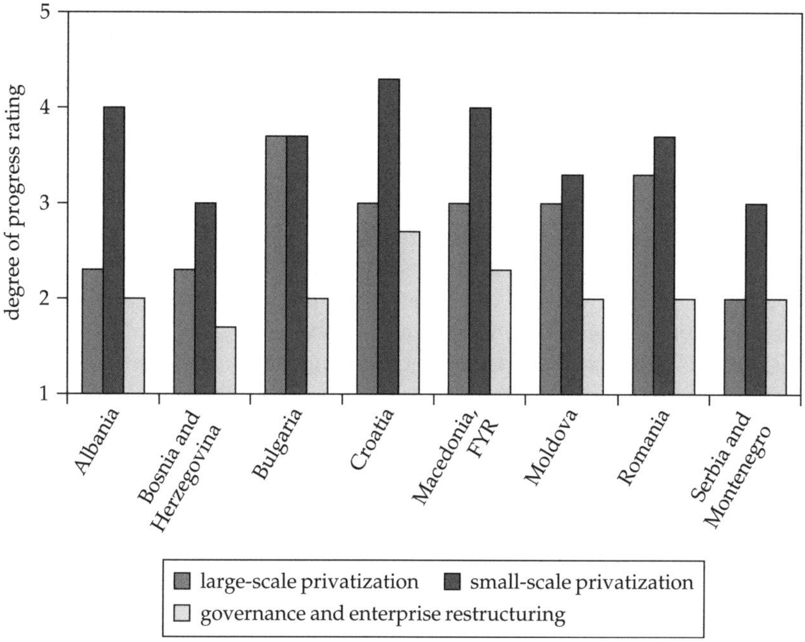

*Source:* EBRD (2002).

---

### Box 5.1  The Mixing of Social and Private Goals: State Ownership in Bosnia and Herzegovina

A venerable industrial firm in Bosnia and Herzegovina, established in the 1930s, provides an illustration of the difficulties posed by continued state ownership of a firm better suited for private ownership. Appointments to the management board are reported to be politically motivated—all appointees are members of political parties—and the firm consequently must pursue the goals of politicians rather than maximizing profits. The intermingling of social and private goals leads the firm to carry excess employees (35–45 percent) on its payroll. Although the firm is fully state owned and called on to carry out social programs by maintaining excessive employment, the firms' managers have reported that the firms are not audited. This firm's experience exemplifies two key shortcomings afflicting the governance of many enterprises in SEE: conflict of interest generated by political interference in firm decisions and lack of accountability generated by the lack of transparency.

The privatization processes chosen by the SEE8 have left an imprint on the economy and on the governance structures of the enterprises, as the discussion in chapter 2 suggests. Voucher privatization schemes (as used in Moldova, for example) have left a legacy of diffuse ownership of the firms that were privatized in this way. Similarly, the dominance of MEBOs in the early privatization experience of Bulgaria and Romania has left many firms insider-controlled (Earle and Estrin 1996). Developing governance structures that ensure effective and appropriate incentives for managers in such environments is essential if privatization is to have an important effect on the economy. Indeed, one notable feature of figure 5.2 is that improvements in privatization have outpaced improvements in developing the institutions of corporate governance and the restructuring of enterprises, at least in the eyes of external observers.

As has been discussed elsewhere (and in this study, for example, chapter 2), the immediate corporate governance environment following privatization was characterized, in many cases, by extremely diffuse ownership. Stock exchanges were set up to facilitate privatization and consolidation of shares and, in many cases, have been successful for this purpose. Firms that were too small to sustain widespread ownership and arm's-length investing were in essence "taken private" as controlling groups bought up shares and the number of shares trading gradually dwindled away. One Bulgarian firm that participated in the case studies described just such an experience (see box 5.2).

---

### Box 5.2  Postprivatization Concentration in Bulgaria

The experience of one large Bulgarian firm exemplifies that of many firms in the region. A single owner held a bare majority of shares immediately after privatization 6 years ago, and the remaining shares (more than 40 percent, initially) were traded on the stock exchange. The controlling owner continued to acquire shares from both workers and institutional owners until nearly all of the shares were acquired. The firm was then delisted from the stock exchange.

Many stock exchanges in the region seem to be in the midst of similar life cycles. Created to facilitate privatization and to allow for postprivatization concentration of shares, the exchanges were intended to ultimately become venues for firms to raise equity capital and for existing shares to be traded by arm's-length investors. For many firms, however, share trading did not play out among arm's-length investors but flowed in a unidirectional way toward concentrated owners, who, motivated partially by weak minority shareholder's rights, were interested in acquiring majority holdings. Thus, as firms have been taken private, there have been few new issues on the stock exchanges to replace them.

## Table 5.1    Origin of Firms in the BEEPS2 Sample
*(percent)*

| Country | Privatized | De novo | State-owned |
|---|---|---|---|
| Albania | 8.1 | 80.8 | 11.2 |
| Bosnia and Herzegovina | 24.7 | 62.6 | 12.6 |
| Bulgaria | 18.4 | 66.4 | 15.2 |
| Croatia | 16.8 | 66.5 | 16.8 |
| Macedonia, FYR | 17.2 | 79.3 | 3.6 |
| Moldova | 20.9 | 63.4 | 15.7 |
| Romania | 15.7 | 69.1 | 15.3 |
| Serbia and Montenegro | 11.3 | 71.1 | 17.6 |
| Total | 16.6 | 69.6 | 13.8 |

*Source:* EBRD and World Bank (2002).
*Note:* Data are based on the full sample of SEE8 firms participating in BEEPS2.

Whereas privatization was the big story early in the transition, the entry of new firms has been the story more recently, as emphasized in chapter 3 (see also table 5.1[2]). Although administrative and other barriers often hinder new entrants to the market, the number of new firms is still notable, many of which rely on individual and family ownership. Among firms that participated in BEEPS2, the primary owner is an individual or a family for more than 60 percent of firms (see also figure 2.6 in chapter 2).

The BEEPS2 sample exhibits remarkable variation in forms of ownership, as shown in table 5.2. Croatia and Romania have few firms that described themselves as sole proprietorships but large numbers that called themselves corporations. Bosnia and Herzegovina and Bulgaria stand out for the large numbers of firms that said their shares were listed on the stock exchanges. Larger firms are, predictably, more likely to report a corporate form of organization and listing on stock exchanges.

Table 5.3 shows how the sample breaks down in terms of ownership. Most firms in each of the SEE8 are completely owned by the state or are exclusively owned by domestic or foreign owners. Mixed ownership (for example, businesses that are partially state owned or are joint ventures) is less common. Among larger firms, however, mixed ownership is much more prevalent.

Although the fusion of state and economy, as well as the conflicts of interest that are integral to that fusion, continues to have lingering effects on enterprises of all legal origins, the effects can be particularly conflicting for partially privatized enterprises. Although the vast majority of firms in the BEEPS2 sample were either fully private or fully state owned, a small number (8 percent) of partially state-owned firms afforded some simple analysis of the effect of partial state ownership on firm performance.[3] The continuation of state involvement in partially privatized

**Table 5.2  Forms of Legal Organization, 2002**

| Country | Sole proprietorship | Partnership | Cooperative | Privately held corporation | Corporation listed on the stock exchange | Other privately owned form | State-owned enterprise | Corporatized state entity | Other |
|---|---|---|---|---|---|---|---|---|---|
| Albania | 51.2 | 36.5 | 0.0 | 1.8 | 0.0 | 0.0 | 5.9 | 4.7 | 0.0 |
| Bosnia and Herzegovina | 50.0 | 9.9 | 0.0 | 12.1 | 12.6 | 2.8 | 8.2 | 3.3 | 1.1 |
| Bulgaria | 47.6 | 16.8 | 3.2 | 4.0 | 13.2 | 0.4 | 11.6 | 1.2 | 2.0 |
| Croatia | 6.4 | 1.1 | 1.1 | 67.9 | 8.6 | 0.0 | 12.3 | 2.7 | 0.0 |
| Macedonia, FYR | 54.1 | 23.5 | 1.2 | 16.5 | 1.2 | 0.0 | 1.2 | 2.4 | 0.0 |
| Moldova | 27.0 | 5.2 | 0.6 | 35.6 | 0.0 | 16.1 | 8.1 | 0.6 | 6.9 |
| Romania | 2.8 | 0.4 | 1.6 | 60.0 | 0.0 | 20.4 | 3.1 | 2.0 | 9.8 |
| Serbia and Montenegro | 42.4 | 18.4 | 2.4 | 16.0 | 3.2 | 0.8 | 13.2 | 3.2 | 0.4 |
| SEE8 | 34.3 | 13.4 | 1.4 | 27.2 | 5.0 | 5.4 | 8.2 | 2.4 | 2.8 |

*Source:* EBRD and World Bank (2002).
*Note:* Data are based on the full sample of firms participating in BEEPS2. See the annex for the subset of enterprises with at least 50 employees.

**Table 5.3  Firm Ownership, 2002**

| Country | Mixed ownership | 100 percent foreign ownership | 100 percent domestic ownership | 100 percent state ownership | 100 percent other ownership | Number of firms in sample |
|---|---|---|---|---|---|---|
| Albania | 10.6 | 5.9 | 61.2 | 8.2 | 14.1 | 170 |
| Bosnia and Herzegovina | 24.7 | 8.8 | 39.6 | 4.4 | 22.5 | 182 |
| Bulgaria | 13.2 | 7.6 | 64.8 | 14.4 | 0.0 | 250 |
| Croatia | 13.4 | 10.2 | 65.2 | 11.2 | 0.0 | 187 |
| Macedonia, FYR | 17.7 | 5.9 | 75.3 | 0.6 | 0.6 | 170 |
| Moldova | 26.4 | 4.0 | 48.3 | 7.5 | 13.8 | 174 |
| Romania | 17.7 | 6.7 | 61.6 | 8.6 | 5.5 | 255 |
| Serbia and Montenegro | 17.2 | 10.4 | 47.2 | 12.8 | 12.4 | 250 |
| SEE8 | 17.4 | 7.6 | 57.8 | 9.0 | 8.2 | 1,638 |

*Source:* EBRD and World Bank (2002).
*Note:* Data are based on the full sample of firms participating in BEEPS2. See the annex for the subset of enterprises with at least 50 employees.

---

### Box 5.3  The Perils of Partial Privatization
### for a Croatian Firm

The experience of one Croatian firm, established in the 1920s, encapsulates the difficult predicament of firms subject to incomplete privatization. This manufacturing firm had a long history of state ownership before it was privatized in the early 1990s. It has since contended with the loss of tariff protection and increased competition concomitant with Croatia's membership in the World Trade Organization.

Attempting to remain dynamic, the firm has diversified its operations and is expanding into new foreign markets. But the historical path that the firm has taken keeps it from fully benefiting from the potential of its dynamism. The privatization process left the state with minority ownership. Managers of the company report that continued partial state ownership exerts a drag on company operations, especially since "the company wastes a lot of time in small bribes (dinners, presents) to state officials to solve business issues." In many cases, retaining minority state ownership does not serve a real purpose and, as this case study illustrates, can be detrimental to the firm's competitiveness.

---

firms does not come without costs. Across the sample of SEE8 firms, firms with partial state ownership made significantly fewer investments in assets than firms that were fully private or fully state owned. Whereas fully private and fully state firms had average growth rates of assets of 22 percent and 24 percent, respectively, firms with partial state ownership had an average growth rate of less than 6 percent. The case studies help explain the performance differential. As box 5.3 illustrates, managers of partially state-owned firms may continue to feel pressured to deliver on the programs of politicians, rather than to deliver profits to shareholders.

## Transparency and Accountability in Firm Finances

Among the many legacies that the old system bequeathed on postsocialist firms was an accounting system that was geared toward planning and control of physical assets, not toward managerial decisionmaking. Although a large amount of information was generally collected, the system did not facilitate systematic analysis. Shortcomings of the socialist accounting system include reluctance to write off bad debts, overemphasis on internal control, and underemphasis on management information. Financial statements may mask the true financial position of the company, thus making it difficult for investors, creditors, and regulators to evaluate different firms with a common metric. Indeed, the problems that can result from inconsistencies in accounting systems have been the subject of many newspaper headlines in the United States, a country with a highly developed accounting system. Systemic problems in the United States with conflict of interest, weak board oversight, and inappropriate executive compensation show that, even in the most developed systems, less scrupulous managers will seek out and exploit weaknesses in the accounting system.

One of the key reforms under way in many countries is the switch from national standards of accounting, particularly those designed for the old socialist systems, toward IAS. Conceptually, a single international standard helps increase transparency of firm finances. Systemwide transparency increases investor and lender confidence. To the extent that the new system also offers more accurate financial statements, the firm managers themselves should also benefit. In June 2003, the South East Corporate Governance Roundtable of the Organisation for Economic Co-operation and Development (OECD), with support from the World Bank and the governments of SEE, produced a white paper on corporate governance in SEE (OECD, South East Corporate Governance Roundtable 2003). The white paper outlined the many differences between IAS and most of the SEE8 systems of national standards. One key difference involves the format of financial statements. Disclosure notes and a description of accounting policies, essential for transparency of financial statements, often are not required under the existing regulations in the SEE8.

Despite the apparent advantages of switching from national standards to IAS, it should be emphasized that the transition will be costly. In the short run, firms are constrained both by the current level of human and organizational capital devoted to the old national standards and by creditors, governmental bodies, and others that persistently demand financial statements based on the old systems. Indeed, the OECD white paper emphasized that a key priority for reforming corporate governance is training relevant professionals, including accountants, auditors, judges, and board members. Firms in Moldova have noted the lack of understanding of accounting rules by firms and inspectors (see box 5.4).

Although one can argue that firms adopting IAS benefit from the greater information content of their financial statements, it must be emphasized that many of the benefits accrue to the system as a whole while the firms directly bear many of the costs of switching. Indeed, expert assessments such as the World Bank–IMF Reports on the Observance of Standards and Codes (ROSCs) often argue that the public's persistent distrust of financial statements leads to very limited demand for improved financial disclosure. It is no surprise, therefore, that firms tend to follow the standards imposed on them by law, rather than adopting IAS of their own initiative. Accounting standards, therefore, are typically imposed on firms and regulated by the government or, in some instances, by professional associations themselves.

An example of collaboration in accounting and auditing reform in SEE was the creation in 2001 of the South Eastern European Partnership on Accountancy Development (SEEPAD),[4] an association of accounting

---

### Box 5.4  The Link between Accounting and Inspectorate Reforms in Moldova

The manager of a small industrial firm in Moldova noted that, because the firm is completely owned by a single person, no external audits were required. The firm's accounts are checked by financial inspectors and need comply only with national accounting rules. The manager complained, however, that fines are imposed for even minor infractions. Tax inspectors are reportedly allowed to come to the firm armed with guns, a situation that the entrepreneur finds particularly disturbing. Despite the small size of the firm, the manager thought it prudent to hire at least two full-time accountants to be sure that taxes are filed on time.

A second, larger, firm echoed these complaints, reporting that financial inspections of accounts are frequent and very time consuming.

The experience of a third firm illustrates the limits of accounting reforms when inspectorates do not keep pace. After consulting with experienced auditors, the firm undertook leasing arrangements because they had tax advantages. The tax inspector, however, was reportedly unaware of the treatment of leasing arrangements under the law. Even though the firm felt itself on solid ground with its choice of financing mechanisms, management found it expedient to simply pay off the tax inspector, rather than go through the disruption of a lengthy inspection process.

---

institutes and bodies from each of the eight nations covered in this study plus Greece, as well as several supporting international organizations. The SEEPAD initiative took as its agenda strengthening regional accounting and audit reform and analyzing obstacles to the development of the accountancy profession.

Leadership in reforming the standards, however, often falls on government regulators, who are themselves constrained by the limited number of trained specialists at their disposal. In some countries, the ministry of finance takes the lead role in developing and revising standards. Given that the traditional focus of these ministries is on taxation and statistics and given that socialist accounting systems are geared toward those goals, leadership by such ministries may lead to standards with important differences from IAS. The Romanian ROSC makes this argument (World Bank 2003a).

Indeed, it is worth reflecting on the meaning of accounting standards in the first place. Many of the countries in SEE have set very ambitious goals of adopting IAS, driven in part by the desire for European Union (EU) accession. However, in most of the countries, the move has not been toward IAS itself but rather toward developing national standards that are based on IAS. The intention of reformers to reduce the burden on firms and the accounting profession by retaining elements of former national standards is certainly understandable. Yet standards that vary from country to country are, after all, not international standards at all.

Although reformers may have eased the reform burden of firms somewhat by retaining elements of national standards, they have also unnecessarily increased the burden on some firms by mandating the use of IAS for an overly broad spectrum of firms. Small and medium-size enterprises, for example, have less to gain by adopting IAS, and, indeed, many EU countries exempt smaller firms from the complexity of IAS. In SEE, by contrast, laws requiring the use of IAS are often applied to many firms beyond the large publicly traded firms that would be the focus in EU countries. In Croatia, the country that is arguably the closest to the adoption of true IAS, plans are under way to scale back some of the coverage of the standards precisely to reduce the burden on small and medium enterprises.

How have firms in SEE progressed toward implementation of IAS? BEEPS1 and BEEPS2 asked firms whether they used IAS, and the responses to this question provide some insight into several issues, but come with a few cautions. First, the question presupposes that adoption of IAS is a matter of firm choice rather than the subject of regulation. Second, given that, instead of adopting IAS completely, most countries have adopted national standards that are based on IAS, the answer to the survey question must technically be "no" for the vast majority of firms. However, the responses firms supplied to this question are interesting both as an indication of how firms understand International Accounting Standards and as a very rough indicator of the prevalence of accounting practices that are related to IAS, if not the same as IAS.[5]

The responses to the BEEPS question on IAS are presented in figure 5.3. In both 1999 and 2002, medium-size and large firms (that is, firms with at least 50 full-time employees) in Croatia and Moldova reported the most widespread use of IAS. For both of these countries, some 90 percent of firms believed that their accounting practices conformed with IAS. At the lower end of the scale are FYR Macedonia, Romania, and Serbia and Montenegro, with less than half of medium-size and large firms reporting the use of IAS.

Within the SEE8, firms' perception that they are using IAS has changed little between 1999 and 2002, except in Bulgaria, which showed a marked increase. Bulgaria's new Accountancy Law, which came into force in the beginning of 2002, calls for the gradual introduction of IAS. Regulated financial companies such as banks and insurance companies, as well as enterprises with publicly traded shares, were to be in full compliance with IAS by the beginning of 2003, whereas other enterprises had until the beginning of 2005 to come into compliance. Bulgaria has also instituted a national program for training accountants and related state officials (Jeliazhov 2002). But adopting a new system such as IAS remains

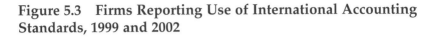

**Figure 5.3    Firms Reporting Use of International Accounting Standards, 1999 and 2002**

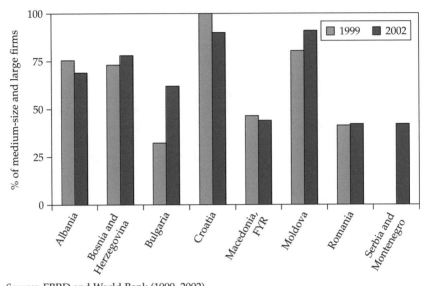

*Sources:* EBRD and World Bank (1999, 2002).
*Note:* Data include only firms with at least 50 full-time employees. Serbia and Montenegro was not included in the 1999 sample.

a challenge. Thirty enterprises in the Bulgarian BEEPS2 sample reported that their shares were publicly traded on the stock exchange, but of these enterprises only slightly more than half said that they used IAS at the time of the survey (mid-2002). By contrast, firms in Croatia, which are subject to similar rules, were more likely to be in compliance. All listed companies are required to adhere to IAS, and indeed, of the 15 surveyed, all reported using IAS.

A series of regressions was run on the BEEPS2 data to explore which firms were more likely to say that they used IAS. The analysis examined the influences on reports of IAS use both for the whole sample of SEE8 enterprises and for each country individually. (Croatia was omitted from the individual country regressions because so few firms had not adopted IAS.) Several explanatory variables were considered, including the concentration of ownership, measured by the percentage of shares owned by the largest shareholder; size, measured by the log of the number of employees; and the legal form of organization. In addition, firm characteristics such as ownership type (foreign, domestic, or state) and industry sector were included in the analysis. The regression results are presented in detail in the annex and simply summarized here.

**Figure 5.4   Firms Reporting Using IAS, by Size and Ownership Type, 2002**

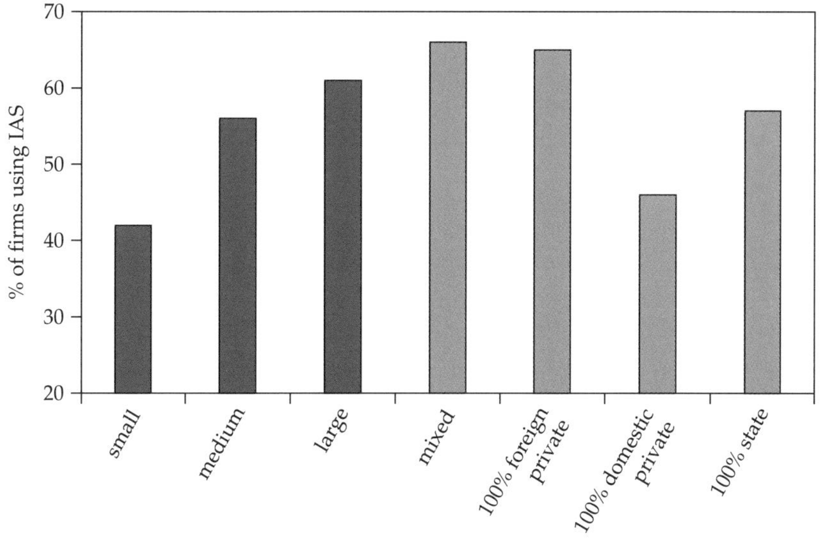

*Source:* EBRD and World Bank (2002).

Across the surveyed firms in SEE, larger firms were more likely than smaller firms to say that they used IAS, and foreign-owned firms were much more likely than were domestic firms to make that claim (see figure 5.4). Neither of these results is particularly surprising. Owners of foreign-owned firms are more likely to demand financial statements prepared in accordance with standards that they can readily interpret. Similarly, larger firms are more likely to be regulated and to deal with foreign partners; therefore, they have more to gain from preparing financial statements according to IAS. It is important to emphasize that these effects were found to be strong even after accounting for other effects. That is, foreign-owned firms were more likely to say that they used IAS than were domestic firms, even after controlling for size.

Even though ownership and size are clear influences on the adoption of IAS, most of the variation in reported use of IAS in the SEE8 is across countries. That is, surveyed firms with a common set of characteristics were more likely to believe they used IAS if they were located in Croatia, for example, than if they were located in Romania. A simple interpretation of this finding is that the drive to adopt IAS is attributable to external factors, such as requirements embodied in laws, rather than to the inward-looking managerial incentives of an improved accounting framework. This concept has important implications, which will be explored later in this chapter.

The variation in use of IAS within a country is also interesting. Consistent with the findings across countries, within most countries in the SEE8 large firms were more likely to adopt IAS, and in several of the countries, the ownership structure correlated significantly with firm reports of IAS use—that is, foreign-owned firms were more likely to say that they used IAS than were domestic firms. Interestingly, legal form of ownership was not a significant factor in any country after controlling for size, and concentration of ownership did not have any significant effect in any of the SEE8.

An independent external audit can also bolster the credibility of a firm's financial statements. Indeed, worldwide such audits are required of publicly traded firms. Again, the accounting scandals in the United States show that the system may break down, for example, when the auditor becomes too cozy with the firm being audited. Notwithstanding this possibility, external audits should provide for financial statements more credible than in the absence of such audits.

How often do firms in the SEE8 report that they make use of external audits? Whereas firms' reports of prevalence of IAS use were relatively stable between the 1999 and 2002 BEEPS, their reports on the use of external independent audits varied considerably. In most of the SEE8, reports of the use of external audits increased between the two periods, the only exceptions being Bosnia and Herzegovina and Croatia, both of which started from a very high level in 1999. In FYR Macedonia, Romania, and Serbia and Montenegro, most medium-size and large firms still do not make use of external audits (see figure 5.5).

It must be stressed in this context that the institutional foundation for truly independent external audits is not easily established. One contributing factor in the U.S. accounting scandals was the potential for conflict of interest on the part of the auditors. In the United States, auditors are paid by the very firms they are auditing, a factor that could encourage the production of misleading accounting statements. The firms interviewed as part of this study voiced some skepticism about the value of external audits, as described in box 5.5. Indeed, the very high percentage of firms reporting that they had external audits suggests that firms in some countries may have erroneously been equating routine preparation of financial statements or reviews by tax inspectors with external audits. In fact, both the OECD white paper and various ROSCs found that, while many of the SEE8 have forged ahead with legislative reform, progress in implementation has been hindered by the carryover of former practices (OECD, South East Corporate Governance Roundtable 2003; World Bank n.d.).

What determines whether a firm reports that it has adopted the practice of external audits? Again, we performed a series of probit regressions to try to address this question, using the same variables described earlier. The full results are presented in the annex and summarized here.

## Figure 5.5  Firms Reporting Using External Audits of Financial Statements, 1999 and 2002

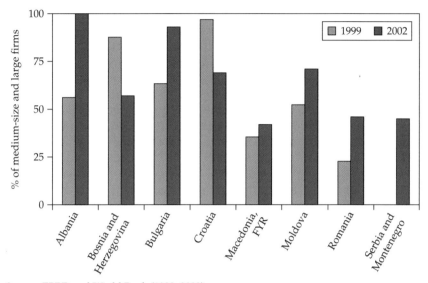

*Sources:* EBRD and World Bank (1999, 2002).
*Note:* Data include only firms with at least 50 full-time employees. Serbia and Montenegro was not included in the 1999 sample.

---

### Box 5.5  Firm Skepticism of Audits in Albania

Although mandatory external audits may help provide independent confirmation of the veracity of firms' financial statements, some firms expressed doubt about their value. The manager of one small Albanian firm, for example, held the view that chartered accountants tend to sign just about anything that a firm gives them, while charging a lot of money for their services. As a manager, he would prefer an auditor who rigorously checks financial statements, thus reducing the chance that they are marred by mistakes.

Businesspeople clearly see the potential benefit of external audits, but they become dissatisfied when the benefits are not realized. Whether the reason for the low-quality service is a lack of human capital on the part of the auditors or a lack of accountability, the dissatisfaction that firms express indicates weaknesses in the system. Mandating that firms use tools such as external audits to help ensure financial transparency and accountability without also attending to the institutional incentives of auditors and to the overall stock of human capital does not help establish true financial transparency.

Most of the results regarding the reported use of external audits mirror those found regarding the reported use of IAS. The cross-country effects are extremely powerful for capturing the variation in firms' reported use of external audits, and the size effect is even stronger than was found for IAS. Larger firms were more likely to say they used external audits, and we again find that ownership makes a difference—domestic private firms were much less likely to adopt external audits than were firms with state or foreign ownership, even after controlling for differences in size, legal origin, and country (see figure 5.6). An important tool for generating financial transparency has yet to take hold as a matter of routine for many domestic firms in the SEE8, a fact that will surely weaken their competitive edge against foreign-owned firms that do take advantage of external audits.

Although the overall pattern for the SEE8 is similar for firms reporting that they adopted IAS and firms reporting the use of external audits, interesting differences exist in individual countries. Ownership concentration, which was not important for explaining the adoption of IAS in any of the eight countries, is important for explaining the use of external audits in both FYR Macedonia and Moldova. In both countries, it is firms with smaller degrees of ownership concentration that are more likely to use external audits, even after controlling for form of ownership. This finding is consistent with the use of external audits by diffuse ownership to check

**Figure 5.6　Firms Reporting Using External Audits, by Firm Size and Ownership Type**

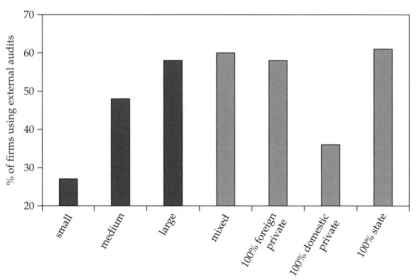

*Source:* EBRD and World Bank (2002).

the performance of management. Surprisingly, however, this pattern held only for a subset of countries. Indeed, although it is often presumed that transparent accounting practices and financial disclosure are particularly necessary for publicly traded companies, the case studies carried out as part of this study suggest that, even for such companies, disclosure is much less frequent than one would imagine. The overwhelming majority of firms in the case studies, including large firms with broad-based ownership, said that they do not produce publicly available annual reports.

It was recognized early on that adopting measures of firm transparency and accountability, such as uniform accounting statements, independent external audits, and public disclosures, would, like many other aspects of transition, be necessary for the proper functioning of the new market economy. As with many areas of institutional reform, however, the challenge of changing the language and culture of accounting proved formidable. Often the push of new rules has preceded the development of capacity to implement those rules. The large number of actors that have an interest in accounting statements and financial transparency complicates the task. Banks, securities markets regulators, tax authorities, and the firm's own internal management and accounting personnel all seek financial statements that they can readily interpret. National accounting standards, though not conforming to IAS and less useful in many ways, are at least understandable to the broad array of professionals that need to understand them. While a country moves to adopt new and better standards of accounting, there is a period during which a uniform understanding of financial statements no longer exists, and asymmetries exist in the penetration of new accounting skills in key government bodies and in the firms themselves. The firms are caught in the middle of this disconnect. The analysis of the BEEPS2 data supports the notion that the push to convert to IAS through national rules can be effective for moving this process along. However, skills development among professionals in both the private and public sectors must also be a high priority, a point that is consistently made in both the OECD white paper (OECD, South East Corporate Governance Roundtable 2003) and in the ROSCs (World Bank n.d.).

Despite the magnitude of the challenge, the recent progress in adoption of IAS, as documented here and in chapter 2, and the general improvements confirmed in the BEEPS provide cause for some optimism. Even the most ambitious reform programs, however, are likely to meet obstacles. A detailed study by the *Financial Times* (Cairns 2000) of accounting practices and annual reports of 125 large international publicly traded corporations found that fewer than half the companies were in full compliance with IAS. The survey found that many companies practice their own brand of "IAS lite" in various respects. Clearly, full adoption of IAS by firms in SEE remains a formidable challenge.

## Access to Finance

In their day-to-day operations, firms face myriad financial decisions. Growing firms decide not only what to produce and where to sell it, but also how to finance the production and which financing terms to accept at sale. Earlier studies of SEE have concluded that the financial systems of the countries of the region were failing to meet the financing demands of the private sector, thereby leaving growing firms to rely far too heavily on internal funds for expansion (Pissarides 2001). In this section, we explore two related sets of issues related to firm financing: the mediums of exchange used to finance sales and purchases and the use of formal and informal financing for both working capital and investment purposes.

### *Financing Transactions*

How do firms in SEE finance their transactions? The BEEPS2 asked firms the percentage of their sales that were prepaid and the percentage that were made on credit.[6] Croatia, the SEE8 country with perhaps the most advanced banking system, had the smallest overall prevalence of sales on credit. Indeed, the responses across countries suggest that firms in countries with less developed formal financial systems are less likely to transact in any manner other than spot exchange. Within SEE, both prepaid and credit sales are strongly negatively correlated with the EBRD indicator

## Figure 5.7   Prepaid and Credit Transactions

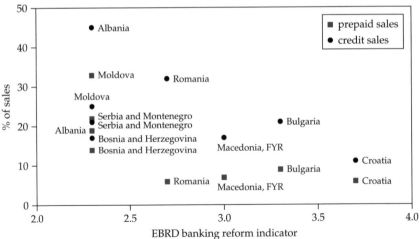

*Sources:* EBRD (2002) and EBRD and World Bank (2002).
*Note:* Data include only firms with at least 50 full-time employees.

## Figure 5.8  Barter, Bills of Exchange, and Debt Swaps as a Percentage of Sales

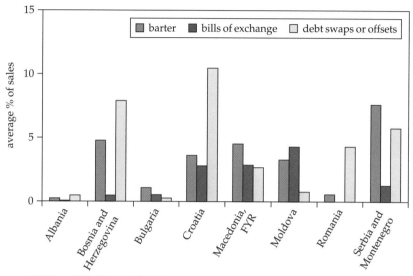

*Source:* EBRD and World Bank (2002).

*Note:* Data for bills of exchange are excluded for Romania because of an inconsistent translation of the term *bill of exchange.*

on banking reform and interest rate liberalization (see figure 5.7).[7] This finding shows clearly the link between financial sector reforms and the use of alternative means of financing by firms.

BEEPS2 asked firms how both sales and purchases were settled. Although the overwhelming share of all sales were ultimately settled in cash, the use of alternative means, such as barter, bills of exchange, and debt swaps, was not uncommon in most countries in 2002 (see figure 5.8). The use of barter for sales and the use of barter for purchases are very highly correlated, indicating that firms that sell using barter also purchase using barter; indeed, this finding is nearly tautological. For the sake of brevity, we will focus only on the use of barter for sales.

Although the overall levels of these alternative means of settlement comprise the minority of sales on average, the percentage of firms that accept such means of payment is much larger (see figure 5.9). Debt swaps and offsets were especially prevalent in Bosnia and Herzegovina and in Croatia. Such offsets may seem innocuous and are not necessarily a sign of underdevelopment, but they ultimately make transactions less transparent. A special auditor's report released in 2003 argued that the extensive use of offsets (known as *multilateral compensations*) among state enterprises in the Republika Srpska disguised the true sources and destinations of

**Figure 5.9　Percentage of Firms Using Barter, Bills of Exchange, or Debt Swaps**

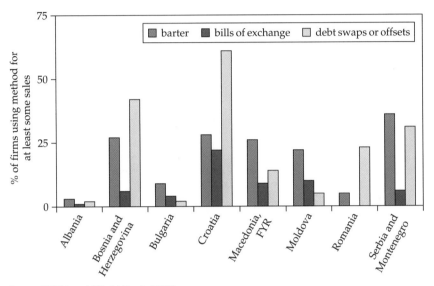

*Source:* EBRD and World Bank (2002).
*Note:* Data for bills of exchange are excluded for Romania because of an inconsistent trans-lation of the term *bill of exchange.*

funds and was even used as a tool for certain ministries to exceed spend-ing limits in the entity's budget (OHR 2003).

A second fact apparent in figure 5.9 is that nontrivial numbers of firms engage in barter. Firms in Bosnia and Herzegovina, Croatia, FYR Macedonia, and Serbia and Montenegro were especially likely to report in BEEPS2 that they transacted by barter. The case studies conducted as background for this study present a similar story: although most of the firms in the SEE8 said that they do not engage in barter, firms in Bosnia and Herzegovina, Croatia, FYR Macedonia, and Serbia and Montenegro all reported significant levels of sales in barter. One firm in Croatia said that it is actively trying to expand the use of barter simply because barter is a fast way of completing transactions (see box 5.6). Interviewed firms uniformly report that there is no tax advantage to barter transactions; they simply use barter to maximize sales and to avoid using credit.

The view presented by firms in the case studies can be tested empiri-cally using the BEEPS2 data. Firms could prefer to use barter for many reasons. For example, problems with the banking system could induce barter. Similarly, firms that choose barter as an alternative to selling their products for credit may do so because they are not confident that the

---

## Box 5.6 The Pros and Cons of Barter in Croatia and Romania

Although most Croatian firms reported that barter is declining, albeit still prevalent, one small manufacturer said that it is trying to expand barter sales because barter is one of the fastest ways of completing sales. That firm reported its sales department spends around 50 percent of its time on the phone trying to arrange payments for late-paying customers, both domestic and foreign. Late and nonexistent payments are the primary causes of business disputes, and the firm reported that resolving disputes through the courts is time-consuming and ineffective. Even if a creditor receives a favorable verdict, the firm reported, not much happens quickly, and some debtor companies go out of business before the creditor can collect. Ultimately, the Croatian firm uses barter as a tool to avoid such difficulties.

Other firms offered a different view, emphasizing the costs that barter imposes. A very large Romanian industrial firm has historically purchased most of its inputs through intermediaries using barter. Recently, however, the company introduced a procurement policy of direct purchases from suppliers on a cash basis. The new policy led to considerably lower prices and better reliability of suppliers. Managers of the company find that cash transactions have made the company more flexible and have increased its purchasing and sales power. Reducing the prevalence of barter was one of the centerpieces of the enterprise's strategy.

---

courts will provide an efficient means of collection. The financing motive has found empirical support in transition countries in the past (Carlin and others 2000; see also Commander, Dolinskaya, and Mumssen 2000; Marin, Kaufmann, and Gorochowskij 2000).

To examine the motives behind barter, we regressed the use of barter on variables capturing the degree to which the firm is hindered by lack of access to finance, by poorly performing courts, by problems with tax rates and tax administration, and by the degree to which customers simply do not pay their bills, as well as on number of other variables and controls. The full methodology and results are presented in the annex. The key results are depicted graphically in figure 5.10.

The results of the analysis largely confirm the anecdotal evidence in the case studies. In the pooled analysis, firms that complained about taxes were no more likely than were other firms to engage in barter, and in the individual country analyses, only Bulgaria demonstrated a weakly significant positive correlation between the problems posed by tax rates and the propensity to use barter. Interestingly, Croatia and Serbia and Montenegro showed the converse relationship: firms that complained about tax rates were less likely to use barter. Taken as a whole, firms do

## Figure 5.10    Factors Influencing the Use of Barter

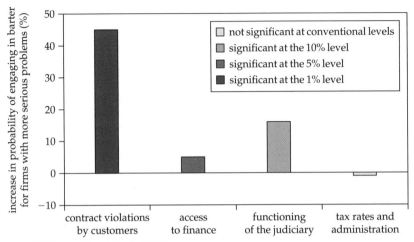

*Source:* EBRD and World Bank (2002).

not seem to use barter to intentionally disguise their activities and thus avoid taxes.

Across the entire sample of SEE8 firms, those that complained about the courts were significantly more likely to engage in barter than were other firms, but this factor was not significant in any of the individual country regressions. By contrast, access to finance was not significant in the pooled regression, but it was a positive and significant factor both in Bosnia and Herzegovina and in Serbia and Montenegro. The findings with respect to the courts and to access to finance stand in stark contrast to the stronger and more consistent findings with respect to contract violations and nonpaying customers. In the pooled analysis and in nearly every individual country regression, firms that complained about contract violations by customers were more likely to engage in barter.

The preceding results are a bit misleading, however, because customers that fail to pay their bills may do so as a result of institutional weaknesses in formal financial arrangements or in the courts. Hence, we analyzed how the problems with contract violations and nonpaying customers are related to such institutional weaknesses. The key results are depicted graphically in figure 5.11 and are presented in detail in the annex.

The results of this analysis are illuminating. Across the SEE8, tax rates are less important than tax administration for explaining the nonpayment problem, but these effects are dwarfed by the influence of the courts and access to finance. In the analysis of patterns within individual

**Figure 5.11   Factors Influencing the Prevalence of Contract Violations by Customers**

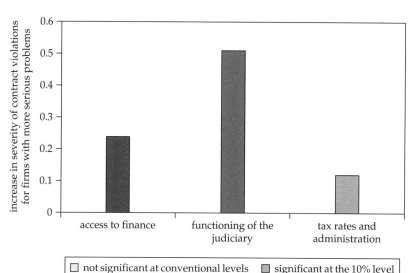

*Source:* EBRD and World Bank (2002).

countries, every one except Bulgaria demonstrated a high degree of correlation between problems with the courts and problems with non-paying customers. Access to finance was a less pervasive influence, although still highly significant in FYR Macedonia, Moldova, and Serbia and Montenegro. Taken as a whole, the results suggest that institutional weaknesses in both access to finance and the judiciary are contributing to the lingering use of barter by many firms in SEE.

Although changes in the BEEPS questionnaire between 1999 and 2002 make it impossible to examine the trend in the use of barter alone, it is still possible to examine the trends in use of barter, bills of exchange, and debt swaps as a group. The results, which are presented in figure 5.12, suggest a decline in most countries in the proportion of firms that some-times use these forms of payment, with the largest decline occurring in Moldova. Indeed, experts have commented that they believe such payments have fallen even further since the 2002 BEEPS. (Figure 5.12 shows the proportion of firms that sometimes use or accept these forms of payment—the proportion of economic activity is even smaller.)

The results described in this section make clear the links between judi-cial reform, financial sector reform, and the use of alternative financing for transactions. As these reforms proceed, firms will benefit from the

**Figure 5.12    Percentage of Firms Using Bills of Exchange, Barter, or Debt Swaps, 1999 and 2002**

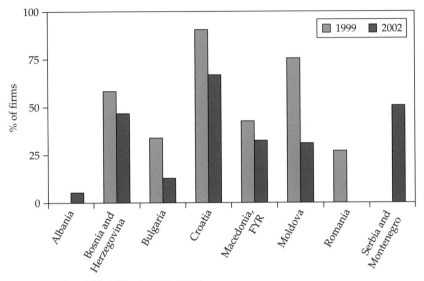

*Sources:* EBRD and World Bank (1999, 2002).
*Note:* Serbia and Montenegro was not included in the 1999 sample. Data for bills of exchange are excluded for Romania because of an inconsistent translation of the term *bill of exchange* in 2002.

more stable and predictable environment. They will also benefit from the reduced transaction costs associated with monetary exchange. Indeed, one firm manager in Romania described in very concrete terms the benefits of abandoning barter (see box 5.6).

## Financing Operations

In addition to the transactional financing discussed in the preceding sections, growing firms need access to financing for capital investment, such as purchases of equipment and other items that will be productive for years into the future, and for day-to-day working capital. Figure 5.13 shows the average percentage of new investment financed by various methods. (Methods of financing working capital were very similar.) In addition to the countries of SEE, several OECD countries are included for comparison. The data for the OECD countries were drawn from the *World Business Environment Survey* (World Bank 2000), of which BEEPS1 was a subset; hence, only 1999 data are included for those countries. It must be stressed that the sample sizes for the OECD countries were a uniform 100, so sampling error plays a role.

## Figure 5.13    Methods of Financing New Investment, 1999 and 2002

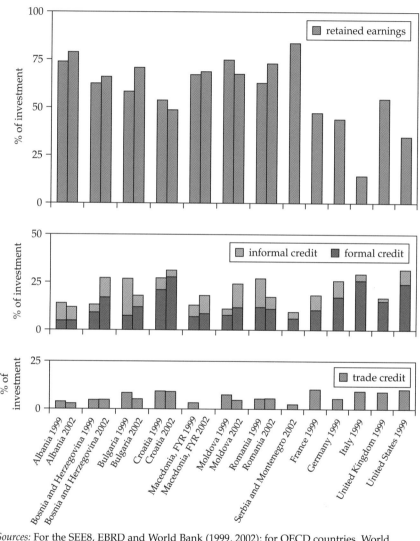

*Sources:* For the SEE8, EBRD and World Bank (1999, 2002); for OECD countries, World Bank (2000), as cited in Beck, Demirguc-Kunt, and Maksimovic (2002).
*Note:* Serbia and Montenegro was not included in the 1999 sample.

In figure 5.13, *formal credit* is an aggregation of the amounts financed by loans from foreign or domestic banks, both private and state owned. *Informal credit* is an aggregation of the amounts financed by loans from family or friends as well as by moneylenders and other informal sources.[8] *Trade credit* represents supplier credit and leasing financing.[9]

For investment purposes, firms throughout the region continue to use primarily their own retained earnings. Croatian firms, with access to a more advanced banking system, were less likely to rely on retained earnings and made greater use of formal financing mechanisms. By contrast, firms in Albania and in Serbia and Montenegro, among others, relied heavily on retained earnings and made very little use of formal credit mechanisms. In the case studies, one Albanian firm attributed this fact to the demanding requirements of formal banks (see box 5.7).

The methods used by firms in the SEE8 to finance working capital largely mirror the methods used to finance investment. Interestingly, new equity is no more likely a choice for financing investment than it is for financing working capital. Even for investment, the degree of reliance on new equity is small in all of the SEE8 and even in the OECD comparators, probably owing to the small sizes of firms. Nevertheless, there were some differences. For most of the countries in SEE, less than 2 percent of new investment was financed by issuing new equity, compared with more than 5 percent for the average of the OECD comparators. The high level of trust in financial statements and investor protections that are the lifeblood of active capital markets apparently requires further institutional strengthening in the SEE8.

---

### Box 5.7  Access to Formal Financing in Albania and FYR Macedonia

A small Albanian construction and agroprocessing firm related its difficulties with financing operations through formal financial channels. Although the firm is growing and is in an industry that traditionally relies on financing, the firm makes little use of formal lending. "Getting credit is an experience in Albania," stated the manager. "The rules are very strict, and often banks require collateral of 200 percent, even though the regulator has determined the benchmark at 140 percent." The manager also lamented that neither equipment nor machinery is accepted as collateral by the banks. Despite having factory equipment worth millions of dollars, the firm is unable to use it as collateral. This factor, combined with the generally unfavorable terms presented by banks, means that the firm finances nearly all of its operations through retained earnings.

A mid-size manufacturer in FYR Macedonia explained that its use of informal financing derives from the unfavorable terms offered by commercial banks. The manager explained that banks require very high levels of collateral, several times the value of the loan, and very high interest rates. Rather than agree to such unfavorable conditions, the firm prefers to simply reinvest its profits. When the firm requires external financing, its manager turns to friends and personal contacts rather than to the banks.

A notable feature of figure 5.13 is the difference in propensity to finance new investment through formal versus informal credit. In most countries, formal financing is used more than informal financing, but Albania and FYR Macedonia are notable exceptions. One Macedonian firm attributed its reliance on informal financing to the high levels of collateral and high interest rates charged by banks (see box 5.7).

On the whole, the data on firm financing decisions present a mixed picture. Firms continue to rely primarily on their own retained earnings as the means of financing their activities. Although nothing is wrong with this method, it does serve as a reminder that financing available for growth is constrained. A key benefit of the corporate form of organization—the ability to finance activities through the sale of equity on the capital markets—will not become available to the vast majority of firms in SEE until the institutions supporting such a system are developed. Reforms must stretch beyond the company laws that describe the forms of organization and reach to the institutions underlying firm transparency and accountability that will give investors the confidence to invest at arm's length.

The use of nonmonetary means of transacting business reflects both the lack of financing and the inefficient recourse available to firms whose customers do not pay their bills. The generalized decline in the use of nonmonetary means in the BEEPS2 data demonstrates that progress is being made in this area. Continued strengthening of the financial sector and improvements in the efficiency of courts will in time further reduce the incentives to use nonmonetary—and ultimately less transparent—means of transacting business.

## Financial Transparency, Investment, and Growth

At the outset of this chapter, we showed the relationship between a rudimentary measure of financial transparency, which was based on survey responses of firms and aggregate GDP growth in the countries of SEE. At a national level, countries with deeper penetration of IAS and external audits tended to grow faster in 2002. Yet the surveys and case studies have shown that building true financial transparency will continue to be a formidable challenge, and the case studies have already suggested that problems with formal financing are pushing firms to look elsewhere for the funds needed for investment and growth. In this section, we will use the BEEPS2 data to examine how the institutions of financial transparency affect investment and growth at the firm level in the countries of SEE.

To examine how investment and growth are linked to financing arrangements and to financial transparency, we analyzed how the percentage change in fixed assets and the percentage change in sales over the preceding 3-year period were related to various factors. Of primary concern were the proxies for financial transparency that have been used throughout this chapter: firm reports of adoption of IAS and use of external audits. The relationship between those measures of financial transparency and firm performance was examined both independently and in ways that controlled for other factors that may influence firm performance (such as ease of access to finance) and for a number of control variables. The number of direct competitors the firm faced, firm size measured by number of employees, and an index of exogenous problems that may have caused the firm to grow more slowly (such as property crimes and loss of power, water, or telephone service) served as proxies for the level competition. Some of the key findings with respect to investment are illustrated graphically in figure 5.14, and the detailed results of these analyses are presented in the annex.

With regard to investment, the analysis suggests several results. First, firm reports of both the adoption of IAS and the use of external auditing are correlated with firm-level investment in simple regressions. In figure 5.14, this relationship is clear from the statistically significant positive bars.[10] However, much of this relationship derives from the fact that countries with deeper penetration of IAS and external audits also had higher levels of investment, on average, among firms in the survey. After controlling for country effects, both IAS and external audits cease to be important for explaining investment. This finding is consistent with the idea that financial transparency has an important external effect: when firms are generally more transparent, the atmosphere of trust that is so essential for

**Figure 5.14  Financial Transparency and Firm Investment, 2002**

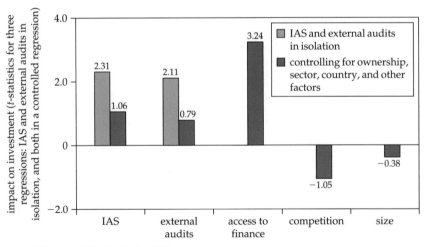

*Source:* EBRD and World Bank (2002).

## Figure 5.15    Financial Transparency and Firm Sales Growth

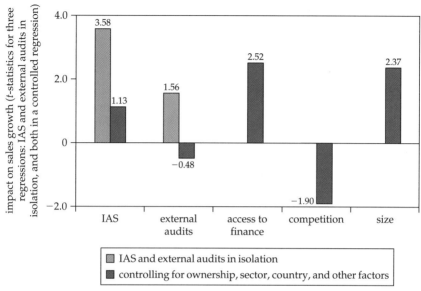

*Source:* EBRD and World Bank (2002).

arm's-length investing is strengthened, and all firms benefit. Second, ease of access to finance is important for explaining investment intensity across surveyed firms, even after controlling for cross-country and other differences. Surveyed firms with more competition and larger firms tended to report lower levels of investment, but the relationships were generally not significant at conventional levels.

The results for sales growth, as depicted in figure 5.15, are similar to those for investment in some ways but different in others. Firms that said that they adopted IAS had much higher average sales growth than firms that did not, a finding that holds even after controlling for country effect. However, after access to finance, size, competition, and other factors are accounted for, the link between IAS and firm sales growth weakens considerably. It is notable that access to finance—itself determined in part by financial transparency—remains significant at a very high level.

## Policy Recommendations

The purpose of this chapter has been to explore the links between the financial transparency aspects of corporate governance and investment and growth in the SEE8, drawing on the case studies and analysis of the survey data. Although country-specific policy recommendations are beyond the scope of this chapter—an array of advisers already provide such advice—the survey data and case studies do provide insights into the direction policies must move if the region is to advance. Many of these recommendations are consistent with the prescriptions found in the ROSCs.

## Deepen the Separation between Politicians and Firms

The case studies showed in very concrete terms how lingering involvement of the state can interfere with the value-producing function of productive enterprises. Managers of partially state-owned firms complained of the amount of time that they had to spend dealing with state officials, rather than pursuing the creation of value. Across firms and across countries, partially state-owned firms invested less than either fully private or fully state-owned firms. Similarly, in the analysis of influences on investment and growth, state-owned firms performed consistently worse than privately owned firms, either foreign or domestic.

Deepening the separation between politicians and firms involves policy measures ranging from further privatization in countries where significant portions of the productive economy remain partially or fully state owned, to establishing clear governance mechanisms that moderate conflicts of interest. With regard to privatization, Albania, Bosnia and Herzegovina, and Serbia and Montenegro all need to continue the work that was delayed by conflict. In connection with the clear need for privatization in many countries, it is worth emphasizing that privatization methods that are open and transparent stand the best chance of shifting ownership to effective owners and minimize the opportunities for corruption.

Similarly, there is a clear link between corporate reform and conflict of interest reform, which is part of anticorruption programs in many countries. Several of the case studies described the politicization of a firm that arose from having politicians on the firm's board. Several countries, including Bosnia and Herzegovina and Romania, have recently adopted conflict of interest legislation that would strictly control such conflicts. The laws are still in the early implementation stage, and it is too soon to know how effective they will be at depoliticizing the firms and reducing the scope for corruption, but in both countries, many politicians are being required to choose between their public office and their board seats. The signal that such measures send about the separation of public and private lives is an essential one.

## Monitor Public Disclosures of Financial Statements

To ensure fuller compliance with public disclosure legislation, the SEE8 must increase their vigilance in monitoring public disclosures of financial statements by firms that are required to make such disclosures. Many small, privately held firms are not required to make public disclosures. However, the case studies revealed that a number of large, publicly traded firms—and even some state firms—that are required to make such disclosures are not doing so. The BEEPS similarly showed that many publicly traded firms said that they do not use external audits. For such firms, public disclosure of financial statements should be the first step in reforms, regardless of whether reforms of the accounting system take place.

## Implement Accounting and Auditing Reforms

With regard to financial transparency, the survey and the case studies provide a rather sobering view of progress in the two areas examined in this chapter: the adoption of IAS and the use of independent external audits. The challenge of bringing about these changes is really no surprise given the accounting and corporate scandals that have come to light in highly developed countries with advanced systems of corporate governance. For the countries of SEE, the challenge of building the institutions of financial transparency is greater still. At the same time, the degree of variation between countries in managers' beliefs that they are adhering to IAS and external audits shows that the benefits of these firms are largely external to the firms themselves. This finding has two implications. First, it provides a very powerful reminder of why the institutions of financial transparency are so important for building systemic trust in financial statements on the part of banks, investors, regulators, and others. Second, the externality suggests that, without some push, most firms will not undertake the institutional reforms that are ultimately called for.

Although progress has been made, the need remains to continue accounting and auditing reforms that build the institutions of financial transparency. It is important to emphasize the need for balance in such reforms. Although the push of legal mandates to revise accounting and disclosure systems is clearly important, the ability of the reforms to generate long-term changes needs to go much further than merely requiring the adoption of new, complex procedures of firm accounting and disclosure.

## Implement Training and Education Programs

Many professionals in the public and private sectors make use of financial statements, and unless the skills for interpreting statements prepared according to new standards are widespread among such professionals, problems will persist. For example, the case studies revealed that firm managers lacked faith in the quality of auditors. The accounting and auditing ROSCs highlight the complex of professionals and organizations that make up the accounting system and profession. The ROSCs also detail practical bottlenecks to progress, such as the only very recent revision of accounting curricula. Maintaining training and education programs that build the stock of professional and highly qualified accountants will be essential for establishing the investor faith in the integrity of financial statements that is necessary for arm's-length investing. Similarly, close attention must be paid to the accountability arrangement for various users of financial statements to ensure that those skills are put to good use.

## Clearly Formulate Rules and Laws on Potential Conflict of Interest in the Accounting Profession

Building the institutions of financial transparency from the ground up gives the countries of SEE the advantage of learning from the experience of other countries. The scandals that have dominated front pages in the U.S. press provide important lessons about conflicts of interest, and reforms are currently under way to rectify them. Those reforms address the conflicts that arise when auditors want to please their customers, when investment-banking firms are also investment advisers, when executive officers of the firms are also board members, and when regulatory authorities such as stock exchanges are governed by the firms that they regulate. Some of these situations are specific to each country, but the general point is that envisioning the ramifications of potential conflicts of interest at the time that laws and regulations are being made may help prevent the damaging erosion of investor confidence that we have witnessed in industrial markets.

## Synergies between Different Institutional and Policy Reforms

The survey and case studies make clear how deeply intertwined different areas of institutional reform are. Many recommendations related to corporate governance and firm finance are located elsewhere in this book. Chief among them are judicial and financial sector reforms. Remnants of barter are driven by concerns about payment, which, in turn, are a factor of both weaknesses in the financial system and the lack of confidence in the judicial system to defend claims in a fair, efficient, and timely manner if payments are not made. Similarly, the high cost and unpredictability of formal financing lead some firms to avoid the financial system altogether and to use informal systems. Staying the course with judicial and financial sector reforms will have amplified effects for firm investment and growth.

The survey and case studies show that areas of policy reform are also intricately intertwined. For firms in SEE to achieve their potential for investment and growth, they need financing. At present, most of their investment must come from their own retained earnings. The leveraging of society's investment funds is a benefit that the economies of the region are not able to exploit. Because many of the benefits of financial transparency are external to the firms, many will not undertake the needed changes in accounting, disclosure, and external auditing until they are required to do so. The survey analysis also showed, however, that although many of the benefits of financial transparency are external, some are internal. In other words, there are direct benefits to the firms themselves in terms of investment and growth from the adoption of transparent accounting and auditing standards. Firms in the region would be well advised to improve their transparency, with or without the government's push.

## Annex: Additional Analyses

This annex presents some additional tables and analyses supporting the discussion in this chapter. It also describes the methods used and presents the full results of the series of formal regressions run as part of this work.

### Form of Organization and Type of Ownership for Medium and Large Firms

Tables A.5.1 and A.5.2 present the BEEPS2 data about the forms of legal organization and type of firm ownership for medium and large firms. For BEEPS2 data for the full sample (including small firms), see tables 5.2 and 5.3.

### International Accounting Standards

A series of regressions was run on the BEEPS2 data exploring which types of firms were more likely to use IAS. Probit regressions were run for both the whole sample of enterprises in all eight countries and for each country individually. (Croatia was omitted from the individual country regressions because so few firms had not adopted IAS.) Several explanatory variables were considered, including the concentration of ownership, measured by the percentage of shares owned by the largest shareholder; size, measured by the log of the number of employees; and legal form of organization. Several fixed effects were also included, such as batteries of dummies for ownership type (that is, foreign, domestic, or state); for sector; and, in the case of the pooled regression, for country. The results are presented in table A.5.3.

### External Audits

To examine what determines whether a firm adopts the practice of external audits, we performed a series of probit regressions using the same

(*Text continues on page 261.*)

Table A.5.1  Forms of Legal Organization: Medium and Large Firms, 2002

| Country | Sole proprietorship | Partnership | Cooperative | Privately held corporation | Corporation listed on the stock exchange | Other privately owned form | State-owned enterprise | Corporatized state entity | Other |
|---|---|---|---|---|---|---|---|---|---|
| Albania | 28.6 | 34.7 | 0.0 | 6.1 | 0.0 | 0.0 | 14.3 | 16.3 | 0.0 |
| Bosnia and Herzegovina | 16.9 | 7.0 | 0.0 | 21.1 | 22.5 | 2.8 | 21.1 | 7.0 | 1.4 |
| Bulgaria | 19.7 | 9.2 | 4.0 | 4.0 | 32.9 | 0.0 | 23.7 | 1.3 | 5.3 |
| Croatia | 4.8 | 0.0 | 3.2 | 41.9 | 19.4 | 0.0 | 25.8 | 4.8 | 0.0 |
| Macedonia, FYR | 28.0 | 10.0 | 0.0 | 48.0 | 2.0 | 0.0 | 4.0 | 8.0 | 0.0 |
| Moldova | 5.4 | 5.4 | 0.0 | 28.6 | 0.0 | 30.4 | 17.9 | 0.0 | 12.5 |
| Romania | 2.0 | 0.0 | 2.0 | 30.7 | 0.0 | 34.7 | 6.9 | 4.0 | 19.8 |
| Serbia and Montenegro | 14.7 | 7.4 | 1.1 | 29.5 | 7.4 | 2.1 | 30.5 | 7.4 | 0.0 |
| SEE8 | 13.8 | 7.9 | 1.4 | 26.1 | 10.9 | 10.0 | 18.6 | 5.7 | 5.7 |

Source: EBRD and World Bank (2002).
Note: Data include only firms with at least 50 full-time employees.

**Table A.5.2  Firm Ownership: Medium-Size and Large Firms, 2002**

| Country | Mixed ownership | 100% foreign ownership | 100% domestic ownership | 100% state ownership | 100% other ownership | Number of firms in sample |
|---|---|---|---|---|---|---|
| Albania | 18.4 | 10.2 | 38.8 | 24.5 | 8.2 | 49 |
| Bosnia and Herzegovina | 52.1 | 2.8 | 23.9 | 9.9 | 11.3 | 71 |
| Bulgaria | 22.4 | 9.2 | 39.5 | 29.0 | 0.0 | 76 |
| Croatia | 19.4 | 12.9 | 45.2 | 22.6 | 0.0 | 62 |
| Macedonia, FYR | 42.0 | 2.0 | 54.0 | 2.0 | 0.0 | 50 |
| Moldova | 44.6 | 7.1 | 19.6 | 17.9 | 10.7 | 56 |
| Romania | 31.7 | 6.9 | 43.6 | 14.9 | 3.0 | 101 |
| Serbia and Montenegro | 29.5 | 6.3 | 28.4 | 29.5 | 6.3 | 95 |
| SEE8 | 32.3 | 7.1 | 36.3 | 19.5 | 4.8 | 560 |

*Source:* EBRD and World Bank (2002).
*Note:* Data included only firms with at least 50 full-time employees.

**Table A.5.3  Factors Influencing the Use of International Accounting Standards, 2002**

| Factor | SEE8 | Albania | Bosnia and Herzegovina | Bulgaria | Macedonia, FYR | Moldova | Romania | Serbia and Montenegro |
|---|---|---|---|---|---|---|---|---|
| Concentration | -0.001 (0.396) | -0.003 (0.465) | -0.004 (0.615) | -0.002 (0.643) | -0.006 (0.269) | -0.001 (0.905) | -0.005 (0.183) | 0.002 (0.607) |
| Corporation | 0.023 (0.814) | -6.231 (0.998) | -0.672 (0.159) | -0.151 (0.598) | 0.348 (0.431) | -0.251 (0.348) | 0.389 (0.110) | 0.474 (0.138) |
| Size | 0.149 (0.000)*** | -0.231 (0.022)** | 0.032 (0.788) | 0.286 (0.000)*** | 0.192 (0.088)* | 0.296 (0.019)** | 0.058 (0.364) | 0.128 (0.087)* |
| Ownership: | | | | | | | | |
| 100% foreign private ownership | 0.296 (0.095)* | -0.155 (0.819) | | 1.122 (0.013)** | 0.533 (0.397) | -0.246 (0.736) | -1.108 (0.018)** | 0.620 (0.188) |
| 100% domestic private ownership | -0.237 (0.037)** | -0.862 (0.079)* | -1.215 (0.005)*** | 0.003 (0.992) | -0.062 (0.871) | -0.539 (0.126) | -0.588 (0.028)** | -0.112 (0.734) |
| 100% state ownership | -0.202 (0.242) | 1.202 (0.157) | -0.428 (0.618) | -0.470 (0.273) | | | -0.194 (0.603) | -0.187 (0.689) |
| 100% other ownership | -0.192 (0.257) | -1.280 (0.021)** | -0.478 (0.260) | | | -0.303 (0.474) | -1.246 (0.015)** | 0.501 (0.260) |

| | (1) | (2) | (3) | (4) | (5) | (6) | (7) | (8) |
|---|---|---|---|---|---|---|---|---|
| **Sector:** | | | | | | | | |
| Construction | −0.950 (0.047)** | −11.449 (0.000)*** | | −6.579 (0.000)*** | 1.196 (0.174) | | −0.438 (0.310) | −0.973 (0.345) |
| Manufacturing | −1.071 (0.021)** | −11.523 (0.000)*** | −6.488 (0.000)*** | −6.458 (0.000)*** | 0.279 (0.734) | −0.969 (0.117) | −0.451 (0.209) | −0.811 (0.375) |
| Transportation, storage, and communications | −1.032 (0.030)** | −11.804 (0.000)*** | −5.939 (.) | −6.376 (0.000)*** | 0.153 (0.872) | −1.864 (0.015)** | −0.095 (0.833) | −0.695 (0.464) |
| Wholesale and retail trade | −1.001 (0.031)** | −12.420 (0.000)*** | −6.821 (0.000)*** | −6.053 (0.000)*** | 0.812 (0.333) | −0.664 (0.238) | −0.302 (0.420) | −0.625 (0.493) |
| Real estate | −0.791 (0.098)* | −12.299 (0.000)*** | | −5.869 (0.000)*** | 1.198 (0.215) | | −0.427 (0.325) | −0.872 (0.361) |
| Hotels and restaurants | −0.884 (0.067)* | −11.319 (0.000)*** | −7.233 (0.000)*** | −6.239 (0.000)*** | 0.660 (0.480) | | | −0.662 (0.508) |
| Other services | −1.029 (0.034)** | −11.678 (0.000)*** | −6.528 (0.000)*** | −6.743 (0.000)*** | | −1.006 (0.102) | −0.009 (0.985) | −0.558 (0.570) |
| **Country:** | | | | | | | | |
| Albania | 0.989 (0.000)*** | | | | | | | |
| Bosnia and Herzegovina | 1.171 (0.000)*** | | | | | | | |
| Bulgaria | 0.249 (0.065)* | | | | | | | |
| Croatia | 0.902 (0.000)*** | | | | | | | |

(Table continues on the following page.)

259

# Table A.5.3 (continued)

| Factor | SEE8 | Albania | Bosnia and Herzegovina | Bulgaria | Macedonia, FYR | Moldova | Romania | Serbia and Montenegro |
|---|---|---|---|---|---|---|---|---|
| Macedonia, FYR | 0.007 | | | | | | | |
| | (0.965) | | | | | | | |
| Moldova | 1.499 | | | | | | | |
| | (0.000)*** | | | | | | | |
| Romania | 0.188 | | | | | | | |
| | (0.175) | | | | | | | |
| Tests of joint restrictions (*p*-values): | | | | | | | | |
| Ownership effects | (0.005)** | (0.028)** | (0.041)** | (0.007)*** | (0.540) | (0.488) | (0.052)* | (0.202) |
| Sector effects | (0.258) | (0.000)*** | (0.000)*** | (0.000)*** | (0.449) | (0.111) | (0.773) | (0.975) |
| Country effects | (0.000)*** | | | | | | | |
| Number of observations | 1,284 | 153 | 97 | 235 | 113 | 160 | 224 | 168 |

*Source:* Author calculations from EBRD and World Bank (2002).

*Notes:* Table shows results of probit estimations; *p*-values are in parentheses. For fixed effects, Serbia and Montenegro was the base country and only the *p*-value of the joint hypothesis that each of the referenced fixed effects is zero is reported. Constants were included but are not reported here. Croatia was excluded from the individual country regressions because more than 90 percent of firms said that they use IAS.

*significant at 10 percent.

**significant at 5 percent.

***significant at 1 percent.

explanatory variables as those shown in table A.5. The full results are presented in table A.5.4.

## Barter

To examine the motives behind barter, we regressed the use of barter on
variables that captured the degree to which a firm is hindered by lack of
access to finance, by poorly performing courts, by problems with tax rates
and tax administration, and by the degree to which customers simply do
not pay their bills. The regressions also included, as a control for the subjective nature of the question, a variable for the degree to which macroeconomic instability is an obstacle for firm business. Because
macroeconomic stability is a country-specific phenomenon, the effect on
firms would tend not to vary too much within a country, hence leaving
much of the variation to be explained by the respondent's propensity to
label things as obstacles. In each of the regressions, the effect of the two
tax-related variables was tested both independently and jointly. In the
pooled regression, country effects were also tested. The full probit regression results are presented in table A.5.5.

We regressed the problems with nonpaying customers on the battery of
right-hand-side variables described above, and the results are presented
in table A.5.6. Whereas earlier regressions had binary dependent variables, which suggested techniques such as probit, the dependent variable
in table A.5.6 takes on five discrete values, and ordinary least squares
regression was used. The table reports $p$-values to maintain consistency
with other tables. Taken together, the system of regressions presented in
tables A.5.5 and A.5.6 is recursive and can be estimated independently.

## Firm Investment and Firm Growth

To examine the effect of financial transparency on firm investment and
firm growth, we ran a series of fixed-effect regressions, with the percentage change in fixed assets and the percentage change in sales over the preceding 3-year period as dependent variables. The explanatory variables
included the proxies for financial transparency that we used earlier: adoption of IAS, use of external audits, and ease of access to finance, as well as
a number of control variables. The proxy for the level of competition is
provided by the number of direct competitors that the firm faced, the size
by number of employees, and an index of exogenous problems that may
have caused the firm to grow more slowly, such as victimization by property crimes and loss of power, water, or telephone service. The full results
for both investment and sales growth are presented in table A.5.7 and
table A.5.8.

**Table A.5.4 Factors Influencing the Use of External Audits, 2002**

| Factor | SEE8 | Bosnia and Herzegovina | Croatia | Macedonia, FYR | Moldova | Romania | Serbia and Montenegro |
|---|---|---|---|---|---|---|---|
| Concentration | -0.001 (0.339) | 0.001 (0.807) | -0.005 (0.306) | -0.011 (0.046)** | -0.010 (0.035)** | 0.004 (0.217) | 0.003 (0.510) |
| Corporation | 0.074 (0.440) | -0.063 (0.863) | 0.010 (0.983) | 0.235 (0.605) | -0.046 (0.853) | -0.300 (0.194) | 0.512 (0.113) |
| Size | 0.279 (0.000)*** | 0.216 (0.042)** | 0.262 (0.002)*** | 0.236 (0.038)** | 0.421 (0.000)*** | 0.214 (0.001)*** | 0.230 (0.003)*** |
| Ownership: | | | | | | | |
| 100% foreign private ownership | 0.397 (0.027)** | 0.366 (0.502) | 0.092 (0.888) | 0.596 (0.363) | 0.237 (0.715) | 0.208 (0.627) | 0.435 (0.361) |
| 100% domestic private ownership | -0.267 (0.017)** | 0.267 (0.510) | -0.081 (0.840) | 0.504 (0.198) | -0.825 (0.005)*** | -0.190 (0.460) | -0.033 (0.928) |
| 100% state ownership | -0.105 (0.539) | 1.468 (0.080)* | -1.014 (0.148) | | -0.080 (0.864) | -0.452 (0.237) | -0.387 (0.412) |
| 100% other ownership | -0.107 (0.525) | 0.149 (0.709) | | | -1.095 (0.004)*** | -0.550 (0.286) | 0.908 (0.056)* |
| Sector: | | | | | | | |
| Construction | -0.576 (0.206) | -5.690 (0.000)*** | -6.136 (0.000)*** | 7.038 (0.000)*** | -0.840 (0.317) | 0.351 (0.429) | 4.870 (.) |
| Manufacturing | -0.679 (0.126) | -6.113 (0.000)*** | -5.844 (0.000)*** | 6.640 (0.000)*** | 0.187 (0.655) | -0.181 (0.648) | 5.039 (0.000)*** |

| | | | | | | |
|---|---|---|---|---|---|---|
| Transportation, storage, and communications | −0.592 (0.194) | −5.936 (0.000)*** | −6.336 (0.000)*** | 6.550 (0.000)*** | | 0.232 (0.624) | 5.413 (0.000)*** |
| Wholesale and retail trade | −0.638 (0.150) | −5.654 (0.000)*** | −6.551 (0.000)*** | 6.788 (0.000)*** | 0.468 (0.285) | −0.076 (0.850) | 5.005 (0.000)*** |
| Real estate | −0.551 (0.228) | −5.769 (0.000)*** | −6.324 (0.000)*** | 7.084 (0.000)*** | | 0.170 (0.708) | 5.100 (0.000)*** |
| Hotels and restaurants | −0.661 (0.152) | −5.710 (0.000)*** | −5.279 (0.000)*** | 7.024 (0.000)*** | −0.036 (0.955) | −0.081 (0.869) | 5.044 (0.000)*** |
| Other services | −0.742 (0.109) | −6.673 (0.000)*** | −4.878 (0.000)*** | | 0.204 (0.714) | | 5.741 (0.000)*** |
| Country: | | | | | | | |
| Albania | 1.944 (0.000)*** | | | | | | |
| Bosnia and Herzegovina | 0.559 (0.001)*** | | | | | | |
| Bulgaria | 0.909 (0.000)*** | | | | | | |
| Croatia | 0.517 (0.003)*** | | | | | | |
| Macedonia, FYR | 0.078 (0.648) | | | | | | |

(Table continues on the following page.)

**Table A.5.4** (continued)

| Factor | SEE8 | Bosnia and Herzegovina | Croatia | Macedonia, FYR | Moldova | Romania | Serbia and Montenegro |
|---|---|---|---|---|---|---|---|
| Moldova | 0.677 | | | | | | |
| | (0.000)*** | | | | | | |
| Romania | 0.142 | | | | | | |
| | (0.320) | | | | | | |
| Tests of joint restrictions (*p*-values): | | | | | | | |
| Ownership effects | (0.000)*** | (0.481) | (0.515) | (0.413) | (0.005)*** | (0510) | (0.054)* |
| Sector effects | (0.814) | (0.000)*** | (0.000)*** | (0.000)*** | (0.000)*** | (0.658) | (0.000)*** |
| Country effects | (0.000)*** | | | | | | |
| Number of observations | 1,349 | 112 | 113 | 123 | 169 | 241 | 178 |

*Source*: Author calculations from EBRD and World Bank (2002).
*Notes*: Table shows results of probit estimations; *p*-values are in parentheses. For fixed effects, Serbia and Montenegro was the base country and only the *p*-value of the joint hypothesis that each of the referenced fixed effects is zero is reported. Constants were included but are not reported here. Albania and Bulgaria were excluded from the individual country regressions because more than 90 percent of firms said that they use external audits.

*significant at 10 percent.
**significant at 5 percent.
***significant at 1 percent.

## Table A.5.5 Factors Influencing the Use of Barter, 2002

| Factor | SEE8 | Bosnia and Herzegovina | Bulgaria | Croatia | Macedonia, FYR | Moldova | Romania | Serbia and Montenegro |
|---|---|---|---|---|---|---|---|---|
| Customer failure to pay bills | 0.226 (0.000)*** | 0.226 (0.076)* | 0.295 (0.013)** | 0.255 (0.029)** | 0.373 (0.012)** | 0.189 (0.090)* | 0.049 (0.749) | 0.182 (0.062)* |
| Access to financing | 0.026 (0.505) | 0.360 (0.003)*** | 0.032 (0.788) | −0.109 (0.241) | −0.045 (0.737) | −0.153 (0.147) | 0.187 (0.218) | 0.184 (0.055)* |
| Functioning of the judiciary | 0.078 (0.088)* | −0.034 (0.803) | 0.045 (0.716) | 0.093 (0.429) | 0.266 (0.113) | 0.153 (0.190) | −0.029 (0.857) | 0.108 (0.287) |
| Tax rates | −0.055 (0.314) | −0.058 (0.748) | 0.257 (0.063)* | −0.236 (0.061)* | 0.029 (0.870) | −0.102 (0.600) | −0.091 (0.718) | −0.239 (0.045)** |
| Tax administration | 0.044 (0.412) | −0.126 (0.466) | −0.229 (0.107) | 0.135 (0.299) | 0.172 (0.358) | 0.191 (0.328) | 0.162 (0.425) | 0.026 (0.804) |
| Macroeconomic instability | −0.059 (0.200) | −0.038 (0.761) | −0.105 (0.418) | −0.011 (0.921) | −0.398 (0.020)** | 0.222 (0.203) | 0.138 (0.538) | −0.110 (0.227) |
| Country: Albania | −1.995 (0.000)*** | | | | | | | |
| Bosnia and Herzegovina | −0.398 (0.007)*** | | | | | | | |

(Table continues on the following page.)

# Table A.5.5 (continued)

| Factor | SEE8 | Bosnia and Herzegovina | Bulgaria | Croatia | Macedonia, FYR | Moldova | Romania | Serbia and Montenegro |
|---|---|---|---|---|---|---|---|---|
| Bulgaria | $-1.061$ | | | | | | | |
| | $(0.000)^{***}$ | | | | | | | |
| Croatia | $-0.269$ | | | | | | | |
| | $(0.061)^{*}$ | | | | | | | |
| Macedonia, FYR | $-0.258$ | | | | | | | |
| | $(0.091)^{*}$ | | | | | | | |
| Moldova | $-0.392$ | | | | | | | |
| | $(0.008)^{***}$ | | | | | | | |
| Romania | $-1.478$ | | | | | | | |
| | $(0.000)^{***}$ | | | | | | | |
| Tests of joint restrictions ($p$-values) | | | | | | | | |
| Country effects | $(0.000)^{***}$ | | | | | | | |
| Tax effects | $(0.574)$ | $(0.367)$ | $(0.105)$ | $(0.170)$ | $(0.425)$ | $(0.611)$ | $(0.722)$ | $(0.094)^{*}$ |
| Number of observations | 1,414 | 145 | 231 | 173 | 131 | 162 | 229 | 208 |

*Source:* Author calculations from EBRD and World Bank (2002).

*Notes:* Table shows results of probit estimations; $p$-values are in parentheses. For fixed effects, Serbia and Montenegro was the base country and only the $p$-value of the joint hypothesis that each of the referenced fixed effects is zero is reported. Constants were included but are not reported here. Albania was excluded from the individual country regressions because fewer than 5 percent of firms reported using barter.

*significant at 10 percent.

**significant at 5 percent.

***significant at 1 percent.

**Table A.5.6  Factors Influencing the Problem of Customers Not Paying Bills, 2002**

| Factor | SEE8 | Bosnia and Herzegovina | Bulgaria | Croatia | Macedonia, FYR | Moldova | Romania | Serbia and Montenegro |
|---|---|---|---|---|---|---|---|---|
| Access to financing | 0.119 (0.000)*** | 0.078 (0.318) | 0.098 (0.130) | 0.019 (0.746) | 0.334 (0.000)*** | 0.254 (0.001)*** | 0.017 (0.784) | 0.238 (0.000)*** |
| Functioning of the judiciary | 0.253 (0.000)*** | 0.239 (0.006)*** | 0.104 (0.159) | 0.247 (0.001)*** | 0.431 (0.000)*** | 0.218 (0.013)** | 0.367 (0.000)*** | 0.268 (0.000)*** |
| Tax rates | 0.046 (0.170) | 0.011 (0.925) | 0.088 (0.248) | −0.055 (0.487) | −0.100 (0.357) | 0.249 (0.071)* | 0.136 (0.135) | −0.084 (0.318) |
| Tax administration | 0.069 (0.033)** | 0.064 (0.586) | 0.107 (0.200) | 0.183 (0.026)** | 0.275 (0.017)** | −0.086 (0.529) | 0.106 (0.159) | −0.008 (0.918) |
| Macroeconomic instability | 0.154 (0.000)*** | 0.292 (0.001)*** | 0.113 (0.121) | 0.125 (0.078)* | −0.057 (0.555) | 0.157 (0.155) | 0.077 (0.345) | 0.149 (0.020)** |
| Country: | | | | | | | | |
| Albania | 0.238 (0.032)** | | | | | | | |
| Bosnia and Herzegovina | 0.107 (0.320) | | | | | | | |
| Bulgaria | −0.001 (0.995) | | | | | | | |
| Croatia | −0.108 (0.301) | | | | | | | |
| Macedonia, FYR | −0.073 (0.510) | | | | | | | |

(Table continues on the following page.)

# Table A.5.6  (continued)

| Factor | SEE8 | Bosnia and Herzegovina | Bulgaria | Croatia | Macedonia, FYR | Moldova | Romania | Serbia and Montenegro |
|---|---|---|---|---|---|---|---|---|
| Moldova | 0.009 | | | | | | | |
| | (0.931) | | | | | | | |
| Romania | 0.149 | | | | | | | |
| | (0.118) | | | | | | | |
| Tests of joint restrictions ($p$-values) | | | | | | | | |
| Country effects | (0.037)** | | | | | | | |
| Tax effects | (0.001)*** | (0.654) | (0.064)* | (0.078)* | (0.043)** | (0.151) | (0.014)** | (0.477) |
| R-squared | 0.228 | 0.285 | 0.096 | 0.198 | 0.432 | 0.196 | 0.270 | 0.236 |
| Number of observations | 1,414 | 145 | 231 | 173 | 131 | 162 | 229 | 208 |

*Source:* Author calculations from EBRD and World Bank (2002).

*Notes:* Table shows the results of ordinary least squares regressions; $p$-values are in parentheses. For fixed effects, Serbia and Montenegro was the base country and only the $p$-value of the joint hypothesis that each of the referenced fixed effects is zero is reported. Constants were included but are not reported here. Albania was excluded from the individual country regressions because fewer than 5 percent of firms reported using barter.

*significant at 10 percent.
**significant at 5 percent.
***significant at 1 percent.

**Table A.5.7 Financial Transparency and Firm Investment, 2002**

*(dependent variable for all regressions is the percentage change in fixed assets over the previous 3 years)*

| Factor | (1) | (2) | (3) | (4) | (5) | (6) |
|---|---|---|---|---|---|---|
| Adoption of IAS | 6.891 (0.021)** | 3.349 (0.290) | | | 5.784 (0.131) | 4.299 (0.287) |
| Use of external audits | | | 6.231 (0.035)** | 2.196 (0.490) | 7.061 (0.081)* | 3.312 (0.430) |
| Easy access to financing | | | | | 30.227 (0.000)*** | 26.309 (0.001)*** |
| Competition | | | | | -7.123 (0.154) | -5.297 (0.295) |
| Size | | | | | -2.414 (0.041)** | -0.517 (0.701) |
| Exogenous problems | | | | | 27.725 (0.027)** | 30.455 (0.015)** |
| Ownership: | | | | | | |
| 100% foreign private ownership | | 22.163 (0.001)*** | | 20.236 (0.002)*** | | 29.576 (0.001)*** |
| 100% domestic private ownership | | 5.186 (0.206) | | 5.898 (0.154) | | 10.093 (0.060)* |
| 100% state ownership | | 6.815 (0.259) | | 7.228 (0.233) | | 8.814 (0.236) |
| 100% other ownership | | 23.801 (0.000)*** | | 23.161 (0.000)*** | | 30.029 (0.000)*** |

*(Table continues on the following page.)*

**Table A.5.7** (continued)

| Factor | (1) | (2) | (3) | (4) | (5) | (6) |
|---|---|---|---|---|---|---|
| Sector: | | | | | | |
| Construction | | -16.286 | | -20.171 | | -1.471 |
| | | (0.296) | | (0.215) | | (0.943) |
| Manufacturing | | -13.247 | | -16.044 | | 1.372 |
| | | (0.375) | | (0.306) | | (0.945) |
| Transportation, storage, and communications | | -3.215 | | -5.975 | | 4.682 |
| | | (0.835) | | (0.712) | | (0.819) |
| Wholesale and retail trade | | -16.619 | | -19.341 | | -4.850 |
| | | (0.266) | | (0.218) | | (0.807) |
| Real estate | | -12.183 | | -11.302 | | 4.328 |
| | | (0.432) | | (0.487) | | (0.833) |
| Hotels and restaurants | | -17.627 | | -21.254 | | -7.284 |
| | | (0.263) | | (0.194) | | (0.724) |
| Other services | | -14.566 | | -18.159 | | 0.053 |
| | | (0.356) | | (0.269) | | (0.998) |
| Country: | | | | | | |
| Albania | | 28.659 | | 28.408 | | 33.132 |
| | | (0.000)*** | | (0.000)*** | | (0.000)*** |
| Bosnia and Herzegovina | | -0.404 | | 1.235 | | 0.864 |
| | | (0.947) | | (0.836) | | (0.913) |
| Bulgaria | | 9.061 | | 9.948 | | 10.723 |
| | | (0.095)* | | (0.065)* | | (0.121) |
| Croatia | | 22.874 | | 25.534 | | 25.827 |
| | | (0.000)*** | | (0.000)*** | | (0.001)*** |

| | | | | | | |
|---|---|---|---|---|---|---|
| Macedonia, FYR | | –4.522 | | –2.345 | | –2.195 |
| | | (0.466) | | (0.699) | | (0.805) |
| Moldova | | 7.596 | | 10.507 | | 8.797 |
| | | (0.204) | | (0.070)* | | (0.242) |
| Romania | | 11.663 | | 16.657 | | 12.852 |
| | | (0.030)** | | (0.002)*** | | (0.054)* |
| Tests of joint restrictions (p-values) | | | | | | |
| Ownership effects | | (0.000)*** | | (0.001)*** | | (0.000)*** |
| Sector effects | | (0.435) | | (0.264) | | (0.762) |
| Country effects | | (0.000)*** | | (0.000)*** | | (0.000)*** |
| Number of observations | 1,399 | 1,399 | 1,481 | 1,481 | 1,015 | 1,015 |
| R-squared | 0.004 | 0.057 | 0.003 | 0.053 | 0.029 | 0.081 |

*Source:* Author calculations from EBRD and World Bank (2002).

*Note:* Table shows the results of ordinary least squares regressions; $p$-values are in parentheses. For fixed effects, Serbia and Montenegro was the base country and only the $p$-value of the joint hypothesis that each of the referenced fixed effects is zero is reported. Constants were included but are not reported here.

*significant at 10 percent.
**significant at 5 percent.
***significant at 1 percent.

## Table A.5.8 Financial Transparency and Firm Sales Growth, 2002

*(dependent variable for all regressions is the percentage change in fixed assets over the previous 3 years)*

| Factor | (1) | (2) | (3) | (4) | (5) | (6) |
|---|---|---|---|---|---|---|
| Adoption of IAS | 12.320 (0.000)*** | 8.313 (0.023)** | | | 7.567 (0.092)* | 5.317 (0.261) |
| Use of external audits | | | 5.378 (0.118) | 4.005 (0.276) | -1.452 (0.758) | -2.329 (0.631) |
| Easy access to financing | | | | | 32.239 (0.000)*** | 23.502 (0.012)** |
| Competition | | | | | -11.598 (0.050)* | -11.182 (0.058)* |
| Size | | | | | 1.255 (0.368) | 3.729 (0.018)** |
| Exogenous problems | | | | | 12.555 (0.394) | 16.214 (0.267) |
| Ownership: | | | | | | |
| 100% foreign private ownership | | 19.155 (0.011)** | | 18.467 (0.014)** | | 22.884 (0.021)** |
| 100% domestic private | | 3.436 (0.469) | | 3.751 (0.434) | | 11.340 (0.070)* |
| 100% state ownership | | -5.684 (0.419) | | -5.652 (0.425) | | -6.781 (0.435) |
| 100% other ownership | | 13.968 (0.054)* | | 12.571 (0.084)* | | 20.457 (0.028)** |

Sector:

| | | | |
|---|---|---|---|
| Construction | -23.245 | -27.641 | -19.502 |
| | (0.178) | (0.116) | (0.386) |
| Manufacturing | -13.070 | -16.097 | -10.330 |
| | (0.430) | (0.342) | (0.635) |
| Transportation, storage, and communications | -6.117 | -10.528 | -5.806 |
| | (0.723) | (0.549) | (0.797) |
| Wholesale and retail trade | -21.601 | -25.609 | -14.014 |
| | (0.192) | (0.131) | (0.519) |
| Real estate | -10.705 | -10.890 | 1.117 |
| | (0.534) | (0.536) | (0.960) |
| Hotels and restaurants | -21.439 | -25.884 | -16.919 |
| | (0.221) | (0.145) | (0.456) |
| Other services | -11.926 | -16.411 | -2.369 |
| | (0.499) | (0.358) | (0.918) |
| Country: | | | |
| Albania | 23.898 | 22.728 | 39.524 |
| | (0.001)*** | (0.001)*** | (0.000)*** |
| Bosnia and Herzegovina | -4.863 | -3.395 | -2.629 |
| | (0.499) | (0.633) | (0.780) |
| Bulgaria | -6.397 | -6.562 | -3.883 |
| | (0.312) | (0.299) | (0.632) |
| Croatia | 17.950 | 20.893 | 22.543 |
| | (0.010)** | (0.002)*** | (0.011)** |
| Macedonia, FYR | -9.009 | -8.037 | -3.529 |
| | (0.219) | (0.263) | (0.738) |

*(Table continues on the following page.)*

**Table A.5.8 (continued)**

| Factor | (1) | (2) | (3) | (4) | (5) | (6) |
|---|---|---|---|---|---|---|
| Moldova | | 9.414 | | 13.896 | | 12.065 |
| | | (0.177) | | (0.041)** | | (0.173) |
| Romania | | 25.963 | | 30.829 | | 29.969 |
| | | (0.000)*** | | (0.000)*** | | (0.000)*** |
| Tests of joint restrictions (*p*-values) | | | | | | |
| Ownership effects | | (0.016)** | | (0.026)** | | (0.018)** |
| Sector effects | | (0.136) | | (0.053) | | (0.396) |
| Country effects | | (0.000)*** | | (0.000)*** | | (0.000)*** |
| Number of observations | 1385 | 1385 | 1469 | 1469 | 1012 | 1012 |
| R-squared | 0.009 | 0.067 | 0.002 | 0.066 | 0.026 | 0.094 |

*Source:* Author calculations from EBRD and World Bank (2002).

*Note:* Table shows the results of ordinary least squares regressions; *p*-values are in parentheses. For fixed effects, Serbia and Montenegro was the base country and only the *p*-value of the joint hypothesis that each of the referenced fixed effects is zero is reported. Constants were included but are not reported here.

*significant at 10 percent.

**significant at 5 percent.

***significant at 1 percent.

# Endnotes

1. Before proceeding with the analysis, we should say a word about the usefulness of the BEEPS2 for examining corporate governance. The BEEPS2 sample was pieced together from different sources in different countries. In addition to official records and databases, telephone books and commercial directories were used to construct the sample frame. The sampling procedures employed quotas for state ownership, foreign ownership, exports, and size. Because the quotas did not cover legal form of organization, and because one country's classification system may not agree with that used in another country, comparisons and inferences based on legal form of organization should be treated with caution. A second shortcoming of the BEEPS2 data for the analysis of corporate governance issues is that the sample is skewed toward small companies. This bias is not inappropriate, given that small companies do in fact dominate every economy, in numbers if not in value. But because corporate governance issues arise from the separation of ownership and control, the dominance in the BEEPS2 of firms without such a separation limits the survey's usefulness for examining corporate governance issues. For some of the analyses that follow, we have restricted the sample to firms with at least 50 employees in order to focus on firms that are more likely to encounter governance problems.

2. The BEEPS2 sampling procedures included a quota for state ownership, among others, so that the percentage of firms with state ownership apparent in table 5.1 and subsequent tables is not reflective of the proportion of state-owned enterprises in the population of firms.

3. At the country level, the percentage of firms with minority state ownership has a strong negative correlation with the EBRD indicator of progress toward small-scale privatization.

4. For more information, see http://www.seepad.org/.

5. As a *Financial Times* survey (Cairns 2000) made clear, compliance with IAS is often not a simple matter of yes or no, but one of varying degrees. Nevertheless, the question captures the overall bent of the accounting system from the perspective of top managers.

6. Presumably, the reference to sales on credit implies some formal credit agreement, as opposed to the standard billing arrangement. Similarly, the reference to prepaid sales is presumed to imply payment in advance of sale rather than at the time of sale.

7. The correlation for prepaid sales is –0.71 and the correlation for credit sales is –0.53. The indicators are available in EBRD (2002, p. 20).

8. BEEPS2 (the 2002 survey) also included the category of credit cards. This category has been omitted to maintain comparability with BEEPS1 (the 1999 survey). Few firms reported using credit cards for this purpose.

9. BEEPS2 (the 2002 survey) also included the category of credit from customers. This category has been omitted to maintain comparability with the

BEEPS1 (the 1999 survey). Few firms reported using customer credit for this purpose.

10. In both figure 5.14 and figure 5.15, the bar graphs show the $t$-statistics from the relevant regressions in the annex. The reason that $t$-statistics were chosen for these graphs is that, unlike some of the earlier graphs, the right-hand side variables had several different scales. The $t$-statistic presented a convenient uniform benchmark that accounts for differences in scaling. A simple rule of thumb that might be useful for interpreting these graphs is that a $t$-statistic exceeding 2.0 in absolute value is statistically significant at roughly the 5 percent level.

## References

Beck, Thorsten, Asli Demirguc-Kunt, and Vojislav Maksimovic. 2002. "Financing Patterns around the World: The Role of Institutions." Policy Research Working Paper 2905. World Bank, Washington, D.C.

Cairns, David. 2000. *The* Financial Times *International Accounting Standards Survey 1999*. Oxon, U.K.: David Cairns International Financial Reporting.

Carlin, Wendy, Steven Fries, Mark Schaffer, and Paul Seabright. 2000. "Barter and Non-monetary Transactions in Transition Economies: Evidence from a Cross-Country Survey." EBRD Working Paper 50. European Bank for Reconstruction and Development, London.

Commander, Simon, Irina Dolinskaya, and Christian Mumssen. 2000. "Determinants of Barter in Russia: An Empirical Analysis." IMF Working Paper WP/00/15. International Monetary Fund, Washington, D.C.

Djankov, Simeon, and Peter Murrell. 2002. "Enterprise Restructuring in Transition: A Quantitative Survey." *Journal of Economic Literature* 40(3):739–92.

Earle, John S., and Saul Estrin. 1996. "Employee Ownership in Transition." In Roman Frydman, Cheryl W. Gray, and Andrzej Rapaczynski, eds., *Corporate Governance in Central Europe and Russia. Volume 2: Insiders and the State*. Budapest: Central European University Press.

EBRD (European Bank for Reconstruction and Development). 2002. *Transition Report 2002: Agriculture and Rural Transition*. London.

EBRD and World Bank. 1999. *Business Environment and Enterprise Performance Survey* (BEEPS1). London and Washington, D.C. Data available online at http://info.worldbank.org/governance/beeps.

————. 2002. *Business Environment and Enterprise Performance Survey* (BEEPS2). London and Washington, D.C. Data available online at http://info.worldbank.org/governance/beeps2002.

Frydman, Roman, Cheryl W. Gray, Marek P. Hessel, and Andrzej Rapaczynski. 1999. "When Does Privatization Work? The Impact of Private Ownership on Corporate Performance in the Transition Economies." *Quarterly Journal of Economics* 114: 1153–91.

Hall, Luzi, and Christian Leuz. 2003. "International Differences in Cost of Capital: Do Legal Institutions and Securities Regulation Matter?" ECGI Working Paper 16/2003. European Corporate Governance Institute, Brussels. Available online at http://www.gsm.ucdavis.edu/faculty/Conferences/leuz.pdf.

Jeliazhov, Dimitar. 2002. "Actions Taken in Bulgaria with Regards to International Accounting Standards (IAS) and International Standards on Auditing (ISA) Implementation." Bulgaria Country Report for the Investment Compact for South East Europe. Processed.

Marin, Dalia, Daniel Kaufmann, and Bogdan Gorochowskij. 2000. "Barter in Transition Economies: Competing Explanations Confront Ukrainian Data." CEPR Discussion Paper 2432. Centre for Economic Policy Research, London.

Mesnard, Mathilde. 2001. "A Comparative Overview of the Corporate Governance Framework in South East Europe." Paper presented at the First South East Europe Corporate Governance Roundtable, Bucharest, Romania, September 20–21.

OECD (Organisation for Economic Co-operation and Development), South East Corporate Governance Roundtable. 2003. *White Paper on Corporate Governance in South East Europe.* Paris. Available online at http://www.investmentcompact.org/pdf/CGWhitePaper.pdf.

OHR (Office of the High Representative). 2003. *Elektroprivreda RS. Report of the Special Auditor.* Sarajevo. Available online at http://www.ohr.int/other-doc/spec-audit-rep/pdf/sar_ers_eng.pdf.

Pissarides, Francesca. 2001. "Financial Structures to Promote Private Sector Development in South-Eastern Europe." EBRD Working Paper 64. European Bank for Reconstruction and Development, London.

World Bank. 2000. "World Business Environment Survey Webtool Interactive." Washington, D.C. Data available online at http://info. worldbank.org/governance/wbes/.

———. 2003a. "Accounting and Auditing." In *Report on the Observance of Standards and Codes (ROSC): Romania.* Washington D.C. Available online at http://www.worldbank.org/ifa/rosc.html.

———. 2003b. *World Development Indicators 2003.* Washington, D.C.

———. n.d. Reports on the Observance of Standards and Codes Web site. Available online at http://www.worldbank.org/ifa/rosc.html.

# 6
# Resolving Business Disputes in South Eastern Europe: The Role of the Courts

The transition economies of South Eastern Europe (SEE) are often cited as a setting where the business environment is one of the main obstacles to higher levels of internal and foreign investment and to higher growth rates. Compared with the more successful economies of Central Europe and the Baltics, the Balkan countries have, so far, proceeded at a slower pace in transforming their economies and have been beset with civil strife and war conflicts.[1] Generally, investment and growth rates recorded in the eight South Eastern European countries that constitute the sample of this study (SEE8) have been lower than in their Central European and Baltic counterparts.

After the resolution of the Kosovo conflict in 1999 and after the change in the regime in Serbia and Montenegro in 2000, the regional economies stabilized. Newly elected governments have been making efforts to improve the business climate and attract inward investment. The purpose of this chapter is to analyze the quality of the investment climate in the Balkans from the perspective of commercial dispute resolution. Obviously, the institutions that (a) promote certainty and confidence when a firm transacts with other firms and (b) serve to enforce contracts (such as the courts, business networks, private protection firms, and government) are a crucial facet of the investment climate and are worthy of special attention.

A spectrum of institutions support contractual compliance and enforcement. Courts are the main institution enforcing contracts and resolving business disputes. Business disputes are inherent in business transactions. In a complex economy involving many buyers and sellers as well as complex goods and transactions, firms necessarily undertake risks in dealing with new clients and suppliers, and face potential disputes with them. Without efficient courts and the expectation that courts will uphold their contractual rights and obligations, firms will be less willing to deal with new clients and suppliers, and fewer transactions will take place. Reliable and efficient courts encourage new business relation-ships because new partners do not fear being cheated. In addition, good courts help businesses undertake more complex business transactions and help them produce more sophisticated goods and services by allow-ing for complex contracts to be written and by encouraging specific investments. Furthermore, courts play an important role in securing social peace.

Despite these functions, companies in many countries seldom use courts.[2] Why does this pattern occur? What are the alternatives to con-tract enforcement outside the courts? Other institutions also serve to enforce contracts and reduce the uncertainty a firm faces when engaged in transactions with other firms. These institutions include both formal and informal mechanisms of enforcement, such as social networks, busi-ness associations, or public information channels to help firms decide with whom to do business and under what conditions. In general, con-tract enforcement mechanisms could be divided into (a) personal rela-tionships based on trust, (b) self-enforcement through repeated transactions, (c) third-party enforcement based on reputation, (d) private enforcement, (e) administrative government intervention, and (f) court enforcement (litigation). Although each of these mechanisms could potentially serve the same purpose, some are inefficient because either they exclude new clients (for instance, the first mechanism listed, which promotes commercially transacting with only known, repeated cus-tomers) or they structure transactions with a goal to avoid business dis-putes (for example, requiring prepayment). Other mechanisms, such as business associations, have been shown to be seldom used.

Although much criticism has been voiced about the use of private pro-tection firms (the Russian rackets) as a substitute for corrupt and ineffi-cient court justice, anecdotal evidence suggests that they are also widely used in the Balkans. However, a detailed and systematic analysis of firms' enforcement strategies does not support this view. Furthermore, those firms providing private protection services for contractual enforce-ment are fraught with their own inefficiencies.

Efficient contract enforcement is fast, fair, and affordable. However, there is a tradeoff between speed and fairness: fast procedures may forgo a certain degree of fairness. Finally, court enforcement must be cheap rel-ative to the value of the dispute; otherwise it will not be used.

This chapter will describe how firms choose to structure their transac-tions and resolve their contractual disputes with other firms in the SEE8. Our starting point is that (a) courts allow for complex exchange to take place and (b) relational contracting and third-party mechanisms of enforcement generate inefficiencies. First, to describe how SEE8 firms avoid disputes, we use detailed business case studies conducted by the World Bank in 2002 in each of the eight countries. In addition, we use data from the two European Bank for Reconstruction and Development (EBRD)–World Bank *Business Environment and Enterprise Performance Surveys* (BEEPS1 and BEEPS2), conducted in 1999 and 2002. The surveys covered more than 6,000 firms in 26 transition economies (EBRD and World Bank 1999, 2002).

Next, we describe the informal, out-of-court ways to achieve settlement of business disputes. Third, we focus on court enforcement of contracts. We explore what determines the use of the courts in resolving commercial disputes. We describe how formal, fast, and costly the enforcement of commercial debt contracts in each of these countries is, and we compare our findings with those for the other transition economies. We argue that firms tend to use the court system when it is less formal, less expensive, and faster in resolving disputes. Available legal survey data (about the exact procedures creditors must go through to collect a debt claim of 50 percent of the country's gross national income per capita, what their legal costs would be, and how long the first-instance process would take) enabled us to identify weaknesses in the functioning of the courts and to propose recommendations for court reform.

Before we proceed with the analysis of contract enforcement, let us first look at how firms in the sample countries perceive their legal systems. Figure 6.1 compares the confidence in the legal system by surveyed firms located in the SEE8 in 1999 and 2002. The data come from firm managers' answers to the BEEPS questionnaire in 1999 and 2002. All the countries of our sample participated in the 2002 BEEPS; in 1999, firms from Serbia and Montenegro did not take part in the survey. Figure 6.1 evaluates to what extent firm managers agree or disagree with the following statement: "I am confident that the legal system will uphold my contract and property rights in business disputes." Firms are given an answer scale from 1 to 6, corresponding to various degrees of disagreement or agreement with the above statement, with higher values indicating a higher degree of agreement. The measures reported in the figure are country averages across all firms that responded to this question, regardless of whether the firm had or had not used the courts in past business disputes.

The results suggest that, in 1999, surveyed firms in Bosnia and Herzegovina and in Croatia felt most confident about their country's legal system, whereas Moldovan firms had the least confidence in their country's legal system. In 2002, firms in Serbia and Montenegro displayed the highest confidence on average, with Moldovan firms again scoring lowest on their confidence in the legal system. Importantly, the trend in confidence between 1999 and 2002 is predominantly downward. Average confidence in the legal system was lower in 2002 than it was in 1999 in Albania, Bosnia and Herzegovina, Bulgaria, and Croatia; confidence

**Figure 6.1    Confidence in the Legal System: Average across All Interviewed Firms, 1999 and 2002**

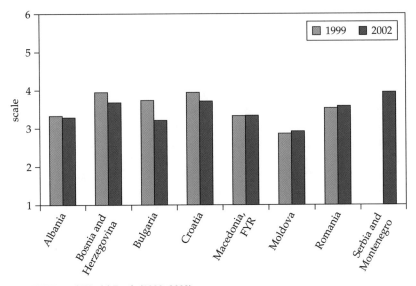

*Source:* EBRD and World Bank (1999, 2002).
*Note:* Respondents were asked, on a scale of 1 to 6, the extent to which they agreed or disagreed with the following statement: "I am confident that the legal system will uphold my contract and property rights in business disputes." A response of 1 indicated a high level of disagreement; a response of 6 indicated a high level of agreement.

stayed at approximately the same level in the former Yugoslav Republic of Macedonia and marginally improved in Romania and Moldova.

This finding is consistent with other current studies of the business environment in this region, including a recent World Bank study (Gray, Hellman, and Ryterman 2004). This study, using data from the BEEPS questionnaires for 1999 and 2002, establishes that, in most South Eastern European countries, corruption measures have worsened over that period. For example, within the group of transition economies, corruption is perceived by business managers to be most problematic in SEE and the Commonwealth of Independent States (CIS). Perceptions of corruption stayed relatively constant at high rates in Albania, Bosnia and Herzegovina, Bulgaria, FYR Macedonia, and Romania. Only Croatia and Moldova recorded improvements in perceptions of corruption between 1999 and 2002. The same report establishes similar results regarding the effect of state capture on firms. With respect to perceptions of state capture, five of the SEE8—Albania, Bosnia and Herzegovina, Bulgaria, FYR Macedonia, and Serbia and Montenegro—had the highest scores among the full sample of transitional economies. In addition, the share of captor firms has increased in several South Eastern European countries, most notably in Bosnia and Herzegovina and FYR Macedonia, but also in Bulgaria and Croatia.

These findings are very much in line with firm managers' perceptions about the legal system and property rights. On average, surveyed managers felt less secure about their contractual rights in 2002 than they did 3 years earlier. Given this assessment, one would expect a less legalistic approach to contract enforcement. Indeed, this trend occurs. The case interviews of firm managers confirm that, to a varying degree, they consider the courts a last resort for resolving disputes, and they describe a way of doing business that very much rests on building mutual trust and long-lasting relationships with suppliers and customers, plus structuring transactions in ways that reduce contractual risk.

## Avoidance of Business Disputes

### Building Good Partnerships and Gathering Information

Disputes are part of contractual activity. Yet, in many countries around the world, firms conduct their business in ways that avoid disputes. This practice is particularly common in places where courts are slow, corrupt, and expensive. Regression analysis using the BEEPS2 data suggests that certain types of firms, such as small firms and firms belonging to the services industry, are less likely to encounter payment disputes. What can firms do to avoid disputes? They can follow several strategies: (a) refuse to extend credit to existing or new customers and even require prepayment before releasing the object of contractual exchange; (b) build long-lasting relationships with suppliers and customers (in other words, rely on so-called relational contracting);[3] and (c) invest not only in collecting information about potential trading partners before engaging in transactions with them but also in monitoring a contractual partner's behavior after an exchange has occurred.

Apart from these bilateral strategies, firms can use business associations, the government, political parties, or private protection firms not only to avoid disputes (by imposing an implicit threat) but also to resolve them when they do arise. The BEEPS2 data and the case studies (as evidenced by box 6.1) reveal that firms actually do employ bilateral mechanisms such as prepayment and nonuse of credit to avoid disputes. Both prepayment and nonuse of credit significantly reduce the probability of payment disputes. Business association membership and donations to political parties, however, are not found to reduce the incidence of disputes, and, in fact, appear to be related to the occurrence of payment disputes arising and the need to resolve such disputes in court.

---

### Box 6.1  How Do Firms Avoid Business Disputes?

One Albanian company interviewed for the case studies stressed the importance of trust in building business relationships. It invests in establishing good relations with its customers and even forgoes signing written contracts. Gathering information about new customers and working toward a good business relationship seem to be working well because the company reports no recent disputes and no use of the court system.

Similarly, a Bosnian software company indicated that it spends considerable time and effort making sure that prospective clients have a good reputation before engaging in business with them. For instance, in 70 percent to 80 percent of cases, the company investigates whether a potential new client is reputable by seeking information from other firms with whom the client does business (for example, banks). This type of advance information gathering and screening, though costly, is seen by the company's management as necessary in a business environment where contractual breaches are common and the court system remains rather ineffective in resolving them. The manager summed up the incidence of contractual disputes by simply saying, "We expect nonpayments." Hence, the extra care being exercised in screening new clients is justified.

A textile firm from FYR Macedonia shared those views. The company invests in forging close working relationships with clients. The manager admitted that "contracts do not mean too much; promise is what counts [when doing business in FYR Macedonia]." Accordingly, the company seldom signs written contracts and avoids disputes by requiring advance payments and by building long-lasting relationships with customers and suppliers.

---

In addition, firms appear to avoid disputes by forgoing trade with third-party, unknown suppliers, even when that trade would be on more beneficial terms than existing suppliers could offer. This practice results in loss of economic value. For example, BEEPS2 asked firms across the region what their reaction would be if their main material input supplier increased its price by 10 percent, assuming alternative suppliers left their price of the same input and all other terms of trade unchanged. In this proposed scenario, only 28 percent of firms across the eight countries would switch entirely to purchasing this input from alternative suppliers. Firms in Bulgaria, Croatia, and Moldova would be most willing to drop the existing supplier and trade with new suppliers, but even in those countries, approximately two-thirds of firms would reject such a bargain and continue to trade, at least partially, with the existing supplier at the higher price.

Table 6.1 presents the share of firms that would be willing to switch to a new supplier if their current main supplier raised its price by 10 percent. The table also shows the share of firms that feared that they would entirely

**Table 6.1   Firms Willing to Switch to a New Supplier When Current Supplier Raises Prices and Firms Fearing Loss of Customers If Prices Are Raised**

| Country | Firms that would switch to a new supplier (% of total firms) | Firms that would fear loss of customers (% of total firms) |
|---|---|---|
| Albania | 23 | 29 |
| Bosnia and Herzegovina | 23 | 29 |
| Bulgaria | 36 | 39 |
| Croatia | 32 | 23 |
| Macedonia, FYR | 24 | 28 |
| Moldova | 34 | 37 |
| Romania | 25 | 26 |
| Serbia and Montenegro | 24 | 19 |

*Source:* EBRD and World Bank (2002).

lose their customers to competition if they raised the price of their main product by 10 percent, assuming that competing firms left the price of the same product unchanged. Again, firms felt quite secure that they would keep their existing customers in such circumstances; only 29 percent of all firms across the region anticipated that a move of this kind would result in customers switching entirely to trade with competing firms. Firms in Bulgaria and Moldova most feared that they would lose customers.

The results shown in table 6.1 indicate that firms attempt to avoid disputes by forging long-lasting relationships with suppliers and customers. However, this practice implies a high cost: lost opportunities to trade with alternative firms on better terms and lost opportunities to support the entry of new firms into the trading arena.

## Business Associations

How are business associations viewed as facilitators of dispute resolution? BEEPS2 asked firms that belong to a business or trade association to evaluate the services provided by that association along several dimensions. Table 6.2 reports firms' assessments of the value of dispute resolution services that are provided by the association to which the firms belong. The evidence demonstrates that, across the region, business associations do not provide much assistance to their members in resolving contractual disputes. On average, only 4 percent of all interviewed SEE8 respondents felt that the business association to which they belonged played a major or critical role in resolving their disputes with other firms, their own firms' employees, or government officials. In contrast, 84 percent of SEE8 firms indicated that the business association to which they

Table 6.2    Business Association Membership

| Country | Firms that belong to a business association (% of total firms) | Firms belonging to a business association that believe it provides no value or negligible value in resolving disputes (%) | Firms belonging to a business association that believe it provides major or critical value in resolving disputes (%) |
|---|---|---|---|
| Albania | 85 | 86 | 5 |
| Bosnia and Herzegovina | 53 | 79 | 6 |
| Bulgaria | 52 | 82 | 5 |
| Croatia | 77 | 94 | 1 |
| Macedonia, FYR | 32 | 85 | 0 |
| Moldova | 36 | 73 | 10 |
| Romania | 55 | 89 | 2 |
| Serbia and Montenegro | 52 | 85 | 3 |

Source: EBRD and World Bank (2002).

belonged provided no value at all or, at best, negligible value to their resolving of disputes with the same third parties. The country case studies reinforce these findings (see box 6.2).

The BEEPS 2002 data on the nonuse of business associations (table 6.2) and the reluctance of firms to switch to new suppliers (table 6.1) are supported by results reported in a study by Hendley and Murrell (2003), which evaluated different mechanisms for supporting contractual agreements in Romania. That study asked firm managers to rate the frequency of use and the effectiveness of six distinct ways to support contracts and resolve disputes when they arise. The results established that (a) informal bilateral strategies such as building personal relationships and relying on trust as well as on the incentives of each party and (b) the use of the formal legal and court system as a last resort are by far the most popular ways to support contracts and resolve disputes. The study found that third-party arrangements such as business associations, services providing private dispute resolution, or the government are seen as being less effective and are used less often to make sure that contractual obligations are met and disputes are resolved.[4] According to the study, informal bilateral mechanisms and the formal legal and judicial system provide the support for contractual agreements in more than 75 percent of cases.

## Use of Prepayment

One method companies use to avoid the risk of customer nonpayment is to insist on advance payment. Advance payment can deter one party in a

## Box 6.2  The Role of Business Associations in Resolving Commercial Disputes

In the case studies, the interviewed firms seldom mentioned business associations as a venue where business disputes are brought and resolved. One of the few companies that did point to the use of business associations for this purpose was a private textile firm from Bulgaria. The firm's managers indicated that they have attempted to resolve a dispute with a foreign client over nonpayment through the Bulgarian Chamber of Commerce. However, they reported, the chamber has done little to settle the dispute. In the meantime, the company has ceased dealing with that particular client.

The level of detail that the firm provided about the foreign client also indicated the close relationship existing between the firm and its customers. For instance, the nonpaying client had been a client for several years before the dispute. We were told that the client was a small retailer and that she tried to delay payment for a particular order by claiming that she had been in the hospital, that she had experienced personal problems, that the retail store had been burglarized, and so forth. Thus, the firm and the client appeared to know each other very well and to have spent considerable time and effort to achieve the relationship.

The same textile firm also revealed how it copes with potential nonpayment when dealing with domestic clients. It produces garments to order for clients, who pick orders every week and pay on delivery. If payment for an order from the previous week is still due, new orders are not accepted. Thus, the risk of nonpayment is lowered. Indeed, the company reported no commercial disputes with domestic clients.

In addition, a textile firm from Croatia reported using the Croatian chamber of commerce to resolve some of its disputes. We were told that courts are slow and that, once a judgment is issued, execution progresses very slowly. The firm explained that it uses the chamber of commerce to arbitrate disputes and implied that it prefers such arbitration to court litigation. The company also indicated that it sometimes voices concerns over public procurement contracts before the chamber. For example, the firm raised a complaint before the chamber of commerce about the outcome of a public procurement tender, which another textile company had won. The chamber sent a letter about this matter to the government. Apparently, however, this action did not produce any tangible results in this case.

business relationship (the buyer) from breaking the terms of a contract with the other party (the seller). When the buyer pays part of the bill in advance, the manufacturer's risk that the buyer will renege on the contract is lowered, and the buyer's risk is increased. Advance payment helps reduce the manufacturer's risk associated with the following business practices: (a) producing goods to order rather than to inventory,

**Table 6.3    Share of Sales . . .**

*(percent)*

| . . . Paid in advance by clients | Share |
|---|---|
| | *Highest share* |
| Moldova | 27 |
| Serbia and Montenegro | 23 |
| Albania | 18 |
| Bosnia and Herzegovina | 17 |
| | *Lowest share* |
| Macedonia, FYR | 9 |
| Romania | 6 |
| Bulgaria | 6 |
| Croatia | 7 |

| . . . Sold on credit to clients | Share |
|---|---|
| | *Highest share* |
| Romania | 30 |
| Albania | 30 |
| Bulgaria | 22 |
| Moldova | 22 |
| Serbia and Montenegro | 21 |
| Macedonia, FYR | 20 |
| | *Lowest share* |
| Bosnia and Herzegovina | 12 |
| Croatia | 10 |

*Source:* EBRD and World Bank (2002).

(b) selling goods across long distances, and (c) selling a large proportion of one's output to a single buyer or to very few buyers (a practice known as *selling in thin markets*).

How widespread is prepayment in the SEE8 economies? The BEEPS2 data show that, on average, interviewed Moldovan firms require payment in advance from their clients for more than a quarter of their sales (see table 6.3). This prepayment reduces the probability of payment disputes arising, but it also limits contractual activity. Prepayment is also quite common among the surveyed firms in Serbia and Montenegro (23 percent of sales on average), in Albania (18 percent of sales), and in Bosnia and Herzegovina (17 percent). Prepayment is less common, on average, in Bulgaria, Croatia, and Romania. For comparison, we can look at similar statistics for Vietnam. McMillan and Woodruff (1999) report that in the years 1995–97 private manufacturing firms in Vietnam used prepayment in 35 percent of their customer relationships; in other words, in 35 percent of sales, some portion of the bill was paid in advance. Box 6.3 illustrates the higher contractual risk associated with producing goods to order and how advance payment is used to reduce this risk.

---

### Box 6.3  Using Prepayment to Reduce Contractual Risk

The companies we interviewed for the case studies often mentioned prepayment as a means of forestalling business disputes. Asking clients to pay a considerable proportion of the price in advance seems to be the norm in many SEE8 firms, regardless of sector, size, or ownership characteristics. A state-owned steel foundry from Bosnia and Herzegovina described three recent cases of business disputes and how it went about resolving them. In two of the cases, the firm was the creditor, and in one case, it was the debtor. One of the former cases is quite telling. The company produced goods to order for a Serbian metalworking company and delivered half of the order in 1995, but the company did not receive payment at the time. Several years ensued, and the Serbian firm closed down production. Even though the Bosnian company attempted to negotiate with the Serbian firm's administration on several occasions, the debt was still due 7 years later. The Bosnian company's management is planning to pursue this case through the Bosnian court system. Even though a written contract exists, the management still faces uncertainty as to the duration and costs of the court procedure.

   The risk associated with contracts for goods made to order is well illustrated in this case. The other half of the goods made to order are still stocked in the steel foundry's warehouse, but they have no alternative commercial use. Given this situation, it is hardly surprising that the same steel company now requires a 50 percent advance payment on its orders, with the remaining 50 percent falling due within 5 days after delivery. Furthermore, new clients must pay the full price of the model good in transactions for which the good is made to the client's order. Subsequent deliveries and payments are scheduled in five installments. In this manner, transactions and payments are structured to avoid the occurrence of payment disputes.

---

## Use of Credit

According to BEEPS2, the share of sales sold on credit to clients is highest in Albania and Romania (at 30 percent) and lowest in Bosnia and Herzegovina and Croatia (at 12 and 10 percent, respectively). These figures, which are shown in table 6.3 alongside those for sales paid in advance, imply that in a large share of sales clients pay at the time of purchase. In most of the SEE8, payment at time of purchase accounts for about half of sales volume. When figures for the sales made through payment at time of purchase are added to prepaid sales, we see that 70 percent to 80 percent of sales are either paid in advance or paid on the spot. Similar results are found in a study by Fafchamps (1996), who reported that surveyed Ghanaian manufacturing and trading firms used cash payment on delivery as the main way to avoid disputes. The practice of granting credit was fairly uncommon; respondents in Fafchamps's study had 34 regular customers on average but extended trade credit to only 6.6 of them.

## Private Protection

Another means of third-party dispute resolution is the private protection firm. Observers have argued that private protection firms have played an important role in contract enforcement in transition countries, most prominently in the Russian Federation. Providers of protection services may be legal or illegal (depending on whether their activities are sanctioned by the state), and they work on a fee basis. The common assumption is that, in the presence of weak and corrupt courts, private protectors step in and assume the tasks of contract enforcement. Indeed, Frye and Zhuravskaya (2000) present evidence based on a survey of Russian shop owners that regulation of businesses by higher levels of government is associated with weaker legal institutions and raises the probability that firms will interact with private protection rackets.[5]

However, other authors have challenged this view. For example, Hendley, Murrell, and Ryterman (2000) contend that use of private protection firms by Russian businesses for enforcement of contracts is in fact quite limited. They report that only 3 percent of the Russian enterprises that they interviewed had used private protection firms to prevent or resolve disputes with suppliers. Furthermore, only 2.5 percent of firms reportedly used private protection firms to investigate a client's ability to pay, further casting doubt on the relevance of these firms for encouraging contractual compliance.

The BEEPS2 survey asked firm managers whether their firms had incurred losses as a result of theft, robbery, vandalism, or arson in the previous year, and it asked for estimates of the value of these losses. This question, therefore, was intended to assess how secure the business environment is. Presumably, the higher such incidences and incurred losses, the less secure firm managers would feel and the more inclined they would be to invest in security or protection services provided by private entities rather than by the state.

Other 2002 BEEPS questions elicited information on (a) whether firms pay for security and protection and (b) what the value of these payments is per year (as a share of annual sales). We use these data to determine which types of firms are more prone to losses from theft, vandalism, and so forth and to discover which types of firms spend more on security and protection.

Table 6.4 compares the value of incurred losses, the value of protection payments, and security payments for newly established private firms

Table 6.4   Statistical Tests for Differences in Firms' Losses Because of Theft, Robbery, Vandalism, or Arson, and for Firms' Spending on Security and Protection Services

| Types of firms | Percentage of total annual sales in 2001 | | |
|---|---|---|---|
| | Incurred losses | Security payments | Protection payments |
| Newly established private firms | 4.15 | 2.70 | 2.46 |
| Old firms (both state owned and privatized) | 2.67 | 2.09 | 2.22 |
| t-statistics | 2.7212 (0.0034) | 3.6231 (0.0002) | 0.7768 (0.2190) |

Source: EBRD and World Bank (2002).
Note: One-tailed t-tests are reported; p-values are shown in parentheses.

and for old firms (both state owned and privatized) across the SEE8. The results indicate that newly established firms are more vulnerable to violent crime against their business interests. These firms, which are mostly small and privately owned, reported significantly higher losses because of theft, robbery, and other forms of violent crime than the other firms. Accordingly, newly established firms spend more on security and protection services, including security equipment, personnel, and so forth, than do old firms. They also spend more on protection services, but the result of the t-test for that variable is not statistically significant.

Security payments are more common than protection payments. About one-quarter of BEEPS2 respondents (24 percent) indicated that they make protection payments, whereas more than twice as many firms (54 percent) said that they pay for security (but not protection). Compared with the findings of Hendley, Murrell, and Ryterman (2000) on Russia, the share of SEE8 firms making protection payments seems high (24 percent), but the two figures are not directly comparable because BEEPS2 does not clearly specify whether protection payments are made only to private protection firms or also to others. Therefore, the BEEPS2 variable may encompass more than purely private protection. Because BEEPS1 did not ask these questions, we are unable to assess how (a) losses caused by criminal activity directed against one's business and (b) spending on security and protection have changed over time.

*Government Intervention*

Parties to a dispute can also rely on bureaucratic recourse; in other words, they can seek government intervention to deal with contractual breaches (particularly in business-to-government business relations). Hendley,

Murrell, and Ryterman (2000) found that few enterprises in Russia use this strategy to resolve contractual disputes with customers and suppliers. However, they did find that prior state ownership influenced an enterprise's reliance on government intervention. Of previously state-owned enterprises, 11 percent used contacts with state officials to solve contractual problems, whereas only 5 percent of enterprises that had never been state owned chose to do so.

BEEPS2 asked respondents about their access to bureaucratic recourse to resolve disputes with government officials. (Specifically, the survey asked, "How often is the following statement true: If a government official acts against the rules, I can usually go to another official or to his superior and get the correct treatment without recourse to unofficial payments/gifts.") Table 6.5 shows differences in access. Old firms, large firms (those with more than 250 employees), and state-owned

### Table 6.5   Statistical Tests for Differences in Firms' Access to Bureaucratic Recourse, Legal Information, and Assessments of the Predictability and Consistency of Legal Interpretations

| Groups of firms[a] | Access to bureaucratic recourse in disputes with government[b] | Information on laws and regulations is easy to obtain | Interpretations of the laws and regulations are consistent and predictable |
|---|---|---|---|
| By age: | | | |
| Newly established firms | 2.74 | 3.74 | 3.15 |
| Old firms (both state owned and privatized) | 3.22 | 4.30 | 3.59 |
| $t$-statistic | −5.6328 (0.0000) | −7.0000 (0.0000) | −5.4533 (0.0000) |
| By size: | | | |
| Small firms | 2.75 | 3.75 | 3.17 |
| Large firms | 3.13 | 4.21 | 3.49 |
| $t$-statistic | −4.7267 (0.0000) | −5.8082 (0.0000) | −4.1032 (0.0000) |
| By ownership: | | | |
| Private firms | 2.84 | 3.83 | 3.22 |
| State-owned firms | 3.18 | 4.45 | 3.68 |
| $t$-statistic | −3.0108 (0.0014) | −6.2167 (0.0000) | −4.3120 (0.0000) |

Source: EBRD and World Bank (2002).
Note: One-tailed $t$-tests are reported; $p$-values are shown in parentheses next to the $t$-statistics.
a. Each of the three groups (by age, size, or ownership) represents a whole sample.
b. Respondents used a scale of 1 to 6 to answer each question, with a response of 1 meaning "never" and a response of 6 meaning "always."

firms are shown to have significantly better access to bureaucratic recourse than newly established firms, smaller firms, and private firms have if they are treated unfairly. Furthermore, older firms, large firms, and state-owned firms have significantly better access to legal information, and they find that interpretations of laws and regulations by the state courts and the government are significantly more consistent and predictable. All the differences in mean responses are significant at the 1 percent level.

## *Other Informal Contract Enforcement Mechanisms*

Apart from being directly involved in resolving commercial disputes of their members, business associations also serve as a reputation-based contract enforcement institution. Reputational contracting is similar to relational contracting in that it rests on the game-theoretic assumption that the one-off gains from reneging on a contractual obligation are lower than the discounted present value of future gain resulting from one's good name.[6] Business associations can provide information about past behavior of members; similarly, credit registries and bureaus supply information about past borrower behavior and payment history.[7]

Related to reputational contracting mechanisms are multilateral punishment systems, including community-driven contract enforcement. These systems work when business takes place in close-knit communities where personal relations matter and the community can easily set sanctions against opportunistic behavior. For instance, this behavior worked in medieval Europe, where, if a party reneged on its obligations, the ensuing sanctions were imposed on the defaulting party's community. The community could then deal with the offending party as it saw fit. Multilateral punishment was also common in the Middle Ages for trans-Mediterranean trade. Merchants had to trade across distance and time, and the institution of the merchant guild was established to deter opportunistic behavior by trading partners and by agents trading on behalf of the merchants.[8] Merchant guilds facilitated trade in the absence of formal, state courts to ensure that involved parties complied with contracts.

However, the importance of these reputation-based enforcement mechanisms declined over time as trade became more impersonal and distant across space and time. Community and social bonds became weaker and could no longer be used to impose credible threats against opportunistic behavior. Furthermore, as economic transactions became more complex, the transaction costs of screening new traders rose and eventually led to the replacement of the merchant guilds with formal national courts in the late Middle Ages.

## Contract Enforcement in Court

How effective and efficient is contract enforcement in court? To answer this question, we rely on data from the Lex Mundi surveys of lawyers at private law firms in each of the SEE8. The methodology for the surveys[9] was developed by Djankov and others (2003) and the survey data for SEE8 were later updated and expanded, with the permission of Djankov and others, by the authors of this chapter.[10]

The Lex Mundi surveys assumed a hypothetical transaction in which a client reneged on the payment of a fulfilled contract, amounting to 50 percent of GNI per capita in that country. Lawyers from the eight sample countries were asked to describe how the creditor would go about recovering his or her payment through the courts. Figure 6.2 shows how long the associated court cases would take not only for these countries but also for countries with more advanced transition economies. In Bosnia and Herzegovina, the process would take the company 630 calendar days from the moment of filing its claim in court to the final enforcement of the court judgment, and the litigants and the judge would have to maneuver through 31 procedural

**Figure 6.2    Duration of Debt Collection Court Cases: A Comparison of Transitional Economies**

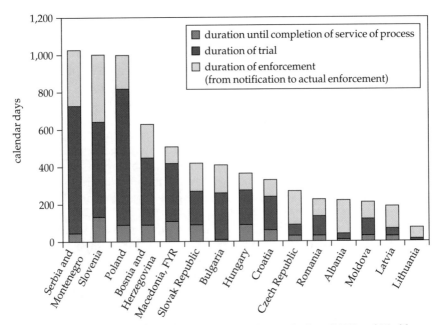

*Source:* Lex Mundi surveys. For background, see Djankov and others (2003) and World Bank (2004).

steps. Similarly, in Serbia and Montenegro, the process would take a little less than 3 years (1,028 calendar days) and would require 40 separate procedures to bring the same lawsuit to completion. In FYR Macedonia, court procedures are also lengthy and involve numerous mandatory procedural steps; the same case would take 509 days from filing until enforcement of the judgment, and it would involve 27 mandatory procedural steps.

Lengthy and burdensome court procedures are not limited to the countries of the former Yugoslavia. The same pattern emerges across the other countries of the region. In Bulgaria, for example, the same assumed case would take 410 days to resolve and enforce, and it would require 26 separate procedures. In Albania, the same case would be resolved in 220 days and after 37 procedural steps.

For comparison, the assumed debt collection case would be resolved in 189 days in Latvia and would involve 19 steps. In Lithuania, the most common mechanism to collect a debt worth 50 percent of GNI per capita would be an out-of-court administrative procedure conducted before a notary public, which would take about 74 days and include 15 procedural steps. In contrast, a first-instance court procedure to collect the same debt would take 150 days and mandate 30 independent actions by the parties and the judge (see figure 6.3). The court procedure would also be more expensive, and plaintiffs would be unwilling to use it, other things being equal.

However, some of the more economically advanced transition countries are also experiencing court delays and do not fare much better in terms of duration and number of procedures. For instance, as figure 6.2 shows, in

## Figure 6.3   Lithuania: A Comparison of Available Procedures in Debt Collection

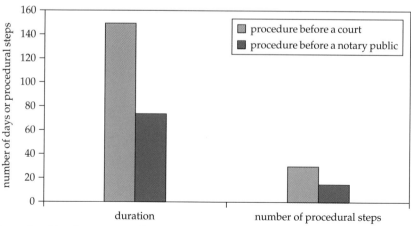

*Source:* Lex Mundi surveys. For background, see Djankov and others (2003) and World Bank (2004).

Poland and Slovenia, the duration of the court procedure is of a similar magnitude to that of Serbia and Montenegro—1,000 and 1,003 days, respectively. In Hungary, duration, although substantially shorter, is still one calendar year.

Lengthy and burdensome procedures cost more. In Albania, the company seeking to retrieve a debt equal to half of GNI per capita would have to pay 1.6 times the debt amount in lawyers' fees and a further 9.5 percent of the claim value in court fees. In FYR Macedonia, attorney fees would also be high—at 71 percent of the claim amount, with court fees adding another 11 percent of the claim amount to total legal expenses. Litigation would also be expensive in Bosnia and Herzegovina and Serbia and Montenegro. Table 6.6 presents the data on legal costs of procedures to enforce contracts in the SEE8 economies. Legal costs, particularly attorney fees, are determined by supply and demand in the market for legal services. Lawyers' fees that are relatively low, such as those in Moldova, for example, may well be the consequence of low demand for legal services (which itself is a function of the country's low income).

Before we proceed with interpreting these data, however, an important caveat is needed with respect to the survey instrument used to gather the data. All the Lex Mundi survey responses were prepared by only one law firm per country, and therefore all data collected reflect the opinions of the respondent lawyers (usually a second lawyer verifies the answers) from this single firm. Consequently, the same survey could have potentially

## Table 6.6 Plaintiff's Costs of Contract Enforcement in a First-Instance Court

| Country | Average GNI per capita, 1999–2001 (US$) | Amount of debt (US$) | Expected attorney fees (US$) | Expected court fees (US$) | Attorney fees (as a % of GNI per capita) | Court fees (as a % of GNI per capita) |
|---|---|---|---|---|---|---|
| Albania | 930 | 465 | 750 | 44 | 80.6 | 4.7 |
| Bosnia and Herzegovina | 1,210 | 605 | 200 | 60 | 16.5 | 5.0 |
| Bulgaria | 1,490 | 745 | 80 | 15 | 5.4 | 1.0 |
| Croatia | 4,583 | 2,292 | 241 | 64 | 5.3 | 1.4 |
| Macedonia, FYR | 1,830 | 915 | 650 | 100 | 35.5 | 5.5 |
| Moldova | 410 | 205 | 40 | 16 | 9.8 | 4.0 |
| Romania | 1,660 | 830 | 120 | 8 | 7.2 | 0.5 |
| Serbia and Montenegro | 940 | 470 | 100 | 100 | 10.6 | 10.6 |
| Mean | 1,632 | 820 | 273 | 51 | 21.4 | 4.1 |

*Source:* Lex Mundi surveys. For background, see Djankov and others (2003) and World Bank (2004).

elicited different answers, at least to some questions, had it been administered at a different law firm or at a company rather than a law firm. Obviously, this possibility raises legitimate issues about the reliability of the collected information—particularly, quantitative data such as duration and costs of court enforcement—and whether valid arguments can be made on the basis of the methodology used. Therefore, those using and interpreting the data—particularly those data that cannot be readily verified—should do so cautiously. At the same time, another point of caution must be stressed: Alternative methodologies for collecting these types of large, comparative, cross-country datasets pose other challenges for researchers of comparative law and court performance. Thus, researchers should fully consider the merits and drawbacks of the Lex Mundi methodology, and contrast those with the merits and drawbacks of alternative methodologies such as firm-level surveys of business managers.[11]

With the above caveat in mind, we move on to the analysis of the Lex Mundi survey data. Three indicators of the efficiency of contract enforcement have been constructed on the basis of the law firms' responses. The first indicator is the number of independent procedures that are mandated by either law or court rules, and necessitate some interaction either between the parties to the dispute or between the parties and the judge or court officer. The second indicator of efficiency is an estimate—in calendar days—of the duration of dispute resolution. Duration is measured as the number of calendar days from the moment the plaintiff files the lawsuit in court until the moment of actual payment. This indicator includes not only the days on which actions take place but also waiting periods between procedures. The participating firms made separate estimates of the average duration until the completion of service of process, the issuance of judgment (duration of trial), and the moment of payment or repossession (duration of enforcement). The third indicator is the cost, as a share of GNI per capita, that is incurred during dispute resolution. This indicator comprises court fees, attorney fees, and payments such as bailiff fees and enforcement fees that are made to various professionals. These estimates are provided by the lawyers who complete the survey.

Finally, a fourth indicator, also based on the survey responses, measures the complexity of judicial process in the first-instance courts in the country's largest city. The complexity index is a composite of several subindices that measure various aspects of the degree of procedural regulations that the parties to the case and the adjudicator must follow. It comprises elements such as the type of court and type of judge having jurisdiction over the case and whether parties must be represented by an attorney in a court of law. The lower the burden of procedural rules, the lower the value of the index. For example, the professional versus layman subindex is an unweighted average of the three components described above (that is, type of court, type of judge, and whether legal representation is mandatory). Each of these components takes the value of 1 when the court is a general jurisdiction court, when the judge is professional, and when legal representation is mandatory; otherwise, their value is 0. The same rules apply to the rest of the components of the procedural complexity index. These subindices include (a) written versus oral stages of process, (b) legal justification of complaint and judgment, (c) statutory regulation of evidence, (d) control of superior review, and (e) other statutory interventions (such as the existence of a mandatory pretrial conciliation procedure as well as requirements for service of process and notification of judgment to be performed by a court officer). (Table 6.7 will later describe each of the components of the complexity index in more detail.)

The following sections examine each of these four indicators of the ease of contract enforcement in court: the number of procedural steps, the duration of contract enforcement in court, the costs of dispute resolution in court, and the complexity of the judicial process.

## Number of Procedural Steps

As figure 6.4 shows, the SEE8 show considerable differences in terms of the number of procedural steps mandated by law or court regulations.

**Figure 6.4   Procedural Steps in the SEE8**

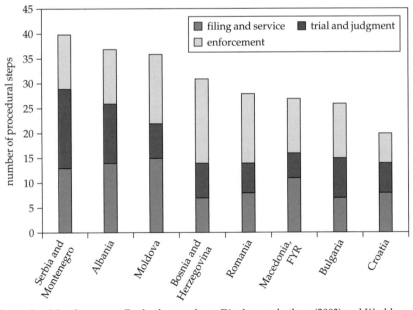

*Source:* Lex Mundi surveys. For background, see Djankov and others (2003) and World Bank (2004).

Serbia and Montenegro imposes the most procedural steps (40), and Croatia imposes the least (20), for resolving what is essentially the same case before a first-instance court in the country's largest city. Albania and Moldova are also among the jurisdictions that impose more procedures, each mandating more than 35 steps in the first-instance trial of the assumed case of debt recovery.

How do the SEE8 compare with the rest of the world and with the rest of the transition economies? The world leader with the shortest number of procedures is Australia, which mandates 11 steps in this assumed case. Generally, wealthy common law countries impose fewer procedures, whereas French civil law countries and, in particular, Latin American countries regulate most heavily and record the highest number of steps through which the parties and the adjudicator must go. Serbia and Montenegro is among the 10 countries with the highest number of procedural steps worldwide.

Compared with the rest of the transition countries, the SEE8 require, on average, the largest number of procedural steps. Figure 6.5 depicts the average number of steps for the assumed case across four distinct transition country groups: the SEE8; the countries in the CIS; the East Asian transition countries (Mongolia, China, and Vietnam); and the Central European and Baltic countries.[12]

As the data show, within the group of transition economies, the SEE8 have the highest number of procedural steps on average, whereas the countries of Central Europe and the Baltic region have the lowest number

**Figure 6.5   Procedural Steps in Transition Regions**

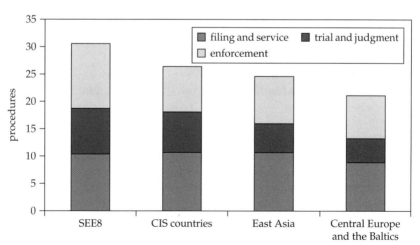

Source: Lex Mundi surveys. For background, see Djankov and others (2003) and World Bank (2004).

of procedural steps. The CIS and East Asian jurisdictions fall in the middle. In each case, we also distinguish between the number of steps during the three main stages of a first-instance court process: (a) from the moment of filing until the process is served to the defendant, (b) from the moment of defendant's opposition until a judgment is rendered, and (c) from the moment of notification of the first-instance judgment to the parties until the moment of its execution.

Why is the number of mandatory procedural steps so important? First, the greater the number of procedural steps, the longer a trial will take. Indeed, more procedures are associated with longer duration (as illustrated later in figure 6.11 for Serbia and Montenegro). Second, a greater number of procedures implies heavier regulation of all aspects of dispute resolution and a more complex overall process in general. Third, a greater number of procedures implies higher costs in terms of lawyers' fees and so forth. Fourth, a greater number of procedural steps breeds more corruption. Moreover, a greater number of mandatory steps leads to the creation of more opportunities for extraction of bribes. Every step is a potential tollbooth for bribe extraction in the countries with high levels of corruption in the public administration.

## Duration of Contract Enforcement in Court

Among the SEE8, resolving the assumed case in a first-instance court would take the longest in Serbia and Montenegro. The entire process would exceed 1,000 calendar days (see figure 6.6). The exemplar in this category is Moldova, where the whole case would supposedly take 210 calendar days from filing until final settlement of the debt and payment to the creditor. Moldova's ranking here is somewhat puzzling given that Moldova regulates court procedure rather heavily and requires one of the highest numbers of mandatory procedural steps.

A cautionary note is in order, however. The Moldovan law firm that completed the Lex Mundi survey provided an explanation in their answer about duration:

> The enforcement, however, could be more cumbersome and could last even years. However, assuming that the conditions of [the] hypothetical case indicate the debtor possesses liquid assets, but simply refuses to pay, then enforcement of the liquid assets, assuming these will be sold at the first or second public auction, [and] assuming that proper diligence is taken by the creditor in his dealings with the court executors (bailiffs), the collection should last a reasonable term from 30 to 90 days from the date of judgment.

## Figure 6.6    Days to Enforce a Debt Contract

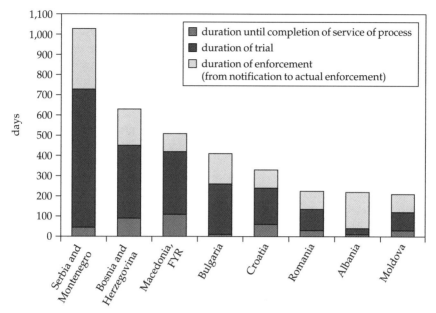

Source: Lex Mundi surveys. For background, see Djankov and others (2003) and World Bank (2004).

The Moldovan firm offered a further explanation in this regard:

> The main delay/obstacle in the debt collection procedures in Moldova is the general state of the Moldovan economy. In most cases, the debtors would either hide their assets, or prove they have no assets, or the assets that would be found would not be liquid, and therefore their sale through public auction could take too long, if at all. Many assets are kept off the books (applicable to legal entity debtors). Individual debtors are often small traders who are formally unemployed, and therefore have no legal income (as all their turnover is maintained outside the Moldovan accounting and tax system, and therefore cannot be proved); their assets would belong to relatives and friends and therefore could not be seized and enforced upon.

These remarks show that the duration of a court procedure in Moldova may well be much longer if the debtor is keen on avoiding payment. The law firm interpreted quite literally the case assumption that at the enforcement stage the debtor possesses sufficient liquid assets to pay but delays payment and, thus, concluded that execution, if pursued properly and with due diligence by the creditor, should not be problematic. If, however, the assumption is relaxed and debtor's solvency is difficult to establish—something that other countries' respondent law firms may have assumed—then Moldova's duration would rise substantially.

An interesting observation is that, in terms of procedural delays, the SEE8 are comparable to some of the Central European countries, whereas the CIS countries tend to report a shorter duration. Worth noting is that four transition economies (Bosnia and Herzegovina, Poland, Slovenia, and Serbia and Montenegro) are among the 10 countries worldwide with the longest procedural delays. Many of the CIS countries have established specialized commercial courts (*arbitrazh* courts), and perhaps this factor could help explain why the duration of their first-instance court procedure appears relatively short.

### Costs of Dispute Resolution in Court

Figure 6.7 shows significant differences in costs of the court proceedings. Albania has the highest costs of legal procedure before the first-instance

**Figure 6.7   Costs of Procedure by Country**

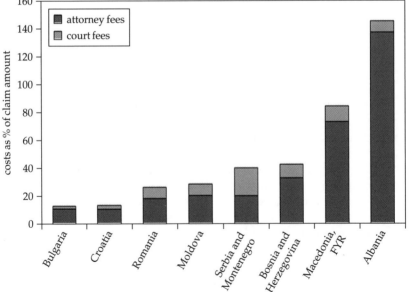

*Source:* Lex Mundi surveys. For background, see Djankov and others (2003) and World Bank (2004).

courts—at 145 percent of the claim amount. Clearly, if fees exceed the claim amount, as in the case of Albania, firms will not take cases to court, unless legal fees would normally be awarded by the judge to the winning party. Indeed, in the country case studies, interviewed Albanian firm managers pointed to a very low use of the courts. Four out of five interviewed Albanian managers indicated that they had not used the courts for resolving business disputes.

Court procedure is also expensive in Bosnia and Herzegovina, FYR Macedonia, and Serbia and Montenegro, with total attorney and court enforcement fees ranging from more than 80 percent of the claim value in FYR Macedonia to 40 percent of the claim value in Serbia and Montenegro.

Court procedure is least expensive in Bulgaria and Croatia, where total costs equal about 13 percent of the claim value. Clearly, legal fees charged by attorneys are determined by demand and supply in the market for legal services. The low fees could reflect a high supply of lawyers and low demand for their services. The way fees are determined is also crucial: whether the lawyer charges by the hour or charges a lump-sum fee affects his or her incentives. The former method clearly produces a proclivity on the part of the lawyer to delay the case, other things being equal.

Fees also depend on whether a party and that party's legal representative are free to negotiate a fee contingent on the litigation outcome. In some countries, fees are also charged by regulation, with minimum fees specified for each stage of a certain court procedure. The specificities of legal fees and attorney compensation are not the subject of this chapter. Yet the costs of procedure, as given by the surveyed law firms, fall in line with managers' perceptions of how costly court resolution of disputes is, as evidenced by the case studies.

How do the SEE8 as a group rank next to the rest of the transition economies? Figure 6.8 demonstrates that the CIS countries bear the highest costs of procedure, close to the value of the claim (97 percent of claim). The costs of court procedure in the SEE8 and the East Asian transition countries (China, Mongolia, and Vietnam) are similar to each other, with total average costs amounting to 34 percent and 30 percent of the claim amount, respectively. The Central European and Baltic countries have the cheapest proceedings among the transition group, with total legal fees at less than 20 percent of the claim.

How do these numbers compare with world averages? Many jurisdictions impose negligible costs of procedure. The cheapest jurisdictions for our assumed case are mostly wealthy common law countries or Germanic civil law countries, where the total fees range from 1 to 5 percent of the claim amount.

**Figure 6.8    Costs of Procedure by Region**

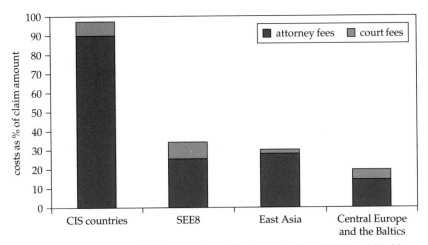

*Source:* Lex Mundi surveys. For background, see Djankov and others (2003) and World Bank (2004).

## *Complexity of the Judicial Process*

Apart from costs, duration, and number of procedural steps, the final measure of the ease of court resolution of disputes is the index of procedural complexity, which is calculated as the sum of certain subindices (described in detail later in table 6.7). Each subindex is an unweighted average of its constituting variables and is normalized to take on values between 0 and 1. The aggregate index varies between 0 and 6. Figure 6.9 presents the procedural complexity for each of the SEE8. It shows that the procedural burden is heaviest on litigants in Albania and least so in Croatia and Moldova.

Figure 6.10 compares how onerous court procedure is in South Eastern Europe in relation to the other groupings of transition countries. The figure clearly shows that, on average, court procedures are regulated most heavily in SEE, followed by Central Europe and the Baltic states. The index of procedural complexity is, on average, lowest in the East Asian transition economies and in the CIS countries.

As we discuss procedural complexity, we need to consider what procedures are common in resolving commercial disputes in the courts. Conversely, we must consider what procedures are featured in only a few jurisdictions. Table 6.7 presents particular procedures used in a standard case of debt recovery (grouped under appropriate subindices) and lists which countries commonly use them.

## Figure 6.9   Index of Procedural Complexity

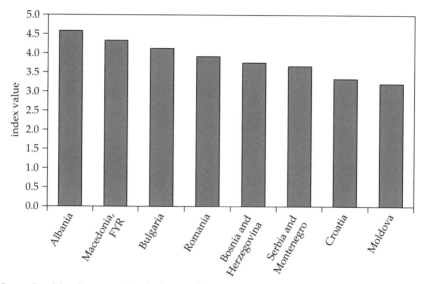

*Source:* Lex Mundi surveys. For background, see Djankov and others (2003) and World Bank (2004).
*Note:* The aggregate index varies between 0 and 6.0, with 0 indicating the lowest level of procedural complexity and 6.0 indicating the highest level of procedural complexity.

## Figure 6.10   Index of Procedural Complexity in Transition Economies, Average by Region

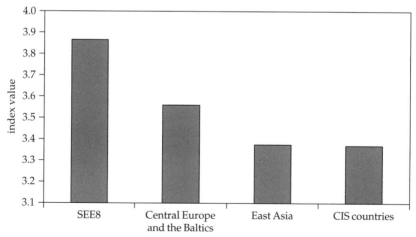

*Source:* Lex Mundi surveys. For background, see Djankov and others (2003) and World Bank (2004).
*Note:* The aggregate index varies between 0 and 6.0, with 0 indicating the lowest level of procedural complexity and 6.0 indicating the highest level of procedural complexity.

## Table 6.7   Complexity of Contract Enforcement: Standard Case of Debt Recovery

| Elements of procedural complexity | Countries that require a specific element |
|---|---|
| Professionals versus laymen subindex: | |
| General jurisdiction court is used. | All SEE8 |
| Professional judge will decide the case. | All SEE8 |
| Legal representation is mandatory in court. | FYR Macedonia |
| Written versus oral arguments subindex: | |
| Filing must be written. | All SEE8 |
| Service of process must be written. | All SEE8 |
| Opposition must be written. | Bulgaria, Croatia, and Romania |
| Evidence normally submitted in written form. | Moldova and Serbia and Montenegro |
| Final arguments normally made in writing. | Albania and Bulgaria |
| Judgment must be written. | All SEE8 |
| Notification of judgment must be in writing. | Bosnia and Herzegovina, Bulgaria, Croatia, FYR Macedonia, and Romania |
| Enforcement of judgment includes mostly written elements. | All SEE8 |
| Legal justification subindex: | |
| Complaint must be legally justified. | All SEE8 |
| Judgment must be legally justified. | All SEE8 |
| Judgment must be motivated on legal grounds and not on equity grounds. | Albania, Bosnia and Herzegovina, Bulgaria, Croatia, FYR Macedonia, Romania, and Serbia and Montenegro |
| Statutory regulation of evidence subindex: | |
| Judge cannot introduce evidence during the case. | Albania and Bulgaria |
| Judge cannot reject irrelevant evidence. | None |
| Out-of-court statements, made by a third party, cannot be used as evidence before the court. | Albania, Bosnia and Herzegovina, FYR Macedonia, Moldova, Romania, and Serbia and Montenegro |
| Judge must prequalify his or her questions before they are posed to the witnesses or parties. | FYR Macedonia, Romania, and Serbia and Montenegro |
| Oral interrogation during trial is conducted only by the judge. | None |

(*Table continues on the following page.*)

## Table 6.7 (continued)

| Elements of procedural complexity | Countries that require a specific element |
|---|---|
| Only original documents and certified copies are admissible as trial evidence. | Albania, Bosnia and Herzegovina, Bulgaria, and Serbia and Montenegro |
| Authenticity and weight of evidence are defined by law. | Albania, Croatia, and Romania |
| A written or magnetic record must be made for all evidence introduced during trial. | Albania, Bosnia and Herzegovina, Croatia, FYR Macedonia, Moldova, and Romania |
| Control of superior review subindex: Enforcement of a first-instance judgment is automatically suspended until resolution of appeal. | All SEE8 |
| Both issues of law and fact (evidence) may be heard during appeal proceedings (comprehensive review). | All SEE8 |
| Interlocutory appeals are allowed during trial.[b] | Albania, Bosnia and Herzegovina, Bulgaria, FYR Macedonia, and Romania |
| Other statutory interventions subindex: Pretrial conciliation or mediation is mandatory before a case may be filed in court. | Albania and Moldova |
| Service of process must be completed by a judicial officer (such as the bailiff or process server). | Albania and Bulgaria[a] |
| Notification of judgment must be completed by a judicial officer (such as the bailiff or court officer). | FYR Macedonia |

Source: Lex Mundi surveys. For background, see Djankov and others (2003) and World Bank (2004).
a. Bulgaria is shown as requiring service of process by a judicial officer despite recent amendments to the Procedural Code to enable service by publication in the Official Gazette or posting of the service papers on the court's announcement board after a first failed attempt at service by a court officer.
b. This procedure does not apply to Serbia and Montenegro.

As table 6.7 shows, in all of the SEE8, the case is handled by a general jurisdiction court and a professional judge. Only FYR Macedonia makes mandatory the use of lawyers for legal representation in debt collection before a first-instance court, although in practice, many plaintiffs in the other countries do hire lawyers in such cases.

Jurisdictions, however, differ significantly on the use of written versus oral arguments during court proceedings. All of the SEE8 impose written requirements for the following stages: the filing, service of process, judgment, and enforcement. However, three of the eight jurisdictions require that the defendant's opposition be in writing and another three require that all evidence be in writing. Furthermore, in two countries, final arguments are normally in written form. Five of the countries require written notification of judgment.

In all eight jurisdictions, the complaint must be justified by citing the relevant parts of the law. This requirement presents an additional hurdle for businesses because they have to seek legal advice before filing a complaint. All jurisdictions also impose a requirement that the judgment be legally justified, with express reference being made to the laws and provisions that have been considered in making the decision. Again, this prolongs the process and increases the burden on the judge after the trial. A related issue is whether a judgment can be made on equity grounds. For example, normally, common law countries do not require legal justification of the complaint, and three-quarters of these countries allow judgments to be made on equity grounds. These percentages are reversed in civil law jurisdictions, including Austria, France, Germany, and Spain. Among the SEE8, all countries except Moldova require that the judgment be made exclusively on legal grounds.

The regulation of evidence is perhaps the area most responsible for causing delays in contract enforcement and is characterized as being the area involving the greatest differences across jurisdictions worldwide. Although three-quarters of the jurisdictions have statutory regulations on out-of-court statements and the recording of evidence, none have regulations on the admissibility of irrelevant evidence and none require oral interrogation exclusively by the judge. The overall regulation of evidence is heaviest in Albania. In all eight jurisdictions, enforcement is suspended if an appeal is filed, and the suspension lasts until the appeal is resolved. Furthermore, all jurisdictions allow for comprehensive review in appeal, and almost all, apart from Croatia and Moldova, allow for appeal during trial. Thus, a debtor who wants to delay execution can file an appeal even if no reasonable chance of a successful outcome is expected.

Finally, pretrial mediation is mandatory in Albania and Moldova. On the positive side, the SEE8 do not impose strict requirements on who serves notice of trial to the defendant and who notifies judgment to the parties. Only Albania and Bulgaria require that a court officer serve the process, whereas only FYR Macedonia requires notification of the judgment by a judicial officer.

For an example that illustrates the evolution of the court procedure for recovery of a debt worth 50 percent of GNI per capita in Serbia and Montenegro, see box 6.4. In addition, figure 6.11 shows the duration and number of procedural steps involved in the process of debt collection for Serbia and Montenegro.

---

## Box 6.4 Example of a Debt Collection Court Procedure

In Serbia and Montenegro, the hypothetical debt collection case would be heard before the Civil Division of one of the five municipal courts in Belgrade. Before beginning court proceedings, the creditor would need to initiate a check protest procedure before a notary public, who would then notify the debtor of the outstanding debt. Once the debtor was notified, the creditor would be able to file a claim with the relevant municipal court and pay the court fees. A court clerk would then register the lawsuit and assign it a case number. After this step was completed, the case file would be assigned to one of the municipal court judges and brought to him or her. The judge would verify that all procedural requirements were met before formally admitting the lawsuit and initiating notification proceedings. In this case, the judge would issue a separate order for service of process to be conducted.

The notice of petition would either be sent by mail by the court clerk or be delivered to the defendant personally by a court bailiff. If unable to find the defendant at his or her address, the postman or bailiff could affix the notice to the defendant's home or business. The postman or bailiff could also leave a copy of the claim with a neighbor and mail the original to the debtor. Also, at this early pretrial stage, the plaintiff would be entitled to apply for attachment of debtor's property to ensure that, once a judgment is issued, the debtor would have sufficient assets to honor the debt. If this step is taken, the judge must decide on the pretrial attachment and issue a corresponding resolution, accepting the plaintiff's request. Thereafter, attachment of the debtor's assets would be carried out.

A defendant is allowed either to raise his or her opposition in writing before the preliminary trial hearing or to answer the plaintiff's complaint orally at the same preliminary hearing. Usually, the debtor will raise some preliminary objections and exemptions that are different from his or her opposition to the complaint and that are generally intended to question the procedure, jurisdiction, and so forth. The judge must then decide on the validity of these exemptions. In our hypothetical case, we assume that the judge would rule against these objections. At this juncture, the judge would review the defense and admit it for trial. The debtor's defense would then be delivered to the plaintiff. The judge would set a term for the plaintiff to file an answer to the defendant's

*(Box continues on the following page.)*

## Box 6.4 (continued)

opposition. Within the prescribed term, the creditor would file his or her answer to the opposition. During trial, the expectation is that the present case would take two separate hearings on two different days. The first hearing would be preliminary in nature; the second one would be the main trial hearing.

Within the main trial hearing, up to 12 sessions of the court would take place. During the trial period, discovery of evidence would take place, documents would be exchanged and delivered to the judge, and written pleadings would be prepared and filed in preparation for the main hearing on the merits. The evidence-gathering stage would actually be declared open by a separate resolution issued by the judge. The parties would be allowed to offer means of proof and evidence to the judge, who would then have to decide and order on these proposed means of proof (for example, bringing forward a witness). The evidence-gathering stage would be closed after all evidence has been submitted and after witnesses have been summoned to testify before the court. On the main hearing day, all interrogations of parties and witnesses and review of all written evidence would be conducted. On that same day, a judgment would be issued.

A judge will deliver a judgment orally on the closing day of trial, after which the decision will be put into writing by the court and the written judgment will be sent to the parties by mail. Our assumption is that the decision would award the debt amount to the plaintiff (creditor); however, the debtor would not pay voluntarily, although he or she has enough liquid assets to settle the debt. In such a case, the plaintiff would have to wait for the expiry of the process of voluntary payment, which is 8 days, to start enforcement proceedings. The plaintiff would then have to prepare a draft enforcement order, plausibly with help from his or her lawyer, and file it for approval with the competent executive court. In addition, the plaintiff would need to pay the relevant enforcement fees. The court would then grant a separate enforcement order for the execution of the judgment. The enforcement order would be delivered to a bailiff, who would request compliance by the debtor.

If, as in our hypothetical case, a debtor will not pay voluntarily, attachment and sale of property are needed. The assets already attached before or during trial will be valued by a specially appointed valuation expert, who will submit to the judge his or her valuation report. The court will then advertise a public auction for sale of the attached and already-valued property, and the auction will take place on the appointed day. Finally, the sale proceeds will be delivered to the plaintiff.

Thus, the first-instance process would take 1,028 days on average (see figure 6.11).

*Source:* Lex Mundi surveys. For background, see Djankov and others (2003) and World Bank (2004).

## Figure 6.11   Duration and Number of Procedural Steps in Serbia and Montenegro

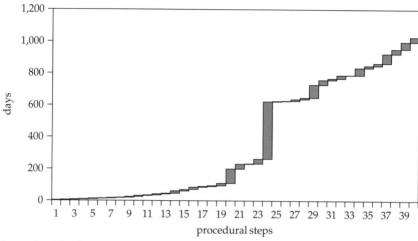

*Source:* Lex Mundi surveys. For background, see Djankov and others (2003) and World Bank (2004).

*Note:* Procedural steps are as follows: (1) the creditor obtains a check protest from a notary public; (2) the plaintiff files the lawsuit with the court; (3) the plaintiff pays the court filing fee; (4) the court clerk registers the claim and assigns a case number to the file; (5) the court clerk passes the case file to the assigned judge, who will hear the case; (6) the judge reviews the case file to verify whether it complies with general requirements for filing; (7) the judge issues a written resolution admitting the case for trial; (8) the judge issues a separate written order for process to be served on the defendant; (9) the court clerk mails the summoning documents to the defendant; (10) service by mail is not sufficient, so a bailiff visits the residence of the defendant and leaves a copy of the summons affixed to the front door or with a neighbor, after which he mails the original to the defendant; (11) the plaintiff applies to the court for attachment before trial of the defendant's property; (12) the court decides whether to grant pretrial attachment of the debtor's assets; (13) the court issues a written decision granting the requested attachment; (14) the defendant files preliminary exemptions challenging the plaintiff's claim on grounds of jurisdiction, procedure, and so forth; (15) the judge issues a resolution on the preliminary exemptions raised; (16) the judge reviews the defendant's main opposition and decides to admit the answer for trial; (17) the defense is delivered to the plaintiff; (18) the judge sets a term for the plaintiff to answer the opposition; (19) the plaintiff files with the court his or her answer to the defendant's opposition; (20) a pretrial process begins involving discovery of relevant evidence to be used at trial and its submission to the court; (21) parties file preparatory submissions and written pleadings before the court; (22) the judge sets the dates for the preparatory and main hearing; (23) a preparatory hearing takes place first; (24) the main trial commences and will take about 10 to 12 meetings in court (the whole process is assumed to take at least 12 months or 360 days); (25) the parties submit offers of evidence or means of proof to the judge; (26) the judge opens the evidence-gathering stage; (27) the judge decides in writing on the admissibility of submitted offers of evidence; (28) the judge summons witnesses proposed by the parties; (29) the judge closes the evidence-gathering stage (this stage precedes the actual trial; the order shown is not chronological);

*(Figure continues on the following page.)*

## Figure 6.11    (continued)

(30) the judge, after reviewing all testimonies and evidence, issues a decision orally, which is then put into writing; (31) a written judgment is delivered to both parties by mail by order of the court; (32) the plaintiff prepares a draft enforcement order and files it with the relevant execution court for approval; (33) the plaintiff pays court enforcement fees; (34) the execution court approves the draft enforcement order; (35) the enforcement order is delivered to a bailiff for execution; (36) the bailiff notifies the debtor and asks him or her to pay the debt within a specified term; (37) the execution court appoints a valuation expert, who values the attached assets and issues a report; (38) a call for a public auction is issued and publicized in the media; (39) the auction takes place, and the debtor's assets are sold; (40) the auction proceeds are transferred to the creditor, who thus receives his or her payment.

## Firms' Use of the Courts

Given the preceding discussion about the ease of court enforcement of contracts, what is the evidence regarding actual use of the courts in resolving disputes in the SEE8? Are the observed trends in the measures of costs, duration, steps, and complexity in line with firms' self-reported use of the court system and their evaluations of the court's performance as captured in their answers to the 2002 BEEPS questionnaire and in the interviews of the country case studies? What types of firms use the courts more often? Put differently, do different kinds of firms experience the courts differently? Why? Is the judicial system discriminating against one or another type of firm? We look at the BEEPS2 and case studies data next to seek answers to these questions.

### Small and Large Firms Compared

Table 6.8 looks at BEEPS2 data about the use of courts by small, medium-size, and large firms across the SEE8 in resolving one particular type of commercial dispute—disputes over payment. The table presents the share of firms in each of the three groups that report having encountered payment disputes but state that none of these payment disputes were resolved through court action. The table demonstrates that, across the region as a whole, small firms use courts the least, with 81 percent of surveyed small firms reporting that none of their payment disputes were decided in court. Medium-size firms indicate a higher usage of the court in solving payment disagreements, yet more than half of those across the region (57 percent) also report no use of the courts in these cases. And although large firms use courts the most in disputes over payments, more than one-third of them (38 percent) indicate no use of the courts.

Furthermore, table 6.8 reveals that 95 percent of surveyed small firms in Albania do not use the courts in payment disputes. In contrast,

### Table 6.8   Firms Reporting Zero Payment Disputes Resolved in Court

*(% of firms that had payment disputes)*

| Country | Small | Medium-size | Large |
|---|---|---|---|
| Albania | 95 | 84 | 79 |
| Bosnia and Herzegovina | 84 | 63 | 45 |
| Bulgaria | 78 | 57 | 36 |
| Croatia | 57 | 47 | 12 |
| Macedonia, FYR | 79 | 45 | 31 |
| Moldova | 79 | 62 | 40 |
| Romania | 91 | 56 | 27 |
| Serbia and Montenegro | 81 | 40 | 33 |
| Mean | 81 | 57 | 38 |

*Source:* EBRD and World Bank (2002).
*Note:* Small firms are defined as having more than 1 but fewer than 50 full-time employees, medium-size firms are defined as having 50 or more but fewer than 250 full-time employees, and large firms have 250 or more full-time employees.

Croatia is the country where small firms use courts the most in payment disputes—with 43 percent of interviewed small firms indicating some payment disputes resolved in court. Medium-size firms in Serbia and Montenegro report the highest incidence of court action over payments (60 percent of such firms report some cases resolved in court), with Croatia and FYR Macedonia ranking close (53 percent and 55 percent, respectively, of medium-size firms in those countries indicate some use of the courts). Albania's medium-size firms are least likely to resolve disputes over payments in court, with only 16 percent of these firms reporting some use of the courts for this purpose. Albania and Croatia are also the countries that report the least and the most use of the courts in payment disputes by large firms, respectively. Although 88 percent of Croatian large enterprises have had payment disputes resolved in court, only 21 percent of Albanian large firms report the same.

Two conclusions emerge. First, because of the costs of procedure and delays in Albania, it is the country where firms of any size use the courts the least. In contrast, Croatia, where costs are comparatively lower, is the country whose firms reportedly use the courts the most. Second, among the three categories of firms, small firms are less likely to use the courts across the region compared with both medium-size and large firms, and large firms have more cases resolved in court than small and medium-size firms do. The case studies further support the BEEPS2 findings on court use. Box 6.5 also presents evidence to this effect.

Finally, the information provided in table 6.8 is instructive with respect to the gaps in court use between specific sizes of firms across the eight countries. For instance, these gaps are largest between large and small

## Box 6.5 Which Firms Use the Courts?

Of the companies interviewed for the case studies that reported using the courts to resolve commercial disputes, most are large or medium-size firms. Very often, these firms are state-owned or privatized companies. Many of the firms that use courts have an in-house lawyer or even a legal department.

One of the Croatian construction companies interviewed reported filing about 10 to 20 court cases on average per year. That company has a legal department with 12 people. Interestingly, the company described the courts as quite efficient in delivering justice. However, it did express concern about the process of execution of judgment. For instance, it reported experiencing difficulties in collecting debts from clients that have gone bankrupt or simply disappeared. Another Croatian firm, a metal-processing plant, also engages in court actions. That firm noted that improvements in the way courts work had occurred over the 12 months preceding the case interview.

Many of the SEE8 firms seem to face problems with bankrupt debtors. For example, a Serbian textile firm described one of its experiences with a bankrupt debtor and the evolution of the case through time. In 1993, the firm supplied an order for a large department store. It did not receive payment and, in 1995, filed a court case. A court decision was issued in 1995, awarding the debt to the textile firm and asking the debtor to pay the firm in 10 equal installments over the next 3 years. In the meantime, the department store had started informal liquidation proceedings. Consequently, its management kept changing, and no payments were made after the court's decision. Having attempted several direct negotiations over the debt, the textile firm filed a new complaint with the court in 2001. In May 2002, the official bankruptcy of the department store was announced. Also in 2002, the court issued an irrevocable decision that the debt should be paid to the textile firm. However, in July 2002, the textile firm was notified that the debtor had no financial resources to pay the debt. At the time of the case interview, the company managers were hoping to recover part of the debt by the end of 2002.

This example illustrates how lengthy debt collection can be. After almost 9 years, the debt was still outstanding. Seven years after the first court decision, collection had not happened. The textile firm indicated that a major reason for the protracted proceedings and inability to collect was that closing down the department store, which employs a large number of people, is politically unpopular.

firms, followed by the gap in court use between small and medium-size firms. Romania displays the largest gaps in court use between large and small firms, Croatia shows the largest gap between large and medium-size firms, and Serbia and Montenegro has the largest gap between small and medium-size firms. Albania has the narrowest gap between large and small firms as well as between large and medium-size firms, a finding

## Table 6.9   Firms Reporting Zero Court Cases Filed between January 2000 and July 2002
*(% of total firms)*

|                          | Small | Medium-size | Large |
|--------------------------|-------|-------------|-------|
| Albania                  | 90    | 60          | 38    |
| Bosnia and Herzegovina   | 79    | 41          | 28    |
| Bulgaria                 | 74    | 50          | 49    |
| Croatia                  | 58    | 38          | 5     |
| Macedonia, FYR           | 76    | 61          | 16    |
| Moldova                  | 86    | 62          | 56    |
| Romania                  | 84    | 49          | 37    |
| Serbia and Montenegro    | 76    | 33          | 25    |
| Mean                     | 78    | 49          | 32    |

*Source:* EBRD and World Bank (2002).

that probably indicates very low use of the courts in general rather than a level playing field among all three types of firms.

Let us turn next to another indicator of court use—the number of cases filed or defended in court by a firm. BEEPS2 asked respondents to provide the number of civil or commercial lawsuits that involved their company as either a plaintiff or defendant over the 30 months preceding the survey interview.[13] This question, like the one about payment disputes, measures court use, but it potentially involves other breaches of contract (for instance, late delivery of products, product deficiency, and so forth) and civil or commercial litigation against firm employees or the government. Table 6.9 provides information on the share of firms reporting no court cases filed.

The results support the conclusions based on table 6.8: Surveyed small firms file fewer civil or commercial lawsuits across the region, surveyed large firms are the most litigious, and surveyed medium-size firms rank in the middle. Small firms in Albania, Moldova, and Romania are least likely to file a case, whereas their Croatian counterparts file the most cases. More than 85 percent of surveyed small firms in Albania and Moldova had not filed a lawsuit during the period studied. Medium-size firms in Serbia and Montenegro and Croatia filed the highest number of cases, and those in Moldova, FYR Macedonia, and Albania filed the lowest number. Among large firms, Croatian ones filed the highest number of court cases, and Moldovan firms filed the lowest number.

These findings are indicative of systematic differences among firms of different size and among firms located in different countries in their use of the courts in resolving business disputes. Country-level differences could be explained in terms of the steps, costs, and complexity of litigation. Differences in terms of size could be attributed to large and medium-size firms not only encountering more disputes, other things being equal, but also using more legalistic strategies in structuring their contractual activities (for example, writing more complex contracts) and in resolving disputes (for example, hiring lawyers, filing lawsuits, and using the courts). Furthermore, large firms are more likely to encounter disputes over large amounts. Therefore, court use is more likely. In addition, these differences may also reflect an investment climate that favors one category of firms over another.

An important point to stress here is that we cannot conduct any analysis of changes in court use between 1999 and 2002 as we do for changes in average perceptions of the judiciary in a later section. Unfortunately, BEEPS1 did not contain questions that were analogous to the BEEPS2 questions about the court cases that were filed and defended or about the prevalence of payment disputes, payment disputes resolved in court, time to disposition, and so forth. A comparison over time would have added valuable information about firms' use of the courts; however, because of these differences in the two surveys, the BEEPS data do not allow for that analysis.

A study of firms in another region of the world also supports the finding that large firms are the principal users of courts. Bigsten and others (2000) examined contractual dispute resolution in six African countries: Burundi, Cameroon, Côte d'Ivoire, Kenya, Zambia, and Zimbabwe. Surveying manufacturing companies in each of these countries, the authors established that contractual flexibility is very common and that relational contracting, based on long-term relationships between firms and their customers and suppliers, is widely used. The study found that legal methods such as filing claims in court and hiring lawyers are used only by large firms and only when negotiations fail. The study also found that firms in Zimbabwe are much more likely to threaten to use the courts against delinquent clients or suppliers. The fact that large firms use courts the most is explained by the proposition that large firms have better access to courts, given that costs of court proceedings are easier to amortize on large transactions. The authors also conjecture that, because Zimbabwe plausibly has the best legal and judicial system among these six countries, good legal institutions encourage rather than prevent firms from using the courts. In this manner, good legal institutions motivate firms to be more willing to take chances with new clients or suppliers, and in so doing, firms consequently encounter more contractual disputes, something that is corroborated by the data. Therefore, the incidence of contractual disputes is higher when the courts operate well and a strong rule of law is present, and the incidence of disputes is lower where legal institutions are less developed and weaker.

How significant are the observed differences between small and large firms' reported use of the courts? We have conducted $t$-tests of differences in means to test whether the share of payment disputes resolved by court action and the number of cases either filed or defended in court differ systematically across small firms, on the one hand, and across medium-size and large firms, on the other. For convenience, we have included both medium-size firms (firms with more than 50 and fewer than 250 full-time employees) and large firms (firms with more than 250 full-time employees) within the category of large firms. Table 6.10 reports the results of these *t*-tests for the region as a whole in 2002 and for each of the SEE8.

The results shown in table 6.10 indicate that, from the perspective of the number of cases filed, defended, or both, significant differences are found between small and large firms. Small firms file and defend significantly fewer court cases than large firms do in each country and across the region as a whole. All results for this measure of court use are significant at the 1 percent level.

In terms of the share of payment disputes settled through court action, small firms again report significantly fewer of these disputes being resolved by court action across the whole sample of SEE8 firms. On a country-by-country basis, small firms also report fewer payment disputes being decided in court; however, the difference in FYR Macedonia is not significant. Nevertheless, the remaining seven countries do show significant differences between small and large firms.

The statistical *t*-test results presented in tables 6.10, 6.11, and 6.12 show differences in mean use of the courts, measured by the number of cases filed or defended and the share of payment disputes resolved in court, across different types of firms. These data can serve as a useful initial indicator of how firms differ in terms of their use of the courts. These characteristics of the firms were then tested in multiple regression analyses for several variables of interest, controlling for other factors. For example, we conducted ordinary least squares regression of court use, measured by the number of cases filed between 2000 and 2002 and by the share of payment disputes resolved in court action, and controlled for firm size, ownership, sector, age, and other characteristics. In different specifications, we found evidence that small firms file significantly fewer court cases than large firms, which supports the findings of the *t*-tests in table 6.10. Similarly, we also found that de novo firms have a significantly lower share of payment disputes resolved through court action than state-owned firms do, as shown in table 6.11. To the extent that we have defined new firms as de novo firms and old firms as state-owned and privatized firms, this finding supports the general findings of table 6.12. The results of these ordinary least squares regressions on court use are presented in tables A.6.1, A.6.2, and A.6.3 in the annex.

## *State-Owned and Private Firms Compared*

To what extent are these differences attributed to different ownership? We next conduct the same tests for differences in court use between state-owned and private firms. These results appear in table 6.11.

## Table 6.10   Statistical Tests for Differences in Court Use between Small and Large Firms

| Country | Number of court cases filed, defended, or both (mean) | Percentage of payment disputes resolved by court action (mean) |
|---|---|---|
| All SEE8: | | |
| Small firms | 1.25 | 4.45 |
| Large firms | 9.11 | 11.46 |
| $t$-statistic | $-10.9280\ (0.0000)$ | $-5.6860\ (0.0000)$ |
| Albania: | | |
| Small firms | 0.21 | 1.66 |
| Large firms | 4.07 | 5.09 |
| $t$-statistic | $-3.0393\ (0.0025)$ | $-1.3943\ (0.0840)$ |
| Bosnia and Herzegovina: | | |
| Small firms | 1.11 | 1.83 |
| Large firms | 13.98 | 7.34 |
| $t$-statistic | $-4.3168\ (0.0000)$ | $-2.3817\ (0.0098)$ |
| Bulgaria: | | |
| Small firms | 1.37 | 4.23 |
| Large firms | 9.06 | 10.23 |
| $t$-statistic | $-3.7086\ (0.0002)$ | $-1.7906\ (0.0384)$ |
| Croatia: | | |
| Small firms | 2.47 | 11.69 |
| Large firms | 15.84 | 18.16 |
| $t$-statistic | $-5.3087\ (0.0000)$ | $-1.4314\ (0.0776)$ |
| Macedonia, FYR: | | |
| Small firms | 1.30 | 6.22 |
| Large firms | 9.76 | 10.53 |
| $t$-statistic | $-3.8636\ (0.0002)$ | $-1.0240\ (0.1546)$ |
| Moldova: | | |
| Small firms | 0.59 | 3.47 |
| Large firms | 3.50 | 14.59 |
| $t$-statistic | $-3.5894\ (0.0003)$ | $-2.4239\ (0.0096)$ |
| Romania: | | |
| Small firms | 0.92 | 2.42 |
| Large firms | 5.45 | 9.36 |
| $t$-statistic | $-5.5805\ (0.0000)$ | $-2.5669\ (0.0057)$ |
| Serbia and Montenegro: | | |
| Small firms | 1.81 | 2.97 |
| Large firms | 11.60 | 14.87 |
| $t$-statistic | $-4.4173\ (0.0000)$ | $-3.9709\ (0.0001)$ |

*Source:* EBRD and World Bank (2002).

*Note*: One-tailed $t$-tests are reported; $p$-values are shown in parentheses next to the $t$-statistics. Ordinary least squares regressions on court use are conducted for the whole sample, controlling for firm size, ownership, and other firm characteristics, and the results are presented in tables A.6.1, A.6.2, and A.6.3 in the annex.

## Table 6.11    Statistical Tests for Differences in Court Use between Private and State-Owned Firms

| Country | Number of court cases filed, defended, or both (mean) | Percentage of payment disputes resolved by court action (mean) |
|---|---|---|
| All SEE8: | | |
| Private firms | 2.80 | 5.78 |
| State-owned firms | 10.81 | 15.34 |
| t-statistic | −5.7337 (0.0000) | −4.4833 (0.0000) |
| Albania: | | |
| Private firms | 0.53 | 1.87 |
| State-owned firms | 6.75 | 9.56 |
| t-statistic | −2.6653 (0.0108) | −1.4810 (0.0790) |
| Bosnia and Herzegovina: | | |
| Private firms | 3.13 | 3.25 |
| State-owned firms | 26.11 | 10.84 |
| t-statistic | −2.9444 (0.0043) | −1.4613 (0.0800) |
| Bulgaria: | | |
| Private firms | 2.64 | 4.31 |
| State-owned firms | 9.54 | 15.21 |
| t-statistic | −1.9932 (0.0270) | −1.9425 (0.0307) |
| Croatia: | | |
| Private firms | 5.69 | 13.47 |
| State-owned firms | 10.71 | 16.84 |
| t-statistic | −1.5044 (0.0720) | −0.5024 (0.3095) |
| Macedonia, FYR: | | |
| Private firms | 3.95 | 6.50 |
| State-owned firms | 10.40 | 31.40 |
| t-statistic | −2.9911 (0.0127) | −1.2719 (0.1356) |
| Moldova: | | |
| Private firms | 1.39 | 5.77 |
| State-owned firms | 2.30 | 20.19 |
| t-statistic | −1.1720 (0.1243) | −1.6818 (0.0558) |
| Romania: | | |
| Private firms | 1.99 | 4.08 |
| State-owned firms | 6.87 | 14.48 |
| t-statistic | −3.3535 (0.0009) | −2.1982 (0.0178) |
| Serbia and Montenegro: | | |
| Private firms | 3.24 | 6.63 |
| State-owned firms | 15.97 | 15.58 |
| t-statistic | −3.1282 (0.0017) | −2.0253 (0.0243) |

*Source:* EBRD and World Bank (2002).

*Note:* One-tailed *t*-tests are reported; *p*-values are shown in parentheses next to the *t*-statistics. Ordinary least squares regressions on court use are conducted for the whole sample, controlling for firm size, ownership, and other firm characteristics, and the results are presented in tables A.6.1, A.6.2, and A.6.3 in the annex.

## Table 6.12   Statistical Tests for Differences in Court Use between New and Old Firms

| Country | Number of court cases filed, defended, or both (mean) | Percentage of payment disputes resolved by court action (mean) |
|---|---|---|
| All SEE8: | | |
| New firms | 1.51 | 3.62 |
| Old firms | 9.07 | 13.53 |
| t-statistic | −9.7914 (0.0000) | −7.2113 (0.0000) |
| Albania: | | |
| New firms | 0.35 | 1.75 |
| Old firms | 3.70 | 7.25 |
| t-statistic | −2.4257 (0.0119) | −1.5523 (0.0652) |
| Bosnia and Herzegovina: | | |
| New firms | 0.94 | 1.45 |
| Old firms | 14.50 | 7.58 |
| t-statistic | −4.5044 (0.0000) | −2.7071 (0.0041) |
| Bulgaria: | | |
| New firms | 0.97 | 3.32 |
| Old firms | 8.29 | 10.26 |
| t-statistic | −3.9673 (0.0001) | −2.1109 (0.0187) |
| Croatia: | | |
| New firms | 3.99 | 9.18 |
| Old firms | 12.29 | 20.33 |
| t-statistic | −3.2986 (0.0008) | −2.3704 (0.0101) |
| FYR Macedonia: | | |
| New firms | 1.25 | 3.91 |
| Old firms | 13.33 | 19.85 |
| t-statistic | −4.5186 (0.0000) | −2.5385 (0.0084) |
| Moldova: | | |
| New firms | 1.02 | 2.80 |
| Old firms | 2.44 | 16.06 |
| t-statistic | −2.2906 (0.0119) | −2.6064 (0.0065) |
| Romania: | | |
| New firms | 1.41 | 2.27 |
| Old firms | 5.65 | 12.70 |
| t-statistic | −4.4605 (0.0000) | −3.1187 (0.0013) |
| Serbia and Montenegro: | | |
| New firms | 2.21 | 4.13 |
| Old firms | 13.84 | 16.19 |
| t-statistic | −4.1500 (0.0001) | −3.3918 (0.0005) |

Source: EBRD and World Bank (2002).
Note: One-tailed t-tests are reported; p-values are shown in parentheses next to the t-statistics. Ordinary least squares regressions on court use are conducted for the whole sample, controlling for firm size, ownership, and other firm characteristics, and the results are presented in tables A.6.1, A.6.2, and A.6.3 in the annex.

As expected, surveyed state-owned firms are found to file more cases and to have a higher proportion of payment disputes resolved in court. The differences for these two variables are highly significant across the full sample of SEE8 firms. Within countries, both differences are statistically significant in Albania, Bosnia and Herzegovina, Bulgaria, Romania, and Serbia and Montenegro. In FYR Macedonia, the difference in number of cases filed is significant at 5 percent, but the difference in share of payment disputes resolved in court is not. The same holds for Croatia, where the difference in cases filed is significant at 10 percent, but there is no significant difference in share of payment disputes resolved in court. In Moldova, there is no significant difference in the number of cases filed or defended, but private firms do have a significantly lower share of payment disputes resolved in court.

Finally, we ran similar tests for differences in court use for old and new firms. We defined new firms as firms established as de novo enterprises, without a state-owned predecessor. The category of old firms comprises both state-owned firms and privatized firms. We ignored the age of the firm in this distinction between old and new firms, focusing entirely on method of establishment.

Again, as with firm size and ownership distinctions shown above, we expected to find that old firms exhibit a stronger tendency to use the court system. This expectation should also be obvious because the majority of new firms are small, private companies. The results of these tests are shown in table 6.12. We found that, across the entire sample, new firms file and defend significantly fewer cases with the courts and that they report a significantly lower proportion of payment disputes resolved by court proceedings. The results remain significant for both variables within each individual country. What causes these observed differences? We explore this question in the next section.

## Perceptions of Court Performance by Court Users

We turn next to some of the BEEPS 2002 data that measure respondents' perceptions about the performance of the court system in their jurisdiction. Perceptions are important because, to a large degree, they would determine use of the courts. Therefore, perceptions would also be a good proxy for performance. We measured the average scores on firms' perceptions about court fairness, honesty, speed, affordability, and ability to enforce decisions across those firms in each country that reported having used the courts either as a plaintiff or as a defendant over the 30 months preceding the survey. In addition, for the same subset of firms, we also measured the self-reported confidence in the legal system in general and firms' views as to how problematic the functioning of the judicial system is for their operation. Thus, we sought out the perceptions of only those

**Table 6.13    Court Performance as Perceived by Court Users, by Country**

| Country | Courts are fair and impartial | Courts are honest and uncorrupt | Courts are fast | Courts are affordable | Courts are able to enforce their decisions | Firm has confidence in legal system |
|---|---|---|---|---|---|---|
| Albania | 2.63 | 2.49 | 2.33 | 2.77 | 3.00 | 3.16 |
| Bosnia and Herzegovina | 2.94 | 2.91 | 2.10 | 2.74 | 2.87 | 3.49 |
| Bulgaria | 3.03 | 2.89 | 1.80 | 3.59 | 3.64 | 3.23 |
| Croatia | 2.97 | 2.90 | 1.74 | 2.62 | 3.18 | 3.93 |
| Macedonia, FYR | 3.00 | 2.84 | 2.46 | 3.35 | 2.99 | 3.37 |
| Moldova | 2.78 | 2.51 | 2.29 | 3.22 | 2.67 | 2.67 |
| Romania | 3.02 | 3.10 | 2.27 | 2.97 | 3.22 | 3.44 |
| Serbia and Montenegro | 3.06 | 3.18 | 2.07 | 3.41 | 3.26 | 3.96 |
| Mean | 2.93 | 2.85 | 2.13 | 3.08 | 3.10 | 3.41 |

*Source:* EBRD and World Bank (2002).
*Note:* Respondents were asked to provide a frequency rating for how often they associate the court system as being fair and impartial, honest and uncorrupt, quick, affordable, and able to enforce its decisions in resolving business disputes. The scale for the rating allowed for responses from 1 to 6, with a response of 1 meaning "never" and a response of 6 meaning "always." The scores shown in the table represent the average of those six values for firms in each country that indicated having used the courts as either a plaintiff or a defendant between January 2000 and July 2002.

firms that had recent experience with the court system. The score on each of these measures, except for problems in functioning of the judiciary, is measured on a 1 to 6 rating scale. Higher values reflect better outcomes in court performance.

Table 6.13 presents the averaged scores per country along the five dimensions of court performance and the general respondents' confidence that the legal system would uphold their contractual and property rights in business disputes. Thus, the latter measure also gauges the efficiency of the judicial system insofar as it captures the notional predictability of judicial decisions.

Table 6.13 illustrates several points, which further the discussion of chapter 2. First, respondents seldom or, at best, only sometimes considered the judicial system of their jurisdiction as performing well (fair, uncorrupt, fast, affordable, and able to enforce its adopted decisions).

Second, court delays are seen as a major symptom of court inefficiency. On average, firms in the region seldom associate their own jurisdiction as having fast-acting courts. Perceptions of low speed in delivery of justice are worst among court users in Croatia and Bulgaria. Courts are seen as least fair and impartial, as well as most corrupt, by court users in Albania and Moldova. They are considered most expensive in Croatia, Bosnia and Herzegovina, and Albania. They are perceived as least equipped to execute their decisions in Moldova and Bosnia and Herzegovina.

Third, despite their generally low assessments of the courts, firms tended to register somewhat higher scores when asked about their confidence in the legal system. The confidence measure uses the same numeric rating scale but different wording of assigned values. How comparable this scale is to the one used to measure perceptions of court performance is not clear, but if we assume that both scales are roughly similar, then we can make direct comparisons between the two sets of scores. Confidence in the legal system is lowest among court users in Moldova, followed by those in Albania. These findings probably reflect the low scores these countries garner on other aspects of court performance. Confidence is highest among firms using the courts in Croatia and Serbia and Montenegro.

Having examined court users' perceptions on court performance in the SEE8, we wanted to see how the region performed compared with the other regions in transition. Comparisons with other transition regions (shown in table 6.14) indicate that the court users of the SEE8 perceive their courts to rank somewhere between those of the Central European and Baltic countries and those of the CIS countries in terms of fairness of decisions and corruption. Compared with the other regional groups, domestic firms using courts in Central Europe and the Baltic countries perceive the courts in those areas to be least corrupt and most fair.

Courts in the CIS countries of Russia, Ukraine, and Belarus are seen as most corrupt and biased in their judgments. Procedural delays are seen as a problem across all transition jurisdictions, particularly in Central Europe, which is consistent with the findings of the Lex Mundi surveys on duration of first-instance procedure in debt recovery. A somewhat surprising finding is that the countries of the Caucasus region—and to a lesser degree the Central Asian CIS countries—perceived their courts as doing better in terms of speed of procedure. This finding is also corroborated by the Lex Mundi data on duration, which establish that many of these CIS countries have commercial courts (*arbitrazh* courts); the Lex Mundi lawyers' estimates of the case duration at first instance are rather short.

Courts in South Eastern Europe are shown to be least affordable compared with the other regions of transition—a finding that, again, is echoed by the data on legal costs from the Lex Mundi surveys.[14] Less variation occurs across the different regions with respect to courts' ability to enforce adopted decisions. The highest scores on average among these perception measures occur for general confidence in the legal system.

## Table 6.14    Court Performance as Perceived by Court Users, by Region

| Region | Courts are fair and impartial | Courts are honest and uncorrupt | Courts are fast | Courts are affordable | Courts are able to enforce their decisions | Firm has confidence in legal system |
|---|---|---|---|---|---|---|
| South Eastern Europe | 2.95 | 2.89 | 2.10 | 3.11 | 3.16 | 3.48 |
| Central Europe | 3.28 | 3.29 | 1.98 | 3.34 | 3.13 | 3.55 |
| Baltic states | 3.35 | 3.22 | 2.17 | 3.47 | 3.12 | 3.50 |
| CIS (Central)[a] | 2.74 | 2.59 | 2.24 | 3.59 | 3.30 | 3.36 |
| CIS (Central Asia)[b] | 3.04 | 2.82 | 2.59 | 3.27 | 3.30 | 3.72 |
| CIS (Caucasus)[c] | 3.01 | 2.92 | 2.91 | 3.31 | 3.12 | 3.37 |
| Mean | 3.05 | 2.97 | 2.18 | 3.31 | 3.19 | 3.50 |

Source: EBRD and World Bank (2002).
Note: Respondents were asked to provide a frequency rating for how often they associate the court system as being fair and impartial, honest and uncorrupt, quick, affordable, and able to enforce its decisions in resolving business disputes. The scale for the rating allowed for responses from 1 to 6, with a response of 1 meaning never and a response of 6 meaning always. The scores shown in the table represent the average of those six values for firms in each country that indicated having used the courts as either a plaintiff or a defendant between January 2000 and July 2002.
a. CIS (Central) comprises Belarus, Russia, and Ukraine.
b. CIS (Central Asia) comprises Kazakhstan, the Kyrgyz Republic, Tajikistan, and Uzbekistan.
c. CIS (Caucasus) comprises Armenia, Azerbaijan, and Georgia.

The case studies generally confirmed the BEEPS2 data with respect to users' perceptions of the legal system (see box 6.6).

## Perceptions of New and Old Firms

Having established that firm characteristics have an effect on a firm's perspective on the use of the courts, we were interested in finding out whether firms' perceptions of how well the courts work depend on firm characteristics such as size, ownership, and method of establishment. We tested for differences in mean perceptions for 2002 for the five aspects of court performance already discussed above and for general confidence in the legal and judicial systems. The results confirm that, across the full sample of SEE8 firms, regardless of whether the firm has used the courts or not, new firms, small firms, and privately owned

---

## Box 6.6  How Are the Courts Perceived?

Most of the companies interviewed during the case studies complained that courts are slow, expensive, and prone to political pressures. Almost no variation in perception occurs across countries, although certain problems appear more pronounced in some countries and industrial sectors than in others. Also, data appear to show that former state-owned firms, which also tend to be large or medium-size, do file more disputes with the courts.

Given that local courts are plagued by problems, firms in SEE might opt to engage in international arbitration or to bring a lawsuit to a foreign court, at least in disputes with foreign clients. One of the interviewed Serbian companies, a private retailer, did just that. It sued a German company for early termination of contract in a German court and won the case. It also sued a Swiss company for breach of an exclusive representation agreement and won that case.

A private, de novo software firm from Romania reported that it usually resorts to direct negotiations in cases of nonpayment and said that it never uses the courts. The firm shared its perception of the court system in Romania: "Ninety percent of businesses do not like to use the courts because they are slow and costly." Moldovan firms echoed that sentiment. One shared the general perception that costs of litigation are too high and often exceed the amount in dispute. Another Moldovan company reinforced that view by adding that court procedures are lengthy and corrupt at all levels. The firm gave as an example its experience as a defendant in a court case. The case took between 3 and 4 years to resolve.

---

firms have significantly worse perceptions of the courts than old firms, large firms, and state-owned firms, respectively.[15]

Table 6.15 shows these results. We can see that the differences are least pronounced in terms of perceptions with respect to how fast the courts deliver justice. Although old firms have a more favorable perception about the speed of court justice than new firms do, the difference misses significance at the 10 percent level. Large firms find the courts faster than small firms do, and the difference is significant at the 5 percent level. Similarly, state-owned firms also believe that the courts are faster than private firms do, and this difference is significant at the 10 percent level. We do not report the results for each country, but they are broadly consistent with the findings for the full sample of SEE8 firms.

### Perceptions about the Courts in 2002 and 1999

At the beginning of the chapter, we established that general confidence in the legal system fell somewhat between 1999 and 2002. What about firms'

## Table 6.15    Statistical Tests for Differences in Firms' Perceptions of the Courts

| Types of firms | Courts are fair and impartial | Courts are honest and uncorrupted | Courts are quick | Courts are affordable | Courts are able to enforce their decisions |
|---|---|---|---|---|---|
| **By age:** | | | | | |
| New firms | 2.75 | 2.65 | 2.20 | 2.92 | 3.17 |
| Old firms | 3.15 | 3.10 | 2.29 | 3.29 | 3.44 |
| t-statistic | −5.2750 | −5.7172 | −1.2556 | −4.5528 | −3.1758 |
| | (0.0000) | (0.0000) | (0.1048) | (0.0000) | (0.0008) |
| **By size:** | | | | | |
| Small firms | 2.75 | 2.67 | 2.17 | 2.91 | 3.19 |
| Large firms | 3.08 | 3.00 | 3.11 | 3.26 | 3.35 |
| t-statistic | −4.5502 | −4.3763 | −2.0724 | −4.3368 | −2.0195 |
| | (0.0000) | (0.000) | (0.0192) | (0.0000) | (0.0218) |
| **By ownership:** | | | | | |
| Private firms | 2.80 | 2.72 | 2.20 | 2.99 | 3.20 |
| State-owned firms | 3.28 | 3.21 | 2.35 | 3.30 | 3.55 |
| t-statistic | −4.9047 | −4.6161 | −1.6058 | −2.7084 | −3.2008 |
| | (0.0000) | (0.0000) | (0.0547) | (0.0036) | (0.0008) |

Source: EBRD and World Bank (2002).
Note: One-tailed t-tests are reported; p-values are shown in parentheses next to the t-statistics.

perceptions of how the courts work? Have they improved or worsened since 1999? This question is one of the few questions on courts that allow for an intertemporal comparison because the 1999 BEEPS did include questions about how courts worked, even though it did not contain questions on court use. Thus, we will compare the average perceptions for all firms in each country in the two rounds of the BEEPS (1999 and 2002), without being able to restrict the samples to court users only. In addition, it would be problematic to analyze how the gaps in perceptions between different types of firms have changed across time because the two surveys used different populations of firms to construct the sample.

Figure 6.12 presents the differences in perceptions of court performance in 1999 and 2002. The figure plots the average perception of how well the courts work. The value for a given country for a given year is the average across all firm responses in that country for that year with respect to the dimension of court performance; the scores along the five dimensions are then averaged to arrive at the overall perception. Figure 6.12 confirms that perceptions of how the courts are doing their job have generally become less favorable since 1999. In most of the SEE8, the average perception has fallen; only Bosnia and Herzegovina and Moldova show

## Figure 6.12    Average Perceptions of Court Performance, 1999 and 2002

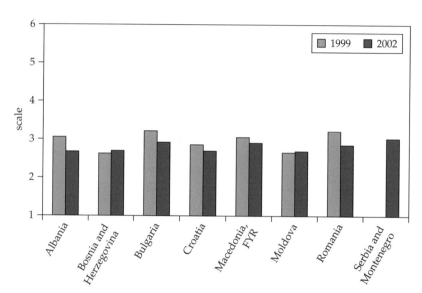

*Source:* EBRD and World Bank (1999, 2002).
*Note:* Respondents were asked to provide a frequency rating for how often they associate the court system as being (1) fair and impartial, (2) honest and uncorrupt, (3) quick, (4) affordable, and (5) able to enforce its decisions in resolving business disputes. The scale for the rating allowed for responses from 1 to 6, with a response of 1 meaning "never" and a response of 6 meaning "always." The values shown in the table were averaged across all firms that provided answers and across all five dimensions of court performance. Thus, they reflect, on the 1 to 6 scale, how often, on average, firms perceive courts to have the features along all of these dimensions.

marginal improvements in perceptions. This finding is in line with the earlier finding that confidence in the legal system in most of the SEE8 fell over the same period.

## Judicial Corruption

BEEPS2 asked several questions pertaining to corruption. In this section, we will focus only on judicial corruption—namely, the incidence of unofficial payments and gifts made to court judges and other court officials to affect the decisions of criminal and commercial court cases. A separate World Bank report (Gray, Hellman, and Ryterman 2004) tackles more generally the issues of administrative corruption and state capture, using the BEEPS data.

First, judging from the case interviews with firm managers, we see that judicial corruption seems to be more of a problem in some of the SEE8 than in others. For instance, one of the managers in FYR Macedonia told us, "Courts do not have a good reputation in FYR Macedonia." Another manager in that country said, "Courts are very corrupt and inefficient, and we would use them only as a last resort." A third manager explained, "Everybody knows that the courts in FYR Macedonia are notoriously slow and politicized." A Bulgarian manager, having a different perspective, was more concerned about the inadequate training and experience of court judges than about their being corrupt:

> Business disputes take a long time to settle. Courts do not have the time to develop efficient court practice to understand the law.... The judges are usually inexperienced recent law school graduates. At the same time, the laws are changing rapidly, which makes it tough for the courts to ensure proper implementation and judgments. [Our firm's] policy is to avoid the courts for several reasons. First and foremost, the process is very long. One would lose years, and justice may not be served.... Some judges are corrupt, but this is not widespread.... Judges are more influenced by political opinions than anything else, especially in large-claim lawsuits.

Thus, while believing some corruption exists in the judiciary, the Bulgarian manager did not see it as a huge problem. In contrast, he cited inexperienced judges, high costs of procedure, and slow judicial process as major impediments.

BEEPS2 asked firms how often they pay bribes in their dealings with the courts. Respondents were given an answer scale ranging from 1 to 6, with higher values signifying a higher frequency of bribe payment. The basic question asked respondents to consider how often their firm would make unofficial payments or gifts in a given year for nine different purposes, one of which was dealing with courts. The other purposes included obtaining business licenses and permits, obtaining government contracts, and dealing with taxes and tax collection.

Another question asked respondents about the effect of unofficial payments, gifts, private payments, or other benefits their firm paid out to judges. The question directed respondents to several areas of bribe payments, including private payments, gifts, or other benefits to judges to affect the decisions of criminal court cases and private payments, gifts, or other benefits to judges to affect the decisions in commercial cases. Respondents were given a 5-point rating scale from 0 to 4, with higher values standing for a higher perceived effect. After the analysis of state capture in Gray, Hellman, and Ryterman (2004), we assumed that this measure would serve as a good proxy for perceived judicial capture. Importantly, the question was worded in such a way that the respondent firm was not asked whether it made such payments itself; rather it was asked whether it had been affected by such payments (perhaps made by other firms). Thus, the respondent was asked to estimate the effect of capture in a specific area.

Interested in determining which types of firms more frequently pay bribes when dealing with the courts and whether firms' capture of court officials and judges depends on firm characteristics, we conducted statistical tests for differences in means between new and old firms, small and large firms, and state-owned and private firms. The tests demonstrated that new firms, small firms, and private firms do pay bribes to court officials and judges more frequently than old firms, large firms, and state-owned firms, respectively. Accordingly, they also indicated a higher perceived effect of payments made to court judges for both criminal and commercial judgments. Table 6.16 reports these results.

## Table 6.16 Statistical Tests for Differences in the Frequency of Bribe Payments to Court Officials and the Effect of Bribes Paid to Judges in Criminal and Commercial Lawsuits

| Types of firms | Frequency with which bribes are paid when dealing with courts[a] | Effect of bribe payments to judges to affect decisions in criminal and commercial court cases[b] |
| --- | --- | --- |
| By age: | | |
| New firms | 2.01 | 0.72 |
| Old firms | 1.77 | 0.61 |
| t-statistic | 3.1963 (0.0007) | 1.9436 (0.0261) |
| By size: | | |
| Small firms | 1.97 | 0.75 |
| Large firms | 1.85 | 0.56 |
| t-statistic | 1.6379 (0.0509) | 3.3247 (0.0005) |
| By ownership: | | |
| Private firms | 1.97 | 0.72 |
| State-owned firms | 1.65 | 0.49 |
| t-statistic | 3.5330 (0.0002) | 3.2802 (0.0006) |

Source: EBRD and World Bank (2002).

Note: One-tailed t-tests are reported; p-values are shown in parentheses next to the t-statistics. Ordinary least squares regressions on the frequency with which bribes are paid by firms when dealing with the courts and on the effect of bribes paid to judges in commercial or criminal lawsuits are conducted for the whole sample, controlling for firm size, ownership, and other firm characteristics, and their results are presented in tables A.6.4 and A.6.5 in the annex.

a. Respondents were given an answer scale ranging from 1 to 6, with higher values signifying a higher frequency of bribe payment.

b. Respondents were given a 5-point rating scale from 0 to 4, with higher values standing for a higher perceived effect.

---

### Box 6.7 Disputes over Land Ownership

In the case studies, many interviewed companies expressed concern about the system of land ownership and registration. This concern is particularly strong among construction firms. A Serbian private construction firm complained that land-use rights are not well defined and that obtaining construction permits is an obstacle to doing construction business. The firm described a case in which it reached an agreement with the Serbian government to build some luxury residential buildings. Under the agreement, the government had to issue the construction permit and provide an advance payment. The advance payment was received, but only in part and only well after construction had begun. However, at a stage when construction was almost complete, a permit had yet to be issued, the government had still not made the full advance payment, and the firm decided to suspend the construction work.

---

Next, we estimated an econometric model of the costs of judicial capture in which we modeled the costs of capture as a function of the frequency of bribe payments and a vector of firm characteristics. The results of these regressions are shown in tables A.6.4 and A.6.5 in the annex. We do find that a higher frequency of bribe payments raises the costs of judicial capture to the firm. Of the firm characteristics, only size and age are found significant. Small and medium-size firms have higher costs of judicial capture, and age, expressed as number of years of firm operation, also affects costs of capture positively and significantly. Interestingly, an index of judicial formalism, which is a composite of judicial complexity and number of procedural steps, is found to significantly raise the frequency with which firms pay bribes to the courts when we control for other factors. This finding lends support to the argument that more procedures and judicial complexity create opportunities for corruption.

Although this chapter focuses only on commercial disputes, many of the firms interviewed in the case studies pointed to administrative disputes with the government as being fraught with problems. Boxes 6.7 and 6.8 give testimony to this view.

## Policy Implications and Conclusions

Contract enforcement mechanisms, both formal and informal, are essential for the smooth functioning of commercial contracts. Therefore, any policy designed to strengthen the enforceability of commercial contracts and the resolution of commercial disputes needs to address judicial reform together with mechanisms for informal enforcement.

---

## Box 6.8    Resolving Payment Disputes with the Government

A software company interviewed for the case studies referred to a commercial dispute with the General Forest Directorate, an Albanian government agency. In 1998, the company won a World Bank tender to supply the information technology (IT) component for a project. According to the agreement, the General Forest Directorate was to cover customs duties and value added tax (VAT) levied on the goods and services in relation to the project. The company delivered, in accordance with the agreement, accompanying invoices and all necessary documents, but the directorate refused to pay the locally incurred costs (customs duties and VAT) for which it was liable.

In the same year, the company filed a lawsuit against the General Forest Directorate to recover the amount of customs duties and VAT that had been incurred in supplying the goods and services. A court decision was issued in the company's favor. After that, the General Forest Directorate paid only the amount of the outstanding VAT but refused to cover the customs duties. The company appealed the decision before two higher courts, but 4 years later, it still had not received the remainder of the amount. The company brought a court order to a bailiff and requested its execution. It had to pay an enforcement fee equal to 7 percent of the sum specified in the court order for the execution to begin. However, the bailiff was unable to execute the court order because the directorate operates under the Albanian Treasury and does not have a separate bank account. Treasury accounts in Albania cannot be assigned in forced execution of court orders.

According to the company's general manager, "The bottom line is that one cannot take money from a government institution." In the company's view, courts are ineffective, are costly, and take a very long time to resolve a case. Therefore, it prefers to settle disputes through out-of-court means. In the manager's view, there is no functioning arbitration court in Albania, and that limits the alternative mechanisms to settle commercial disputes out of the courts.

---

Policymakers could pursue several types of reform that have been found to improve the enforcement of commercial contracts in various jurisdictions worldwide. Those measures include establishing information-sharing systems such as credit reporting agencies, and ensuring that judicial decisions are publicized and that information on judicial cases in various stages of resolution before the courts is collected and used to identify bottlenecks in judicial enforcement. In addition, non-contentious matters such as firm or property registration should be removed from the domain of the courts and transferred to appropriate administrative agencies. Also, judicial procedures should be simplified, particularly in terms of filing, gathering evidence, and processing appeals. Specialized courts such as commercial courts or small claims courts could also be established. In addition, measures to introduce and enhance alternative mechanisms for formal dispute resolution (such as arbitration and mediation) could also improve contract enforceability. Finally, measures should be taken to improve court resources. We will look at each of these areas of reform in turn and discuss their relevance for the SEE8.

## Establish Information-Sharing Institutions

As discussed earlier, once trade is conducted impersonally, intertemporally, and from a distance, the role of informal contract enforcement mechanisms lessens and the role of formal state enforcement through courts increases. Yet even in countries where state-run courts work well, informal contract enforcement institutions (such as credit bureaus, the media, and nongovernmental organizations) and reputational intermediaries (such as accountants and auditors) perform important functions in ensuring that contracts are enforced and that obligations between business partners are met. Credit bureaus, for example, provide information about a potential business partner's past credit history and thereby alleviate the informational asymmetry in doing business with an unknown customer or supplier. In so doing, credit bureaus provide an incentive to parties to observe the contractual agreement. Another reputation-based enforcement mechanism operates through institutions such as the media and nongovernmental organizations. To the extent that the media detect and publicize illegal actions of various economic actors, businesses, or the government, they not only provide the necessary information about potential business partners but also provide a check against opportunistic behavior. In addition, the media provide information about the courts and the outcomes of court cases.

Establishing credit-reporting agencies such as public credit bureaus may be one way of strengthening contract enforcement in the SEE8. According to a recent World Bank (2004) report, only Bosnia and Herzegovina among the SEE8 has a private credit information bureau in operation. Public credit registries are more common, and Bulgaria, Romania, and Serbia and Montenegro have all established one. A public credit registry is also being established in Albania. Croatia and Moldova are reported to operate neither a public credit registry nor a private credit bureau.

Messick (1999) points out that, although many scholars recommend establishing information-sharing institutions such as credit bureaus, potential free-rider problems and other market failures could be an impediment. In particular, he refers to the origins of private credit bureaus in the United States and argues that most were set up as small, nonprofit organizations, often run as part of the local chamber of commerce. Members generally belonged to a tight-knit business community, and this mechanism provided the right incentives to overcome free-rider problems and other market failures.

As evidenced by World Bank (2004), some of the SEE8 have already undertaken steps to foster information sharing by setting up public or private credit registries. Yet more could be done. For instance, the same report ranks countries in terms of the regulatory environment for information sharing. Moldova and Serbia and Montenegro both rank among the 10 countries worldwide in which the legal and regulatory environment is least conducive to information sharing. Moldova is found to lack the legal basis for a private credit registry to operate. Moldovan bank secrecy laws prohibit the sharing of information on borrower behavior. Only publicly listed companies are subject to broad financial disclosure requirements. Furthermore, access to public information sources such as court judgments, notary records, and so forth is greatly restricted. Therefore, the Moldovan laws and regulations effectively rule out successful information sharing. In addition, the quality of Serbia and Montenegro's public credit registry and of its performance is low. Therefore, reforms should target these laws and regulations.

## Establish Judicial Statistics

One universal policy recommendation with respect to improving the operation of the courts is to gather information about the flow of court cases through the system. It is useful to collect reliable data about numbers of cases filed at various stages in the judicial process as well as information about court users, nature of claims, monetary size of commercial disputes, use of appeals, legal fees, and so on. This type of empirical data is necessary to identify bottlenecks in court performance and give policymakers information about where reforms are needed most. Collecting judicial statistics is also necessary to improving the court administration and case management systems, which are often cited in transitional countries as requiring modernization and reform.

A diagnostic study of the legal and judicial systems in Serbia and Montenegro (World Bank 2002) finds that one of the overarching problems associated with the country's courts is the length of court procedures. For instance, the study mentions that it takes 3 to 4 years to reach a judgment in court and more years to obtain execution of the judgment. This finding is in line with measures of duration of court process discussed earlier in the chapter. The study attributes court delays to complex and cumbersome rules of judicial procedure, insufficient human and administrative resources in the courts, and lack of properly aligned incentives for performance by court judges. However, it also acknowledges that a better understanding of why courts take so long could be achieved only through collection of judicial statistics.

Collecting reliable data on court performance as well as on the types of cases that reach the courts and that get through the process past the filing stage has been very informative and helpful to policymakers in other parts of the world. These data could outline priorities for judicial reform in the SEE8.[16]

## Remove Non-Contentious Cases from the Courts

One of the reasons for court delays and case backlogs is that, very often, courts are responsible for dealing with what are essentially non-dispute matters such as company or property registration. Often judges rather than court clerks are the ones who are exclusively dealing with these kinds of registration procedures. In countries where courts' human resources are already stretched thin, this practice burdens the system further. Therefore, many legal scholars have recommended transferring these types of non-contentious matters away from the courts to the relevant administrative agencies (Delaey 2001; Messick 1999). This type of transfer is found to work well and to free up judges' time so they can deal with proper disputes.

Bulgaria is an example of a jurisdiction where company registration is performed by a judge. According to a World Bank (2004) report, the registration procedure involves (a) submission of the necessary documents, (b) review of documents and approval by a judge, and (c) technical processing of the submitted information and issue of the court registration decision certificate. Apparently, the judge's resolution takes the most time in this process. Given that there are many company registrations, courts have to dedicate a high proportion of their judges to deal with registrations. For example, 8 of the 23 judges who are competent to resolve all types of cases at the Sofia District Court deal exclusively with business registration and reregistration. There is a clear need to eliminate court approval in the business registration process, introduce an equivalent administrative procedure, and, thus, increase judges' time and shorten times to disposition.

Similarly, the courts in Serbia and Montenegro also deal with business registration. For example, in Belgrade, 18 of the 95 commercial court judges work exclusively on company registration and re-registration cases. A draft law is seeking to transfer these registration procedures to a separate agency, a change that is expected to free up judicial time and resources so that judges can deal with actual disputes.

In Romania, judges are also performing tasks that are not related to dispute resolution, such as registration of property. Judges seconded to the local chambers of commerce also perform registration of companies.

A report by the American Bar Association (ABA, Central and East European Law Initiative 2002c) on the state of the Romanian judicial system considers the performance of these tasks as one of the main reasons for judicial inefficiency and procedural delays in Romania.

## Simplify Judicial Procedures

Making judicial processes less burdensome and simpler for the parties is seen as a way of improving the speed and transparency of litigation. As discussed earlier and demonstrated in figure 6.10, the SEE8 jurisdictions are the most procedurally cumbersome within the group of transition economies. This type of procedural complexity or formalism is shown to be detrimental rather than beneficial for court performance. Islam (2003) argues that complexity raises the costs of dispute resolution and makes judicial processes more opaque. For example, Djankov and others (2003) find that judicial formalism is associated with lower judicial efficiency, longer duration of process, more corruption, and less access to justice. Therefore, Islam (2003) recommends and discusses extensively simplifications of judicial procedures for different world regions. These reforms include measures along several dimensions of procedural laws.

One point must be emphasized, however: calls for procedural simplification should not be interpreted as meaning that judicial processes be stripped of all formality. In a judicial process, a tension always exists between (a) the time and costs of adjudication and (b) the quality and accuracy of adjudication. Many procedural steps are put in place to ensure the quality of the judicial process. These steps will be discussed further in the following sections.

ORAL PROCEDURE

First, some move away from written toward more oral procedures may bring some benefits. It is argued that, in jurisdictions where written elements dominate, judges do not have direct contact with witnesses and other sources of evidence. This situation arguably causes interruptions, thereby delaying the process. In addition, written elements usually necessitate lawyer involvement in the process. A World Bank (2001b) judicial sector assessment of Argentina, for example, discusses how lawyers would have an incentive to use procedural delays as a way to benefit their clients. Presumably, lawyers benefit from the preeminence of written procedures over oral ones because this situation allows them to handle more cases. The study suggests that introducing oral procedures could be one way of solving this dilemma. In this respect, the study gives as an example the reduction of the average duration of criminal cases from 3 years to 6 months. The expectation is that the same move to oral procedures could also reduce times to disposition in civil cases.

Of course, reducing the written elements of the process does not mean that written procedures do not have a role in the judicial process. Some legal scholars argue that written and legally motivated complaints help the judge to prepare for a hearing and avoid delays and surprises. Oral procedures may even protract proceedings because they require personal interviews of parties who fail to appear before the judge. Furthermore, introduction of oral proceedings requires additional resources such as proper audio court recording systems, lay judges, etc. Therefore, any move in favor of oral procedures should be made after a careful and thorough analysis of its costs and benefits.

Bulgaria, Croatia, and Romania are found to be jurisdictions that rely mostly on written procedures in the civil case of debt collection, as reviewed above. All three require that the defendant's opposition be presented to the court in writing rather than verbally; all three require a written judgment and that this written judgment also be notified to the parties in writing; Bulgaria also mandates that closing arguments by the parties or their lawyers also be given in writing. Evidently, some move away from written procedures could speed up the judicial process and may also improve access to justice in smaller and simpler cases.

LEGAL JUSTIFICATION

The need for legal justification of the complaint and the final judgment in court procedures is linked to the reliance on written or oral procedures. In jurisdictions where written elements dominate, it is very likely that the plaintiff and the adjudicator will be required to have legally motivated reasons for the claim and the judgment, respectively. These motivations, although designed to ensure that due process and the law are followed, are often thought of only as raising the cost of procedures and delaying the time until judgment. If a legally motivated complaint is needed, the plaintiff must hire a lawyer to prepare it for him or her, thereby raising costs and limiting access to justice. When a judge issues the decision of the case at the hearing but the law requires a legally motivated decision, the judge will need to take extra time to put the judgment in writing and to provide reasons together with the law articles that pertain to the decision.

Again, some legal experts opine that legal justification is an important element of a court decision. It provides parties with the legal rationale for the decision, increases transparency and predictability of court decisions, and raises legal awareness.

All the SEE8, as shown in table 6.7, require that both the plaintiff's claim and the first-instance judgment be justified in law. Limiting the need for legal justification in straightforward commercial cases could be one way to streamline the process.

## STATUTORY REGULATION OF EVIDENCE

Albania is found to regulate evidence most heavily, followed by Romania. For example, six of the jurisdictions (the exceptions are Bulgaria and Serbia and Montenegro) mandate that presented evidence be recorded (in writing or on tape), which is done to facilitate the appellate court's control over the first-instance judge. Furthermore, Albania, Bosnia and Herzegovina, Bulgaria, and Serbia and Montenegro impose the restriction that only original documents and certified copies be admissible as evidence before the courts. In addition, in Albania, Croatia, and Romania, a law determines the level of authenticity and weight that would be attached to evidence presented by the parties in court, which again limits the judge's discretion. Other differences among the SEE8 arise from whether hearsay evidence (statements of fact heard by a third party) can be admitted as evidence in the process. In a quarter of the sample, hearsay evidence is not admissible in a court of law. Changes in procedural laws designed to allow for more discretion on the part of the judge in admitting evidence and making use of it could potentially ease the judicial process.

## CONTROL OF SUPERIOR REVIEW

In all of the SEE8, the enforcement of judgment is automatically suspended until the resolution of the appeal, which substantially reduces the importance of the first-instance judgment. In addition, all eight countries allow for both factual and procedural issues (issues of fact and of law) to be reviewed by second-instance appellate courts, thereby expanding the options for appeals made solely to delay the execution of the first-instance decision. Most of the eight jurisdictions are also lenient toward the filing of interlocutory appeals (appeals and motions raised during first-instance case trial before a judgment is issued). Only Croatia and Moldova prohibit these types of interlocutory appeals. Not prohibiting these appeals leads to frivolous appeals and motions that are directed at interlocutory decisions by the judge and that are intended to interrupt the process and delay execution.

Reforms in this area could improve the enforceability of the first-instance judgment and limit the scope for appeals without due cause. Romania, for example, has made efforts in this direction. According to an American Bar Association study (ABA, Central and East European Law Initiative 2002c), revisions were adopted in the Code of Civil Procedure in 2001. Those revisions limit the number and levels of appeal allowed to litigants.[17] The changes reportedly have led to improvements in court performance and have reduced case backlogs.

## NOTIFICATION

The rules on other statutory interventions, which comprise rules on notification of complaint and judgment, are found to be closely associated with court use, as evidenced by the econometric results presented in the annex. Notification of court claims and judgments also varies across countries. In this area, however, most of the SEE8 allow the complaint to be notified to the defendant directly by the plaintiff or the plaintiff's attorney, or simply by mailing a letter. Only in Albania (and, until recently, Bulgaria) is the defendant not held accountable unless he or she is served with the claim by a specially appointed court officer. Because a defendant who wishes to avoid service of process can undertake measures to do so, rules of notification should be fairly simple and should allow for completion of notification through alternative means (such as affixing a notice of petition to the defendant's home or depositing the claim with a neighbor, at the place of work, or with the relevant municipal authorities) when the defendant cannot be found.

Reforms to improve the system of court notifications of parties and witnesses have been under way in the SEE8. For example, revisions were made to the Bulgarian Code of Civil Procedure in 2000 after it was found that notification of defendants had been causing long delays of commercial cases. Before the revisions, a court officer had to notify the defendant in person before court proceedings could begin. Under the new regime, if the first notification by a court officer fails, it is sufficient to post a second notification on the court's announcement board and in the Official Gazette. Service is then considered complete. This example illustrates that countries have been already moving in the direction of reducing the burden of procedural notifications.

Notifications of parties and witnesses could be cumbersome and problematic even when a court officer is not required to personally serve the claim to the defendant. For example, a report on Croatia prepared by the American Bar Association (ABA, Central and East European Law Initiative 2002a) identifies complex and cumbersome notification procedures as considerably delaying civil litigation. High absentee rates by litigants and lawyers at trial hearings, said to reach 33 percent in some courts, occur because of these deficiencies in procedural notifications. For instance, service of process is accomplished by mail, but defendants wishing to delay trial can evade service by changing their registered addresses or by avoiding the local mail delivery person. The report also mentions that affixing is not permitted, so the defendant must be at home and willing to answer the door when the delivery person rings. Because notifications are usually attempted during normal business hours, litigants are normally at work at the time. Similar problems with subpoenas and notifications of parties and witnesses are typical of the Serbian court system (ABA, Central and East European Law Initiative 2002d).

## Establish Specialized Courts

Specialized courts are considered useful institutions to lessen the burden of the general jurisdiction courts. Specialized courts deal exclusively with certain types of disputes; for example, commercial courts deal exclusively with commercial disputes. Small claims courts are also specialized courts that have jurisdiction over civil and commercial claims up to a certain amount.

Both small claims courts and specialized commercial courts are associated with less procedural complexity (procedures are mostly conducted orally, and notification and evidence rules are simplified) and faster times to disposition. Legal costs are also lower. In some countries, for instance, legal representation is prohibited or strongly discouraged in small claims tribunals. This condition eliminates litigants' attorney fees, which can be very high in the general courts. Today, small claims courts are common in high-income countries such as Australia, Canada, France, Germany, Japan, New Zealand, and the United States as well as in low-income, common law jurisdictions such as Nigeria, Thailand, Uganda, Zambia, and Zimbabwe. They have also been set up in some civil law, emerging market economies such as Brazil and Mexico. At present, there are no small claims courts in the transition countries.

Specialized commercial courts are also credited with speeding up judicial process by simplifying procedures and allowing judges to specialize and develop expertise in the area of commercial litigation. For example, a commercial court was established in Dar es Salaam, Tanzania, in 1999 as a specialized division of the regular High Court. The new court has jurisdiction over commercial disputes in which the value of the claim exceeds 10 million Tanzanian shillings. The court has proved to be faster than the regular courts, with times to disposition averaging 3 to 4 months.

It must be stressed, however, that specialized courts also have some disadvantages. They may lead to quality differentiation, geographical barriers to access, inconsistent legal practices, easy capture, and smaller economies of scale. In addition, establishing specialized courts could be expensive. A more feasible option for developing countries could be to institute specialized judges within a unified system of regular courts.

Specialized commercial courts or specialized judges in the general jurisdiction courts could prove useful for litigants in the SEE8. For example, a report by the American Bar Association on FYR Macedonia (ABA, Central and East European Law Initiative 2002b) finds that one of the reasons for the substantial backlogs of cases and delays in litigation in that country is, at least in part, because of a 1996 reorganization of the judicial system whereby specialized courts such as commercial courts were eliminated and the general courts assumed first-instance jurisdiction over most disputes. Judicial statistics provided in the report indicate that backlogs mainly affect the first-instance courts and that the number of civil cases from prior years pending resolution with the first-instance courts fell in absolute terms between 1998 and 2000. However, the ratio of civil cases resolved to the total number of civil cases outstanding (including cases filed in previous years and in a given year) declined between 1999 and 2000 (from 55 percent to 51 percent). Therefore, backlogs in Macedonian civil cases at first instance still persist and are, in fact, on the rise. The same report also establishes that an average civil case reportedly takes one and a half to two years to complete (ABA, Central and East European Law Initiative 2002b). This estimate is close to the duration of the hypothetical debt recovery cases featured earlier (which involved an average duration until completion of 509 days).

Within the SEE8, Croatia, Moldova, and Serbia and Montenegro have specialized commercial courts. In Moldova, as in most of the CIS countries, the commercial courts are known as *arbitrazh courts* and were established as a successor to the *Gosudarstvennyi Arbitrazh* or *Gosarbitrazh* (the central administrative agency where enterprises could bring contractual breaches during the Soviet era) to exercise jurisdiction over business disputes between legal entities.[18]

## Introduce Alternative Dispute Resolution

Policymakers in the SEE8 could also improve contract enforcement through reforms designed to endorse the use of mediation (also known as *conciliation*) and commercial arbitration. Under those mechanisms, the resolution of a dispute comes from the parties themselves under the guidance and control of a third party (a mediator or arbitrator).

Mediation has grown in popularity in some emerging market jurisdictions that typically have overburdened courts and significant case backlogs. Essentially, it is used to move civil cases away from the general courts. Mediation can be voluntary or mandatory. For instance, Argentina introduced mandatory mediation for civil cases as a pilot program in 1996. A special law was enacted requiring that cases filed in civil and commercial national and federal courts in Buenos Aires go through mandatory mediation at the beginning of the lawsuit. Mediators are assigned to cases by a lottery, which the court conducts at the time of filing. The court also assigns a judge to the case, who will eventually decide the case if mediation fails. Mediation cannot last longer than 60 days, and parties must personally attend mediation proceedings. Lawyer representation is mandatory, and parties must also pay the mediator for his or her services. The pilot has achieved great success in bringing mediated cases to resolution. For example, only 21 percent of civil cases and 31 percent of commercial cases returned to the formal judicial procedure after mediation in the first year of the pilot's operation. Among the SEE8, pre-trial mediation is mandatory in Albania and Moldova.

## Improve Court Resources

Judicial sector assessments by the American Bar Association's Central and East European Law Initiative in the SEE8 have also pointed to other areas in need of reform, such as the training of judges and judicial support staff, the poor state of judicial buildings and office equipment, the budgets of the courts, the case assignment system, and the case filing and tracking systems. Some steps have already been undertaken to make improvements in these areas. For example, most of the SEE8 have introduced a lottery (random) case assignment system, which limits the opportunity for bribes to be offered to court presidents to assign a case to a particular judge. Foreign donors have assisted in renovating court buildings and supplying computer equipment. Judicial salaries in many of the SEE8 have been raised in an effort to root out corruption and better align judges' incentives with court performance objectives. Yet much remains to be done. For instance, the American Bar Association's report on Bosnia and Herzegovina (ABA, Central and East European Law Initiative 2001) reveals that most Bosnian courts lack sufficient funding for trivial tasks such as mailing summonses, paying the court's electricity bill, or even purchasing folders for the case files. Some courts report also being unable to cover expert witness fees. Many courts have substantial debts. This type of situation clearly undermines the work of the courts and their independence from the executive branch of government.

Although reforms such as introducing new technology and case information systems have proved very successful in similar countries such as the Slovak Republic, other legal experts and observers note that increasing legal resources and the number of judges might not improve court performance.[19] They surmise that the problem lies in the complicated and burdensome judicial procedure, not in the number of actual judges. Available evidence shows that often reforms such as increasing the number of judges are not associated with improvements in judicial efficiency.

## Conclusion

For the SEE8, where courts are considered a last alternative in resolving business disputes and enforcing commercial contracts, reforms that both improve the procedures within which courts work and better align the incentives of all interested parties for fast and predictable disposition of cases could probably improve the performance and perceptions of the courts. Not all disputes can or indeed should go to court, and, most certainly, the majority of firms will continue to rely on informal ways to enforce contracts. Nevertheless, further efforts to establish specialized or small claims courts or to move cases to mediation could help alleviate the burden of the judiciary and could provide parties with simpler and cheaper options for resolving disputes. Comparative international evidence could guide these reforms. However, judicial reforms in all areas discussed above should be accompanied by reform of the informal mechanisms to do business and solve disputes. In this respect, information-sharing institutions are critical.

## Statistical Annex

### *Determinants of Firms' Use of the Courts in Resolving Business Disputes*

We explored the BEEPS2 data for the SEE8 to identify the determinants of firms' use of the courts in resolving business disputes. The survey has a section devoted to dispute resolution and asks respondents about their perceptions of the quality of the court system. Three of the questions deal with use of the courts. They ask about the number of civil and commercial cases filed and defended between January 2000 and July 2002, and about the share of payment disputes that ultimately are resolved in court. In addition, the section asks firms about the use of prepayment and about the reluctance to grant customers credit. Finally, a separate question gauges the incidence of payment disputes and the amount of time required to resolve (in any manner) an overdue payment. Our dependent variables measuring court use are "cases_filed" and "court_use." The former equals the number of cases filed between January 2000 and July 2002; the latter equals the percentage of payment disputes resolved through court action.

We specify the following regression equation, which is estimated by the ordinary least squares method:

$$C_{ij} = \alpha + \beta X_{ij} + \chi Y_j + \varepsilon_{ij}$$

where $C_{ij}$ represents the use of the courts by firm $i$ in country $j$; $X_{ij}$ represents the characteristics of firm $i$ (including size, sector, and ownership dummies, age, and foreign ownership dummy); and $Y_j$ represents country-specific measures of the quality and costs of using the courts. (The main variables are based on the Lex Mundi survey data, which are outlined in the chapter. They include the judicial formalism index, which incorporates the judicial complexity index and the index of procedural steps; the subindex of other procedural interventions; and the average expected attorney fees payable in a standard debt collection case, as a percentage of GNI per capita.) In the equation, $\alpha$ is a constant and $\varepsilon$ is a standard error term.

The ordinary least squares estimates of the above specification demonstrate that judicial formalism has a significant negative impact on the percentage of payment disputes resolved in court (court_use), controlling for firm-specific characteristics, business association membership (ba_member), and political party donations (pol_part_d). It also has a negative impact on the number of court cases firms file but just misses significance at the 10 percent level. The results are reversed for the subindex of other statutory interventions (other_interv). It is significant for the number of court cases filed, but misses significance in the regression on share of payment disputes resolved by court action. Finally, attorney fees (attorney_fees_pc) have a significant (at 10 percent) negative impact for both the number of court cases filed and the share of payment disputes resolved in court. The variable jud_form means the aggregate index of judicial formalism, which is the sum of the subindices presented in table 6.7 plus the index of independent procedural steps.

Among the various controls, size and ownership dummies are significant in the different specifications. The regression results are presented in tables A.6.1, A.6.2, and A.6.3.

## Corruption Regressions

For corruption regressions, the basic equation is

$$C_{ij} = a_0 + a_1 F_{ij} + a_2 X_{ij} + \varepsilon_{ij}$$

where $C_{ij}$ represents the costs of judicial capture by firm $i$ in country $j$; $F_{ij}$ represents the frequency with which firm $i$ in country $j$ is paying bribes to the courts; and $X_{ij}$ represents firm characteristics such as size, ownership, sector, foreign ownership, foreign holdings, and age.

The costs of capture are measured by the BEEPS2 question about what perceived effect on the firms results from the unofficial payments, gifts, private payments, or other benefits that are made to judges to affect the decisions of commercial and criminal cases. The extent of these capture practices is measured on a 0 to 4 scale, from no impact to decisive impact. The judicial capture variable (jud_cap) is a simple average of the effect of bribes to affect commercial and criminal judgments.

The frequency of paying bribes is measured by the BEEPS2 question that asks how often in a given year firms pay bribes to deal with the courts. It is measured on a 1 to 6 frequency rating scale, from "never" to

## Table A.6.1   Ordinary Least Squares Regression of Firms' Use of the Courts on Judicial Formalism

| Independent variables | Dependent variables | |
|---|---|---|
| | cases_filed | court_use |
| small | −5.768 | −3.988 |
| | (−3.36)** | (−1.83) |
| medium | −2.794 | −3.387 |
| | (−1.79) | (−1.16) |
| (large) | | |
| de_novo | −4.037 | −7.182 |
| | (−1.72) | (−5.60)*** |
| privatized | −3.158 | −1.779 |
| | (−1.72) | (−0.70) |
| (state_owned) | | |
| foreign | 0.650 | 0.421 |
| | (1.56) | (0.26) |
| mining | 2.486 | 4.631 |
| | (0.82) | (0.77) |
| services | 0.483 | −0.590 |
| | (0.94) | (−0.51) |
| (manufacturing) | | |
| age | 0.016 | 0.030 |
| | (0.88) | (−0.85) |
| jud_form | −1.484 | −3.847 |
| | (−1.79) | (−2.80)** |
| ba_member | 1.196 | 1.983 |
| | (1.61) | (1.12) |
| pol_part_d | 1.450 | −0.138 |
| | (2.77)** | (−0.10) |
| Constant | 15.321 | 30.339 |
| | (2.85)** | 4.22*** |
| Observations | 1096 | 847 |
| R-squared | 0.15 | 0.09 |

*Source:* Author calculations from EBRD and World Bank (2002).
*Note:* Robust *t*-statistics are in parentheses.
*significant at 10 percent.
**significant at 5 percent.
***significant at 1 percent.

"always." The respective variable (bribe_courts) is rescaled to assume values between 0 and 1.

The results for 2002 indicate that a higher frequency of paying bribes results in significantly higher costs of judicial capture, when we control for other factors. Small and medium-size firms are found to bear significantly

## Table A.6.2   Ordinary Least Squares Regression of Firms' Use of the Courts on the Index of Other Statutory Interventions

| | Dependent variables | |
|---|---|---|
| Independent variables | cases_filed | court_use |
| small | −5.558 | −3.784 |
| | (−3.28)** | (−1.77) |
| medium | −2.787 | −3.174 |
| | (−1.54) | (−1.11) |
| (large) | | |
| de_novo | −4.190 | −7.694 |
| | (−1.80) | (−6.28)*** |
| privatized | −3.076 | −1.573 |
| | (−1.67) | (−0.63) |
| (state_owned) | | |
| foreign | 0.674 | 0.996 |
| | (1.64) | (0.61) |
| mining | 2.378 | 4.560 |
| | (0.76) | (0.74) |
| services | 0.579 | −0.317 |
| | (1.07) | (−0.25) |
| (manufacturing) | | |
| age | 0.013 | 0.029 |
| | (0.67) | (0.83) |
| other_interv | −4.797 | −4.738 |
| | (−2.93)** | (−1.33) |
| ba_member | 1.237 | 2.021 |
| | (1.71) | (1.23) |
| pol_part_d | 1.422 | −0.274 |
| | (2.80)** | (−0.19) |
| Constant | 9.613 | 14.284 |
| | (2.81)** | (5.11)*** |
| Observations | 1096 | 852 |
| R-squared | 0.15 | 0.08 |

Source: Author calculations from EBRD and World Bank (2002).
Note: Robust t-statistics are in parentheses.
*significant at 10 percent.
**significant at 5 percent.
***significant at 1 percent.

higher costs of judicial capture than large firms. Among the other control variables, only firm age is found to be significant. It affects the costs of capture positively and significantly.

Using the 2002 data, we also estimated the determinants of the frequency of bribe payment. We used the same firm characteristics as in

**Table A.6.3    Ordinary Least Squares Regression of Firms' Use of the Courts on Attorney Fees Payable at First Instance**

| | Dependent variables | |
|---|---|---|
| Independent variables | cases_filed | court_use |
| small | −5.661 | −3.924 |
| | (−3.38)** | (−1.88)* |
| medium | −2.733 | −3.163 |
| | (−1.76) | (−1.12) |
| (large) | | |
| de_novo | −4.078 | −7.434 |
| | (−1.74) | (−6.05)*** |
| privatized | −3.154 | −1.540 |
| | (−1.73) | (−0.62) |
| (state_owned) | | |
| foreign | 0.675 | 0.798 |
| | (1.61) | (0.51) |
| mining | 2.500 | 4.551 |
| | (0.81) | (0.73) |
| services | 0.469 | −0.428 |
| | (0.90) | (−0.34) |
| (manufacturing) | | |
| age | 0.016 | 0.027 |
| | (0.82) | (0.79) |
| attorney_fees_pc | −0.023 | −0.050 |
| | (−1.99)* | (−2.05)* |
| ba_member | 1.285 | 2.218 |
| | (1.68) | (1.26) |
| pol_part_d | 1.327 | −0.295 |
| | (2.47)** | (−0.22) |
| Constant | 9.119 | 14.275 |
| | (2.73)** | (5.43)*** |
| Observations | 1096 | 852 |
| R-squared | 0.14 | 0.08 |

*Source:* Author calculations from EBRD and World Bank (2002).
*Note:* Robust *t*-statistics are in parentheses.
*significant at 10 percent.
**significant at 5 percent.
***significant at 1 percent.

the costs-of-capture specification and added as independent variables the country-specific judicial formalism (jud_form) variable and firms' access to bureaucratic recourse (bur_recourse). We also included a dummy variable (for_hq), which assumes the value of 1 when the firm's headquarters are located in a foreign country and 0 when they are not located in a foreign country. It is thus a proxy for the firm having foreign owners.

The results show that judicial formalism has a significant positive effect on the frequency with which bribes are paid in dealing with the courts. Access to bureaucratic recourse has a negative effect on the frequency of bribe payments to the courts, but this effect is not statistically significant. Private firms are found to pay bribes to the courts significantly more frequently than state-owned firms. Sector characteristics are also found to be significant. Industrial firms pay court bribes with a significantly higher frequency than firms in the service sector. These results are reported in tables A.6.4 and A.6.5.

## Table A.6.4 Ordinary Least Squares Regression on Firms' Capture of Courts

| Independent variables | Dependent variables jud_cap |
|---|---|
| small | 0.221 |
| | (2.66)** |
| medium | 0.062 |
| | (2.15)* |
| (large) | |
| (state_owned) | |
| private | 0.086 |
| | (1.23) |
| for_hq | 0.244 |
| | (1.17) |
| sector | 0.063 |
| | (1.61) |
| age | 0.003 |
| | (4.96)*** |
| for_hold | 0.000 |
| | (0.01) |
| bribe_courts | 1.900 |
| | (7.86)*** |
| Constant | 0.033 |
| | (0.38) |
| Observations | 1158 |
| R-squared | 0.25 |

Source: Author calculations from EBRD and World Bank (2002).
Note: Robust t-statistics are in parentheses.
*significant at 10 percent.
**significant at 5 percent.
***significant at 1 percent.

## Table A.6.5   Ordinary Least Squares Regression on Frequency of Bribe Payment

| Independent variables | Dependent variables bribe_courts |
|---|---|
| small | −0.012 |
|  | (0.83) |
| medium | −0.032 |
|  | (1.90)* |
| (large) |  |
| (state_owned) |  |
| private | 0.066 |
|  | (5.16)*** |
| for_hq | −0.054 |
|  | (−0.95) |
| sector | 0.020 |
|  | (2.77)** |
| age | 0.000 |
|  | (0.41) |
| for_hold | −0.014 |
|  | (−0.54) |
| jud_form | 0.075 |
|  | (2.41)** |
| bur_recourse | −0.013 |
|  | (−1.52) |
| Constant | −0.155 |
|  | (−0.93) |
| Observations | 1276 |
| R-squared | 0.04 |

Source: Author calculations from EBRD and World Bank (2002).
Note: Robust $t$-statistics are in parentheses.
*significant at 10 percent.
**significant at 5 percent.
***significant at 1 percent.

# Endnotes

1. Central Europe comprises the Czech Republic, Hungary, Poland, the Slovak Republic, and Slovenia; the Baltic States comprise Estonia, Latvia, and Lithuania; and South Eastern Europe comprises Albania, Bosnia and Herzegovina, Bulgaria, Croatia, the former Yugoslav Republic of Macedonia, Moldova, Romania, and Serbia and Montenegro (that is, the SEE8).

2. See Macaulay (1963) for an early study of commercial exchange without legal contract enforcement among manufacturing firms in Wisconsin. See also Clay (1997) for a discussion of how trade prospered in the absence of legal court enforcement in California in the 1830s and 1840s. For a comprehensive survey of

the literature on the evolution of contract enforcement institutions, see Greif (2003).

' 3. *Relational contracting* refers to doing business only with firms with which relations are already established. It is supported by the premise that the long-term benefits of maintaining the business relationship outweigh the one-off benefits from cheating. For a discussion of the importance of relational contracting for manufacturing firms in five transition economies, see Johnson, McMillan, and Woodruff (2002).

4. Similarly, a study by McMillan and Woodruff (1999) of contract enforcement mechanisms used by privately owned manufacturing firms in Vietnam established that trade associations are not seen as providing significant contract enforcement services. In that study, of the interviewed firms belonging to a trade association (47 percent of the total number of interviewed firms), only 28 percent said that the trade association provided "information about the trustworthiness of customers and suppliers," and only 13 percent said that the trade association provided "contract and/or dispute resolution" services.

5. For a discussion of the different types of private protection schemes in Russia, including criminal groups, see Frye and Zhuravskaya (2000) and Volkov (1999).

6. For a theoretical model and an empirical investigation of the effect of firm reputation on contracting, see Banerjee and Duflo (2000). Their study shows that, among Indian software firms, characteristics such as firm age, previous experience with a client, and certification by the International Organization for Standardization, all of which plausibly measure firm reputation, affect the choice of a particular contract and the outcome of that contract.

7. A good example of the role of trade associations in providing information about past behavior of firms is given by Woodruff (1998). He shows that, in a closed economy, Mexican footwear producers relied on information about past behavior of retailers that was provided by the manufacturers' trade associations. His work also illustrates how greater openness to international trade can break down some of these informal mechanisms for ensuring contractual compliance.

8. See Greif, Milgrom, and Weingast (1994) for a theoretical model of the origins and functions of the merchant guild. See also Milgrom, North, and Weingast (1990) for a model of the law merchant in medieval Europe.

9. The surveys were designed in cooperation with scholars from Harvard University and Yale University and with advice from practicing attorneys from Argentina, Belgium, Botswana, Colombia, Mexico, and the United States. The questions cover the step-by-step evolution of a debt-recovery case before local courts in the country's largest city. The respondent firms were provided with detailed assumptions about the case, including the amount of the claim (equivalent to 50 percent of GNI per capita), the location and main characteristics of the litigants, the presence of city regulations, the nature of the remedy requested by the plaintiff, the merit of the plaintiff's and the defendant's claims, and the social implications of the judicial outcomes. These standardized details enabled the

respondent law firms to describe the procedures explicitly and in full detail. The survey was divided into two parts: (a) a thorough, step-by-step description of the procedure used to resolve the hypothetical case and (b) multiple-choice questions. The following aspects of the procedure were covered: (a) step-by-step description of the procedure, (b) estimates of the actual duration at each stage, (c) indication of whether written submissions were required at each stage, (d) indication of specific laws applicable at each stage, (e) indication of mandatory time limits at each stage, (f) indication of the form of the appeal, and (g) the existence of alternative judicial or administrative procedures. Multiple-choice questions were used both to collect additional information and to double-check the answers. In addition, the survey asked questions about the incentives of judges, attorneys, and the litigants as well as questions on regulation of evidence and appeal.

10. Djankov and others (2003) calculated a judicial formalism index for a case of small debt collection (where the amount in dispute is 5 percent of GNI per capita) for a sample of 109 countries around the world, and this original sample covered Bulgaria, Croatia, and Romania. The database was later expanded to cover 25 additional jurisdictions, including Albania, Bosnia and Herzegovina, Moldova, and Serbia and Montenegro. The factual and procedural assumptions of the case have been kept the same; however, a larger debt claim was assumed (50 percent of GNI per capita) and the parties to the case are now explicitly assumed to be legal entities. With the permission of Djankov and others, the authors of this chapter then ran the survey instrument in FYR Macedonia in October and November 2002. Finally, the authors of this chapter updated the results for Bulgaria, Croatia, and Romania in January 2003 to reflect a larger debt amount (50 percent of GNI per capita). The law firms provided new answers to the survey, assuming the larger debt claim.

A new World Bank (2004) report on doing business in more than 130 countries around the world covers the topic of contract enforcement and uses the same assumed case of collecting a debt worth 50 percent of a country's GNI per capita. The Doing Business database on contract enforcement is built on the original Lex Mundi data and covers all of the South Eastern European countries studied in this report. The sources of the data and case assumptions are identical.

11. Among the merits of the Lex Mundi methodology are the following: (a) the methodology involved repeated interactions with the respondent law firm (three rounds of Lex Mundi data collection at a minimum), (b) the lawyers surveyed have dealt with debt collection court cases on a regular basis, (c) a senior law firm partner always checked and verified the answers given, (d) laws and regulations applicable to the hypothetical case were collected, and (e) much of the information provided can be double-checked.

The major drawback of this methodology is the small sample size (one respondent firm per country). An alternative to the Lex Mundi methodology would be one that relied on firm-level surveys to collect information about the operation of the courts in a country. An appealing feature of firm-level surveys is that they generally rely on a large sample of respondents comprising plaintiffs and defendants rather than lawyers. The drawbacks are the following: (a) these surveys are generally one-off survey interviews on a number of different topics (the operation of the judiciary is usually a small portion of the questionnaire); (b) the interviews are normally conducted with the firm's chief executive officer or general manager, who, though familiar with the firm's use of the courts in general, most likely has never been in court; and (c) the level of detail and depth that is afforded by the Lex Mundi surveys may not be possible to achieve in a firm-level survey.

12. For the purposes of this chapter, we have considered Moldova as part of the SEE8 rather than as a CIS country. The CIS country group comprises Armenia, Azerbaijan, Belarus, Georgia, Kazakhstan, the Kyrgyz Republic, the Russian Federation, Ukraine, and Uzbekistan. The Central European and Baltic states are the Czech Republic, Hungary, Latvia, Lithuania, Poland, the Slovak Republic, and Slovenia.

13. BEEPS1 did not ask this question.

14. The Lex Mundi data show the courts in the CIS countries as most expensive, followed by the courts in the SEE8 region.

15. Definitions of firm characteristics are the same as in the previous section.

16. Latin American countries such as Brazil, the Dominican Republic, and Mexico have all recently set up systems to manage court cases, and these systems have provided information about types of cases, the number of cases that go through the entire first-instance process, and so forth. Information gathered in this manner has proved to be indispensable in improving the work of the courts.

17. Romanian civil procedure allows normally for two levels of appeal for judgments issued by the local courts (*judecatorii*). These levels are intermediate appeal (*apel*) before the county tribunals and a final appeal (*recurs*) before the courts of appeal.

18. For a discussion of the role of the arbitrazh courts in resolving business disputes between Russian enterprises, see Hendley, Murrell, and Ryterman (2000, 2001).

19. See World Bank (2001a) for discussion and analysis of the reform of the court case management system. See also Dakolias (1999) and Buscaglia and Dakolias (1999), of which the latter cross-country study of court performance finds that court clearance rates and times to disposition are significantly affected by the adoption of information technology by the courts and higher capital budgets, among other things.

# References

ABA (American Bar Association), Central and East European Law Initiative. 2001. *Judicial Reform Index for Bosnia and Herzegovina.* Washington, D.C. Available online at http://www.abanet.org/ceeli/publications/jri/home.html.

———. 2002a. *Judicial Reform Index for Croatia*. Washington, D.C. Available online at http://www.abanet.org/ceeli/publications/jri/home.html.

———. 2002b. *Judicial Reform Index for Macedonia*. Washington, D.C. Available online at http://www.abanet.org/ceeli/publications/jri/home.html.

———. 2002c. *Judicial Reform Index for Romania*. Washington, D.C. Available online at http://www.abanet.org/ceeli/publications/jri/home.html.

———. 2002d. *Judicial Reform Index for Serbia*. Washington, D.C. Available online at http://www.abanet.org/ceeli/publications/jri/home.html.

Banerjee, Abhijit, and Esther Duflo. 2000. "Reputation Effects and the Limits of Contracting: A Study of the Indian Software Industry." *Quarterly Journal of Economics* 115(3):989–1017.

Bigsten, Arne, Paul Collier, Stefan Dercon, Marcel Fafchamps, Bernard Gauthier, Jan Willem Gunning, Abena Oduro, Remco Oostendorp, Cathy Patillo, Mans Soderbom, Francis Teal, and Albert Zeufack. 2000. "Contract Flexibility and Dispute Resolution in African Manufacturing." *Journal of Development Studies* 36(4):1–37.

Buscaglia, Edgardo, and Maria Dakolias. 1999. *Comparative International Study of Court Performance Indicators*. World Bank Report 20177, Legal and Judicial Reform Unit, Legal Department, World Bank (August 31).

Clay, Karen. 1997. "Trade without Law: Private Order Institutions in Mexican California." *Journal of Law, Economics, and Organization* 13(1):202–31.

Dakolias, Maria. 1999. "Court Performance around the World: A Comparative Perspective." Technical Paper 430. World Bank, Washington, D.C.

Delaey, Francis. 2001. "Enforcing Contracts in Transition Countries." *Law in Transition* (Autumn):17–22.

Djankov, Simeon, Rafael La Porta, Florencio Lopez-de-Silanes, and Andrei Shleifer. 2003. "Courts." *Quarterly Journal of Economics* 118(2):453–517.

EBRD and World Bank. 1999. *Business Environment and Enterprise Performance Survey* (BEEPS1). London and Washington, D.C. Data available online at http://info.worldbank.org/governance/beeps.

———. 2002. *Business Environment and Enterprise Performance Survey* (BEEPS2). London and Washington, D.C. Data available online at http://info.worldbank.org/governance/beeps2002.

Fafchamps, Marcel. 1996. "The Enforcement of Commercial Contracts in Ghana." *World Development* 24(3):427–48.

Frye, Timothy, and Ekaterina Zhuravskaya. 2000. "Rackets, Regulation, and the Rule of Law." *Journal of Law, Economics and Organization* 16(2):478–502.

Gray, Cheryl, Joel Hellman, and Randi Ryterman. 2004. *Anti-Corruption in Transition 2: Corruption in Enterprise-State Interactions in Europe and Central Asia 1999–2002.* World Bank, Washington, D.C.

Greif, Avner. 2003. "The Emergence of Institutions to Protect Property Rights." Paper presented at the Annual LACEA Congress, La Puebla, Mexico, October 11. Forthcoming in Claude Menard and Mary M. Shirley, eds., *Handbook of New Institutional Economics*. Dordrecht, Netherlands: Kluwer.

Greif, Avner, Paul Milgrom, and Barry R. Weingast. 1994. "Coordination, Commitment, and Enforcement: The Case of the Merchant Guild." *Journal of Political Economy* 102(4):745–76.

Hendley, Kathryn, and Peter Murrell. 2003. "Which Mechanisms Support the Fulfillment of Sales Agreements? Asking Decision-Makers in Firms." *Economics Letters* 78(1):49–54.

Hendley, Kathryn, Peter Murrell, and Randi Ryterman. 2000. "Law, Relationships, and Private Enforcement: Transactional Strategies of Russian Enterprises." *Europe-Asia Studies* 52(4):627–56.

———. 2001. "Law Works in Russia: The Role of Law in Interenterprise Transactions." In Peter Murrell, ed., *Assessing the Value of Law in Transition Economies*. Ann Arbor, Mich.: University of Michigan Press.

Islam, Roumeen. 2003. "Institutional Reform and the Judiciary: Which Way Forward?" Policy Research Working Paper 3134. World Bank, Washington, D.C.

Johnson, Simon, John McMillan, and Christopher Woodruff. 2002. "Courts and Relational Contracts." *Journal of Law, Economics, and Organization* 18(1):222–27.

Macaulay, Stewart. 1963. "Non-Contractual Relationships in Business: A Preliminary Study." *American Sociological Review* 28(2):55–70.

McMillan, John, and Christopher Woodruff. 1999. "Dispute Prevention without Courts in Vietnam." *Journal of Law, Economics, and Organization* 15(3):637–58.

Messick, Richard E. 1999. "Judicial Reform and Economic Development: A Survey of the Issues." *World Bank Research Observer* 14(1):117–36.

Milgrom, Paul, Douglass North, and Barry Weingast. 1990. "The Role of Institutions in the Revival of Trade: The Law Merchant, Private Judges, and Champagne Fairs." *Economics and Politics* 2:1–24.

Volkov, Vadim. 1999. "Violent Entrepreneurship in Post-Communist Russia." *Europe-Asia Studies* 51(5):741–54.

Woodruff, Christopher. 1998. "Contract Enforcement and Trade Liberalization in Mexico's Footwear Industry." *World Development* 26(6):979–91.

World Bank. 2001a. *Administration of Justice and the Legal Profession in Slovakia.* Poverty Reduction and Economic Management Unit, Europe and Central Asia Region, Washington, D.C.

———. 2001b. *Argentina: Legal and Judicial Sector Assessment.* Washington, D.C.

———. 2002. *Federal Republic of Serbia and Montenegro: Legal and Judicial Diagnostic.* Washington, D.C.

———. 2004. *Doing Business in 2004: Understanding Regulation.* Washington, D.C.

# Index